William Sidney Gibson

**Miscellanies, Historical and Biographical**

Being a Second Series of Essays, Lectures, and Reviews

William Sidney Gibson

**Miscellanies, Historical and Biographical**
*Being a Second Series of Essays, Lectures, and Reviews*

ISBN/EAN: 9783337074517

Printed in Europe, USA, Canada, Australia, Japan

Cover: Foto ©ninafisch / pixelio.de

More available books at **www.hansebooks.com**

# MISCELLANIES

## HISTORICAL AND BIOGRAPHICAL;

BEING A SECOND SERIES OF

## ESSAYS, LECTURES, AND REVIEWS:

BY

WILLIAM SIDNEY GIBSON, ESQ. M.A.

OF LINCOLN'S INN, BARRISTER AT LAW ; FELLOW OF THE SOCIETY OF
ANTIQUARIES OF LONDON, AND OF THE GEOLOGICAL SOCIETY ;
HON. MEMBER OF THE ACADEMIE DES SCIENCES ET
BELLES LETTRES DE DIJON, AND FELLOW OF
THE ROYAL SOCIETY OF ANTIQUARIES
OF THE NORTH, COPENHAGEN,
ETC.

LONDON:
LONGMAN, GREEN, LONGMAN, ROBERTS, AND GREEN.
NEWCASTLE-UPON-TYNE: F. AND W. DODSWORTH,
AND ROBERT ROBINSON.

1863.

WESTMINSTER:
PRINTED BY J. B. NICHOLS AND SONS,
25, PARLIAMENT STREET.

# CONTENTS.

## DIVISION I.

### TOPOGRAPHICAL ESSAYS.

| | PAGE |
|---|---|
| MEMOIR OF NORTHUMBERLAND . . . | 1 |
| AUCKLAND CASTLE—THE RESIDENCE OF THE BISHOPS OF DURHAM . | 71 |
| FINCHALE PRIORY, NEAR DURHAM | 96 |
| BYRON AT NEWSTEAD ABBEY . . | 109 |
| THE PERCY'S STRONGHOLD—ALNWICK CASTLE | 120 |
| SUMMER DAYS IN SCOTLAND . . . | 127 |
| SCANDINAVIAN TRAVEL—JUTLAND AND THE DANISH ISLES . | 144 |
| THE MEDITERRANEAN | 159 |

## DIVISION II.

### ESSAYS, SCIENTIFIC AND MISCELLANEOUS.

| | |
|---|---|
| SCIENCE AND ROYALTY UNDER HIGHLAND SKIES . . | 181 |
| THE BRITISH ASSOCIATION AT OXFORD . . . | 203 |
| MINERAL SPRINGS—THEIR MEDICINE AND MYTHOLOGY | 232 |
| RIVERS AND THEIR ASSOCIATIONS | 261 |
| HAILSTORMS AND THEIR PHENOMENA . . | 279 |
| IMPRESSIONS OF THE INTERNATIONAL EXHIBITION, 1862 | 292 |
| ART TREASURES AT SOUTH KENSINGTON | 305 |

## DIVISION III.

### BIOGRAPHICAL AND HISTORICAL ESSAYS.

| | PAGE |
|---|---|
| AUGUSTUS CÆSAR; HIS COURT AND COMPANIONS | 317 |
| CANTERBURY AND ITS ARCHBISHOPS—SAXON PERIOD | 342 |
| CANTERBURY AND ITS ARCHBISHOPS—NORMAN PERIOD | 357 |
| EMINENT JUDGES OF ENGLAND—A LECTURE | 369 |
| DESORMAIS: A STORY OF SKIPTON CASTLE | 411 |
| JAMES HOWELL, THE FIRST HISTORIOGRAPHER ROYAL | 422 |
| THE STORY OF RICHARD SAVAGE, DRAMATIST AND POET | 432 |
| LIFE OF PROFESSOR EDWARD FORBES, THE NATURALIST | 441 |

### ERRATA.

Page 10, line 2, *for* Romans *read* Normans.
Page 143, lines 26 and 29, *for* ravines *read* moraines.
Page 333, line 25, *for* Romans *read* Germans.

# MEMOIR ON NORTHUMBERLAND.

NORTHUMBERLAND affords a tempting field not only to the naturalist and the sketcher, but to the antiquary and the student of county history. The wild and mountainous nature of a great part of the county, the peculiarities of its architectural monuments, the dialect and character of its population, all mark Northumberland by striking features. Its remoteness, the separate nationality (so to speak) which it retained during many centuries, and the slight intercourse with the rest of the kingdom formerly enjoyed by its inhabitants, combined, moreover, to give this part of England many distinguishing peculiarities. Then, too, its traditions and associations with by-gone times are full of character and interest; and perhaps there is not a county where the present is seen in more striking contrast with the past, for works of "the stone age" constructed by British tribes—probably the contemporaries of the unknown founders of Stonehenge and Carnac—enduring remains of Roman military occupation, feudal structures and towers of refuge and defence, are here the characteristic representatives of times gone by. But the Celtic inhabitants of Northumbria have been succeeded by a hardy and industrious people, who, instead of fashioning rude weapons of war and chase in earthy huts, raise coal, build ships, and manufacture iron for the world; and a walled town, and thinly scattered villages that were ravaged by the moss-trooper, have given place to crowded haunts, spreading habitations, and a rapid extension of commercial enterprise and mining industry. To the stony ways that were traversed by the Roman legions, turnpike roads and railways have succeeded; lands formerly swept by the border robber now adorn a tale of peace and plenty at local agricultural meetings; and the waters of the Rede and the North Tyne, that in former times often reddened to the beacon fires on Scottish foray, flow through pastoral and even fertile landscapes. Thriving plantations wave on lands that continued to be wastes at the beginning of even the present century, and on many a height the plough traverses camps and graves of ancient Britons. Agriculture—pursued in the days of the Romans and in the feudal ages under protection of stone walls and towers—now obliterates in its progress the defences which it no longer needs. At the mouth of the Tyne, in places where, so lately as a century ago, crops of corn were raised amidst the rude "schelings" of fishermen, a populous seaport has risen, which draws its harvests from the deep, and has at length wrested from Newcastle independence and a share in the conservancy of the river; and that town, which was defended through the middle ages by massive walls, has spread within the last thirty years far and wide beyond their circuit, and become a centre of railway traffic and manufacturing industry, with a population numbering a hundred thousand souls.

*Natural features.* Before entering on the historic monuments of Northumberland, its natural features demand some description.

In its northern, central, and western regions, it is a country of mountainous hills, broad tracts of sombre moorland and brown heathery wastes, indeed a third of the county may be said to consist of moorlands, having an average elevation of from 500 to 1,000 feet. These vast hilly moors rise on the western and south-western frontiers of Northumberland into bold and mountainous forms of very picturesque character, but not marked by the steep and rugged grandeur of the Highlands of Scotland or the mountains of the English lake district. The lofty range of hills, or Pennine Chain, stretching with little interruption from the borders of Scotland, through Northumberland, into Derbyshire, attains its greatest elevation in the wild and sterile heights of Cross Fell. To the north-west, from the high frontier moorlands of Cumberland, this range presents successive elevations, which in Northumberland culminate in the Cheviot mountains—the highest eminences in the county. The scenery in all the high regions is remarkable for breadth rather than the softness of outline of the chalk downs in the South of England, and the sterile wastes derive impressiveness of aspect from their solitude and extent.

"Cheviots' mountains lone" are the well-known eminences of an elevated region of porphyritic and pyrogenous rocks, about equal in area to Dartmoor, and extending from Chew Green and Coquet-head, on the north-western frontier of Northumberland, to Flodden-field on the north-east, and from near the vale of Whittingham (on their south-eastern slope) to Kelso on the Tweed. Perhaps the Cheviots cannot be better described than by saying that they form a tripled range of rounded massive hills, some of which have a perfectly conical form; the highest attains 2,680 feet; next is Hedgehope, and then comes Yevering Bell, which attains nearly 2,000 feet, and forms a dome-shaped mass, eminent above the lesser elevations. It overlooks scenes to which the genius of Scott has given an undying charm, and many a spot celebrated in border annals, besides Homelhaugh—the Homildon under which Hotspur and Douglas fought in 1402, and Percy-lawe, another height associated with the memory of Hotspur's valiant race. But the great Cheviot Forest is gone, and the red deer that occasioned the celebrated chase have vanished.

*The Cheviots.*

One of the lower eminences detached from the range is the hill of Flodden, and below it stretches the memorable field. With its green hillocks are now mixed flourishing plantations, and it retains few of the characteristic features described by Scott. "King James's Chair" has been destroyed, but its site is marked by a clump of firs. The

*Flodden field.*

country then was bare and open: inclosures now stretch on the uplands, and the straggling patches of natural wood are gradually yielding to cultivation. On the adjacent ridges, heather has given place to corn, habitations have risen amid green pastures, and broad plantations border the river Till. The slopes of the Cheviots are covered for some distance from their base by a sort of copsewood, but on their greater heights this verdure dwindles to brushwood, bracken, and thin turf. The whole range is intersected by wild glens and sequestered denes, and many a secluded spot is still clothed by remains of primeval forest. In some of the ravines the reddish porphyritic cliffs are exposed,* and through them flow the tributaries of the river Till—shallow sparkling burns that murmur over a stony bed, or fall in little cascades through their rocky channel. Among the Cheviot hills the tourist is in an impressive region of natural wildness—one of those few remaining realms of solitude where

> Lone Nature feels that she may freely breathe;
>   While round us, and beneath,
> Are heard her sacred tones: the fitful sweep
>   Of winds across the steep;
>
> \*   \*   \*   \*
>
> The wheeling kite's wild solitary cry,
>   And—scarcely heard so high—
> The dashing waters when the air is still,
>   From many a torrent rill
> That winds unseen beneath the shaggy fell,
>   Track'd by the blue mist well.

Rothbury Forest.    The wild moorlands of Rothbury Forest, which culminate in the dark rugged slopes of Simonside, a hill 1,400 feet in height, form, with Ottercaps, a series of lofty hills distinct from the Cheviot range, and not of their mountainous character. Remarkable for their precipitous and picturesque

---

\* The porphyries and sienites of the Cheviots are seen at Wooler in proximity to the lower sandstone of the carboniferous formations.

crags rather than for their height, are the basaltic formations which cross the county from the north-east to the south-west, and rise into precipitous eminences on the line of the Roman Wall. In the south-western part of Northumberland are the elevated regions of the lead-mining district, and the sterile lonely fells of millstone-grit and limestone rock. Knaresdale—which is perhaps the most picturesque part of the valley of the South Tyne—winds amidst lofty massive hills, and is the pass into the lead-mining district of Alston Moor and Nenthead, surrounded by wild heights that stretch southward to Cross Fell. This hilly region of the lead-mines extends from the Cumberland frontier at Alston round the southern boundary of Northumberland, and is continued in the commons of Allendale and Hexhamshire. The counties of Northumberland, Durham, and Cumberland join near Allenheads in an elevated region of moorlands and mosses from 1,000 to 2,200 feet above the sea level; and on the northern declivity the sister streams of Allen have their birth, while on the declivities to the south and east rise the Wear and the Tees.

The lead-mining districts form a tract about twenty miles in diameter in each direction, comprising the border districts just now mentioned, the manor of Alston Moor and the mountainous region stretching to Cross Fell, the higher dales of the Wear and the Tees in Durham, the valleys of the East and West Allen, the Tyne, and the Derwent. The aspect of the higher portion of this mining district is almost unrelieved by cultivated lands; the heights are for a great part of the year commonly wrapped in mists, and snow lies on the higher fells until summer. Yet, in favourable weather, the mining settlements are far from presenting a dreary wilderness or Siberian climate. The great centre of lead-mining in Northumberland is Allenheads—which is 1,400 feet above the sea, and can boast the highest residence in England. Alston, the highest market-town, is on the Cumbrian side of the boundary. Here the population is almost wholly employed in mining, and much secluded

*margin:* Lead-mines of South Tyne and Allendale.

*margin:* Allenheads.

from the rest of the world. In the school maintained at Allenheads by Mr. Beaumont, a gossiping writer says he found, out of fifty children assembled on some occasion a year or two ago, only five boys who had seen wheat growing, and three who had beheld the sea. The inhabitants of the district were correctly enough described * more than thirty years ago, as "an industrious and loyal people, moral, intelligent, and of simple habits, whose seclusion from the rest of the country, and whose occupation, lead them to inquiries which quicken their understanding and induce them to seek knowledge from books." They appear still to deserve this character, and to have availed themselves eagerly of opportunities for improvement.

A branch of the Newcastle and Carlisle Railway has for some years past opened to the rest of the world the adjacent mining district of Alston Moor, and Allendale will probably ere long be penetrated by a railway.

The prevailing features of this part of the country are bleak wild fells, traversed by few roads, with patches of fir planted here and there on the steep slopes. It is stated by Mr. Sopwith, F.R.S., and President of the British Meteorological Society, that the maximum temperature of the district of Allenheads is nearly coincident with the minimum temperature of Bywell,—a place seated about twenty miles distant in the valley of the Tyne, and about twelve miles westward from Newcastle. In the elevated region described, the quantity of rain is in some years double that which falls in Middlesex; insomuch that Mr. Walter White, in his book already quoted, congratulates the inhabitants on having employment underground out of the way of bad weather! But Nature, if not remarkable for geniality as regards sky and climate in this high moorland country, has been bountiful beneath the surface. The quantity of lead produced from Mr. Beaumont's mines at Allenheads,

---

\* By Mr. Locker, in one of his Reports to the Commissioners of Greenwich Hospital, the lords of the manor.

and at the adjacent mining settlements of Coalcleugh and St. John's, Weardale (a part of the parish of Stanhope), is understood to have amounted to nine or ten thousand tons annually. Galena (from which as is well known the lead of commerce is derived) is the most abundant of the minerals; and some of the ores are exceedingly rich in silver. An economical process for the separation of silver from lead, founded on the simple natural law that melted lead will crystallise while silver remains fluid, was invented in 1829 by the late Mr. Hugh Lee Pattinson, a distinguished native of Alston Moor—a practical chemist and electrician, who in his latter years liberally devoted to the cultivation of astronomy much of his leisure and of the fortune acquired in the alkali works he established on the Tyne. In one year the ores of a mine called the Hudgill Burn Mine yielded, by refinement from the lead, silver worth 8,000*l*. The mineral veins prove to the adventurous miner sometimes only slender threads of hope that lead to ultimate disappointment: more commonly, they conduct him to arteries of mineral wealth. There seems to be no doubt of the existence and value of copper ores in the Alston district, but they have not been worked with success. Iron ore is abundant in the shale formations of the lead-mining country; and at Nunstones, near Tynehead, there is a great sulphur vein * in a hill which was denominated in a lease "the back-bone of the earth:"—it is remarkable as a mineral vein, being at one part 300 feet in width, and throwing up the strata 60 feet. The lead-mines of Alston Moor, which in 1734 were vested by Act of Parliament in Greenwich Hospital after the attainder of the ill-fated Earl of Derwentwater, have yielded a considerable proportion of the great annual revenues of that national institution, besides fortunes to private lessees of mines worked in the manor of Alston Moor.†

\* It is described as containing amorphous white quartz, several strong ribs of sulphur, and some yellow copper-ore.
† A notable example of mining enterprise was in progress in April 1859 : a

All the engine work of the mines is done by hydraulic power, and one of the most interesting things in the district is this application of natural force to the aid of human labour. Not a steam-engine is used in any of Mr. Beaumont's mines. Springs rising in the caverns of the hills become arteries of industry; and on the river Allen itself, the economy of water-power is something quite instructive.

This important mining-field was certainly known to the Romans, of whose station at Whitley, (near the town of Alston, and on the "Maiden Way" from Caervoran on the Wall to Kirby Thore,) there are some interesting remains. When the Roman legions penetrated from York to Carlisle, their path took them from the rich mining-fields of Yorkshire and Durham to cross this yet richer land of mineral wealth beyond; and the mines of the Derwent Valley (now proposed to be made accessible by a railway), the mines of Allendale and Tynedale, and those of the Cumbrian frontier, all lay within the province guarded by the Roman Wall. In the days of the Anglo-Norman kings, the mines were profitably worked under protection of the crown, and yielded surprising quantities of silver. In those days the miners found their fuel in the forest tracts around, and until comparatively recent times the hill-sides, now so barren and hardly yielding scanty pasturage for sheep, were clothed with their native wood.

*Basaltic formations.*

Northumberland owes much of its picturesque scenery to the basaltic rocks. They form some of its most remarkable eminences, especially on a part of the line of the Roman Wall; they occur also amongst stratified formations, and they traverse the county in the form of dykes. Extending from

---

new level was being driven seven miles underground, running north and south, to explore for the veins of lead which run in an opposite direction. Mr. Sopwith, in speaking of the celebrated aqueduct of "Nentforce Level," which was projected by Smeaton, remarks that among the great improvements it has effected in the practice of mining is the general use of horse-levels, by which easy access to the mines is gained—a mode of working said to have been introduced by Sir Walter Calverley Blackett a century ago.

Ettrick Water by the north-west of Hawick, a dyke crosses Northumberland in almost a right line to the sea-coast, a little to the south of Warkworth, a course of about sixty miles. Another remarkable basaltic dyke is that great and continuous fracture or line of dislocation which extends from the coast at Cullercotes, a fishing village to the north of Tynemouth, westward through the valley of the Tyne, and then southward by the Cumberland frontier, Brough, Kirby Stephen, and Kirby Lonsdale, ending in what is called the "Craven Fault," near Settle, a course of 110 miles, placing the whole section of the strata on one side of the dyke much above the corresponding beds on the other side, and forming one of the most remarkable dislocations known. A great range of basaltic rock also traverses Northumberland from south-west to north-east; it begins in the dale or "forest" of the Lune, sweeps round the great limestone escarpment of Crossfell and Tynedale-fell, and, curving towards Thirlwall on the border of Cumberland, runs from thence in a north-easterly direction, in a hilly range with precipitous declivities on the northern face; crossing the North Tyne, it extends to the sea coast at Howick; it then rises in masses nearly a hundred feet thick at Bamburgh, having the rocky group, or "seventeen sister-satellites," of Farne, for its seaward prolongation; and ends in the hills called the Kyloe Crags. Basaltic veins or dykes also appear on the coast at Holy Island, Beadnell, Tynemouth, and other places, and seem to have a direction transverse to the great ridge above described. On the line of the Roman Wall we find that its builders availed themselves of the bold, precipitous escarpments, and carried the wall in many places over the basaltic crags. A crest near Wall-town, which was formerly crowned by a mile-castle of the wall, is 800 feet above the level of the sea. In this district, populous in the days of Roman military occupation, but now an almost uninhabited waste, the lonely sheets of water known as the Northumbrian Lakes reflect the basaltic cliffs. In the northern part of the county also, the basalt forms rocky eminences of great height (in one place 500 feet above the level of the sea), on some of which elevations Saxons or Romans raised their castles, as at Bamburgh, Holy Island, and Dunstanburgh, where the magnificent rocks of columnar basalt rise a hundred feet above the surging waves. At Bamburgh, to the northward, (an important citadel from the days of the Northumbrian kings,) the draw-well was excavated through seventy-five feet of basaltic rock and a like thickness of the underlying sandstone—a fine-grained reddish-tinted rock. The basalt is even thicker on the adjacent rocky islets of Farne * The isolated, metamorphic, and dislocated condition of the limestone, sandstone, and shales, on some of these islands, seems to indicate that the antient lavas flowed over those lower groups of the carboniferous limestone series. In many places the rocks appear to have been disturbed by an eruption of the basalt, which occurs both as an injected dyke and an overflowing lava. Thus, on the coast at Howick, a few miles to the south, basaltic dykes intersect the carboniferous limestone cliffs. In some localities the basalt rests conformably on those formations; for example, near Alnwick, a bold cliff of columnar basalt, called Ratcheugh Crag, is capped by the carboniferous limestone, changed here and there, by the contact, into granular marble. Another basaltic eminence, between Alnwick and the coast, rests on beds of blue limestone and metamorphic shale, which has been converted in some localities into a porcelain jasper, or, where in contact with the basalt, into a black mineral of conchoidal fracture.

Boulder-clay. Another formation that is conspicuous in Northumberland, especially in the northern and eastern regions, is the Boulder-clay. It covers the eastern side of the range of sandstone hills which extends in a south-westerly direction from Kyloe to Alnwick Moor; in some places it forms long hilly slopes, in others it is heaped in isolated mounds resembling gigantic tumuli. Then there are hills and ridges of diluvium (gravel,

---

* A valuable paper on the geology of the Farne Islands, by Mr. Geo. Tate, of Alnwick, F.G.S., will be found in the Proceedings of the Berwickshire Nat. Club, 1857, p. 231.

clay, and pebbles), which certainly resemble lateral moraines, and have been attributed to glaciers. A tortuous ridge of hills at North Charlton, between Alnwick and Belford, is an example; and similar mounds occur over considerable portions of the country at the foot of the eastern valleys of the Cheviots. The boulders and fragments of Scottish mountains which occur in the boulder-clay, and are scattered over Northumberland, especially on the shores of the sea and rivers, can hardly have been transported by any other agency than that of floating ice, which probably bore the ponderous and far-travelled boulders to the places where they rest, at a time when the climate of this part of the island was of an Arctic character. Beneath an overlying boulder-clay in the Hawkhill quarry, probably once an icy shore, the limestone bed *in situ* is in some places polished, scratched, and grooved; the markings having generally a direction from north to south.*

*Traces of glacial action.*

The chalk, greensand, and associated formations are absent in Northumberland; so that there are not in this county the water-reservoirs of the south, and the supply seems to depend on the actual rainfall.

The carboniferous limestone formations stretch from the Northumberland side of the Tweed at Kelso to the sea; they extend along the coast to the mouth of the Coquet, and pass under the northern and western boundary of the great coal field.

*Carboniferous limestone formations.*

The coal series, which are of course regarded as the formations most characteristic of Northumberland, and which hold the first place in regard to its mineral wealth and maritime trade, must now be adverted to; but it would require a separate Essay to give any adequate description of mining operations, or of the coal-field itself.† The car-

*The coal-field.*

---

* Proceedings of the Berwickshire Nat. Club, p. 102.

† An ample description of the coal field of Northumberland and Durham, the different qualities of coal, and a catalogue of organic fossils, may be found in Mr. Winch's paper, published in the fourth volume of the *Transactions of the Geological Society* of London. And in a recently published work, entitled *Our Coal Fields*, much information relating to the pits and pitmen of the Newcastle and Durham coal field will be found.

boniferous sandstones certainly cannot be said, however, to contribute to the picturesque features of the county, except in river-valleys, for low rounded hills, and a generally flat coast, mark the extent of the coal formations. It will be sufficient here to say, that the northern extremity of the great coal field of Northumberland and Durham reaches to the mouth of the Coquet, and that it is circumscribed by a line following the coast of Northumberland, and running in a southerly direction from the mouth of the Tyne, bordered by the magnesian limestone formations of the Durham coast, and passing by Ferry Hill nearly to Pierse Bridge on the Tees; thence, running diagonally across the counties of Durham and Northumberland to their northern limit on the Coquet river, Bywell on the Tyne being the western boundary of the coal field in the last named county.*

The coal worked further to the west—in the millstone-grit and carboniferous limestone formation, near Haltwistle and adjacent places—belongs to isolated coal formations quite independent of the great field above described. Through this vast basin fifty-seven different seams or beds of coal lie in succession; the thickest and most important of which are respectively about seventy-five fathoms and one hundred and thirty-five fathoms deep, a little to the eastward of Newcastle.† The most important of the beds worked in the productive "Steam Coal" district between the Tyne and the Blyth lie from ninety to one hundred and ten fathoms deep, and the workings in some instances extend a mile and a half from the pit-shaft. The "High Main" seam lies under one hundred and sixty fathoms of beds of stone at Jarrow, but rises to the cliffs beyond Tynemouth, only two miles to the northward; as regards geological succession, the mountain-limestone and the strata of the lofty hills of Alston Moor lie under the deepest coal mines of this great basin.

Coal-mining.

The quantity of coal now annually raised from it exceeds

---

* The extreme length of the coal field is therefore about forty-eight miles, and its extreme breadth about half its length.

† The lowest seam worked in the whole "Newcastle Coal Field" is on the Wear at Monkwearmouth, at a depth of 1,700 feet.

sixteen millions of tons.* It is unnecessary to dwell on the wondrous impetus given to the production of coal by the introduction of steam machinery in collieries; it works the pumps that are constantly moving to free the mines from water,† lifts the coal to the pit mouth, and propels the wagons that convey it to the ships.‡ A colliery, with the peculiar machinery it arrays upon the surface, the neighbouring settlements of the pitmen, the uncouth looking objects with which it blackens the rural landscape, the dark underground economy of a coal mine, and the character of the people engaged in this occupation, all afford matter of curious interest to a stranger. And how striking are their commercial results! When one reflects that its coal field has covered the banks of the Tyne in Newcastle, and for some miles above and below the town, with factories and ironworks, has converted the walled mediæval town of monks and merchants into a busy emporium of commerce inhabited by a hundred thousand people, and has concentrated in adjacent places that were rural a few years ago, a population equal to that of many an old county town of England, it is curious to compare such an extent of coal production with its state in days when the use of coal was prohibited in London, or even thirty years ago, when the whole quantity produced in Great Britain was not equal to what is now consumed in the manufacture of iron. When Edward the Third's works at Windsor were in progress, no coals could be bought in the metropolis, and the king's master of the works was obliged to obtain the king's writ to the sheriff of Northumberland for the purchase of a cargo direct from a colliery upon the Tyne. He bought 726 chaldrons, which cost seventeen-pence a chaldron, at Winlaton, whence

* The total produce from all the British coal-mines appears to be about 68,000,000, which is four times the quantity raised thirty years ago.

† In one colliery on the Tyne, now abandoned, the weight of water raised is computed to have exceeded by thirty times that of the coal.

‡ In some small collieries in remote parts of the Northumberland coal-field mining operations are still, however, almost as primitive as in the days of Wykeham; the machinery is rude, and pack-horses convey the produce.

they were taken in barges for shipment at Newcastle; and, a great part of the cargo having been thrown overboard during a storm, the small residue which reached Windsor cost, besides the barge-hire to that place, 165*l.* 5*s.* 2*d.*!* The fortunes of coal-mining, the princely incomes realised from successful speculations, the capital hopelessly sunk in others, would form a curious chapter in the history of industrial enterprise. Here, as in many other fields, science, energy, and perseverance have won their triumphs; but, nevertheless, hopes have often been disastrously destroyed. All the layers or seams of coal together bear in their aggregate thickness but a small proportion to that of the rocks with which they alternate; and a large proportion of the beds are too thin for profitable working; so that many unfortunate speculators have derived nothing from the laborious, slow descent, but the lesson which the succession of many hundred feet of sedimentary rock must teach as to the enormous duration of the globe. At the doors of a local museum (at Newcastle) may be seen the warning trunks of two gigantic coniferæ—all that ever rewarded the heavy cost of sinking a certain pit in search of coal.

*The sylva of Northumberland.*

From this glance at the carboniferous formations in which we find stored up the remains of forests that in some pre-Adamite condition of our globe waved in tropical luxuriance on the area now forming the county of Northumberland, it is time to pass to the existing sylva of this part of England. To the regret of the lover of forest trees and ornamental woodland, there are few localities in which Northumberland can boast of fine old timber. Remains of gigantic oaks that grew in its primæval forests have been found in peat-mosses, in spots now either destitute of timber, or where the largest living trees are dwarfs compared to them, or in alluvium of the river banks from Newcastle to the sea, now crowded by objects very unlike forest timber, and more familiar with glowing coke ovens than glistening

---

* To the metropolis alone 1,200,000 tons of coal went sea-borne from the Tyne in the year 1859.

leaves. In the north of the county, hawthorn and holly, which latter often attains great size and ornamental character, enrich the denes; and in many a hilly ravine the snowy blossoms of the thorn in spring, the bright coral berries of the mountain ash in autumn, and those of the holly in winter, contrast with the deep green foliage of the pine and fir. Many fine whitethorns also flourish near old mansions, and on river-meadows; but, within the last eighty years, quickset hedges have been generally planted, and the roads and hedge-rows of Northumberland too generally want the adornment and shade of trees, and are destitute of the lines of snowy blossom that in spring perfume the roads in the midland and southern counties. The yew is not common, but some rural churchyards in this county are fitly shadowed by its venerable form, and by the dark perennial foliage that seems so symbolic of duration, and of a life beyond decay. At Beltingham, for example, (the native parish of Bishop Ridley, a pleasant rural seclusion not far westward from the confluence of the Allen and the Tyne,) there is a fine old yew, that companioned through storm and sunshine the little church of Norman days, and is still green beside the more modern edifice that has succeeded to it.

Flourishing plantations are scattered over the county; those of fir are now quite a conspicuous feature, whereas a century ago this tree was seen only in exposed situations, and in gloomy isolated groups; but the cultivation of the common larch in the north of England within the last seventy-five years has surpassed that of any other tree, and its wood is in extensive use. The silver fir also been planted with advantage, and there are some noble specimens of it that have stood for more than a century as ornamental forest trees—*e.g.* those in Alnwick-park and in the glebe land on the river bank at Hartburn, where a silver fir planted about the accession of George III. is nearly 140 feet in height and 12 feet in circumference. Within the last fifty years an immense extent of land in this county has been appropriated to the raising of timber; but, in ornamental woodlands Northumberland cannot vie with southern counties. Its chief seats and castles are however surrounded by their parks; and, in natural as well as artificial beauty and extent, Alnwick Park is one of the chief sylvan glories of the kingdom.\* About seventy years ago, the beech began to be extensively planted in this county, less, however, for its ornamental character than for the value of its timber; but noble beech trees, and woods and avenues of beech, surround some of the old castles and mansions of Northumberland. It has been remarked with apparent truth that, the further we go northward from Yorkshire, the later the elm seems to have been introduced; but, where there is deep rich soil in Northumberland near to some " well-watered shore," many a fine wych-elm grows luxuriantly. The evergreen or holm-oak flourishes even within the influence of the sea-breeze, and the Spanish chestnut attains a large size when planted in a free loam, or other favourable soil, but there are few remarkable avenues of chestnut trees:—those at Dilston, Shawdon, and Rock, seem the most noticeable. The birch has been much cultivated, for it attains a profitable size in less than twenty years, and is in demand for making fish-barrels and the clogs used for shoes by the peasantry. The Oriental plane is seldom seen; but of the sycamore, as well as of the ash, there are in this county some fine specimens. The holly flourishes in native luxuriance; the alder borders many of the rocky, swift-running streams; and there are groups of large willows, as at Elishaw (*i.e.* the willow-wood), a place where the Watling-street crosses the river Rede.

Rivers.

And now the rivers claim some notice, after detaining the reader so long amongst the hills and rocks, the minerals and forest trees. It is in the river valleys of Northumberland that its most pleasing landscapes are found, and the region of the

---

\* It was here that Hugh Duke of Northumberland planted the original tree of Athenian poplar, which he had brought from America with other kinds during the Colonial war, and from which the trees disseminated in the North of England have been derived.

carboniferous rocks is that in which the picturesque beauty of its river-scenery is greatest. In the central and western parts of the county the rivers generally wind through country of a bold and mountainous character. In the hilly regions of the Tyne, the Derwent, the Allen, the Coquet, and the Wansbeck, the river in many places flows under lofty banks which rise sometimes to a considerable height clothed to the summit with native wood; in one place some gray, weather-tinted cliff or scar of rock tufted with trees throws its shadow on the stream; in another, a succession of ledges of stone breaks its current into narrow rapids and murmuring falls; elsewhere we see it leave the deep embrowning shade for sunny meadows, and flow past them in a bright tranquil current, or wind through a broad shingly bed. The lover of " Potamology " might revel amidst the swift rivers of Northumberland, or by the many burns and rivulets that,

With fitful sound
Wafted o'er sullen moss and craggy mound,

descend through sequestered dells to join the better-known historic streams, and might listen with delight to its dreamy carol as below some heathery bank the rivulet " goes on for ever " in its gladsome course, with many a little cascade in the " dimpled linn," and many a winding in the sunshine or beneath the shadow of purple fox-glove and pendent fern. From its rise on the eastern declivity of Cross Fell, at a spot not far from the source of the Tees, the South Tyne is but a slender rivulet until it has passed the dark fells of Hartside and Alston Moor, and received the Nent below Alston; thence flowing northward through the picturesque and fertile valley of Knaresdale, it is bent to its eastward course by the high border lands to the west of Haltwhistle. It then receives the waters of the river Allen, whose sister streams, descending from the moorlands that separate Allen-dale from Weardale, have flowed on the eastern and western sides of the high ridge of Allendale Common, and met under the grey old tower of Staward Peel, in scenery hardly inferior to that of some wooded passes in the Tyrol. Although

*Marginalia: South Tyne. East and West Allen.*

c

intersecting a wild moorland region, the banks of these rivers are full of natural beauty, and the ravine that forms the course of the river is often marked in the landscape by its deep natural wood. The North Tyne rises at the opposite extremity of the county,—indeed some of its springs are in Roxburghshire across the border, and its native region is a district of lonely fells; but the wild graces of Tynedale are gemmed by many bosky burns, and the North and South Tyne meet in a valley (not far to the north-west of Hexham, and now opened to the tourist by the Border Counties Railway), which has few rivals in the beauty of its pastoral and wooded scenery. Many a trout-stream sought by the angler has its source in the Cheviot hills—many a

*marginal note:* North Tyne.

> River to whose shallow falls
> Melodious birds sing madrigals.

The chief of these is the Beamish, afterwards known as the Till, which rises, on their eastern slope, in the mountainous moorlands that give birth to the river Aln; but unlike that river, which flows eastward to the sea, the Till pursues a curiously winding course through many a bright vale to the north and west round the eastern declivities of the range, and, passing Flodden Field and the historic sites of Ford and Etal, meets the Tweed in very imposing scenery at Twizell, where the bridge, a semi-circular arch of ribbed stone, presents

*marginal notes:* The Till. Tweed.

> One bow, but great and strong,

as when Surrey with his vanguard and artillery passed over it on the morning of the battle of Flodden. Here, too, the gray old border-tower of Twizell until lately crowned the lofty rock crested with wood that still looks down upon the stream.\* From its first appearance in the Northumberland landscape, the silver Tweed, dear to archæologist and lover of the picturesque—is marked by scenery of great beauty,

---

\* It is certainly not matter for regret that the modern Castle above it was never finished ; and one hopes that ivy and creeping plants may ere long hide its frightful rows of Georgian windows.

and it flows by " Norham's castled steep," and several monuments of religion and chivalry. Its banks are crowned by many old churches and ruined towers; and shady fishpools, and the music of many a brook tempt the angler and pedestrian to its shores. The picturesque banks of the Aln are likewise dignified by historic associations, for it passes the sites of the ruined abbeys of Hulne and Alnwick, and reflects the princely towers of Alnwick Castle. Next comes the river Coquet, which traverses some of the finest scenery in Northumberland; amid the deep woods that clothe its banks it surrounds the grey ruins of Brinkburn Priory and laves the monastic meads of Guyzance; and then the river, passing the hermitage " deep hewn within a craggy cliff and overhung with wood," which is commemorated in the well-known ballad, flows seaward past the feudal towers of {.mark} River Aln. {.mark} Coquet.

> Warkworth, proud of Percy's name.

Between the Coquet and the Tyne low sandhills for the most part form the coast; but the lesser streams of the Wansbeck and the Blyth still {.mark} Wansbeck.

> Rush to the sea through sounding woods;

and Wallington, Morpeth, Mitford, and Bothal, mingle objects of historic interest and picturesque character with the sylvan beauty of the Wansbeck valley.

Glancing from natural features to works of human industry, a curious contrast to these quiet streams and to the secluded wildness of the higher regions of Tynedale, is presented by the noise and restless traffic on the banks of the Tyne for fourteen miles before it joins the sea. Signs of trade and manufacturing industry accumulate on either bank of the river for some distance above Newcastle: there is the hydraulic-engine and ordnance factory at Elswick, lately extended and made famous by the manufacture of the Armstrong gun; then come the older manufactories of lead and shot, and Stephenson's great locomotive engine works; and acres of workshops standing where not half a century ago were {.mark} The Tyne in its lower course.

shady walks to which the citizens resorted for rural views; then, below the quays, warehouses, manufactories, and murky smoke of the town, a succession of blast-furnaces and iron-works, ship-building yards, rope-works, coke-ovens, alkali-works, and manufactories of glass,* of pottery, and fire-bricks meet the eye on either side of the river.† Wallsend—once familiar with the eagles of Roman legions and the raven-banner of Danish sea kings, is now surrounded by the smoke of furnaces and the sounds of industry. Midway between it and the sea, are the new "Northumberland Docks;" and looking thence across the Tyne to Jarrow, we see other new docks (second only to the Victoria Dock in extent), which have been formed in the slake or bay where the Saxon Ecgfrid's little fleet was wont to ride; and now, busy workshops and a forest of masts surround the gray old church tower of the monastery at Jarrow, which Venerable Bede made so famous through the Christian world. And nearer the sea, the populous towns of North and South Shields, vessels on the stocks, and a crowd of shipping afloat, wharfs, coal-staiths, piles of timber, tall chimneys pouring forth smoke, coke-ovens glowing, hammers resounding, and thousands of sooty faces, mark the busy traffic, the active industry, and material riches of the Tyne.

Agriculture. Hardly less striking than the vast developement of min-

* Glass-works seem to have been first established on the Tyne in the reign of James I., and the artisans were emigrants from the Low Countries.

† In what is called "The Newcastle District," thirteen iron furnaces were in blast at the beginning of the present year, producing iron at the rate of 118,000 tons per annum. A large proportion of this enormous produce leaves the district in the shape of engines, both those of war and those of peace; in machinery and manufactured articles; and an immense quantity is transformed upon the Tyne into iron steam-ships. The first iron-ship seen in the Tyne arrived about twenty years ago, and now scores are built every year, some of which are really noble and gigantic vessels. From the works of one enterprising firm alone, a fleet of powerful iron steam-ships have issued, and those which are employed in the coasting trade have quite changed the character and fortunes of that traffic. Here also two express steam-ships, larger than the ill-fated Royal Charter, have been built for the Atlantic, besides a frigate for government, and vessels for the navigation of Indian waters.

ing and manufacturing industry seen upon the river is the advancement of agriculture in Northumberland; and very striking is the contrast between the high cultivation for which the agricultural districts of the county are now generally remarkable, and the state of natural wildness in which a great part of Northumberland remained even within the time of living memory—a state attributable to the former isolation and disturbed condition of the county, its remoteness, and the difficulty of communication from its want of roads.

It would seem that after the departure of the Romans, the populous colonies which the conquerors from Italy had raised up—even on the bleak regions bordered by the Wall—decayed, and that Northumberland relapsed into a desolate and unproductive condition. It was a wild and impenetrable territory in the days of William the Conqueror, and if a Domesday Survey of this part of England had come down to us it would present, no doubt, a rugged picture. The ancient lakes, woods and morasses of which we have the remains in the bog and black peat-earth that fills up many a basin-shaped depression throughout the valley of the Till, probably continued to occupy parts of the alluvial district eastward of the Cheviot hills in the days when Saxon chieftains held sway at Bamburgh; and Milfield plain (near Wooler), was probably a swamp, or covered by tangled forest, in and long after the days when adjacent eminences of the Cheviots were the abode of a British tribe who wandered in skins of the wolf and the elk. The beaver—which occurs in 1188 apparently for the last time in any of our historical records—certainly lingered in streams of the North of England long after it had disappeared from those of Wales and the southern counties, and the wolf undoubtedly inhabited Northumberland down to the time of Henry III., if not later. From the fact that the picturesque basaltic rocks of Spindlestone near Bamburgh, and some other localities in northern counties, are the scenes of strange legends about a voracious serpent or dragon by which they

*Long-continued wildness of the county.*

are said to have been formerly inhabited, it would appear probable that tracts of primeval rock and forest lingered in those parts of the country down to the Anglo-Saxon reigns. The period is not perhaps many centuries more remote when the last hippopotami and elephants ranged the river banks of Yorkshire; and there is now the authority of Professor Owen himself for the belief that we once had our native British lion, and that it may even have been contemporary with the aborigines of Britain. But whether any of the great carnivorous animals now living only within the tropics, whose remains are found in bone caves in England, did or did not linger down to the time of the Roman invasion, it is certain that there existed in Britain in the time of Julius Cæsar two species of gigantic ox and one of reindeer, which are now extinct in this country; and it is highly probable that a species of the great fossil ox (*Bos primigenius*) was seen living in the wild forests of Britain, and in those of Germany, when they were penetrated by the Roman legions.*

In localities, then, of primeval rock and forest, such as Spindlestone continued to be in the time of the Heptarchy, may there not have co-existed with the species of animals that were living in Cæsar's time, but are now extinct, a reptile having such saurian affinities as to have been invested by popular terror with attributes of the dragon of legendary tale? Not only Rhodes, Naples, and Arles had their legendary dragon: in many a less renowned locality popular tradition commemorates the exploit of a hero who delivered the territory from the dragon's ravages. The dragon of Arles seems to belong to the time when a great crocodile, or other saurian, inhabited the estuary of the Rhone and other rivers flowing into the Mediterranean. Legends of conflicts with dragons are widely spread through northern

---

\* Remains of the *Bos primigenius* were recently found about three miles westward from Spindlestone in a post-pleiocene deposit of whitish clay, gravel, and water-worn stones, reposing on a peaty soil known as the Adderstone Mains Bog, which is traversed by the North-Eastern Railway.

Christendom, and are among the fabled feats of Teutonic heroes; they are connected with many antient churches, and are commemorated in sculptured stone as well as in rustic legend; as, for example, in Devonshire, where local folk-lore asserts that the stone avenues on Dartmoor, like the hut-circles and the kistvaens, were erected in far-distant times when *winged serpents* frequented the hills, and wolves inhabited the valleys. The dragon of "Spindlestone Heugh" was probably an equally substantial adversary: but the legend no further concerns the present subject than as indicating the primeval wildness retained by the locality in question within the time of tradition.

The name of Chevy (Cheviot) chase is a memory of the wild forests of this county: many another waste of rock and wood retained its primeval state even in the middle of the seventeenth century; and a large tract of the Border country continued until a much later period in a state hardly less primitive than it was when the monks from Iona, or St. Cuthbert from Melrose, journeyed through it, intent on their apostolic mission to the pagan natives. Thus, within the memory of some who are still living (as Lord Macaulay in his History of England remarks,) the sportsman who wandered in pursuit of game to the sources of the Tyne, found the heaths round Keeldar Castle peopled by a race hardly less savage than the Indians of California, and heard with surprise the half-naked women chanting a wild measure while the men with brandished dirks danced a war-dance. Of the lawless state of this part of the border country from the middle of the thirteenth to the middle of the seventeenth century, history affords a terrible picture. One of the oldest documents illustrative of this state of things, is a roll of pleas held at Wark, in North Tynedale, in 1279, before justices itinerant of Alexander III. of Scotland, to whom that regality then belonged; and the various deeds of robbery, violence, and encroachment recorded, exhibit a general disregard of the rights of persons and property. Four centuries afterwards, in the reign of James II. of

*Lawless state of the Borders.*

England, North Tynedale was still looked upon as a waste of evil repute, the haunt of border thieves, and a country which no king's messenger dared enter.* Camden had to leave his task unfinished when he reached Thirlwall on the Cumbrian border. Other parts of Northumberland, which had been centres of Roman civilization, were swept by the moss-troopers through those four centuries, and were in the wild, uncultivated condition naturally resulting from such a state of social insecurity. Notwithstanding the rude laws by which the townships were charged with the pursuit and apprehension of malefactors and the loyal inhabitants of the country united for its defence, the reports of the Lords Warden of the Marches, even down to the Union, afford a melancholy picture of the barbarous state of things, the insecurity of life, and the atrocious forays which harassed the owners of property. The State Papers, during the administration of Cardinal Wolsey, abound in complaints on the state of the Borders, and portentous anathemas were fulminated in aid of the civil power. Robert Carey, Earl of Monmouth, Governor of Norham, and Warden of the Middle Marches, writing in the seventeenth century, from Alnwick Abbey, where he had taken refuge with his family and household, says that, amongst the malefactors he had captured and hung, were "two gentlemen thieves" who robbed travellers. The priest and curate of Newcastle are both included in a list of " Border thieves," early in the reign of Elizabeth; and Fox, bishop of Durham, writing a few years before, describes the priests of Tynedale and Redesdale— themselves thieves, and chaplains of landowners who were thieves—as too unlettered to read the service-books, and as persons of scandalous lives. In a Border survey in 1550, we read—" the whole countrey of Northumberland is much given to riotte, specially the young gentlemen or head men,

---

\* The spirit of insubordination was not wholly quenched until a later reign, and, in North Tynedale, the king's authority was defied until late even in the last century.

and divers also of them to theftes and other greater offences." In a will made by an inhabitant of Morpeth, in 1583, the testator describes himself to be dying of the wounds murderously inflicted by four of the Ogle family and their accessories, in consequence of his having presumed to say that " the Dacres," then lords of Morpeth, " were of as good blood as the Ogles." At this time, even Hexham market was attended by " a hundred strong border-thieves," who overawed the country people they robbed. So wild and insecure was the country between Newcastle and Carlisle, that the judges of assize were escorted by an armed force. When Lord Chief Justice North came the circuit in the days of Elizabeth, the village of Bywell, through which the road passed, was inhabited by expert handicraftsmen who worked in iron—" village blacksmiths," who became inured to bear arms; and, the tenants of each manor in the barony of Bywell being bound to guard the judges in their progress, the service devolved on these stout and hardy men. The Lord Chief Justice describes his attendants as wearing long beards, short cloaks, and long, basket-hilted broadswords hanging from broad belts, and mounted on horses so small that the riders' feet and swords touched the ground. The state of the road then, and until the road-making achievements of Marshal Wade, was such that it would have been difficult to give effect to the traditional usage mentioned by Lord Campbell—that a jury, who had not agreed by the end of the assizes, were to be carried in a cart after the judge to the boundary of the next county, and there shot into a ditch—as that result was likely to be much sooner arrived at. All the communication in the way of trade between Newcastle and Carlisle, now denominated " goods traffic," was undertaken in single-horse carts by carriers, who always journeyed in company, in the fashion of an Eastern caravan, for mutual protection—a state of things which, in these days of railway travelling, it is curious to contrast with the ease and swiftness of our transit through the picturesque scenery and over the cultivated lands between

*Former want of roads.*

those towns.* And, if the road between Newcastle and Carlisle was often nearly impassable until Marshal Wade overthrew many miles of the great Roman barrier to construct his military way upon the line and with the materials of the wall, it may be imagined in what condition those parts of Northumberland remained in which there were no roads at all, and in which the violence of the moss-troopers had prevented cultivation and improvement. The frontier-lands were not reclaimed from their lawless state until the stern rule of that picturesque old chieftain and Warden of the Marches Lord William Howard (" Belted Will ") procured for him the honourable title of " Civilizer of the Borders," and restored peace to the country.† But it was not until a century after his time that the old roads through Northumberland were improved, and new roads formed to render accessible the country which had been so long impenetrable.

The first Turnpike Act for Northumberland was obtained about 1746, on a representation by the grand jury that the high post-road from London to Edinburgh had become so deep and ruinous by reason of the heavy carriages passing over it, that it could not be traversed without danger.‡ Soon afterwards, " the military road " (as it was called) from Newcastle to Carlisle was taken in hand. On the road between Hexham and Penrith a public conveyance appeared for the first time thirty years ago. About the same time, road-trustees in this part of England became so enterprising as to form plans for widening and levelling the high roads and reducing the steep hills and vexatious windings which

* *Festina lente* seems nevertheless to be the motto of the Railway Company.

† The Courts of the Wardens seem to have been regulated during the sixteenth and seventeenth centuries in a spirit of justice, and to have administered the rude border-laws with judicial forms. A complete cordon of defence was also maintained, with watchers at fords and passes.

‡ It has been suggested that the first wheeled-carriage capable of conveying travellers, that ever crossed the Tyne, was probably that in which the ladies of the Princess Margaret, daughter of Henry VII., accompanied her on her nuptial journey into Scotland. Remembering what the roads then were, and that the carriages were without springs, it is surprising how travellers could survive such a journey.

retarded traffic through the central parts of the county: large sums were then expended on the roads through Alnwick into Scotland, and on the road from Newcastle by way of Weldon Bridge and Wooler to the Tweed at Coldstream. But now the railway whistle will ere long be heard among the lonely border hills where (as at Keeldar) the inhabitants still derive their supplies through carriers from Hawick, some of whom are stated to combine the trades of draper, grocer, baker, stationer, and hardware and crockery dealer. The border regions are no longer the uncultivated lands in which the lawless freebooter defied the arm of justice:—

> Long rolling years have swept those scenes away,
> And peace is on the mountain and the fell;
> And rosy dawn and closing twilight grey
> Hear but the distant sheepwalk's tinkling bell.

With security of property and facility of communication the era of improvement and agricultural production began, and Northumberland stood honourably foremost in adopting the improved system of agriculture which was introduced on this side of the border about thirty years ago. Weedy wastes were reclaimed; thorough draining began to be practised extensively; the value of lime in agriculture was recognised by Northumbrian farmers; and in time improved implements appeared, and even thrashing machines driven by steam or water power were set up. Within the last ten years much has been done in draining, and it is estimated that 170,000 acres have been drained in that time; still, however, much remains to be done. Landlords wisely fostered the spirit of improvement, and the agriculturists of Northumberland have for some time past shown themselves not behind their mining and manufacturing brethren on the Tyne in the spirit of enterprise. Long leases and liberal covenants as in the South, capital, and intelligence, are now the recognised requirements for successful farming in this part of England also, and much has been done of late years to enforce the conviction that the highest state of cultivation is the most productive to the tenant. A traveller through

*Agricultural improvements.*

the border district north of Wooler, formerly the scene of constant forays, and where on many a hill the purple heather hides the black stains of ancient battle, cannot fail to be struck by the extension of agriculture: cultivated fields stretch for hundreds of acres where no villages and few human dwellings are seen, and up the slope of steep hills agriculture bravely holds its own. It says much for the "peace and plenty" picture drawn by Mr. Grey, the agent of the Greenwich Hospital Commissioners for their estates in Northumberland, at a meeting of the Hexham Farmers' Club, in the summer of 1859, that on those large estates, the rental of which exceeds 42,000*l.* a-year, there were only 30*l.* in arrear at the last audit. The condition of the peasantry as well as of the farmers has improved rapidly. The farm-buildings and the labourers' cottages have shared in the general improvement, and within the last ten years the wages of farm-labourers and hinds have increased by nearly one fifth. In the cottages where, not long ago, wheat-flour was seldom seen and meat was almost an unknown luxury, white bread is common, and the butcher's cart even is said to have now become a regular visitor in Northumbrian villages. It is not many years since the primitive agricultural cart with solid wooden wheels might be found in Northumberland just as it is now seen in Spain. The improvement has reached even the remote districts of Tynedale, where, from the time of Henry III. down to the present century, there existed the tenure "in drengage" (the service of ploughing, harrowing, and sowing the lord's land), which seems to have been common in, if it was not confined to, the territory that constituted the old kingdom of Northumberland; and, for a long time past, rents have come to be paid in money instead of the primitive forms of farm produce or bond-service. There is a remarkable proportion of large holdings in the farms of Northumberland. In 1851 there were returned thirty-four farms of 2,000 acres and upwards. The whole arable land of the county is about 270,000 acres, and the cereal produce amounts to about two millions and a half annually. In the pastoral division of the county an immense improvement has been made. There are sheep-farms of grass-land of immense extent, the scanty herbage and ungenial climate of the high moorland tracts rendering those parts of the county fit only for grazing, and large flocks of the native breed of sheep—" a hardy race on Cheviot bred"—are there maintained. The proportion of meadow-land is small. A considerable breadth of the level tract of country extending along the coast is devoted to the culture of wheat, the soil being for the most part a strong clayey loam. The corn produce in Northumberland amounts to about a million and a quarter annually. A large proportion of the arable lands, especially in the carboniferous sandstone districts, are of a moist loam with a subsoil of retentive clay, and are, of course, appropriated chiefly to the raising of grain. A sandy or gravelly dry soil, favourable for raising turnips, is found on the river banks of Northumberland, and also on the uplands and in the valleys of the Cheviot district. Sir Hildebrand Osbaldistone laments (as the reader will remember) that the new turnips, with the rats and the Hanoverians, the French antics and book-learning, had changed the world which he had known in old England. Turnip cultivation has however become a considerable feature of Northumbrian farming, and the common white turnip as well as Swedes are successfully raised on even the heaviest lands, for retentive. soils have been converted into rich loam by a judicious system of cultivation. Only a century ago no turnips were grown in Northumberland, and the culture of potatoes was then first introduced in this county by the vicar of the border parish of Norham.

To glance from potatoes to population: we find that at the last census the population was returned as follows:—

| | | |
|---|---|---|
| Unmarried males (all ages) . . | 97,356 | |
| Husbands . . . . . | 46,655 | 149,515 |
| Widowers . . . . . | 5,504 | |
| Unmarried females (all ages) . . | 93,441 | |
| Wives (many husbands were probably at sea) | 48,403 | 154,053 |
| Widows . . . . . | 12,209 | |

Of the 303,568 total inhabitants, only 232,826 were returned as natives of the county. The agricultural labourers greatly exceeded the coal-miners in number.

*Labourers' homes.*

The condition of the labourers' cottages on some of the great estates of Northumberland has been deplorable, but considerable improvement in this respect also has been made in its agricultural districts within the last few years; Lord Grey's Howick cottages are models of neatness, and the Duke of Northumberland has spent immense sums on his estates. His Grace set about the improvement of his labourers' homes in a business-like way; and an immense number of cottages marked by fitness and utility, and by a wish to benefit the occupiers, have consequently risen—a permanent improvement to the property and an honour to the noble owner. The mountainous and moorland regions, which are about equal in extent to the arable division of the county, are, of course, vast solitudes; and even in the central districts the county appears very thinly inhabited,* the villages being few and far between, many land-owners having been accustomed to clear the peasants' cottages from their estates.

It is in the agricultural districts generally that the Northumbrian character is the most favourably displayed. Manly independence, shrewdness, honesty, and hospitality, are the common characteristics of the peasantry; and there is many a village the very remoteness and isolation of which seem to promise that those good old-fashioned qualities will be found—a village where (as a late historian remarked) the weaver and the smith work only for the farmer, where the mill is a corn-mill only, where the ale-house is not "licensed to let post-horses," and the tailor is not "from London"—a place girt by small inclosures, intersected by briery lanes, and telling altogether in its aspect that it belongs to an ancient race of yeomanry, jealous to preserve their little patrimony and tenacious of the habits and tra-

---

* In the parish of Elsdon, for example, one of the largest and least populous in Britain, a population of 2,000 is thinly scattered over an area 21 miles long by 5 miles broad.

ditions of their sires. Nevertheless, the aspect of most of the villages of Northumberland, even in the agricultural districts (excepting, perhaps, some old villages of rural districts in the north of the county), does not bespeak anything attractive or pleasing in the inhabitants, or reflect much credit on the former disposition of the land-owner. And as to the new settlements (the endearing name of villages seems hardly applicable to them) that sprang up when waste lands came to be divided, when men no longer dwelt under the protection of castles, and population increased with the advance of peaceful industry, there certainly is not anything imaginative, or (as in the case of most old British names) descriptive of locality, in the names that were given to them. Of this very modern class of appellations we have the following ridiculous examples in Northumberland:—Blink-bonny, Brandy-well Hall, Breadless-row, Click-him-in, Cold-knuckles, Delicate Hall, Delight, Fell-him-down, Glower-o'er-him, Maccaroni, Make-me-rich, Mount Hooley, Philadelphia, Pinch-me-near, Pondicherry, Portobello, Quality-corner, Skirl-naked, Twice-brewed, Windy-nook, &c. *Absurd modern names.*

The agricultural villages, and the labourers' homes generally, as well as the population of agricultural districts, stand, however, in favourable contrast to the chief part of the pit-villages (as they are called) and the mining population. Long rows and aggregations of unsightly cottages, peopled only by those who earn their living from the adjacent pits, mark too many of the colliery districts; and the cottages, especially where the property is leasehold, are generally hideous, sordid, barrack-like abodes, not indeed destitute of cleanliness and homely comfort, but totally wanting in the humanising though humble adornments of southern rustic homes: no flowers grace these dwellings of dusky toil, no verdure relieves the bare cindery earth around them, no church diffuses its hallowed influence and associations; and, if we were to judge of the coal-mining population of Northumberland and Durham by comparing their dwellings with the cottages of the mining population of Cornwall, a con- *Colliery villages.* *Character of mining population.*

clusion very unfavourable to the Northumbrian miners would be drawn; but, although the pitmen are an unpolished race, and as regards religious and secular instruction have too generally been left as uncultivated as their dialect is uncouth, they share the Northumbrian energy of character, and, where they have acquired any education at all, there are constant examples of their desire for knowledge, especially in applied sciences. Great allowances must be made for this Troglodytean class of labourers, for they spend their youth and vigour cramped in close and impure air in a high temperature, are liable to instant destruction from the "fire-damp" and equally fatal "choke-damp" of the mine, and lead a cheerless life which almost separates them from the world of breeze and sunshine. Where libraries have been formed for the colliers, or the workmen in the great iron, alkali, and other manufactories upon the Tyne, the men readily avail themselves of such advantages, and it appears that works of imagination are especially in demand. Allotment gardens, too, are becoming very generally cultivated in the colliery villages. The wages of the pitmen are good, and sufficient for their wants, and there are few colliery villages where a school is not maintained besides a reading room or mechanics' institute. The lead-mining districts, however, are much in advance of most colliery districts in regard to educational provisions. Allusion has been already made in particular to the system of industrial polity established at Mr. Beaumont's lead-mines. The comforts of the labourers and the education of their children are well cared for; schools and libraries are established, benefit societies are in operation, and the miners enjoy such physical comforts and leisure that they can profit by the educational provisions made in their behalf. It is really worthy of remark, that, at one of these mining settlements called Coalclough, in Weardale, some miners published a selection of poems, and four conjointly wrote a pamphlet on the benefits to be derived from well-conducted friendly societies. The lead-miner's day is for eight hours only, and he works for five days in the week, his wages varying from 15s. to 20s. Some of the leisure time of the miners is employed in cultivating cottage-gardens, and their ambition is to possess a small freehold. In the coal-mining districts, unfortunately, a boy is no sooner able to earn some wages than he is taken from school; and, as regards benefit societies, the helpless widows and children of coal-miners have still to lament the want of a provident or assurance fund, a provision which the coal-owners ought to assist their labourers in making,* for, although of late years, from greater care and improved ventilation, there have been fewer of the frightful explosions that used to bring sorrow and destitution to scores of families at once, there is an increase in the number of deaths in coal-pits in proportion to the number of tons of coal now raised. So much for the physical condition of the labouring population.

The peasantry of Northumberland cherish the local traditions of the county; they very generally retain the feelings of clanship which in former days bound the tenants and dependants of an estate or family to its hereditary owner or representative: and they hold in memory, as part of the folk-lore of Northumberland, the stirring events of Border history. In ballad-poetry Northumberland is richer than some other counties, and it seems as if the natives had been tenacious of their oral traditions in proportion to the former want of books, education, and intercourse with the rest of the world. *Legendary lore.*

The student of folk-lore finds, therefore, much to interest him in Northumberland. Many old superstitions linger among the peasantry, and in this county, as in the South-West of England, much of heathendom survives, but with this peculiarity in Northumberland, that there are traces of Scandinavian as well as of Celtic and Saxon superstitions. In some Northumbrian customs, however, we seem to have

---

* That strange amphibious race, the " keelmen " of the Tyne, formerly a very numerous class, but who are gradually becoming extinct, have a provident fund arising from a tax of a farthing a ton on all coal shipped in the Tyne.

D

Old customs.

Superstitions.

vestiges of the Romans: thus, the image called "the Harvest Queen" or "Corn-baby," which has been deemed the representative of the Roman Ceres, continued, in the latter half of the last century, to be dressed up and carried from many a village on the last day of harvest to the field, where it remained to the end of reaping; again, the sword-dance, which though Scandinavian also, some antiquaries have connected with the *Saltatio armata* of the Roman militia on their festival *Armilustrium*, is or lately was practised in some Northumbrian villages; the Roman feast of the Lares, when their couch was adorned with flowers and placed before the houses, was represented late in the last century by exhibiting a cushion covered with flowers at cottage doors on Midsummer-day; and at Allhallows, too, there was still the rural sacrifice of nuts which has been deemed the relic of a pagan festival in honour of Pomona. Although the belief in witchcraft, which in the first year of that accursed usurpation of fanatics called the "Commonwealth," sacrificed fourteen unhappy women in one series of executions at Newcastle-upon-Tyne, now seldom takes a form that is anything more than ludicrous; it lingered, with many less mischievous superstitions, down to later times. It is not alone at Housesteads, by the Roman Wall, on a meadow once occupied by a suburb of the military station of Borcovicus, that the fairies come from an adjacent cave for their moonlight dances; the "good people" figure in many another rural locality, and are quite familiar objects in the folk-lore of the county. It has been remarked, with much truth, that where popular tradition associates fairy legends with any spot, it is highly probable that such tradition has been derived from Celtic inhabitants of the locality. The parish registers in Northumberland—most of which begin after the Restoration,[*] afford many traces of the gross ignorance and superstition of the people. The condition of the peasantry in Northumberland during the old days of violence and

---

[*] The registers of only five parishes, viz.: Newcastle, Berwick, Hexham, Morpeth, and Earsdon contain any entries that go back to the time of Elizabeth.

insecurity may be easily inferred. Even in later times, education continued to be sadly deficient on the Border lands, but at the beginning of the seventeenth century the gentlemen of property and old family were often unable to write or read. At that time there appear to have been only twenty-one schoolmasters * in the whole county, of whom eleven were employed at Newcastle; sixteen gentlemen of old family were discharging the duties of parish clerk; and in the early part of the reign of Elizabeth, out of 146 Northumbrian landowners who combined to defend the borders, only fifty-four could write their names; but in regard to education at that period Northumberland probably was not much behind other and more peaceful parts of England. A century ago, in the time of Hutchinson, the historian of Northumberland, Cumberland, and Durham, the Solstitial " Beltein" fires were still raised on Midsummer eve on the top of high hills, and the people danced around them; the rustic inhabitants still carried lighted torches about their fields on the eve of St. Peter's day, and at May-day practised a kind of divination by fishing for a wedding-ring in a syllabub: the Christmas fire is still lighted with the yule log in this county, and there are relics of the rock and river worship of Celtic tribes. Of course stories of the supernatural are connected with several of the Border towers. For example, Meldon Tower, in the vale of the Wansbeck, is the scene of the ghostly wanderings of a personage celebrated as Meg of Meldon,† who for her covetous habits, and practice of unearthly arts, was doomed after her death to wander seven years and rest seven years alternately, and her phantom—the terror of the neighbourhood—haunts the place where she had deposited a bull's hide full of gold; but the former lady of Meldon does not come, like Lady Howard of Okehampton, nightly to her park in a gilt coach

* One of the Berwick pedagogues in 1578 was Aristotle Knovsley, and another was John Wacke.

† Supposed by Hodgson to be Margaret, wife of Sir William Fenwick.

attended by her black hound. Perhaps the Wansbeck Valley Railway, now commenced, may produce the gold and banish the phantom. Again, the ruins of a mansion of the Orde family, built at a place called Sandybank, is attributed to a ghost of such terrific character as to have rendered it uninhabitable. But enough of these popular legends; it is time to turn to things more substantial.

*Celtic or ancient British antiquities.*

The monuments of the pre-historic period in Northumberland are so numerous, as to show that this part of our island must have been the scene of populous British settlements. Earthworks and encampments, stone-circles and sepulchral remains, abound in the north of the county, and occupy localities that are now mountain solitudes and hills where now only the moorfowl dwells among the heather. Here, as in Wiltshire, it was the high lands, and not the valleys, that were inhabited by the aboriginal people; forests seem to have overspread the vales, and the earthworks and other traces of the long residence of Celtic tribes occupy the heights. Northumberland does not present any such monuments as the grey Cyclopean monoliths of Stonehenge; but single and double stone-circles, of the kind which used to be called Druidical, occupy wild solitudes in the northern part of the county, amid the camps, villages, and graves of the rude tribes with whom the Romans came in contact. Some inclosures, containing circular foundations, which are found in Redesdale, resemble those existing on Ingleborough in Yorkshire, and at several places in Cornwall. The top of Yevering Bell is crowned with circular mounds and fosses, and with the remains of circular walls of stone that are supposed to have formed temples for Celtic worship or conspicuous altars for the Baaltein fire; and almost every lesser eminence of the Cheviots is crested with remains of the early inhabitants who chased wild animals in the adjacent forest. Numerous cromlechs, tumuli, stone obelisks and circles are marked on the admirable maps of Watling Street recently prepared by direction of the Duke of Northumberland; and at Old Bewick, and various other places in the north of the county, are camps and entrenchments of circular and of half-moon form.*

Northumberland preserves in many local names the traces of its former Celtic language. The British names of places were generally, as is well known, descriptive of some natural characteristic, and many of them have survived in their primitive form, or as modified by the language of conquerors: *ex. gr.*—the names of Tyne and Tweed, of Aln and Derwent, of Lindis and Low, are British; and some names of hills in the Cheviot range, as Yevering, Steroch, and Yenshcon, indicate a similar derivation. Again, the name of a spot called " Petty-may " or " Pity-me," which is situated among some remarkable knolls on the Watling Street, and seems to have been a place of sepulture, is perhaps, as some one has suggested, derived from *Beddau-maes*—a field of graves; so too, " Foul-play " from *Foel-blae*—the bald, blue hill. Most of the Roman names of stations on the Wall are evidently Latinized forms of the descriptive British names, but few or no other traces of Roman speech are found in the county.

It is, of course, to the enduring sway of the Saxons in England that we have to attribute the greatest part of its local names. Those of Saxon derivation greatly preponderate in Northumberland, but the Danes, also, have left many similar memorials. Long, however, as was the Danish rule in the North of England, its only monuments are found in local names, and in the Scandinavian element visible in

---

* In this locality some remarkable stones have been found, which are incised with figures sculptured in the rudest forms, and bearing resemblance to some of those Pictish or early sculptured stones of Scotland, which form the subject of a very interesting paper, with illustrative drawings, printed in the fourth volume of the Spalding Club books. The incised markings of the Old Bewick stones are of so primitive a character that they seem to belong to a more remote era than the very early crosses of Caledonia. Some circular figures on the rock, near the site of two hill-forts in the Old Bewick district, correspond remarkably with some sculptures of unknown purport which are engraved in " *The Sculptured Stones of Scotland,*" and are stated in the last part of the Proceedings of the Scottish Society of Antiquaries to resemble figures in the Mound at New Grange in Ireland, and others that are found in Britany.

the dialect and population, especially in the people who derive their living, as their forefathers did, from the sea.

The Norman scribes of the Domesday Survey (which, unfortunately, does not extend to Northumberland), corrupted the Saxon and Danish names, both of places and persons, much in the same way that the Romans had altered the British names; but of the Norman, as of the Roman speech, few traces are left in English topography.

*Monuments of Roman period.* The historical monuments of the Roman period in Northumberland consist, not only of the remains of art, the military weapons, the altars and votive-tablets that have been found in once populous military stations, but of paved roads, and, above all, of considerable fragments of the great barrier-wall which forms so imposing a monument of the Roman power. The surveys of the Roman Wall, and of the Watling Street, lately made by Mr. MacLauchlan for the Duke of Northumberland, and, by the liberality of his grace sumptuously produced for private distribution, accurately illustrate the two greatest military works of the Romans in Northumberland, and have done for these celebrated monuments what has not been done for Roman remains in other parts of England.

*Watling Street.* Watling Street has a course of sixty-nine miles from Pierse-bridge (where it enters the county of Durham,) to Chew-green on the Scotish border, the intermediate stations being Binchester, Lanchester, and Ebchester, in the county of Durham; and Corbridge, Risingham, and Rochester, in Northumberland; all, save Chew-green, being inclosed by walls of masonry, and the whole line being bordered more or less by remains of British occupation. The Watling Street, and the Roman roads that joined it, have been obliterated in many localities in Northumberland, even within the last hundred years, by the progress of cultivation, and the former way is traceable by only faint remains through large portions of its course.*

* A county map which was published a hundred years ago, when few of the roads that now traverse Northumberland had been made, delineates this great

It is striking and suggestive to discover, amid grassy mounds in remote solitudes far from the haunts of men, memorials of the former residence in those places of martial legions; and strange and exotic, on lonely Northumbrian hills, seem the inscriptions which were set up there by soldiers from sunny Mediterranean shores, by legionaries from Italy and Spain, Belgium and Gaul. And more suggestive still are those lapidary monuments—some in such preservation that they seem as if chiseled yesterday, others scarcely legible; names that once carried terror to nations as nearly obliterated on the stone as in human memory; some in which a line is pregnant with the genius or faith of antient Rome: often a few letters reveal a whole fable of heathen mythology; and it is touching to find amongst the overthrown military edifices of the Roman soldier an inscription to a "beloved wife," another, set up by a Belgic tribune, in memory of a "charming daughter,"—memorials of their love that have outlived mighty monuments of their sway.

The most wonderful of the Roman military works in Northumberland was the Barrier Wall, and most imposing must have been its appearance, when, with its commanding stations, it stood in all its strength, scaling the heights of the rugged cliffs, and descending the valleys, in its course across the country from sea to sea. Portions of this great monument may still be traced through a considerable part of the line from Newcastle to Carlisle, for, though it was generally resorted to as the stone-quarry for any farm-buildings in its vicinity, a line of masonry eight feet broad, and twelve feet high, has not been easy to demolish. The stations *per lineam valli*, which seem to have been cities on a small scale (containing, as they did, temples and baths, and the buildings of a garrison,) were twenty-three in number; and, besides these fortified stations, there were mile-castles along the whole line, with watch-towers between

*The Roman Wall.*

military way, and certain branches of it, as then existing in localities in which it has now been obliterated for many years.

them on the wall. Some of the stations were of considerable magnitude; one of the largest was Borcovicus (now known as Housesteads), garrisoned by the first cohort of the Tungrians from Belgic Gaul, which, from the foundations of streets and ruined buildings still visible, and the descriptions left by Hunter, Gordon, Horsley, Gale, Stukeley, and other antiquaries, seems to have deserved its appellation of " The Tadmor of Britain." The station called Chesters is remarkable for extensive and almost perfect remains of the baths of a luxurious villa. Perhaps the largest and best naturally defended of the stations is Amboglanna, which, from its modern name of Burdoswald, seems to have become the citadel of a Saxon king. It occupies a large quadrangular plateau, beneath the steep slope of which flows the rocky Irthing; and the interest of the fine view from it is much enhanced by the similarity (which Lord Carlisle has suggested,\*) to the scenery of the celebrated place supposed to be the site of Troy. But it is not within the scope of the present Memoir to describe the Wall or its stations.† The question " Who built the Wall? " was much debated by northern antiquaries a few years since, but it is not necessary to throw upon these pages the " cold shade " of that frigid and pedantic controversy.‡

It has always been a question whether the Wall, and the works connected with it, are to be attributed to three distinct periods,—whether Agricola constructed the stations as well as the military-way; whether Hadrian built only the ditch and southern mounds of the vallum; and Severus the wall of stone? Whatever conclusion may be the correct one, Mr. MacLauchlan's careful survey greatly augments our

\* In his " Diary in Turkish and Greek waters."

† " The Roman Wall in Northumberland " is the subject of an able and interesting article in the *Quarterly Review* for December, 1859.

‡ The reader who may be interested in the question, will find a long chapter devoted to its discussion in a work recently produced under the auspices of the Antiquarian Society of Newcastle, entitled *A History of Northumberland*, in three parts ; Part I. containing the general history of the county. 4to. 1858.

knowledge of these stupendous works themselves. It is curious to contrast with what we now know about the Wall, the idea entertained in Horsley's days (when it had been very imperfectly explored,) as to the extent of the command held by the Roman legions over the country beyond it. Horsley had not been able to discover any gates in the Wall or passes through it, excepting at the stations or the intersection of the military ways; but, it appears that in each of the mile-castles recently excavated, important passes through the wall have been found, and the remains of massive gates. In the valley, eastward from Borcovicus, a passage in the Wall was found, defended with double gates, having a guard-room on each side, and in the middle an upright stone such as is found in other gateways of the stations and likewise in the streets of Pompeii.

The territories of five British tribes extended from the Wall to the Forth and Clyde, and formed the province of Valentia in the reign of Valentinian. Bremenium (the only one of Ptolemy's towns to the north of the Wall which occurs in the Itinerary,) was the chief seat of the Otadeni —a tribe that does not seem to have been subdued until the return of Agricola from his campaign in Caledonia in A.D. 84, and commands the upper part of the valley of the Rede on the line of the great Roman road. It lately attracted some attention on account of excavations in progress there; and it is curious that, amongst Roman remains found in this remote station, is a metallic mass which has proved to be wholly composed of chain-mail, hauberks of which are represented on the base of Trajan's column at Rome. In the same part of the province are remains of another remarkable centre of British settlement—the Mote Hill of Elsdon, perhaps the most perfect earthwork of the kind in Northumberland. It is surrounded by entrenched works not only of the British inhabitants but of their Roman conquerors, who seem, indeed, to have occupied the Mote Hill itself, for in it two altars bearing the name of Aurelius Antoninus were found. From the antient British inhabitants has been

*Roman towns north of the Wall.*

derived the name of Otterburn, which is near the line of the Watling Street, and retained until lately some British earthworks. In the same district was Habitancum (now Risingham); and remains of nameless outlying Roman camps are found on the branches of Watling Street that traverse this part of the Roman province. But from Roman military works and altars, it is time to turn to those monuments in Northumberland which belong to the mediæval period of its history, and are more interesting to ourselves.

<small>Saxon period.</small> Of the dark interval between the departure of the Romans and the conversion of Edwin, it is of course not to be expected that any monuments can be found, unless some of the remains of British settlement already referred to should really belong to that period. The followers of Woden seem to have raised a temple to their deity at the mouth of the Aln, for a Christian-edifice, now in ruins, which was probably its successor, was known even down to a century ago by the name of "Woden's Church." It is more interesting as the probable locality from which the royal embassy sailed forth to invite St. Cuthbert from his island hermitage on Farne: in modern times, this little port of the Aln acquired very different associations, for there was, during many years, a considerable shipment from it of corn and other agricultural produce; but the wasting sea has nearly swept away the antient church of Alnmouth that rose above the sand-hills; the railway has diverted its trade, and almost its only visitors are those few who come hither to woo Hygeia amid the sea-born gales.

<small>Ecclesiastical antiquities.</small> The ecclesiastical monuments of Northumberland have quite a peculiar character. It has a prominent place in the annals of the church and nation from the very earliest times, for its inhabitants were converted to Christianity before those of the West of England, and in its fountains Paulinus baptised converts soon after the mission of Augustine. In the far-off morning of Northumbrian Christianity, Aidan and Cuthbert, Oswald and Oswin, form a saintly and regal constellation; and religion, arts, and letters were cultivated by

Northumbrian monks—or perhaps by Scotish monks in Northumbrian monasteries—long before the days of Alfred, and in times when some other parts of England seem to have hardly emerged from barbarism. The Anglo-Saxon church had not a more fruitful field than this distant province, nor a period of greater historical lustre than that in which Northumberland was ruled by a monarch of its own. Sunny uplands on the slopes of Cheviot now traversed by the lonely shepherd were then seats of Saxon royalty; Bamburgh was the citadel of kings, and Hexham the dowry of a queen; and the site of many a parish church in Northumberland, now neglected and remote, was consecrated by its first apostles. The light of the Gospel, cherished by a regal convert, shone from Bamburgh while Christianity was being spread amongst its pagan natives. Hexham—the fifth church that was built of stone in Britain, and one of its chief glories—was the masterpiece of St. Wilfrid, the greatest of Anglo-Saxon church-builders; and near to it St. John of Beverley had lived a hermit beneath the "Eagle's Mount." The then royal abbey of Tynemouth was famed far to the Cleveland hills and northward to the Tweed; and the sanctity of Cuthbert gave a line of bishops to Lindisfarne. In that remote island, moreover, arts flourished from the seventh century, as we may see in the celebrated book of the Gospels, called "The Durham Book," now in the Cottonian Library, which was written and illuminated at Lindisfarne. The history of Northumberland during the Saxon period is more ample than that of any other part of England, but its architectural monuments cannot claim so high a degree of antiquity. Notwithstanding the picture drawn in *Marmion* of Lindisfarne, standing with the "deep walls" that had defied the Dane, the "ponderous columns short and low," and all the "Saxon strength"—

> That could twelve hundred years withstand
> Winds, waves, and northern pirate's hand;

and notwithstanding the belief of an enthusiastic ecclesiologist, who visited the county a few years ago, that he recognised Saxon work in the grey old towers of the sister-churches at Bywell and of Ovingham upon the Tyne, it does not appear there is any undoubted Saxon architecture standing above ground in any part of Northumberland, save such fragments as are built up with later work in various churches; but on many ecclesiastical sites in this county Saxon foundations have been laid bare in the course of rebuilding or other alteration.

Norman churches.

The Norman period was the most important era for church-building in Northumberland. A large number of its parish churches date from the twelfth century, and in many of them the actual fabric is of that period. Norman piety also rebuilt the Saxon monasteries of Hexham, Lindisfarne, and Tynemouth, and founded five other abbeys. Northumberland, however, cannot boast a Tavistock or Woburn; its monastic foundations was generally more remarkable for antiquity than magnificence, and for saintly associations than for architectural splendour. Its parochial churches, too, are plain and stern; no lofty spires adorn the landscapes of "mountainous Northumberland," nor are its religious edifices enriched by much architecture of the Decorated style. None of its villages or way-sides, and few of its churchyards, afford an example of those gray antique crosses which, abounding in the West of England, for example, consecrate the spot to Christian memories, nor does monumental sculpture enrich many of its churches. All the monastic edifices in the county are in ruins excepting the choir and transepts of the noble abbey church of Hexham, which became the parochial church some time after the dissolution of monasteries.*

Monastic remains.

The monks must have owned no small part of Northumberland. The Augustine Canons flourished at Hexham,

---

\* The nave was burnt by the Scots in 1296. In Hexham Abbey Church is preserved, however, one venerable and curious monument of its Saxon privileges—the stone chair called "Frith-stol," or seat of peace.

also at Alnwick (where the Abbey was founded by that martial predecessor of the Percys of Alnwick, Eustace FitzJohn, the husband of Beatrice heiress of Ivo de Vesci); and at Brinkburn, where, girded by the Coquet, and sheltered in deep woods, the walls of their church, a work of Norman and Transition architecture, remain. The Benedictines flourished on the bold sea-beaten cliffs of Tynemouth, and northward at Lindisfarne; the Carmelites at Hulne, (the first monastery of that order founded in England,) and the Præmonstratensians at Blanchland on the wooded Derwent. The Cistercians—those pious

————men who from ambition's pathway stole
To give their whole lives blamelessly to God———

were established at Newminster, eldest, and for a long time only, daughter of princely Fountains;—Newminster, whose abbat Robert was canonized as of the holy company of heaven, and whose gray walls rose near Morpeth, on a secluded sunny meadow of the Wansbeck, set in an amphitheatre of woods, and half-encircled by the peaceful shining stream. Many of the religious houses of Northumberland were defended in the manner of a castle, having their strong outer walls, and fortified gate-towers; others, like Blanchland and Brinkburn, seem to have relied for safety on their seclusion in deep-wooded river valleys, surrounded by wild and lonely moorlands, and far from the highways of the Northumbrian marauders. The island monastery of Lindisfarne was defended by a castle, but seems to have owed its exclusive immunity from pillage to the respect which even the Scots could own for Cuthbert, its patron saint.

The monastic remains in Northumberland may be briefly described. The grand old Romanesque church of Lindisfarne, round which such memories crowd of Saxon bishops, wild sea-kings, and Norman monks, is the oldest monastic church in Northumberland. The episcopal dignity having been transferred to Durham before the Conquest, Lindisfarne was subsequently refounded as a priory or dependent

Lindisfarne.

house of the great Benedictine monastery upon the Wear. Here on Holy Isle no sound of strife or martial armament disturbed the recluses' prayer; from the cares of state and policy that beset the thorny splendour of Durham the monks of Lindisfarne were free; their cloister long resounded only to the cry of the waterfowl or the roar of the waves, and in the reign of Henry II. was celebrated as the "school of saints." The Surtees Society has published that interesting series of "Account Rolls" of Lindisfarne which remain at Durham, and in these we may read the story of the house from year to year, and see the monks at their employments, at one time dispensing a yearly income equal to 2,000*l.* in our money, and at another by the failure of crops reduced to the very low ebb of 32*l.* They maintained a great sea-fishery, and sold to their brethren at Durham porpoises and other fish then esteemed as delicacies for episcopal feasts. They protected, and never presumed to destroy, those eider-ducks of which Farne has been the abode from the earliest times—a bird about which they cherished the harmless superstition that it had been miraculously preserved from the days of St. Cuthbert. These feathered children of the wave seem, like themselves, to have loved quiet, yet not to have shunned the society of man. It is very remarkable that on the barren Farne islands the wild waves have not the sole dominion, for, on several of these rocky islets, though swept by storm and sea-spray, the gentle eider-ducks, besides various tribes of noisy sea-fowl, breed and dwell.*

*Hexham Abbey Church.* The finest example of Transitional architecture in Northumberland is the stately abbey church which the Augustine Canons raised at Hexham near the end of the twelfth century, above the curious crypt constructed partly with stones bearing Roman inscriptions, which, from its resemblance to

---

* Their protection is highly creditable to Archdeacon Thorp. Besides the eider-duck, the dotterel and rare roseate tern may now be seen on the Farne islands. But ornithologists have to lament that the local catalogue of birds is elsewhere diminishing, and that rare birds are too often wantonly destroyed.

the crypt at Ripon, seems to have been a subterranean part of Wilfrid's cathedral.

At Tynemouth some portions of the early-English choir, a structure of peculiar beauty, and considerable portions of the Norman church, remain, though the great waves have rolled beneath them and the wings of the sea-birds have swept them, for seven hundred years. But none of the buildings of the monastery exist, the site and circuit having been a garrison from the time of the Dissolution—a strange contrast to the state of the priory in its palmy days, when its monks enjoyed a kind of separate regality, owned parishes and manors scattered from the Tyne almost to the Cheviots, entertained sovereigns, and maintained a splendid hospitality. *Tynemouth.*

The ruins of Hulne Abbey crown a wooded height of enchanting beauty upon the river Aln, and the remains, as well of the buildings as of the church of the Carmelites, are considerable.* Of Alnwick Abbey, however, in the adjacent park, a fine gate-tower is all that remains. At Newminster there is only a solitary archway, amid grass-grown lines and mounds of ruined wall, to mark the site of that once famous Cistercian house. Of Brinkburn Priory the church alone exists, but it stands comparatively entire, and presents fine examples of Transitional work, as stern in aspect as it is secluded from the world in situation. *Hulne. Alnwick. Brinkburn.*

In the Anglo-Norman reigns England saw an age of castle-building and of warlike manners, but an age which *Military antiquities of the feudal age.*

* The foundation of Hulne is attributed to somewhat romantic circumstances. John de Vesci, lord of Alnwick, visited Mount Carmel with a companion Crusader before he succeeded to his inheritance, and there found that another Northumbrian knight, who had signalized his valour, had preceded him

" To Bethlehem's glade, and Carmel's haunted strand,"

and had taken the vow and the Carmelite robe among the fraternity on the Mount. The ardent Crusaders, however, obtained permission for their countryman to return with them, on their promising to found a house of Carmelite Friars; and, being struck by the resemblance to Mount Carmel of the secluded hill on which the ruins of Hulne Abbey now stand, they selected it for the site of their monastery.

marked its wonderful vigour by also building churches; just as in France, where many cathedrals, even, were completed in the time of Philip Augustus, notwithstanding the wars that characterise his reign. The parish churches of Northumberland are, for the most part, built with more of strength than ornament; and, in this respect, resemble the churches of Cornwall. They have generally low, square, heavy towers, which seem also to have been used as places of defence; and other architectural features bear the impress of the days of Border warfare,—*ex. gr.* narrow, deep-splayed windows, few and high, in the Norman walls, sometimes a roof of stone, and such other features (common in castellated architecture, but seldom seen in churches in the southern parts of England), as the square-headed trefoiled arch, and considerable massiveness in the walls. In many instances we have a campanile instead of a western tower, where a castle is adjacent, lest a church-tower should have afforded to the Border enemy a place of strength; and where there is not an adjacent castle a tower stood detached in the church-yard.

Parish churches.

The most noticeable parish churches in the county are, those of Norham, Bamburgh, Warkworth, and Alnwick, in the northern division; Mitford and Morpeth on the Wansbeck; Hexham, Bywell, Ovingham, and Ryton, upon the Tyne; and St. Nicholas in the town of Newcastle. Norham church is remarkable historically for its connection with the early bishops of the once princely see of Durham, lords of "Norham's castled steep," and the frequent residence there of Edward I. in his wars with Scotland. The church, which stands amidst trees in a beautiful situation, is a Norman fabric, massive and solemn in aspect, and almost cathedral-like in proportion. Bamburgh church is a fine early-English edifice with a beautiful crypt, and its earlier history is associated with the regal memories of the adjacent castle, now the chief seat of the charities founded by Bishop Crewe. Warkworth has a chancel of late-Norman work with vaulted roof of stone; and the fine church of the Augustine Canons of Alnwick (St. Michael's, now the parish church) has good Middle Pointed work. At Ovingham (an early-English transeptal church) and at Bywell, we have examples of a class of towers of, at all events, early-Norman date, with single belfry windows rude and severe in character.* At Newcastle, the small church which Osmund "the good," the Conqueror's nephew, is said to have built within the Roman Station, probably amidst the ruins of Saxon "Monkchester," was rebuilt on an enlarged plan in the reign of Edward III., and this edifice, famous for its light and graceful coronal spire, which surmounts the lantern-tower of Lancastrian days, is one of the largest (but, in the interior, most puritanical looking) parish churches in England. There are three other parochial churches in the town, one of which (St. Andrew's) is partly Norman; and formerly the walls of Newcastle inclosed also many monastic edifices; but, of these, few vestiges remain.

In few of the churches of Northumberland are preserved sepulchral monuments earlier than the sixteenth century; but in the church at Chillingham a noble sepulchral monument, which presents good examples of the armour and costume of the period, and has only one equal in the northern counties, commemorates Sir Ralph Grey of Chillingham Castle, who died in 1443, and Elizabeth his wife. In Bothal church there are recumbent figures of somewhat later date upon an altar tomb; and here and there, as at Warkworth, Hexham, and a few other churches, we come upon cross-legged effigies bearing on their shields of stone the heraldry of Northumbrian chieftains and Crusaders.

Many of the parish churches have not recovered from the

* In the peaceful churchyard of Ovingham rest the remains of Thomas Bewick, who perpetuated so many charming traits of Tyneside scenery in his characteristic engravings; and opposite to this spot, on a bold wooded slope, is Cherryburn, once the Bewicks' home. Not far to the eastward of Ovingham, also on the Tyne, is the birth-place of George Stephenson. It is an ordinary rude double cottage, but pleasantly situated near wooded knolls, and within sound of the rippling of the broad stream.

forlorn and dismantled state in which they lay for a century and a half after the Reformation, a period during which some were without glass to their windows, and some without font, priest, or congregation. Many an interior has still a cold, poor, and meagre aspect from the general want of stained glass and of architectural enrichment, and the prevalence of whitewash, and of pews "more suggestive of sleep than supplication;" several edifices have suffered moreover from ignorant churchwardenisms hardly less destructive than fanatical zeal or Border hostility. But the revived taste for ecclesiastical architecture, which has been for more than thirty years past so beneficially active in other parts of England, has at length gained some ground in Northumberland; new churches have risen, old churches have been restored, and the taste for church building and church restoration is seen even in remote localities. Thus, in the northern division of the county, Ford church has been restored; at Etal a chapel designed by Mr. Butterfield has been built; the Norman church of Kirk Newton, at the foot of Yevering Bell, has been saved from ruin; and at the more famous church of Lindisfarne further dilapidations are (at least for the time) averted. The ruins of Brinkburn priory church, moreover, have been preserved, and Hexham abbey church has been freed from some tasteless and hideous defacements. Many costly churches in good architectural taste have been built—St. Peter's at Newcastle, St. Mary's (the Roman Catholic cathedral), St. James's at Morpeth, and St. Paul's at Alnwick, deserve particular mention. Warkworth too, as well as Lesbury, Cheswick, Bamburgh, the Farne island, and Kyloe, all present evidences of the revived feeling for the preservation of the ecclesiastical edifices and the revival of the ecclesiastical architecture of mediæval days.

*Revival of architectural taste.*

But it is time to glance at the Military and Domestic Architecture of Northumberland.—

*Castles and towers.*

There is not any class of historical monuments in this county so characteristic of past times as the remains of its feudal architecture; indeed, to the eye of a traveller, the distinguishing features of Northumberland seem to be the many grey towers that mark its landscapes, and its larger baronial castles. Of the latter class of buildings, the castles of Alnwick, Warkworth, and Prudhoe, Dunstanburgh, Morpeth, and Bothal, (of all which, only Alnwick is maintained entire,) Ford, Chillingham, and Langley were the chief examples; and, besides these, there are the once-royal castles of Newcastle-upon-Tyne, Bamburgh, and Wark (the latter now reduced to a green mound), and Norham—once the northern stronghold of the mitred lords palatine of Durham.

The castles and pele-towers of Northumberland were the only domestic buildings that had any permanence or strength, and they form almost the only visible remains of its inhabitants during the middle ages. For example, in the extensive Border-parish of Elsdon, which is twenty miles in length, there is not a house a century old, excepting the fourteenth-century pele-tower immemorially appropriated as the rectory-house, nor is any old dwelling except the tower of Otterburn remembered. Indeed the whole county hardly affords a house like the Tudor mansion or manor-house so common in southern counties,* although there are houses that were built, and some pele-towers to which mansions were added, in the seventeenth century. The pele-towers or lesser strongholds have a character of their own; their aspect seems in keeping with their situation, and many a tower now crumbling in decay is the scene of some stirring Border legend. They are, generally, square massive buildings, the ground floor vaulted, and the upper chambers reached by a narrow newel staircase; many are in fact built like little fortresses, in which the chieftain and his neighbours might defend their moveable goods on incursions of the enemy.†

*Their general character.*

---

\* Denton Hall, an old manorial-looking house with gabled roofs and mullioned windows, which stands about three miles westward from Newcastle, is however deserving of mention, and it has some associations of interest, inasmuch as it was the residence of the literary Mrs. Montagu, in the family of whose husband it now remains, the house being the property of Lord Rokeby.

† Even in the time of Dr. Dutens, rector of Elsdon, who died in 1812, the

Many a fortalice had for its owners an old family of Northumbrian gentry, slow to abandon it for the comforts and accommodation afforded by the manorial residence of southern type; and it is, no doubt, for this reason that in Northumberland scarcely any residences as distinguished from towers of defence are found of a date earlier than James I.

In this respect, Northumberland affords a striking contrast to some other counties—Somersetshire, for example, where there is hardly a village that has not its sixteenth-century house.

The lawless and insecure condition of the Border lands until a much later time than even the days of the Stuarts delayed the progress of improvement, and the dwellings of the yeomen, farmers, and peasantry retained a rude and primitive character, while those of the landowners continued to be lonely towers. In the reigns of Henry VIII. and Elizabeth, as appears from the accounts of the "ministers" or crown receivers after the dissolution of monasteries, thousands of acres remained wholly waste and unproductive, owing doubtless to their liability to be ravaged by the Scots and Moss troopers of the Border. Camden describes the herdsmen on the wastes of Northumberland as a sort of nomadic race, living in huts called *scheles*, from collections of which ancient schelings some places in the county derive their names, and, amongst them, even the populous port near the mouth of the Tyne, the site of which was occupied formerly by dwellings of the fishermen. But, with the civilization of the Borders, modern dwellings often came to be joined to the old tower. A good example of this addition is seen at Belsay, originally a square pele-tower of the time of Edward II., remarkable as the finest specimen of that kind of fortress in the county. And at Dilston—a place to which the sad fate of the chivalrous and devoted young Earl of Derwentwater has given a

---

ground-floor of his rectory tower there, remained the dark vault in which the cattle of preceding rectors had been housed by night; the floor above, paved with stone, being used for kitchen and servants' lodging, and the upper floor for study and bedroom.

melancholy interest—Sir Francis Radcliffe, his ancestor, built, early in the seventeenth century, a stately mansion which he annexed to the more ancient stronghold. At Cresswell, too, which still belongs to the Cresswell family, a long, low hall of two stories, of the time perhaps of Queen Anne, was added to the massive old tower.* It was not until after the Restoration that their dangerous vicinity to the Scotish border ceased to influence the domestic economy of inhabitants of Northumberland, and from that period many of the modern additions to old fortress-houses date.

It may be said, therefore, that all the domestic architecture of Northumberland which belongs to former ages is of a military character; and that at this day most of the chief seats in the county are either mediæval castles and towers, characteristic of the old times of insecurity and strife, or mansions adapted to modern elegance and refinement. Besides a few mansions and eighteenth-century halls not pretending to castellated style, such as Wallington and Howick, Cresswell and Bywell, or Eslington (Lord Ravensworth's charming seat in the wooded vale of Whittingham,) some imposing new structures have been built more recently in the form of old castles, such as Blenkinshope and Beaufront, the latter of which is on the site of the old mansion of the Erringtons. Northumberland, however, can boast but few of those attractive seats surrounded by ancestral trees which abound in other parts of the country, and fewer still of those antique manor-houses—those old historic sixteenth-century houses—which, with shadowy gables, perhaps with battlement and moat, and royalist memories clustering round them like their ivy, adorn the stately parks of England in the South.

No fewer than thirty-seven castles and seventy-eight towers are enumerated in a list of the castles and towers of Northumberland which was drawn up in 1460. Of the castles which then existed, eleven have disappeared, eighteen

---

* The present residence, which was built adjacent to it during the present century, acknowledges the more elegant requirements of modern times.

are more or less in ruin, and only eight are maintained for use and habitation.

<small>Castles formerly royal.</small> The Crown had a fortress at Bamburgh—

"King Ida's castle, huge and square,"

now private property, and modernized in the interior for residence; also at Newcastle, the keep-tower of which is a conspicuous and well-known feature of the town; at Wark upon the Tweed the bishops of Durham (who, as lords palatine, exercised a sovereignty of their own,) had the stronghold of their Northern home (Nort-ham)

"On Tweed's fair river, broad and deep,"

a building which even in its ruin has not lost its imposing grandeur; and a castle was built at Tynemouth by Robert de Mowbray, the Norman Earl of Northumberland, who refounded the monastery there; but the garrison buildings now called the Castle of Tynemouth have no claim to antiquity, and few portions remain of the ancient surrounding walls that were maintained by the monks for their defence. Three of the castles in Northumberland date from a period even earlier than the reigns of Stephen and Henry II., in which such a great architectural movement took place throughout England; but several of the most important castles in this county were built in those reigns, and generally upon the model which was first introduced in the White Tower of London, and derived from certain castles in Normandy.

<small>Bamburgh.</small> The largest and most imposing in situation, if not the oldest, of the Northern castles, is the once regal pile of Bamburgh, built probably in the reign of Henry I. Here, as at Dover, outer walls (which at Bamburgh follow the irregular outline of the precipitous basaltic crags,) inclose an area, in the centre of which rises the square massive keep. A steep road, winding under the tower-crowned cliffs, leads to the citadel, and on the southern edge of the fortified inclosure stood the hall and chapel. Down to the time of the Union a constable of high rank governed the

castle for the Crown,* but, it having been sold by James I., and, in little more than a century afterwards, forfeited by Thomas Forster, the Northumbrian squire who made so unfortunate a figure in the Jacobite rising of 1715, Bamburgh was purchased by Nathaniel Lord Crewe, Bishop of Durham, and by him bequeathed to charitable uses. In the hands of his trustees, this old historic fortress, no longer armed against a foe, has long spread forth hands of mercy to mankind: there the young are educated and the destitute relieved, and charities are maintained which were aptly enough described as being to sailors shipwrecked on that coast what the convent of St. Bernard is to travellers on the Alps.† The chief room in the keep is applied to a purpose that its Norman builders never contemplated, for there a noble but little-known library reposes. Something should be done to restore the mediæval character of Bamburgh Castle, the repairs executed in the last century being in the worst possible taste.

The fortress which gave its name to the town of Newcastle-upon-Tyne may be said to have commanded the northern frontier of England. Its erection is attributed to Robert Duke of Normandy, and it occupies a plateau where probably he found some buildings of the Roman castle then in existence. The Norman stronghold before long looked down upon a rising town to which ships resorted as in the Roman days; and in the reign of John it had become a port of some importance,‡ and seems to have then had some

The New Castle on Tyne.

---

* In the thirteenth and fourteenth centuries it was the subject of an interesting series of mandates, highly illustrative of Northern history, which are preserved among the Liberate Rolls at the Tower of London.

† Qu. Rev. xxxix. p. 399, where the charities of Bamburgh are characterised as the most extensively useful, as well as munificent, of our eleemosynary foundations: whether as extensively useful as they might be is, however, doubtful.

‡ Out of 4,958l. contributed to the Crown in King John's reign by all the ports of the Eastern and Southern coast, Newcastle paid 158l. Mr. Hodgson Hinde estimates the population of Newcastle 150 years afterwards, viz. in 1377, at nearly 4,000, and in 1548 at 10,000. The latter estimate seems beyond the mark. The population of Newcastle now, however, approaches 100,000. The customs duties received at the port in 1852 amounted to 327,577l.

trade with Norway. Skins of beavers, sables, squirrels, martins, foxes, and goats, besides wool, were then exported from the Tyne. Under Edward I. the Norman fortress was expanded somewhat on the plan of Conway and Carnarvon, and surrounded by walls defended by nine towers, which were called after baronies in Northumberland charged with their maintenance; but of these surrounding defences there are no remains excepting a gate-tower in which old-clothes dealers have succeeded to armourers and warders. In the Scotish campaigns this castle had particular importance, and here the kings of England often resided; but after the Union its dignity departed: James I. sold it into private hands, and for a long time the keep of the Plantagenets became a county prison, and their royal free chapel was suffered by the Newcastle municipality to be used as a beer-cellar; but happily it is now the fashion to respect and preserve historical monuments, and the old castle after all its vicissitudes is in the care of the local Antiquarian Society, and appropriated to its collections and meetings. The dark, frowning keep, still entire, forms an interesting example of the military architecture of the Norman days. The town itself was probably walled as early as the reign of Edward I., at all events it was then inclosed by a circuit of massive walls with gate-towers, considerable portions of which remained down to about thirty years since, when, however, the defences that had withstood Time, the Scots, and the Civil Wars yielded to town-improvement, before whose march the many religious houses that once flourished in Newcastle have also fallen. But on the river-bank called the Sand-hill, formerly and still the merchants' quarter, there are some many-storied timber houses, with overhanging fronts and casemented windows, which have stood for perhaps three centuries. From their former inhabitants many families now received amongst the gentry of Northumberland have sprung. In one of these houses lived Mr. Surtees the father of the first Lady Eldon, and from it she eloped with the future Chancellor. In Sandgate—an adjacent locality—

lived Scott the prosperous yeoman, whose son William became Lord Stowell, and whose younger son John became Lord Eldon; but, although he followed the trade of "fitter" (a sort of coal-broker) on the Tyne, he it is said could boast among remote ancestors no less a person than Sir Michael Scott the Wizard, whose fame has been perpetuated by a more lawful magician. The Grammar-school in which these distinguished brothers were pupils was then held in the chapel of the old hospital of St. Mary in the West-gate (to which it had been removed when the school became a royal foundation in the 42nd of Queen Elizabeth), and there Hutton was mathematical master. In the same school, Cuthbert, afterwards Admiral Lord Collingwood (also a native of Newcastle,) was educated until, at the age of eleven, he went to sea; and there Akenside not many years before received the first part of his education; but, notwithstanding its associations and the remonstrances of archæologists, the building was demolished a few years ago for approaches to the new Railway Station. In the higher part of Newcastle, a new town of tall stone-fronted houses—overspreading what had been the secluded garden of a nunnery—rose about twenty-five years ago, and the new streets in many places intersect those of the old town, so that Newcastle presents a strange combination of buildings; it may well be called a "surprising place for its history, trade, buildings, social economy, and smoke."

In striking contrast to the spreading town upon the Tyne, with its noisy traffic and busy population, stands the time-worn dark-red sandstone pile of Norham upon the Tweed, which was built by a Bishop of Durham in the reign of Henry I., not long after the new castle on the Tyne. The privileges which the episcopal lords of Norham granted to their little town were such as might have made it the Newcastle of the Tweed, if they could have only brought the tide so far. Traces of military architecture of various periods are found in this ruined castle. But the square and massive keep— Norham.

"Where whilom kings did make repair,"

is now reduced to a mere shell crumbling on its steep and rocky banks—a scene of ruin and repose that recals some old-world town of Normandy, and Tennyson's picture of a decayed castle—

> "Here had fallen great part of a tower
> Whole, like a crag that tumbles from the cliff,
> And like a crag 'twas gay with wilding flowers;
> And, high above, a piece of turret stair
> Worn by the feet that now are silent, wound
> Bare to the Sun."

It is much to be lamented that, while a taste for architectural improvement has been manifested in so many of the old historic buildings of Northumberland, Norham Castle, like Dunstanburgh, Etal, Edlingham, and some other castles, is falling more and more into decay.

*Wark.* Upon a steep precipice above the Tweed stood another royal castle, viz. Wark, originally built by Walter Espec, the noble founder of Rievaulx Abbey, but reconstructed in the reign of Henry II. This frontier fortress became of great importance to the Crown during the wars with Scotland, and was in 1342 the scene of a somewhat romantic incident described by Froissart.\* David of Scotland and his army, on their return from slaughtering the monks and people of Durham, encamped under Wark Castle, laden with church-plate and spoil. The Earl of Salisbury, constable of the fortress, was absent when it was beleaguered by the Scots, and the little garrison fell to the command of the youthful countess, the beauty of the age, who defended it while the King of England was advancing against the enemy, and there she entertained Edward and his chivalry right nobly, but much to the disturbance of the young monarch's peace, who according to some historians not only instituted the Order of the Garter in her honour, but did so in commemoration of this event. The castle afterwards came to the chivalrous family

---

\* c. 77. The story is related in Brady's Hist. of Edw. III. p. 254.

of Grey, and in 1623 Sir William was created Lord Grey of Wark, but the dignity became extinct in 1706. Of Wark Castle little but rubble of the foundations now remains.

The chief baronial castle in Northumberland is that of Alnwick, which was built by Eustace de Vesci about 700 years ago, and still retains some portions of the Norman fortress. The castle and barony were acquired by Henry de Percy in 1309, and it is at this day a residence of the noble inheritor of the dignities and possessions of that great historic family. The most important portions of the existing castle were the work of the second Henry de Percy, lord of Alnwick, who defeated David king of Scotland at Neville's Cross—a nobleman who, seen in his deeds of martial valour and his works of architectural splendour, forms a very commanding figure in the history of his time. An adequate idea of the importance of these old Percys in the age in which they lived can only be derived from the public records of the realm: their power and prominence were such that their history is almost the history of England, and their piety and munificence constantly meet us in the churches and monastic chartularies of the North, just as we see at this day the Percy crescent sculptured on many a building in Northumberland—and very suggestive is the contrast between the peaceful dominion which that badge now marks and the time when it gleamed on the banner of the earls in the pride of warlike array, or when the " Percy's silver crescent set in blood."

It would be foreign to the scope of this memoir to sketch the genealogy of the Percy line from the time when William Le Gernons, the Conqueror's companion in arms, exchanged the slopes of his native Percy for Northumbrian moors. Suffice it to say that Henry, son of the Henry de Percy who acquired Alnwick, and died in 1315, succeeded him as second lord, and in the service of Edward III.—to whom he seems to have been hardly inferior in importance—ran a career full of honour. It was he who superseded the square Norman keep by a picturesque cluster of seven semicircular

*Alnwick Castle.*

towers, inclosing a large court-yard, and surrounded by an area defended by curtain-walls with towers, and entered through a strong barbican and between lofty walls. His grandson, who became the first Earl of Northumberland, was the father of Hotspur, the hero whose ardour shone on the field of Otterburn, and with whom the Lion of Northumberland fell in the fatal conflict at Shrewsbury. The family honours were restored in 1414 to the Earl's grandson, and he became the second great builder of his race, for he repaired the decay into which Alnwick Castle had fallen, and built the keep at Warkworth, which castle and manor had been acquired by the second Lord Percy. Its chief feature is the magnificent octagonal keep which this nobleman (the second Earl of Northumberland) added to the Norman castle of the FitzRichard family, and its walls and the vaulted chambers of its lower story are still strong and massive. In the adjacent area are impressive remains of the Norman and the Edwardian structures, where now

*Warkworth Castle.*

> " Through fractured arch and doorway freely pass
> The sunbeams into halls o'ergrown with grass;
> The floors unroofed are open to the sky,
> And the snows lodge there when the storm sweeps by."

But the grey old keep has not lost all its feudal dignity. Its aspect, notwithstanding that it is roofless and is surrounded by ruined walls, seems worthy of the associations which history and Shakespeare's *Henry the Fourth* connect with Warkworth Castle; for, unlike the keep of Alnwick which was almost rebuilt about ninety years ago, its mediæval structure and character have at least remained unimpaired by any modern alterations, and,

> "Like veteran worn but unsubdued,"

it looks forth on land and sea as if still maintaining the pride of the ancient Percys. The interior presents a very characteristic and unexpected scene, for the guard-rooms and other gloomy vaulted chambers on the entrance-floor (beneath which are still more rayless dungeons) remain perfect and in their former strength, like shapely caverns hewed in a rock of solid stone; and the walls of the once beautiful chapel, of the dining-hall, and the various chambers and domestic offices connected with it, which occupy the floor above the floor of entrance, are still massive and entire, and, though now open to the sky and a resting-place of the sea-birds, afford an impressive example of the baronial state of other days. The imposing fragments of the older keep, the chief tower of entrance, and the curtain-walls that surround the whole plateau of the fortified inclosure, are for the most part of Norman date.

But at Warkworth the castle is not the only interesting monument of the Past, for, on the opposite side of the river, among the deep woods seen from the rampart, are the cells —excavated like a grotto in the sandstone cliff, and overhung by trees—to which the well-known ballad gives romantic associations as the work and former abode of the " Hermit of Warkworth:"—

"The chief, a chapel, neatly arched,
On branching columns rose;"

a chantry, probably, that was founded by the third Earl Percy for Mary Plantagenet his wife. Castle and hermitage, wood, rock, and water, combine so many picturesque features at Warkworth, that it has long been a favourite subject with artists; and, as the keep with its tall watch-tower is seen far and wide over the country and the coast, it is quite a familiar object to the traveller.

While the feudal pile rises at the higher end of the acclivity on which the wide street of Warkworth is built, the still older edifice of religion—the parish church—stands at its lower end upon the river bank. The church is a Norman structure built on foundations of the earlier church of Saxon days. With its venerable associations and its Norman features (the most striking is a vaulted stone roof to the chancel), some defacements of the Georgian era—such as sash-windows, sordid pews, hideous galleries, decaying wood-work, whitewash, and green mould, were sadly out of keeping; but these have lately been swept away — a welcome though tardy proof that the revived feeling of reverence for churches, and of taste for church architecture, is now extending in Northumberland.

*Works in progress at Alnwick Castle.*

In the long and disastrous interval before the ancient honours of the Percy family were revived with the ducal coronet of Northumberland, Alnwick Castle suffered great dilapidation, and in the latter half of the last century it was still more injured by alterations in what was at that time supposed to be the Gothic style. The towers clustered in the central keep were then converted into large reception rooms, and the whole castle underwent such an injurious transformation that it lost its ancient feudal dignity of aspect without acquiring either comfort or fitting splendour. The present duke, who may be called the third great builder in the Percy family, therefore formed and is now completing a magnificent design for the purpose of restoring to the exterior of his castle its mediæval dignity, and providing a new and sumptuous interior, which is being enriched with carvings and decorations designed from churches and palaces of Italy. These costly works are naturally attracting much attention to Alnwick, and the fitness of a Renaissance style of ornament for the interior of a feudal castle in Northumberland has been much debated; but at all events the architecture of former times really worthy of preservation has been carefully preserved, and Alnwick Castle is acquiring the splendour which the greatest historical edifice in the North of England should display.

*Dunstanburgh.*

The other baronial strongholds may be briefly mentioned. Dunstanburgh Castle, which was built by Thomas Earl of Lancaster in 1315 (about the time of the completion of the Edwardian works at Alnwick), is one of the most picturesque objects in Northumberland. It is built on basaltic crags on a rocky peninsula, beneath whose precipices the billows " leap and fall,"—a situation well adapted for defence: the entrance is guarded by two circular towers of a height and breadth exceeded only by the "Eagle Tower" of Caernarvon; but the archway is the only part of the castle that is not in ruins.

The ruins of Prudhoe Castle, crowning a green eminence on the south bank of the river, are familiar to all travellers in the valley of the Tyne. To the ancestor of the Umfravilles — Robert-with-the-beard — the Conqueror gave the barony of Prudhoe and that of Redesdale, which was then a wild forest tract, to hold by the honourable service of defending that part of the country from wolves and the king's enemies, with the sword which King William wore when he entered Northumberland. The castle was originally built in the reign of Stephen, by Odonel de Umfraville, and resisted a siege by William the Lion of Scotland; but at no very distant period from the days of its Norman strength the castle, like the family, declined from its high estate. The ruins present interesting architectural features, especially a domestic chapel of the end of the thirteenth century, remarkable for the earliest known example of an oriel window. In 1381, Gilbert, the last of the Umfravilles, died, and, his widow marrying Henry de Percy, first Earl of Northumberland, the castle and barony of Prudhoe became a property of the Percys, and gave a title which was borne for many years by the present Duke of Northumberland, who has given it fame in the annals of science. With Prudhoe is connected the early history of Harbotle ("the high dwelling"), which lies on the verge of a wild and unfrequented district in Redesdale, for it was anciently a stronghold of the Umfraville family. After becoming a refuge for the Redesdale men, and a prison for their Border foes, the castle fell into decay.

In a situation of great strength and picturesque beauty, near the confluence of the two bright streams of the Wansbeck and the Font, is Mitford Castle, which was built between 1150 and 1170, upon the model of Gisors in Normandy, by William Bertram the noble founder of Brink-

*Prudhoe.*

*Mitford.*

burn Priory. From a remote period this fortress, whether in English or Scotish hands, was conspicuous in history; in it William the Lion resided; in it Roger Bertram confederated with the Barons against Henry III.; and to it Gilbert de Midelton, a Northumbrian chief and freebooter, conveyed his princely captive Louis de Beaumont, Bishop of Durham, in the reign of Edward II. Mitford stands on a lofty rock in a moated plateau: the keep is in ruins, and the ramparts that environed the hill lie in shattered masses overgrown by trees. Of the adjacent Norman stronghold of the De Merlays, at Morpeth, only some curtain-walls remain: a later gate-tower has recently been repaired for offices of the agent of the noble owner, Lord Carlisle. A similar but finer gate-tower, and fragments of surrounding walls, are all that remain of the neighbouring castle of Bothal; formerly a barony of the Bertram family, and of the Lords Ogle in the reign of Elizabeth, but now inherited by the Duke of Portland.

*Morpeth.*

*Bothal.*

*Ford.*

Ford Castle, in the north of the county, stands on an eminence above the river Till, and in view of the hills of Flodden. It is an edifice of imposing aspect; but two massive corner-towers, apparently of fourteenth-century date, are its only ancient portions: high up a turret-stair in one of these towers is the chamber in which King James is said to have slept on the night before the battle of Flodden Field. It attained castellated dignity early in the reign of Edward III. when its owner was Sir William Heron, who married the heiress of Odonel de Ford, and from whom the baronial family of Heron of Ford descended.

*Langley.*

At Langley, which is near Haydon Bridge upon the Tyne, a mere shell remains of the baronial stronghold of the lords of Tynedale—a picturesque building of grey stone, of imposing appearance, and much resembling a Norman keep, but of the date 1345 to 1365. It was confiscated after the so-called rebellion of James last Earl of Derwentwater.

*Chillingham.*

Chillingham Castle (the property of the Earl of Tankerville, as representative of the ancient family of Grey of

Wark,) concludes the list of the castles of feudal ages of which any considerable portions remain, but it is not of much interest to the antiquary. The park, however, is celebrated for the formidable wild cattle which have been its inhabitants from time immemorial. These animals are similar to the herd of wild cattle still inhabiting the antient forest tract of Cadzow, near Hamilton Palace, supposed to represent the aboriginal race of the Scotish forests, to which Sir Walter Scott alludes:—

> Mightiest of all the beasts of chase
> That roam in woody Caledon,
> Crashing the forest in his race,
> The mountain bull comes thundering on :
>
> Fierce on the hunter's quivered band
> He rolls his eyes of swarthy glow,
> Spurns with black hoof and horn the sand,
> And tosses high his mane of snow.

These animals are of middle size, and are perfectly white except at the ears, but the hoofs and horns are black. They are remarkable for symmetry of form and gracefulness in action, but are perfectly wild and untamed, and dangerous when exasperated. Professor Owen has remarked on the essential differences between the white cattle of Chillingham and our domestic cattle, and he considers the colour, the dewlap, and other characteristics, to indicate that they are descendants of the sacred Brahmin bull. He seems disposed to regard them, not as belonging to an aboriginal stock of British cattle, but as probably obtained from India through the Egyptians, the Greeks, and the Romans, and introduced to Britain by the Roman colonists. The present number of the herd at Chillingham is about sixty.*

One would not expect to find upon a lonely eminence by the river Till, the former home of the great family of

---

* A bull lately slaughtered weighed between five and six hundred pounds. The flesh is dark, but tender and juicy, and is said to have a game flavour.

Etal.

Bywell.

Seaton Delaval.

Manners: their ancestors, however, had their stronghold from the time of Henry II. at Etal Castle. It was deserted by its owner Sir Thomas Manners, ancestor of the Duke of Rutland, for the more peaceful and splendid halls of Belvoir, on his marriage with the heiress of De Roos, and the antient stronghold has disappeared.

A gate-tower called Bywell Castle is the only architectural monument of the Barony of the Balliols, and even this tower was raised after the property had come to the Nevilles, Earls of Westmerland, whose possessions were forfeited on the rising in 1569. It is now the property of Mr. W. B. Beaumont, whose Tyneside mansion, Bywell Hall, stands adjacent in pleasing woodland scenery.

Five miles to the northward from Tynemouth on the Seaton Delaval estate, now inherited by Lord Hastings, there formerly stood a castle of the Delavals, but the only relic is a Norman chapel, with double chancel arch, which stands amidst the trees that surround the ruins of the modern hall. The family flourished in Northumberland from the coming of the Normans. At the time of the Restoration, it was represented by Sir Ralph Delaval, who has left a curious monument of his enterprising character at his little port of Seaton Delaval, for he built piers, and cut a sluice through the solid sandstone cliffs to form an entrance to the harbour, closing the seaward opening with booms of timber after the manner of a portcullis. The honours of the family had become extinct when Admiral George Delaval (of the Dissington branch), who was employed on embassies to Portugal and Morocco in the reign of Queen Anne, purchased the Seaton Delaval estates, and, with Vanbrugh for his architect, began to build the stately hall of Italian architecture, which in the latter half of last century was the scene of the hospitalities of the later Delavals. In their time it was famous for strange practical jokes, of which their guests were frequently the victims; but of these once gay halls of pleasure a destructive fire, which occurred in 1822, has left only a scathed and ruined shell.

Of the lesser strongholds or Border towers many have disappeared within the last four hundred years; some have been incorporated with modern buildings; a few are maintained in habitable condition, but the greater part are in decay. Of those which are kept up for residence, Belsay, already mentioned, is architecturally the most interesting; and Haughton Castle, in the valley of the North Tyne, is also remarkable as a fine specimen of this kind of fortalice. The old tower of Featherston, on the wild and wooded banks of the South Tyne, formerly the inheritance of an historic family of Northumberland, is a good example of a pele tower, merged, so to speak, in a modern castellated mansion. For beauty and natural strength of situation, none of these old buildings are more remarkable than Staward Pele, which like a pharos-tower crowns a narrow promontory where the eastern and western branches of the Allen river meet under those wooded banks, on which, nearer to the Tyne, are formed the sylvan walks of Ridley Hall. Some of these old fortress towers stand as if still guarding lonely passes in the Border hills; some, that formerly saw the frequent inroad of hostile forces, stand dismantled and decaying by highways that are now seldom trod; some, half hidden by trees, crown a precipitous bank above a rocky stream now sought only by the angler or the lover of scenery; and here and there upon the coast is a tower that now looks upon no other enemy than the wasting sea; but all, in their stern character and structure, mark the lawless ages through which they stood;—all take back our thoughts to times when life and property were insecure, and when the owner depended on his own vigilance and his weapons for his daily food.

Yet in this county a large number of the estates continued hereditary in one line of succession for centuries.* The confiscations which followed the events of 1715, pro-

*Lesser strongholds.*

*Vicissitudes in ownership*

---

\* Probably, however, there are not many such examples as the estate of Angerton near Morpeth, which descended from the Bolbecks, its owners in the time of Henry I. to the Howards Earls of Carlisle, and was held by that family until the late Earl sold it to Mr. Ralph Atkinson.

duced a greater change in the ownership of landed property in Northumberland than all the vicissitudes of time since the Norman Conquest, and caused the destruction not only of many an ancient family of gentry, but of many an ancient fortalice. So fell

——— — the tower of Widdrington—
Mother of many a valiant son ;

so fell the Radcliffe's towers of Dilston and Cartington and Langley, and the houses of many other families in whom loyalty was as hereditary as land.* The Northumberland gentry seem to have suffered beyond those of any other county for their fidelity to the Stuart cause. Yet it is curious to find amongst the freehold tenants in North Tynedale six centuries ago many names still found in that district; for example, William de Swinburne (who was treasurer to the English princess Margaret, Queen of Scotland) held the lands now possessed by Sir John Swinburne, his representative, and Charlton holds what Adam de Charleton held.

Some pele-towers seem to have been themselves perpetuated by the church they were built to protect, as at Hexham, where there is a strong tower of the days when the Archbishops of York held their regality of Hexhamshire; and at Corbridge, on the Tyne, where a tower of the time of Edward II., formerly the priest's residence, stands adjacent to the church, and affords an interesting specimen of this kind of fortified dwelling; at Elsdon, too, the tower of the Umfravilles is preserved as the rectory, and the fortified tower at Rothbury has been the rector's residence from early times.

No longer needed for defence, these Border-towers, so characteristic of the rude and troubled times gone by, are now mere picturesque objects in a peaceful landscape, where

* The ruined fortalice of Cartington, which stands, in beautiful scenery, three miles northward from Rothbury, has historical associations of some interest, for in the 29th Hen. VI. it belonged to John Cartington, whose only child, heiress of Cartington and Dilston, carried those estates, with other lands, to the family of Radcliffe of Derwentwater, by her marriage to Sir Edward Radcliffe, ancestor of the short-lived Earls of Derwentwater.

their existence only serves to bring the past in striking contrast with the present, and to heighten the gratitude of all dwellers on the Border-lands for the peace and security they now enjoy. "In such houses," said Lord Monboddo to Dr. Johnson when they were standing before his wild-looking tower in Scotland, "our ancestors lived, and they were better men than we." "No," said the Doctor, "we are as strong as they, and a great deal wiser."

With this rapid glance at the chief historical monuments of Northumberland, it is time to bring the present Memoir to a close. Upon a retrospect of the objects to which the reader's attention has been directed, few things, perhaps, are more striking than the fact that in this county British chieftains, Roman governors, Saxons, Scandinavians, Normans, and feudal lords have all left their characteristic monuments. As to the far-off time when a Celtic people brought hither their Gaulish traditions, some of the earliest works of man may be seen in this county; probably, indeed, no rock-sculptures, stone-circles, mote-hills, or graves can be found in Britain older than those that remain in Northumberland. Hilly regions, that are now lonely solitudes, must evidently have been once a most populous part of this island; and the British camps, gray monoliths, stone-circles, and green sepulchral mounds, that still border the Watling Street and are scattered on the hills in adjacent localities, are but a small part of what the Roman legions saw when Cæsar invaded Britain. Then, of the Roman period, the remains are characteristic as well as numerous, and, to crown them, there is the Roman Wall. Even of the dark period following the departure of the Romans and before the Middle Ages began, Northumberland, as the reader has seen, possesses monuments; and when we come to the feudal age, from which period its most memorable localities were battle-fields, and during which history draws so dark a picture of its state, we find a distinguishing feature of this county to be the stern monuments of mediæval times that rise in almost every part of it. Then, turning to its inhabitants, we see that those turbulent and warlike ages have not passed without leaving their impress on the character of the people as well as of their buildings. The scenes marked by Border chivalry and national conflict in former days, the ancient superstitions, and the legends handed down from sire to son, are commemorated in ballad poetry and popular tradition; and highly interesting is this folk-lore in Northumberland, as might be expected from the character and variety of the people who have contributed to it. As regards the Christian antiquities of this part of England, the reader will have observed that the connection of most of them with the Anglo-Saxon church surrounds those sacred monuments with its own historic splendour, but that their present condition is little in keeping with their associations. Finally, if the mutability of all things on the earth is seen in the edifices of religion, so the student of genealogy finds that there is no part of this country in which the vicissitudes of families read a more impressive lesson of the evanescence of human glory.

# AUCKLAND CASTLE.

A Paper read before the Architectural and Archæological Society of Durham and Northumberland, assembled at Auckland Castle by invitation of the Lord Bishop of Durham, Sept. 29, 1862.

[*Ecclesiologist*, February, 1863.]

THE architectural importance of this old historic building cannot be regarded, in its present state, as at all commensurate with the dignity of its associations, although its chapel is a very noble relic of the ecclesiastical art of other days; but there is enough in the history of this ancient seat of prelates to render it well worthy the attention of an archæological, if not of an architectural, association.

Auckland Castle—the only one of the many castles, halls, and manor-houses formerly belonging to the see which now remains the bishop's residence—is remarkable not only for having been a favourite abode of the see of Durham for more than seven centuries, but for the memories which some of the most illustrious of her bishops have associated with this ancient seat of piety, munificence, and learning. Although now and for long past termed a castle, it was not dignified by that appellation until late in the fifteenth century, and it has not been the scene of any very memorable events in national history. It did not stand forth during the middle ages in the Norman might of the castle of the bishops at Durham, nor did it resemble the fortress of Norham, their northern home upon the Tweed. At Auckland no dark, massive keep frowned defiance on beleaguering foes; nor from its gates did the mitred earls of the palatinate lead forth a martial band. Auckland appears to us in history rather as the spot to which, in turbulent and warlike times, the bishops loved to withdraw from strife, to seek the peace of God, and to rejoice in His gifts of natural beauty amidst the lonely and tranquil woodlands of the Wear.

In a long previous age the green dells of the park were the resort of the Roman soldiers who maintained their camp on the adjacent mount, now called Binchester, by the Watling Street or great military way; and their sepulchral urns have been found by the rocky stream of the Gaunless, not far below the castle. It has been conjectured that the Romans also fortified the ridge on which Auckland Castle itself stands, and maintained there an outpost subsidiary to their great camp on the opposite hill at Binchester; but, be this as it may, Auckland first appears in history very soon after the see had been founded at Durham, for it is mentioned as part of the gift conferred on the see of Durham by Canute the Dane.

Of Auckland during the Norman era history affords hardly any glimpse. But in the survey called Boldon Book, compiled in the year 1183 by order of Hugh Pudsey the powerful and magnificent Bishop of Durham, we have proof that Auckland had then become an episcopal abode. The definition there recorded of services rendered by tenants in lieu of rent gives a pleasant picture of the simple manners of the time, and of the residence of the early bishops on this spot. The record brings before us provisions for the enjoyment of the chase, and for the exercise of hospitality; we see the oxen of the bishop's neighbouring tenants ploughing his land, or carting his wine, or carrying his wood for fuel; the husbandman sowing seed, or making hay, or reaping the bishop's crops; the miller grinding the bishop's corn, and other tenants bringing eggs, poultry, and other produce. Then, too, we almost behold, in records of another kind, viz. the mortuary rolls or inventories of each bishop's personal possessions at his death,—the rich plate and the illuminated manuscripts, which, even in those early ages, accompanied the prelate as he moved about from castle to castle or manor to manor, and which generally came afterwards to enrich his abbey-church,—we see the bishop surrounded by his court and his retainers; and here, far from camps, and oblivious of the thorny state and splendour of the feudal castle, celebrating high festivals of the Christian year.

That the duties of religion were not forgotten amidst the amusements of secular life we see from the noble domestic chapel that has come down to our times at Auckland, and from the inventory rolls extant at Durham from the death of the second Norman bishop to the death of Cardinal Langley. These almost bring before our eyes the commanding figure of Carileph himself, in his gold-embroidered robe ornamented with gryphons and other quaint devices, and faintly shadow forth many another noble form in the long line of Durham's sovereign prelates. In these records, too, we see them only as bishops, habited in the vestments of church ceremonial, and divested of the coats of mail and warlike attributes in which we meet them in our national history.

What kind of building stood here in Bishop Pudsey's day we can only conjecture. That it was a fabric with massive stone walls, though not having the form and characteristics of a castle or any important chamber except a great hall, is probable; for in those times of turbulence and insecurity all great men dwelt in fortified houses. Perhaps the architectural works of Bishop Pudsey that remain in other parts of his diocese, and the dignified character of such features of the chapel as connect it with his time, justify the inference that there was some corresponding stateliness in the bishop's palace at Auckland even in Pudsey's day. But history throws not a ray of its pale light on those forgotten walls.

The Bishop of Durham was often not only the King's chief minister of state and companion in his wars, but also his host when the King came into the North. The first royal visit to Auckland of which we read is that of King John, who came here on the 18th April, 1209, in which year he led a great army against Scotland, and frightened the King into paying eleven hundred marks of silver, and delivering over his two daughters as hostages for securing the treaty. The restless King of England came again on the 11th of April in the following year, and soon afterwards we find the name of Ernald de Auckland connected with King John; for Ernald's dogs captured a wolf in the park at Freemantle, and his groom received five shillings from the King on bringing him the wolf.

Frequently as succeeding kings of England were in the North, especially during the wars with Scotland, Auckland—probably because of its situation, or perhaps because it was not a defensible castle—escaped the costly honour of again receiving the sovereign and his followers until the time of Edward III. But, meantime, let us glance at its state under early bishops of Durham.

The architectural history of Auckland is connected with one of her greatest prelates—the magnanimous Anthony Beck, son of Walter lord of Eresby in Lincolnshire, who became Bishop of Durham on the 9th of July, 1283, and was (somewhat curiously) celebrated as "the most valiant bishop of the realm." The life of Bishop Beck seems to have been spent chiefly in the court and the camp. One of his exploits in the Scottish wars was to attend Edward I. with a large army arrayed under the banner of St. Cuthbert; and he held dignities which no one of the other bishops of Durham ever attained, or perhaps desired, inasmuch as he was Patriarch of Jerusalem and King of the Isle of Man (for the shadowy crown of that island kingdom, which, after the death of Magnus, last King of Man of the old Norwegian dynasty, is seen at one time worn by a Scottish monarch, and at another bestowed by Edward of England as Lord Paramount of Man, rested afterwards on this warlike prelate and lord palatine of Durham): so that one would think he had little time for building. Graystanes (the monk of Durham who wrote in the reign of Edward III.) says, however, that Beck "constructed the manor-house of Auckland, with a chapel and chambers, in a most sumptuous way;" and that he made provision for chaplains to serve for ever in the chapel. Godwin adds (but I do not know on what authority) that this bishop "incastellated" the ancient manor-place of Auckland; "and he built," continues Godwin, "the great hall, wherein were divers pillars of black marble speckled with white; also the great chamber and many other rooms adjoining; and erected a goodly chapel there of well-squared stone, and placed in the same a dean and twelve prebendaries, allotting the quadrant in the west side of the castle for their habitation." The roll of Bishop Beck, containing an account of his receipts and expenses apparently for the year 1308, contains, moreover, the following item:—"To Geoffrey, the bailiff of Auckland, for building the chapel of Auckland, 148*l.*;" and that large sum, be it remembered, is equivalent to more than 2,000*l.* of the money of our day.

It was probably on the dedication feast that the Archbishop of York came to Auckland: at all events, the same roll contains an entry of 34s. 1d. for " the expenses of the archbishop at Auckland for one night." From the same roll it would appear, that, out of the savings of Beck's enormous income, he deposited, in little more than a year, in the hands of foreign bankers, a sum total equivalent to little short of 80,000l. in our money. Edward I. seems to have admired Bishop Beck's plate, embroidered vestments, and paraphernalia very much; for, after his death, cups and flagons of gold, tents, and a cloth of embroidered work, were bought by the King, and the purchase-money, represented in our currency, is little short of 20,000l. The bishop's vestment of red cloth of Tartary, embroidered with archangels in gold, had been lent to the King of England on his way to Scotland, and there lost in the war.

Nothing memorable concerning Auckland occurs for the next thirty years. The northern counties were, during all that period, incessantly harassed and wasted by the wars begun by the mighty and invincible Edward, and continued by his feeble successor; and the bishops, even when they retired to Auckland, did not escape

the sound<br>
Of wars and tumults far away.

The stately cathedral church of Durham, completed by the care of a line of prelates and priors reaching back to the days of Carileph, had now acquired the height of its splendour; and Edward III. had not long attained the throne, when Richard de Bury, the foremost statesman of his age, the most learned man in England, and the greatest minister of the Crown in the most brilliant reign of English history, was elected bishop of this regal see.

The young King, intent on his campaign against the Scots, came to Auckland in October, 1336, and was entertained by Bishop de Bury, who was at that time enjoying the society of his beloved books and his learned chaplains in this ancient wood-environed home. One dwells with pleasure on the picture of the learned prelate in his retirement; for Auckland must have stood pre-eminently forward as a seat of learning in his day. He took advantage of his frequent embassies on affairs and treaties of state to visit the library at Paris, and ransack the slender libraries of the foreign monasteries at which he rested on his way; and year after year, with undiminished pleasure, he returned to these repositories of books, " to quench the fever of political strife in the calm fountain of the muse." On these embassies he managed to collect an enormous number of manuscripts, and is said to have possessed more books than all the other bishops in England. He also maintained a staff of transcribers, correctors, illuminators, and binders, and filled his chambers with his books wherever he resided. The historian of his life tells us that the bishop had such an accumulation of manuscripts, that the floors were covered with them, insomuch that persons who came into his presence could not with due reverence approach him; and it was difficult to move in his sleeping-room without treading on a book. And he was not only surrounded by these silent friends collected in his house from all parts of Christendom, but he loved to keep around him men of ability and learning.

The food of the bishop and his companions was not, however, wholly literary, neither did they "cultivate literature on a little oatmeal." From the roll of a steward of Auckland for the year 1338, it appears that, although the bishop resided there for only five weeks in that year, there was consumed a fat ox per week, beside fat pigs, and the sheep and poultry which were found by the tenants, and the venison from the bishop's park, and thirty-one quarters of wheat, and seventy-eight quarters of malt. John de Whitchurch, a grave archdeacon, the bishop's commissary during his absence from the diocese, conducted the chase in Weardale; and, when he and his followers went to the forest, they took with them three quarters of wheat baked into bread, and a plentiful supply of ale, to accompany the venison on which they were to feast. And, when a whale or a sturgeon was taken on the coast of the bishop's manor of Howden, portions of the royal fish were duly brought to Auckland. It was not uncommon for bishops to keep monkeys for their amusement at table; and Bishop Beck having kept an old and a young monkey to divert his cares, we have an amusing picture of the greediness with which the younger animal appropriated the blanched almonds from a silver plate on the bishop's table, and was deprived of them by the elder. But

De Bury seems to have preferred monks to monkeys, and a chaplain read to him during dinner.

This lover of literature found time also to be an author, and it was at Auckland that he wrote the " Treatise on the Love of Books," which is a unique monument of literary ardour, and has long been known as one of the most remarkable of the intellectual productions of the middle ages. It shows how anxious he was to remove the obstacles which in his time stood in the way of learning, and it may be regarded as a foundation charter for the public library which he founded in the University of Oxford, and to which he bequeathed his immense collection of books,—

> Sure that the works of mighty men—
> The good, the faithful, the sublime,
> Stored in the gallery of Time,
> Repose awhile, to wake again ;*

and at Auckland on the 14th April, 1345, the good bishop died.

The first yearly account that has been preserved of a steward of the manor embraces twelve months from Michaelmas in the fourth year of De Bury's pontificate, and the document is interesting, not only as illustrating the domestic economy of Auckland, and showing that it was at that time a long-established place of residence of the bishops, but because it refers to the house itself sometimes as the Manor House, and sometimes as the Hall, but never as the Castle, and indicates that considerable works were then in progress. Mention is made in it of various buildings, offices, and chambers. A cottage " at the gate of the manor house " is mentioned, and the rent accounted for. There is a payment to the plumber for work " in the great chapel " and " in the little chapel;" to a carpenter, " for repairing the turret;" to various workmen, for " repairs to the great hall," to " the great stone wall on the west side of the manor-house," to the " glass windows of the great chapel," and to " the gable of the hall." This part of the building, and also the kitchen, appears to have been covered with timber, and Norway timber was bought for the kitchen door and windows. Mention is made of " my lord's chamber," and of " the king's chamber;" and the brewhouse was duly recognised, and was " put in order against my lord's coming." " The king's

* Goethe.

chamber," mentioned in this account of the year 1338, again occurs in 1350 and in 1459, and very probably derived its name from having been the place of lodging of Edward III. himself, when he was the guest of De Bury for two or three days in October, 1336, only two years before the date of the roll in which mention of " the king's chamber" first occurs.

In the year 1346, when Thomas de Hatfield was Bishop of Durham, Auckland Park is connected with an event ever memorable in English history. David of Scotland, who had long menaced the English frontier, seized the opportunity of Edward's absence with the chivalry of England, in the campaign which was crowned by the victory of Creci, to invade the northern counties with a great army. On the night of the 16th October, 1346, while David, threatening Durham, lay at Beaurepaire, a country-house of the monks, the Archbishop of York (who with the Lords Henry Percy and Ralph Neville had been appointed arrayers of the northern forces) assembled the English army in Auckland Park, without the knowledge of the Scots, and the following day saw the victory of Neville's Cross and the capture of the fugitive Scottish King.

About thirty years after this time, an account of the clerk of the works for 1378 refers to work " in my lord's chamber on the north of the small garden within the manor house," and to " the parlour," which seems to have had a window towards the Wear; but nothing worthy of mention concerning Auckland occurs until the spring of 1381, in a roll of Bishop Fordham's time, when many payments occur for wine, for wax bought for candles, and for various other articles taken to Auckland, apparently for the entertainment of John of Gaunt, Duke of Lancaster, who was on his way to the Borders as a commissioner of the crown, and was escorted by the bishop, and was accompanied to Gateshead by " the bishop's archers of Durham."

Walter Skirlaw, the succeeding bishop, is not otherwise connected with the architectural history of Auckland than inasmuch as he erected a great stone gateway which led to the manor-house, which was standing in the reign of George III., and also constructed a bridge over the Wear. It was at Auckland that he made his will, on the 7th March, 1405, and the document indicates, as Dr. Raine has remarked, the splendour of the see of Durham at the period of its highest magnificence, and affords us a gorgeous list of the plate, the vestments, the books, and the embroidered cloths which surrounded the bishop at Auckland. The prelates, from early times, maintained considerable state, and we derive from the records at Durham many glimpses of the manner in which they lived. The windows had long been filled with glass; the bare walls were hung with tapestry; and their table was served with dishes and plates of silver, although the trenchers and platters, used by persons of inferior rank, were of wood. Bishop Skirlaw bequeathed to his friends fifteen silver and silver-gilt cups, the design and ornaments of which are described, and he was attended by esquires, valets, grooms, pages, clerks, cellar-keepers, chamberlain, and chaplain.

Some repairs and works were in progress at Auckland during the pontificate of Cardinal Langley, but they do not seem to have been important. In the roll of his clerk and surveyor of works for 1423 mention is made of the postern gate opening to the highway on the south side of the chapel, and of a passage extending from the parlour to the east end of the chapel; but such scattered notices as these do not enable us to form any clear notion of the arrangement of the buildings in that day. It was in what was called " the inner chamber" at Auckland that Cardinal Langley made his will, on the 11th Dec. 1436, and he died there on the 10th Nov. in the following year.

Perhaps, inasmuch as the belfry or upper stage of the tower of St. Andrew's church, which, although distant a mile, is the parish church of Auckland, is not only contemporary with Langley's pontificate, but was built by his gift,—and inasmuch also as the collegiate foundation which formerly flourished in St. Andrew's became, after its establishment within the walls of the bishop's palace, connected with the history of Auckland Castle, this may be a fitting place to advert to that foundation. The parish church itself had been endowed at a period of remote antiquity, and it existed long before the time at which Auckland first occurs as an episcopal abode. It was this church that was made collegiate by Bishop Beck, but his statutes seem to have been only a revival of an older foundation, for Carileph himself is said to have instituted a sort of collegiate foundation for secular priests in St. Andrew's, Auckland. At all events a collegiate establishment of canons was existing in 1292, when Beck refounded it, and charged the dean with providing for divine service daily " in the chapel within his manor-house of Auckland;" and so much earlier as 1239 the deanery of Auckland is mentioned. It is interesting to look upon those Early English features of the existing fabric which saw the ecclesiastics of the great bishop's day. Before 1314 an endowment had been assigned for the officiating priest of the domestic chapel, and Bishop Skirlaw bequeathed many valuable robes and vestments to what is described as " his collegiate church of Auckland." Other bishops paid persons for teaching the choristers to sing in the chapel, and Cardinal Langley revived the statutes of Bishop Beck.

Subsequently, however, the dean and his canons appear to have obtained a residence, which came to be known as " the College," within the walls of Auckland Castle; and inasmuch as in 1460, and again in 1470, the fabric is called " The New College," it seems probable that the arrangement was made by Booth, the bishop of that day. In his chancellor's roll repairs to the New College are mentioned, and he built the stone gateways of the College. It occurs again in 1498;* and in the following year Bishop Fox constitutes the priest of the chantry of the Blessed Virgin in the parish church sacrist " in the collegiate chapel within the manor-house of Auckland," and seems to recognise the domestic chapel as having become the collegiate church of the dean and canons. The collegiate establishment, at all events, became removed from the vicinity of the parish church to that of the bishop's hall, and, when Leland visited the North in 1538, it would appear that nothing remained near the parish church but the dean's great house and barns, and other houses of husbandry. But the college of Auckland was an educational as well as an ecclesiastical foundation, and it was the school in which many of the young nobility and gentry of the North of England were educated.

At the dissolution, the college fell to the Crown, and it be-

* In the inventory of the implements and books of the College, taken on the accession of Wm. Thomason to the deanery in this year. Wills and Inv. Surt. Soc. p. 101.

came the private property of the bishops. Repairs to its buildings are frequently mentioned in the account rolls of the time of Elizabeth. It is a grave accusation against the sacrilegious Pilkington, the first post-reformation Bishop of Durham, that in 1561 he broke up the college bells of Auckland and sold and converted them to his own use. He is also stated to have made a bowling-alley where divine service used to be celebrated, from which the inference would seem to be that the chapel of the college was not the present chapel of the castle, and that it had been actually destroyed. The spoliations of the college did not end with Pilkington's life, for he was buried at Durham under the marble slab which had been the monument in Auckland College of one of its deans, and which was brought to Durham for this new duty. After the Restoration, the land and buildings of the college were conveyed by Bishop Cosin to the see. The walls that remain have been so altered and modernised that they afford no indications of its former architecture or plan; but the shape was that of a quadrangle, of which Mr. Gresley's house occupies the southern front.

To return, however, to the general history of Auckland Castle. From the time of Cardinal Langley, the buildings seem to have remained much in the state in which they were left by that bishop, and it does not appear that Auckland was the scene of any event memorable in our history during those devastating wars of the Roses—

> When the Percys, Veres, and Nevilles left their castle-halls and revels
> To rush like raging devils into the deadly fight,
> And Loyalty and Reason were confounded by the Treason
> That cast into a prison the king of yester-night.

Events then followed events with startling rapidity, and England's nobles were in a state of change; but, though kingly dynasties were falling, bishop tranquilly succeeded to bishop at Auckland,

> Where valour bowed before the rood and book,
> And kneeling knighthood served a prelate lord;

and in the still domain of their cathedral church religion continued to celebrate her stately rites and hail the returning seasons of the year, as much undisturbed by the agitations of the world as the sunlight that decked their park in the glories of spring or the calm splendour of the autumn day.

The bishop's residence is still called "the Manor-house of Auckland," in 1457, when, in the month of July, Robert Neville, Bishop of Durham, who was the fifth son of Ralph, Earl of Westmoreland, and had for his mother, Catherine, daughter of John of Gaunt, Duke of Lancaster, here made his will and died.

In the rolls of his successor, in 1471, repairs of "the great chapel," as it is there called, occur; and new glass was brought in 1475 from Newcastle for repairing the windows of the manor-house. In the same year, rushes were bought for strewing the hall and other chambers. In January, 1489, Bishop Sherwood subscribes a letter "written at my castel or manoir of Auckland," and at this period the appellation of "castle" seems first to occur.

In the year 1480, "wild cattle and other untamed animals" are first mentioned as denizens of the park. The stock-keeper accounts in that year for the farm of the herbage of part of the park, and states the rest to be occupied and depastured by the wild cattle. It is worthy of remark that this wild race survived all the storms and changes that fell during the next hundred and fifty years upon the Church of England and upon the lords of Auckland, and that thirty-two head of the wild cattle remained in the park on the 24th September, 1627. In 1634, too, Sir William Brereton, on his visit, saw twenty-nine wild white cattle in the park. Fallow deer inhabited it, as well as the wild bulls and kine, when Leland came to Auckland in 1538; but from a much earlier period the park was as well stocked with deer as the fish-ponds were with fish and the thickets with fowl. The old pomarium episcopi or bishop's orchard occurs as early as the time of De Bury. In the year 1338, however, his steward had no produce to account for, and he gives the sufficient reason that "there is neither fruit nor tree." The almost unique fig-tree of Auckland Castle, which was planted by Bishop Barrington and is still flourishing and fruitful, is, at all events, a becoming representative of the old orchard of the bishops, whether it does or does not grow upon the site. Long may it flourish, and may its branches never be less!

A letter from Bishop Ruthall, written at Auckland in 1513, in the month after the battle of Flodden, affords a lively picture of the hospitality of Auckland: the bishop had been urged by the Crown to repair his castle at Norham, which the Scots had seized before the conflict, and writing to Wolsey, then almoner, says: " *The hospitalitie of this countray agreth not with the buylding so greate a warke, for thate I spend here wold make many towris, and refreshe my ruynous howses. I broght hider with me viij tunne of wyne, and, our Lord be thankyd, I hafe not two tunne left at this howre, and this is faire utteraunce in two monethes, and schame it is to saye how many befs and motons have bene spent in my hous, besids other fresh meats, whete, malt, fysche, and such baggays: on my fayth, ye wold marvayle, if my pastures had not been sum what stockyt byfore behynd, for ccc. persons some day is but a small numbre, and of these days have I many, besides 60 or 80 beggers at the gate; and this the way to keep a man poore.*"

In the preceding month of September the bishop contributed 800*l.* to the Earl of Surrey, then on his road to the borders: it was carried to Newcastle on three horses, and three men were employed four days in telling the money and delivering it to Surrey. Bishop Ruthall nevertheless made great additions to the house at Auckland during the thirteen years of his pontificate (1509 to 1522). He built from the ground the whole of the dining chamber of his day. But the upper part of the gable window of this great dining-room was left incomplete by Ruthall, and finished by Bishop Tunstall, his successor. The lower window which gives light to the present servants' hall, and the panels above it containing the armorial bearings of the See and of Ruthall, are the work of that bishop. The upper part of the structure, with its rich ornamental work, is Tunstall's, and his arms are represented in the same way. Between the works of the two bishops Wyatt inserted the incongruous modern windows of the present dining-room, but all the rest of the gable is a very elegant and characteristic piece of work. This portion of the buildings itself proves that the Parliamentarian usurper Haslerigg did not really demolish the castle, as he is stated to have done, deeply as " ravenous sacrilege " has injured the secular as well as the ecclesiastical buildings of this venerable pile.

In 1538, when Leland was here, the great hall was standing, for he saw it in what he describes as "divers pillars of black marble speckled with white." The material probably was the same shelly limestone, capable of high polish like Purbeck marble, which is used in the piers of the noble chapel. Leland mentions, too, "the exceeding fair Great Chamber, with other chambers there." Skirlaw's "goodly gate-house at entering into the castle" was likewise then standing.

We have now arrived at the pontificate of Tunstall—a bishop who made great contributions to the learning and science of his country, as well as considerable additions to his house of Auckland during the long eventful years of his rule, which extended from 1529 to 1558. He saw the happy union of the Red and the White Rose in the person of Henry VII.; he lived through the destructive and sanguinary reign of Henry VIII.; saw the brief reign of Edward, and the still shorter but perilous reign of Mary, and died in the year in which Elizabeth succeeded to the throne. Tunstall in his will says, he found the houses and dwellings belonging to the bishopric in such almost total ruin, that "he had not a house at his first coming to lye dry in," and that he had, "by great cost and labour," repaired them. Accordingly, in 1531, very soon after he became bishop, the roll of the clerk of the works contains an entry of 42$l$. 3$s$. 4$d$. paid for "repairs in the manor house of Auckland." He appears to have built the gallery, in which there is a range of bed-chambers, as well as to have finished the great gable of the dining-room begun by his predecessor. That gallery or wing (which stretches in a straight line westward, and is called "Scotland") is built above a range of cellars, which, however, may be older than Tunstall's time. The bed-chambers have succeeded to his "long gallery," which was seen a century later by Brereton when he came to visit Bishop Morton in 1634. The origin of the traditional name of "Scotland" for this part of the building is unknown; but, as Scottish hostages were in and from Beck's time occasionally committed to the custody of the bishop, it may have acquired its name from the older chambers which occupied its site having been set apart for their reception. It certainly adds a more gloomy horror to the dark range of cellars, fit as they are for dungeons, if we can imagine that here Scottish captives were occasionally confined—

> Doomed, in sad durance pining, to abide
> The long delay of hope from Solway's farther side;

but Auckland is not a likely place to have long detained prisoners, and nothing has been observed in the stone walls or roof of these cellars to connect them with the time

> When English lords and Scottish chiefs were foes,

or to show that they ever held in confinement any potentate less friendly than the family of Sir John Barleycorn. The long gallery was materially altered when appropriated to its present uses by Bishop Trevor. Tunstall not only found Auckland in decay, but clear of any furniture, and he seems to have recognized the fitness of instituting heirlooms in this episcopal residence, for he bequeathed for the use of his successors all his tapestry, tables, and bedsteads, expressly to invite succeeding bishops to hospitality and residence in the diocese. That his injunctions were not neglected, we have many proofs; and towards the close of the century Bishop Toby Matthew seems to have begun his rule at Auckland by providing (amongst other things) three hogsheads of Gascony wine, which was bought at Newcastle at 5*l*. a hogshead, and brought to Auckland.

In 1611, during the pontificate of Bishop James, a fair and illustrious guest was intended to be the unwilling recipient of the hospitality of Auckland. The Lady Arabella Stuart, the heroine of one of the most melancholy love stories in real history, having incurred the resentment of her kinsman James I. by marrying without the king's consent Mr. Seymour, afterwards Marquis of Hertford, the Privy Council determined to transfer the custody of the lady to the Bishop of Durham at Auckland. But she (of course) had a will of her own, and viewed with despair, as we read, her removal to "a place so out of the world as Durham;" so, when the bishop had conducted her and her attendants at great expense to Mr. Conyers's house at Barnet, she escaped in man's attire, and was on the sea when she was overtaken and recaptured. She was then conducted to the Tower of London, where she died.

Bishop Neile, whose pontificate lasted from 1617 to 1627, is stated to have expended nearly 3,000*l*. in repairing and ornamenting the palace of Auckland. His works must have been very considerable, if they really cost so large a sum of money; but we know that he delighted in building, for while Dean of Westminster large sums were expended on the abbey under his superintendence.* Beef and beer seem to have been the basis of all architectural energy at Durham, for this prelate, too, wrote to his agent in 1622, to desire that there should be "a brewing of beare at Awkland in regard of my purpose of lieing there, God willing, some part of this sommer; and I wish it should be well hop't for keeping it the better from sowering; but the brewer must be charged to look well to the sweetness of his caskes, for there is never a yeare but I lose much beare by the mustines of his caskes."

In 1628, on Bishop Neile's translation to Winchester, an inventory was taken, in which the following, amongst less important parts of the palace (it is still the manor house) are mentioned:—

The hall;
The chamber on the north side of it;
The great chamber;
The dining-room, well wainscotted round about;
The earl's chamber;
The chancellor's chamber;
The knights' chamber;
My lord's study;
The long gallery, and
A chamber at the end;
My lord's chamber, and
A chamber within;
The new library;
The buttery, and the chamber above it.

Mention occurs a hundred and forty years before of a chamber called "the Wyndesore chamber," and of "the high chapel;" and again, in 1548, "the high chapel" is mentioned in an item for taking down the stalls, and helping to convey them to Durham. Within three years of Bishop Neile's translation, the great kitchen was pulled down by his successor, who seems to have been

* A minute account of the expenditure on the works at Westminster remains, curiously enough, in the Library of the Dean and Chapter of Durham.

a destroyer; for the bishop who succeeded him recovered 333*l.* for dilapidations, which sum appears to have included 300*l.* for the estimated cost of rebuilding the kitchen as it was before.

And now we have arrived at the pontificate of the excellent Morton, a learned man and the patron of learning, who was prelate during a sad and eventful period of our history, for he became bishop in 1632, was deprived of his see by the usurpers in 1646, and, retiring into a life of poverty and content, died at a great age in 1659; exiled, as Dr. Raine has justly said, by the strong arm of successful treason, from a home ennobled by his munificence, and consecrated by his piety.

In 1634, when Bishop Morton was living at Auckland in peace, Sir William Brereton, already mentioned, visited him there; and his letter not only gives a lively picture of Auckland in his day, but is important for its mention of the two chapels. " This very worthy reverend bishop," he writes, " maintains great hospitality in an orderly, well-governed house. The castle, as it is a stately, pleasant seat, of great receipt, so it is of great strength, compassed with a thick stone wall, seated upon the side of an hill, upon a rock, a river running below, and good store of wood (though little of timber) encompassing above. Here," continues Brereton, " is a very fair, neat hall as I have found in any bishop's palace in England. Two chapels belong hereunto, the one over the other; the higher a most dainty, neat, light, pleasant place, but the voice is so drowned and swallowed by the echo, as few words can be understood. The lower is made use of upon Sabbath days, and there is great resort hither by the neighbourhood. Here are three dining-rooms, a fair matted gallery, wherein there was placed on both sides these pictures ;" and then he enumerates the portraits of Reformers, adding, " and none but of this strain." " A dainty, stately park," he continues, " wherein I saw wild bulls and kine, which had two calves runners. There are about twenty wild beasts, all white; will not endure your approach, but, if they be enraged or distressed, very violent and furious." And in conclusion he says, " Here we rested the Lord's Day, and were very generously and nobly entertained."

It was Bishop Morton who appropriated for the free grammar-school which King James I. had instituted shortly after his accession, the old chapel of S. Anne, in the market-place. An older history attaches to that desecrated little building; for in the parish church of S. Andrew there existed formerly a guild or fraternity, to which pertained a chapel of great antiquity dedicated to S. Anne, and situated in the market-place. This chapel seems to have been resorted to by parishioners of Auckland, and it was enlarged in the time of Richard II., and again in 1482. This edifice was standing when Bishop Morton appropriated it for the school-house of the free grammar-school. It had probably fallen into decay before 1781, for a wretched structure then succeeded to it, which seems to have served for the grammar-school and the chapel; and the lower part of an unseemly tower at the west was converted into a market-house. But these buildings were all removed in 1847, when the present edifice, designed by Mr. Salvin, was built.

But, to revert to Auckland Castle in the time of Morton. Here, on the 31st May, 1633, he received King Charles I. on his progress to his realm and crown of Scotland. This was not his first visit; for, when a mere boy, he sojourned for a while at Auckland, on his way to the South. He saw it again before his untimely death; but his third and last visit was made in 1647, when he came to Bishop-Auckland as a prisoner, having been shortly before sold by his Scottish subjects to their fellow-rebels in England. But the success of armed rebellion had then driven the learned and munificent Morton from his see, and the king was surrounded by rude soldiers in a small inn kept by one Christopher Dobson in Bishop-Auckland, and the castle of the prelates was in the hands of "insulting rebel powers."

In 1647 a survey was made for the Parliament, preparatory to the sale of Auckland. It is returned as "a very stately manor-house, called the castle or palace of the late Bishop of Durham, with two chapels to it, one over the other, built of stone, and covered with lead; the site of the house walled about with stone, and in some places embattled, having thereto a stately gate-house, stables, brewhouse, bakehouse, and other offices, all which are in dilapidation."

The castle and manor were conveyed by the Parliamentarian Commissioners to Sir Arthur Haslerigg for 6,102*l.*, and he began to build a new mansion-house upon the spot. Haslerigg is stated by Dugdale to have disliked the old-fashioned buildings at Auckland Castle. The fanatics of the usurpation days desired, we know, to trample out all the monuments of the past, as well as the Church and Monarchy of England, and to begin the affairs of mankind anew; and no doubt Haslerigg found the old buildings too characteristic of the ecclesiastical traditions of Auckland to be agreeable to his taste. So he resolved on building, says Dugdale, "a new structure of a noble fabric, all of one pile, taking for his model the curious and stately building at Thorpe, near Peterborough," a large, square, four-storied edifice, which Chief Justice Oliver St. John, after the murder of Charles I., erected partly out of the cathedral at Peterborough. Haslerigg accordingly demolished a considerable part of the buildings of Auckland Castle, and out of the materials built what is described as a magnificent house; and it seems to have stood on the ground to the south of the chapel, the destruction of which he seems, however, only to have begun. And so

> The reverend pile lay wild and waste,
> Profaned, dishonoured, and defaced.
> Through storied lattices no more
> In softened light the sunbeams pour;
> Gilding the Gothic sculpture rich
> Of shrine, and monument, and niche.
> The civil fury of the time
> Made sport of sacrilegious crime;
> And dark fanaticism rent
> Altar, and screen, and ornament.

But the reign of the usurper was short; and he had not completed his stately mansion when his place knew him no more. Upon the Restoration the zealous and learned Cosin was appointed Bishop of Durham; and the twelve years of his pontificate were fully occupied in removing all Haslerigg's buildings, and in carrying out his design of reinstating Auckland Castle. The buildings of his time remained for a century much as he left them; and although the alterations made in the latter half of the last century have been such as to deprive most parts of the castle of any original character, its plan and form seem to be what Cosin left. The two oil paintings now hanging on the staircase in the porter's lodge, and Buck's engraving in 1728, probably represent with substantial accuracy the walls and arrangement of the courtyards as they stood in Cosin's time.

He seems to have begun with the chapel. In a letter to Robert Morley, of the craft of Freemasons, he gives minute directions as to buttresses and rustic ashlar work, and sends a pattern; so that the bishop seems to have been his own architect, and to have directed the works from his house in London. Gothic achitecture, civil as well as ecclesiastical, was in his day at its lowest debasement; and little as the munificent bishop knew of church architecture, his chapel would probably have been much worse, but for his directions. The work of his time may be open to our criticism, but not its motives; for he laboured for the honour of God, and evidently felt that "artistic splendour of costly decoration forms a natural, right, and scriptural tribute for thankful man to lavish upon the holy and beautiful houses of the Giver of all Good."

Cosin rebuilt the south wall; added a clerestory to the body of the chapel, and a new roof; put in new windows throughout, raised the sills of the windows of the north aisle to suit the levels of his new windows on the south; repaired and ornamented the eastern gable; repaved the nave, the aisles, and the altar-platform, and put in new screens and woodwork. He ordered marble stones from Amsterdam for his chapel; and in 1663 entered into contracts with two glaziers at Durham and two at Auckland for glazing the windows with blue and white glass. For decorative painting, John Baptist Van Ersell, of the city of Durham, was employed; and the sculptor was Hendrick de Keyser, of Bishop Auckland. The roof was to be painted a blue ground, and the coats of arms in their colours, decorations which are said to have been obliterated in the time of Bishop Barrington.* Cosin also entered into a contract in 1664 for work at the holy table, none of which remains.

It is strange that Haslerigg should be stated to have destroyed the chapel of Auckland Castle in order to build his mansion, and

---

* It is stated that the chapel was at some time during the Georgian era used for a school, and that the gilded and coloured ornaments were found to divert the attention of the boys from their books.

that credit should be given to Bishop Cosin for building "another and a beautiful chapel" on the north side of the castle, with the stone of Haslerigg's mansion. The various ancient features of the existing edifice show that if Haslerigg destroyed any chapel, it stood elsewhere; and it was probably that upper or lesser fabric, which is mentioned in 1338, which seems to have been used for divine service in the time of Charles I. which contained the stalls that Bishop Tunstall removed, and which would seem to have stood to the north of the present drawing-room, above the porch of the existing chapel, in a part of the castle now converted into bedrooms.

At all events the masonry of the north wall of the chapel is ancient; the original stones of the window jambs remain, though the windows were partly blocked up by Cosin's windows being placed at a higher level. At the east end too, on the exterior, two buttresses and parts of the original wall remain. Inside the chapel, however, the most ancient portions of the fabric are to be seen. The westernmost piers are in the style of Bishop Pudsey's time, and strongly resemble those in his Galilee at Durham. The rest of the pier arches also seem earlier than Bishop Beck's time: they are fine, and rest on clustered columns, banded, and having moulded capitals. The corbel-shafts and aisle-corbels of the original roof remain. The polished Stanhope marble shafts, which seem to have been coupled with freestone shafts in the piers, were unadvisedly covered with whitewash in the time of Bishop Van Mildert, when also, according to Dr. Raine, the tracery of the windows was filled with the tasteless coloured glass that now defaces this beautiful edifice.

Passing from the chapel, to revert to the work of Cosin in other parts of the castle, we find that the bishop speaks of "the new hall" in a letter of 1662. Probably what is called "the great hall or chamber" of his time is now the noble drawing-room of the castle. It had a lantern; and this appears to have been finished by the bishop's desire in the form of the lantern which he found over the chapel. A lantern in the centre of the roof is represented in Buck's view. Cosin contracted for windows to be opened on the west side of the hall, but these are now closed by masonry. He stipulated that the buttresses should be built up to the battlement, on the model of those which he built on the south side of the edifice which he calls "the new chapel." The ornamental woodwork which Cosin added to the great hall was removed in Bishop Barrington's time by the injudicious advice of that arch-destroyer Wyatt.

The very remarkable oak-panelled room with armorial bearings, now called the store-room or housekeeper's room, is probably the chamber which Cosin destined for his library, inasmuch as its mullioned window is probably the same bay or three-light window which, by a contract dated 1st Sept. 1664, was "to be taken out of Sir Arthur Haslerigg's building, and set into the wall of the room where my lord intends to make his library." The panel in the upper part of the bow has the arms of Queen Elizabeth, with a lion and rouge dragon as supporters, and in the corners we have a Tudor rose and a pomegranate crowned. Along one side of the room at the top are shields bearing what purport to be the arms of contemporary sovereigns of Europe, Asia, and Africa, and "a strange assemblage of potentates" they may well be called. On another side of the room are shields bearing the arms of several English earls of the reign of Elizabeth, decorations which may very probably have given to this room the name of "the earls' chamber." A room in the castle bore that name in 1628. This curious apartment was probably a room of dignity in later times, for the arms of Lord Crewe, Bishop of Durham (who gave the organ now in Auckland Castle Chapel), and the arms of several of the sees of England, are represented in the window.

If Dr. Raine was right in his opinion that the present kitchen was an original part of the building, and that if any portions of Bishop Beck's great hall remain, they are to be found in this kitchen, it cannot have been the "great kitchen" which Bishop Morton's immediate predecessor is recorded to have pulled down. At all events, it is old as well as spacious; but it has been spoiled by the modern flat ceiling which cuts off half its proper height, and only one of the old fireplaces remains in it. The present servants' hall was destined, as we have seen, for a dining-room by Tunstall, whose crest is carved in the ceiling.

The buildings of Auckland Castle seem to have remained much

as Cosin left them until the time of Bishop Trevor, who built the suite of rooms on the south front, which are so important to the comfort and convenience of the house. Trevor is stated to have spent 8,000*l.* on Auckland Castle. In that amount is included the purchase-money of the house now the porter's lodge. Trevor did not live to complete the additions he began to build, and they were completed by Bishop Egerton. When Pennant came here in Egerton's time, he found that Skirlaw's Gate Tower had been destroyed, and replaced by Bishop Trevor's attempt at Gothic. Pennant gives such dimensions of the "old hall" which he found standing (and mentions by that designation), as seem to show that the present ante-room was, before Barrington's time, part of that noble structure; for he says,—"The principal apartments are an old hall 75 feet by 32, the height 35, and a handsome dining parlour ornamented with portraits of Jacob and the twelve patriarchs, presented by Bishop Trevor." The present drawing-room retains its original breadth only, its length being reduced to 60 feet, and its height to 27. Auckland Castle was described by Pennant as having lost its castellated form, and as then resembling some of the magnificent foreign abbeys. Probably it never had a really castellated form; but even Wyatt's transformations could not deprive the building of the picturesque irregularity and mediæval aspect which were so striking in Pennant's day. To Egerton's work succeeded the pseudo-Gothicising of the great drawing-room and other parts of the structure, under the unhappy direction of Wyatt, that prince of sham and stucco; when Cosin's old timber roof, if not destroyed, was masked by a tasteless groining in plaster; when the great staircase was altered and enlarged, and alterations were made which destroyed the original character of the house. At the same period the gateway was built, the line of screen-work on the south front of the castle put up, and the turret of the old courtyard walls removed. And here the story of Auckland Castle ends.

It has been truly said that we live in days of returning reverence for the structures that link our age with bygone periods of English history; and certainly, in most cases, when we do venture to meddle with the historic monuments of our country, we are careful to show that reverent love for the past which can preserve and appropriate what was excellent in it, while acknowledging a necessity for change. Excepting the ancient and dignified chapel, few portions of this building have been left to appeal to us for preservation on architectural or on sentimental grounds; but let us not forget that upon this spot illustrious men have lived and died; that here some of the greatest of the princely bishops of this see with pious zeal planned and directed many of the great and useful works which elsewhere at this day claim our grateful remembrance; and that here, in a turbulent age, they might be seen calmly founding noble institutions of charity and learning, or maintaining the liberties of the Anglican Church; that here they gave their thoughts, and time, and wealth, to build for posterity, and to let their light so shine before the world, that the Father in heaven might receive the more glory and honour amongst men. May a time never come when in this ancient diocese of Durham her people will be indifferent to the historic traditions and the dignified memories which are garnered up in Auckland Castle!

Mr. Frederick R. Wilson of Alnwick, Fellow of the Royal Institute of British Architects, having, after the foregoing paper was read, kindly offered to prepare and present a ground-plan and other illustrative details to accompany it on its publication, visited Auckland Castle, and traced out the remains of an ancient curtain-wall fortified with towers. The results of the survey so made by Mr. Wilson have been, at the author's request, stated by him in the following letter addressed to the author in January, 1863:—

Dear Sir,—My archæological survey of Auckland Castle, made on the 14th and 15th inst., brings me to the discovery that Bishop Beke must have built here a veritable Edwardian castle. I am enabled to say there was a keep, and a castellated circumvallation, 'garnished with towers,' as the chroniclers have described. The Bishop of Durham, who most hospitably and ably furnished me with every assistance in the survey, drew my attention to two ancient views of the castle hanging in the gateway tower. One of these depicts a central mass of building, surrounded by an embrasured wall, on which there are towers at intervals. Although this evidence was not very old, it confirmed me in my impression that a site possessing such military advantages would not have been disregarded by a martial prelate like Anthony Beke. I, therefore, in conjunction with his lordship, prosecuted my search, and ultimately ascertained the positions of several of the wall-towers and the barbacan. By reference to the plan, which I have great pleasure in sending, you will perceive there is a large square tower at the south-west angle, now used as the entrance-lodge. This, I find, occupies the site of a large Edwardian tower; although, from the fact of its having been rebuilt by Skirlaw, and rebuilt again by Ruthall, and again by Tunstall, since that period, it presents a Tudor instead of an Edwardian appearance. Near the stables are the remains of the entrance-barbacan, which faces the coevally principal street of the town. Attached to this are the two modern gate-pillars, walled across, indicating that it continued to be the principal entrance to the castle; and beyond this again, at the north-west angle of the curtain, on the verge of the declivity of the bank, there is a square platform, much modernised, which indubitably marks the site of a corresponding tower to that at the south-west angle, which would leave the barbacan, as at Alnwick, mid-way between the two lengths of curtain fortified with towers. From this north-west angle the ancient north curtain-wall, now represented, for about half its ancient length, by a low modern one, skirted the edge of the precipitous bank. About two hundred feet from the angle, the low wall in question takes a semicircular form, marking the existence of a semicircular tower; and at the same interval again there is a projecting belt of trees, in a similar form, which, I conclude, marks the site of a second tower. The eastern curtain-walls and towers shown in the view have disappeared: a carriage-road to the park occupies their site, and a modern wall now curtails and circumscribes the outer ward.

I have carefully gone over all the apartments of the keep, and have traced the ancient lodgings. I show these on my plan; and as I have distinguished all modern partitions, you can perceive exactly all that remains of the ancient configuration of Auckland Castle.

To the above letter the author ought, perhaps, to add that he does not know in what " chroniclers " any mention is found of " a keep and a castellated circumvallation." That the " central mass of building " could ever have been called a Norman or an Edwardian " keep," the author presumes his able correspondent does not mean to assert. As to the curtain-wall, it will be remembered that, in the reign of Charles I., Auckland Castle is described to be " encompassed with a thick stone wall." From Skirlaw's time, at all events, the great gate-house seems to have been the entrance to the castle. The author desires to add his acknowledgments, and to express his satisfaction that Mr. Wilson has made the discoveries which he so clearly describes.

# FINCHALE PRIORY.

ALTHOUGH closely connected with the great priory at Durham from the time of Richard the First, Finchale has a history earlier than that of Durham itself, and seems to have been a place of some importance in days when the primeval forest still overspread the hill on which the remains of St. Cuthbert finally rested,—

> Where his cathedral, huge and vast,
> Looks down upon the Wear.

There is reason to believe that in St. Cuthbert's life-time, and subsequently during the reigns of Anglo-Saxon princes, Finchale was a monastic if not a royal abode. It is mentioned in history as the place where synods of the Church of Northumbria assembled in the years 788, 798, and 810—a period when the bishop's see was at Hexham; and it is worthy of remark, that in the reign of William Rufus, when Finchale had relapsed into a state of wildness and solitude, the foundations of forgotten buildings and the remains of men were often uncovered by the spade. We have no certain information as to the building to which these foundations belonged; and whatever dignity Finchale may have known in Saxon times, it had certainly become the abode only of wolves and noxious animals at the time of the Norman Conquest, and at the time (A.D. 1110) when Godric, afterwards celebrated as its hermit-saint, came to dwell amongst its solitudes and give to it a new and more enduring fame.

The biography of Godric was written by his friend Reginald, a monk of the Benedictine fraternity which had then been established for more than a century at Durham. From this memoir it appears that he had been a sailor for sixteen years; and that having in the course of his travels visited St. Andrew's in Scotland, as well as Lindisfarne and the sea-girt hermitage of St. Cuthbert, he began to emulate the devotion of that holy recluse.

He made a pilgrimage to Jerusalem as well as to Rome, and on his return sold his property and began a hermit's life; but this wanderer of the sea did not begin that life in any fixed dwelling-place, for he roved amongst woods and inhabited caves in the vicinity first of Carlisle and then of Wolsingham. After passing two years in this way, he believed that St. Cuthbert himself directed him to take up his abode finally at a place in the forest near Durham indicated to him by the name of "Finchalech," but he was first to make another visit to the Holy Land. He obeyed these directions; and returning to Durham—where the cathedral of the magnificent Bishop Carileph was then rising in Norman strength, and where the monastery had been founded that was afterwards to become so renowned—Godric after a short stay journeyed forth from Durham, and is recorded to have found the spot which was to be his final resting-place, by the same means that had directed the monks who were wandering with St. Cuthbert's body to Dunholme, which had been indicated to them as his chosen place of rest. St. Cuthbert, as we have all read, was to be carried to Dunholme; but where this place lay the monks in those pre-chorographic days had no idea. As they proceeded, however, a woman looking for her cow called aloud to another peasant, who replied she was in Dunholme, and the monks hearing this were directed to their journey's end, and there the good brethren most wisely and with the best possible taste remained.

Equally wild was Finchale when Godric first came hither, and he is said to have experienced a most discouraging reception, for he was attacked by a wolf, and found he was to become, like Job, "a brother of serpents and a companion of owls." He nevertheless began to build of wood an oratory and a cell for his abode. These were situated on a plot of ground which is many hundred yards higher up the river than the site of the priory of Finchale and is still called "Godric's Garth." Reginald gives a curious account of the austerities he practised and of the pertinacity of the Evil One in harassing and interrupting him in various ways and tempting shapes. He was moreover robbed and nearly killed by the Scots—probably on the invasion of England in 1138. But kind and holy comforters were not wanting; and good Reginald relates that Godric was visited not only by monks and eminent ecclesiastics who came to his hermitage as to a shrine, but that he even received encouragement in visits from some of the holy company of heaven.

In 1149 he built a larger chapel of stone, probably on the site of the existing ruins of Finchale Priory, in gratitude for deliverance from a flood, the raging waters of which in that deep rocky vale had quarried stone for his work by detaching blocks from the cliffs on the opposite side of the river. And in that chapel, which was dedicated in honour of St. John the Baptist, a priest came from Durham every Sunday, and on many holy days, to celebrate divine offices for the country people of the secluded region around St. Godric's dwelling. The chapel of his hermitage was dedicated to the Blessed Virgin. These little edifices were connected by a cloister, and there were other buildings, and near to them welled forth a spring afterwards known as Godric's fountain. He planted an orchard and reaped harvests from his corn-land; he ground his wheat and made his own bread; and though he probably did not indulge himself by practising "the gentle craft" of the angler, he drew from the river an abundant supply of fish.

At length on the 21st of May, 1170, when from this sequestered dell he had marked in the starry skies the flight of sixty summers, his body yielded to decay of nature and his spirit put on immortality. He had attained more than ninety years of age. His remains were interred in a stone coffin in the chapel of St. John in the presence of a large assembly, and a plate of lead was inscribed to his memory.

Finchale continued to be a hermit's dwelling for some years after Godric's death. The hermitage with its fields and fishery were in the gift of the prior and convent of Durham, and two monks named Reginald and Henry, the former of whom is believed to be identical with Godric's literate friend and biographer, succeeded; and it may be reasonably supposed that in this valley of deep retirement the learned monk wrote some of the historical works known to have proceeded from his pen which have come down to our own days, and which present to our view those in which he lived with a freshness of portraiture unimpaired by time.

Finchale, after witnessing for three hundred and fifty years the daily life and works of the populous monastery which ere long succeeded to the hermitage, has become again a solitude, and has been so for a period of more than three hundred years; but still the same natural walls of beauty and peace that formed to the Hermit-Saint and to the reverend pair who succeeded him their bounds of monastic seclusion, seem, even to the casual visitor of to-day, to exclude the "jarring world;" still the rapid stream, by whose waters they took their pensive way, encircles the green turf they trod and sweeps by the shadowy recesses where they dwelt; still at summer eventide the sunlight gilds the woods that wave upon the river's bank; and when the broad moon climbs the neighbouring heights, the silvery lustre falls upon the river still flowing through sylvan shadows to the unchanging sea.

In the reign of Richard I. the time had arrived when the modest hermitage was to acquire the dignity of a convent. This it did through the act of that very great prelate Hugh de Pudsey, who is memorable as one of the greatest of the mitred Counts Palatine of Durham. It was this bishop who built the Galilee Chapel and some other parts of the Cathedral Church of Durham, and accomplished many enduring and costly works in his diocese. He had a son named Henry, who derived from his mother, Adelis de Percy, property in Yorkshire, and who was owner of Wingate, and Haswell, and Hetton, in this county of Durham—then rustic vills, but now populous and smoke-enveloped colliery settlements. Under the protection of this Henry de Pudsey, or FitzHugh, certain canons of the Augustine Priory of Guisborough migrated from their convent in the Cleveland hills to a sheltered and beautiful spot, about a mile from Durham, on the little river called the Browney; and upon this brotherhood he conferred those three Saxon villages.

But the Benedictine monks, who had then acquired much land in the county, and were becoming rich and powerful, were jealous of the settlement of monks of another order in such near proximity to themselves; and accordingly they brought Henry de Pudsey to repent of what he had already done, and to agree with them that he would expiate his too-hasty liberality towards the monks of Guisborough by building a church or monastery at Finchale instead, and by transferring to the Benedictines of Durham the endowments he had destined for the Augustine canons of Guisborough who were to be conciliated by receiving possessions elsewhere. Father Stephen, the superior of the little colony of canons who had been invited to the glades of the Browney was, however, extremely unwilling to accede to this arrangement. Representations were addressed to the Holy See; negotiations took place, but ultimately the monks of Durham prevailed. And so, in the Norman Chapter-house of the black-robed Benedictines came Father Stephen, on behalf of the little fraternity of White Monks, and relinquished into their hands all the possessions of his short-lived convent. To the Durham monks also Henry the founder transferred his foundation gifts, and the bishop confirmed the arrangement and gave his charter for the foundation of a priory at Finchale. This was done in 1196, and thus—

——In the antique age of bow and spear
And feudal rapine, clothed in iron mail,
Came ministers of peace intent to rear
Their holy church in this sequestered vale.

Within the first fifty years from this time, the monks of Finchale received the greater part of their endowments, but they were unable to begin the erection of a larger church and monastery until about 1238. In 1213, King John extorted from the poor prior a sum equivalent to 1,000*l.* of our money, besides two good palfreys, for delivery of Yokeflete, in the East Riding, and some other lands which had been conferred upon his convent; and it is not surprising that they were unable to begin the building of their priory church, if they had to submit to many such exactions in order to obtain possession of their land. However, during the half century from 1238 to 1288, distinct traces of their proceedings are afforded in a series of documents preserved at Durham, which consist for the most part of "Indulgences," granted by different English and Scottish bishops for the purpose of inducing the men of the North to contribute to the new fabric, money, if they had it, and labour and materials if they had not money. In 1242, the work of building the new church was in progress, and the early English portions of the existing ruins are its remains. Soon afterwards, three altars were dedicated in this new church. In 1260, Robert, Bishop of Dunblane, exhorted his flock to visit devoutly "the Church of Saint John the Baptist at Finchale, and the tomb of St. Godric;" and his shrine had then become an object of pilgrimage. It would be curious to know whether any Scotsmen were really induced to cross the border for such a purpose; but other Scottish bishops certainly took Finchale under their care. It is to be remembered that the realm of Alexander III. of Scotland then extended into the county of Northumberland. In 1266, Archibald, Bishop of Moray, granted an indulgence "towards sustentation of the lights and ornaments of the chapel of St. Godric, in Finchale, and towards the building of the window that was to light it from the east;" and the series ends in 1288 with an indulgence granted by Alan—a bishop whose diocese was the remote and storm-swept land of Caithness. But the last of the indulgences in which the building is mentioned as unfinished bears the date of 1264.

The only portions of the older church that seem to have been then preserved were discovered in the south transept a few years ago, and appear to have belonged to the Norman shrine of Godric. The early-English work that remains is very characteristic of the style which prevailed during the period embraced in the indulgences referred to; but it is of an austere simplicity, and almost wholly without those elaborate ornaments that enrich the architecture of the period in churches built by wealthy fraternities. When the monks of Finchale were beginning to construct this church, Thomas de Melsonby, the great prior of their parent house of Durham, was completing the transept of the nine altars in the cathedral—an elaborate and stately fabric, which still stands as unrivalled and unspoiled as the Norman portion of the cathedral, and forms an enduring monument of the taste and the resources of church architects in the thirteenth century.

The chief architectural features of the existing priory church at Finchale may be described in a few words. The plan of the church is cruciform, and originally there were aisles to the nave and to the choir, as far as the third bay eastward. The great cylindrical piers at the intersection of the transepts are still massive and imposing; they supported, of course, a tower, and the spire that crowned it (or a later spire) was standing a hundred years after the Dissolution, but of the tower even, not a vestige now remains. The eastern end has a pointed gable with flanking turrets. All the piers of the choir are cylindrical with roll mouldings: those in the nave are alternately round and hexagonal. The western front retains the original lancet lights, which here, as in the transepts, are well proportioned and very characteristic. The canopy of the sedilia remains, and Finchale is remarkable for a double piscina of the high altar.

Two events, of some advantage to the monks of Finchale, occurred while the construction of the church and the monastic buildings of Finchale was in progress, or soon after their completion. Two of their superiors were successively elected Bishops of Durham, namely, Robert de Stichill, elected in 1260, who died in France on his return from a general council at Lyons in 1274, and desired that his heart might be deposited among his beloved fraternity in the Chapter-house of Durham ; and Robert de Insula, his successor, who carried the piety and humility of the cloister to the episcopal throne.

But before a century elapsed from the time of these bishops, the edifice of the priory church of Finchale underwent great changes and curtailment. The cause is not known; but when we remember the troubled state of this realm during the first half of the fourteenth century, the outrages committed by the Scots, and the consumption by armies of the produce of the convent lands of England, we may conjecture that in some of these devastating inroads the priory sustained losses which its inmates were unable to repair, except by contracting the original proportions of their church.

The piers between the choir and aisles and the nave and aisles were (probably at this time) filled with rough masonry, and windows of Decorated work were inserted between the piers.

The material used in these repairs is a freestone of perishable quality, and very inferior to the ashlar work of the early-English fabric. The "Account Rolls" of the monastery for several years before 1369 contain disbursements for materials and amongst workmen, which show that some considerable works were then in progress; and the fabric of this time is seen not only in the church, but in adjacent buildings of the convent. In some years, 1374 for example, the expenditure of the monks exceeded their income, and the excess is set down as " due to creditors."

The monks were again employed in repairing their church after the sun of Plantagenet had set, and while princes of the House of Lancaster were on the throne; but at this time the convent was no doubt much impoverished. However, the monks had become so luxurious that they actually wore linen shirts—an indulgence not contemplated by the Benedictine Rule ; and not very long before, they had been reproved for keeping a pack of deer-hounds—a custom then common among the secular clergy, and which the prior probably justified on the old ground that venison was good for sick monks, and that deer-skins were useful for binding their books.

And *apropos* to books, I must advert to the literary labours that were carried on within the walls of Finchale. The Scriptorium—as the place was called where books were transcribed—was an important feature of most monasteries ; and to the industry with which the work of transcribing and illuminating was prosecuted by the monks, posterity is indebted for many inestimable manuscripts that have survived the wreck of the religious houses—a legacy for which we used to express our gratitude by stigmatizing as " the Dark Ages " the times in which those manuscripts were produced. At Finchale the scriptorium and the library were on the south side of the church, and occupied the tower now standing to the eastward of the refectory, but separated from it by the passage which led to the orchard, and they communicated with the apartments of the prior. The monks of Finchale expended considerable sums in materials for books, and there is a remarkable instance which shows that they procured the services of the best transcribers the age afforded. That instance occurs during the reign of Edward the Third, in the priorate of Ughtred de Boldon, an eminent and learned monk who was a preserver of learning, and himself an author. He brought William de Stiphel, of Bretagne, to Finchale, and there employed him for some time as a transcriber. Two of the manuscripts which he wrote at Finchale in 1381 are in the British Museum, and the splendid folio copy of Nicholas de Lyra's Commentaries, still remarkable as one of the finest manuscripts in the unrivalled collection of the church of Durham, was finished by him at Durham in 1386. We derive, therefore, some glimpse of the life of the monks in the cloistered seclusion of Finchale; and this is not all, for a most valuable series of "Account Rolls" of Finchale are preserved at Durham, in which we find much to illustrate the former state of the priory and the life of its monks. Not that they committed to writing even their own names, or any particulars relating to themselves. Unknown to the world except in the instances in which monks were selected for the high places of ecclesiastical rule and were compelled to move in the turbulent scenes of the world's ambition, they only desired so to pass through things temporal that they might not lose the things eternal. The lapse of centuries has obliterated even the sepulchral monuments of the monks of Finchale, and overspread with grass-grown ruins the very cemetery in which, beneath the shadow of their beautiful church and by the flowing waters of the Wear, their brethren committed them to the final rest, and their personal history is veiled for ever from the world. Some of the customs of the monks and of the neighbouring country, the condition of their monastery at different times, the prices of various articles of commerce, and the wages of labour, receive, however, considerable illustration from the Account Rolls of Finchale. They exist from 1303 down to nearly the time of the Dissolution, but the series, unfortunately, is not unbroken. It is curious that, while ages have overthrown the massive walls of the priory, and covered them in many parts with trees, we can read in those fragile written memorials—those dry leaves that have rustled to the winged feet of Time—a picture of what was going on year by year at Finchale, and may almost behold its inmates engaged in their innocent labours.

The monastic buildings of Finchale Priory are in such a state of confused ruin, that it would be very difficult to give any description of them. In many parts we find only—

> Cypress and ivy, weed and wall-flower grown,
> Matted and massed together; hillocks heaped
> On what were chambers; arch-crush'd columns strewn
> In fragments, choked-up vaults, and frescoes steeped
> In subterranean damps.

The cloister square is on the south of the nave, and it had originally a vaulted roof, as appears by the early-English columns remaining. The chapter-house adjoined the south transept, as at Durham. The dormitory was on the opposite side of the cloister square; and the refectory, which has been built on a remarkably fine early-English crypt, and must have been a noble looking structure, occupies the south side. There is a deeply recessed doorway to this hall, and six windows lighted it from the south. To the eastward stood the scriptorium and the prior's chambers, the guest house, and the various domestic offices. The fine early-English doorway which stands on the south-side of the church was no doubt the great entrance to the guest hall. There was somewhere in Finchale Priory an apartment which was called " the Placr chambre," and was appropriated to the miracle plays of the age, and to the performance of minstrels and gleemen who were always welcome visitors at the monasteries. It is to be hoped that the monks of Finchale did not follow the bad example which was sometimes set by the court of Henry VII., in the value placed upon minstrels and players as compared with poets. A " Household Book " of that monarch has the following entries:—

> Paid to a dancing lass from Spain . . . 12*l.*
> To my lord of Oxon's players . . . 1*l.*
> To a blind poet . . . . . One shilling.

I have mentioned the Guest House, and may as well remark, that the expenses of the convent at Finchale (like those of other convents) for hospitality were considerable. Of course these payments varied greatly; but, in every year, " the kitchen " was a formidable head of expenditure. In 1374 the prior's account shows that no less than 84*l.* 6*s.* 8*d.* was expended on the kitchen alone; a sum worth, probably, 800*l.* at least in the money of our day. It must be remembered, that not only noblemen and travellers resorted in those times to the monasteries for lodging and entertainment, but that the indigent received support at the convent gate in days when poor laws were unknown. On a visit of Edward II. to Battle Abbey, in 1324, so laborious was travelling, and so rare were the means of hospitality, that the king had to bring his own rice, ginger, cloves, and almonds; while bread, pigs, "muttons," capons, and peacocks, were contributed for the royal table by the abbot and the neighbouring landholders. No doubt the difficulty of travelling and the want of luxuries were still greater in the north country. One instance of a prince's visit to this remote convent is on record. It is that of Edward Earl of Lancaster, second son of King Henry III., who was at Finchale on the 4th Dec. 1285, with a large company of nobles, knights, and clerics. He conferred on the priory an annual rent from his mills of Emildon, in Northumberland, "towards sustentation of the lights in the church." Lights are mentioned in 1353 as burning by Godric's shrine. Probably Earls of Douglas were amongst their visitors, for the tower, in which there are the remains of a bay window overlooking a beautiful sweep of the Wear, eastward of the priory, and well known to visitors, is called "the Douglas Tower." To return once more to the conventual kitchen, though, unfortunately, only upon paper. We find that among the contents of the larder enumerated in 1411 were 3,500 salt herrings, 140 salmon trout salted, and two pots of honey, besides abundance of corn in the granary, and good store of convent ale. But people now know better than to adopt the vulgar idea that the monastic revenues expended by the monks on their kitchen went to provide good eating and drinking for themselves. It was once the fashion for us to vindicate our Protestantism and enlightenment by sneering at the monks as incarnations of laziness and gluttony; but that bigotry has given place to more just convictions amongst educated men. The fasts of the monks are known to have been frequent; their diet was a continued round of frugal simplicity; their devotions may have been formal, but occupied the chief part of their time; and the monastic wealth, of which they are said to have been so greedy, went to raise the noble edifices which no modern art has rivalled, to maintain a stately splendour in the worship of Almighty God, and to promote good works of education and charity amongst men.

Of the charities, indeed, that were dispensed at Finchale, we have an interesting memorial. In a survey made after the suppression, in the reign of Henry VIII., we find that the amount distributed annually under the head of " alms," at Finchale, was 34*l*. 3*s*. 11*d*. ; and the dole or daily distribution of food ordained by the charter of Henry de Pudsey, their founder, " for the relief of all indigent persons resorting to the monastery of Finchale," appears to have been fulfilled from the reign of Richard I. down to 1535, when the sum of 9*l*. 10*s*. yearly appears to have been the amount of the charge upon the monastery for Pudsey's gift alone. Here then was a charity flourishing continuously for a period of 350 years! The place where these charities were distributed appears to have been the building called the ' Exchequer,' or ' Celarer's Lodging ;' and the gate-tower and chapel on the approach from Durham, which stand apart from the monastic buildings, were connected with the great resort of strangers and indigent people to Finchale Priory.

But Finchale is now a silent region of the past. The antiquary, with inquisitive eye, here treads above the buried footprints of a once active monastic community, and stands—

Within the shade
Of ruined walls, that have survived the names
Of those who reared them.

Here are the altars before which the pious knelt, and here are the choral walls that so long witnessed day by day the ritual solemnities of their faith; but cold, and silent, and deserted are the buildings within which throbbing hearts, with all their griefs and hopes, have beaten, and where voices daily raised on high the songs of praise.

Early sovereigns, and a long succession of religious men, desiring the prosperity of Finchale, had fenced it round by grants, and fondly hoped that it would flourish till the end of time. But Henry VIII. decreed that Finchale should become again a solitude, and should yield up all the dedicated property that could be sold for the use of the crown. The gross yearly income was valued at the time of the suppression at a sum equivalent to perhaps 1300*l*. of our money. The fraternity then numbered thirteen monks, and a large body of dependants. The plate, jewels, vestments, bells, and lead were sold for the crown; but the landed possessions were granted to the newly-founded chapter of Durham, and are attached to a prebendal stall recently held by the Rev. Henry Douglas, and previously by the Bishop of Bristol.

The fallen masonry and rubbish which had accumulated in long years of neglect and desecration choked up the ruins of the church, until a few years since, to the depth of ten feet; and even in 1830 a large sycamore tree grew on the site of the high altar, and the nave and chancel were filled by ash-trees, elders, and thorns. But after that time the ruins were cleared and became the object of some care; yet they are now allowed to suffer dilapidation and injury from any crowd of irreverent visitors who choose to desecrate them. But, roofless and shattered as they are, these decaying works of man mingle with the enduring beauties of nature, and stand thickly mantled by ivy of ancient growth;

> Which now with rude luxuriance bends
> Its tangled foliage through the cloister'd space;
> O'er the grey windows' mouldering height ascends,
> And fondly clasps them with a last embrace.

# BYRON AT NEWSTEAD ABBEY.

[*Chambers's Journal*, 4 Oct., 1862.]

IN a far-off time during the middle ages, when the old forest of Sherwood still spread as wild and wide as it did before the coming of the Normans or even of Julius Cæsar, when its thickets were still the home of the red deer, and seldom knew the foot of man, when the Norman castle had not long risen at Newark by the flowing Trent, or the noble minster of St. Mary at Southwell, a little colony of black canons, who followed the rule of St. Augustine, came to raise, amidst the wild solitudes of the forest, that holy and beautiful house which, under the name of Newstead Priory, flourished until the general dissolution of monasteries.

Newstead, however, owes its celebrity not to its ecclesiastical associations, nor to the high place it held in English history while it stood as a religious house, but to the splendour of a recent owner's name; for it was the inheritance, and, during part of his short life, the home of Byron—a modern episode, indeed, in the history of a house which had Henry II. for its founder. Newstead, from a very early time, owned almost a principality, and was often the abode of the royal hunters who came to enjoy the chase in Sherwood; and their regard for the good ale and larder of the monks seems to have extended to the pious recluses themselves. But, although Newstead was architecturally remarkable for the beauty of many of its features, especially the graceful western front of the church, that portion is now the only relic of the edifice—a fragment which is still the most striking and picturesque ornament of the priory buildings, and has perhaps no rival save in St. Mary's Abbey at York. How transitory does Newstead, in its whole duration as a religious house, appear, when compared with the steadfast and enduring oaks amidst which it rose, and which were still vigorous when it fell ! And still more transitory was its ownership by the ancestors of the poet, since whose succession to this property it has twice passed to strangers!

On the Dissolution in 1540, the priory, and all its possessions in lands and tithes, were bestowed by the crown on Sir John Byron, lieutenant of Sherwood Forest, grand-nephew of the knightly " Byron with the Long Beard" who fought beside Richmond at Bosworth. The anecdote relating to the sons of the first lay-owner of Newstead, which is given by Burke on the faith of its tradition in the Byron family, affords an example of the strange fatality supposed, even by the noble poet in his time, to attend the Byrons. Each of the sons married, and their wives are described as models of female excellence; but the elder son having married beneath his own rank, John, the younger son, became the object of his father's preference. The elder, when going out to hunt one day, fell from his horse in a fit, and died immediately. The younger son ultimately succeeded to the inheritance, but only to experience a life of sorrow. His beautiful and beloved wife lost her reason at the birth of her daughter Margaret, who became the wife of Colonel Hutchinson the regicide, and within a few minutes of her death, Sir John, her husband—who is said to have become conscious of the event by some mysterious spiritual sympathy—also expired.

Although the newly acquired home of the Byrons suffered much from the brutality of the Roundheads during the Great Rebellion, the domestic buildings of the monastery were not in ruin a century afterwards; for in 1760, when Horace Walpole, " with great delight," as he says, visited Newstead, he found it still " the very abbey . . . the hall entire, the refectory entire, the cloister untouched. The park, which is still charming, has not been (he adds) so much unprofaned, the present lord has lost large sums and paid part in old oaks; five thousand pounds' worth have been cut near the house. The refectory, now the great drawing-room, is full of Byrons, and the vaulted roof remains." The room here referred to appears to have been the dormitory of the monks, their refectory having been used as a hay-loft until Colonel Wildman acquired the property, and converted it into the dining-hall. The fine roof of what was the dormitory is not vaulted, but is of oak, in which stucco ornaments, in a seventeenth-century style, have been inserted between the timbers. "The Byrons" have vanished.

But the owner mentioned by Walpole as "the present lord"— namely, William, fifth baron, who had succeeded in 1736, and was the grand-uncle and immediate predecessor of the noble poet—suffered the buildings as well as the estate to fall into deplorable decay. The refectory was, as already mentioned, full of hay, and there was hardly a chamber of which the roof did not admit the rain. He not only cut down the oaks—insomuch that the noble and spreading tree which stands alone before the entrance to the park from the Nottingham and Mansfield road, is almost a solitary relic—but sold all the deer of the park, which is said to have sheltered two thousand seven hundred head. It has been suggested that this was probably the topic on which his memorable duel with Mr. Chaworth, in January, 1765, arose. A club of Nottinghamshire gentlemen dined at the Star and Garter Tavern in Pall Mall, and a dispute arose whether Lord Byron, who took no care of his game, or Mr. Chaworth, who was a strict preserver of it, had most game on his manor. Mr. Chaworth having been mortally wounded, Lord Byron was tried by his peers, and found guilty of manslaughter; and he passed the latter years of his strange life in austere and almost savage seclusion, dreaded and unpopular, but surrounded by a colony of crickets, which, it is said, were seen on the day of his death to leave the house in such numbers that a person could not cross the hall without treading on them.

On the death of this old lord of Newstead without issue, George Noel Gordon Byron, then in Scotland, succeeded to the title and estates. This was in May, 1798, when the "young heir of fame" was in the eleventh year of his age; and it was in the following autumn, when his mother brought him from Aberdeen to take possession of Newstead, that he for the first time beheld, as he has said, "its woods stretching out to receive him." Its state of ruin might well have called forth the lament he penned at a later period:

> Through thy battlements, Newstead, the hollow winds whistle;
> Thou, the hall of my fathers, art gone to decay.

His college-friend, Mr. Charles Skinner Mathews, in describing (in 1809) his recent visit, gives some notion of the state in which Byron found the mansion: "Newstead," he says, "though sadly fallen to decay, is still completely an abbey, and most part of it is still standing in the same state as when it was first built. There are two tiers of cloisters, with a variety of cells and rooms about them, which, though not inhabited, nor in an inhabitable state, might easily be made so; and many of the original rooms, amongst which is a fine stone hall, are still in use. Of the abbey-church, only one end remains; and the old kitchen, with a long range of apartments, is reduced to a heap of rubbish. Leading from the abbey to the modern part of the habitation is a noble room, 70 feet in length, and 23 in breadth; but every part of the house displays neglect and decay, save those which the present lord (the poet) has recently fitted up."

Such of the buildings of the monastery as were still standing in Byron's time remained, probably, much in the state in which the monks had left them; and in the days of the poet they seem to have been still so little altered that the whole aspect of the priory spoke less

Of the baron than the monk.

The church, however, had been almost destroyed, and only the buildings that were suitable for residence had been at all preserved; but the domestic architecture of the monks was so far retained, and a monastic style has been so far adopted in the additions of modern times, that the feature of Newstead which to a stranger seems the most characteristic is the transformation of a monastery into an inhabited and elegant mansion of the present day. The picturesque cloisters, with the vaulted chapter-house of Transition architecture, now the domestic chapel; the low, arched dining-room, formerly the prior's chamber; and the fine crypt, now the servants' hall, are the most antique portions of the old buildings that have been incorporated with the house. The crypt is as entire as when it was the eleemosynary of the charitable monks.*

* The adjacent lake, known as "the Eagle Pond," shares the romance which surrounds everything at Newstead. When it was drained in the time of the noble poet's immediate predecessor, the workmen fished up a fine brass eagle, mounted as a reading-desk, on a pedestal (and, as Colonel Wildman always said, two candlesticks

While the buildings of Newstead have been thus altered, Sherwood Forest itself has undergone great change. Washington Irving represents the house as standing in " a legendary neighbourhood," and amidst the forest-haunts which the exploits of Robin Hood have for ever associated with ballad poetry; but, around the park, few portions of the forest remain uncleared, and " the greenwood " is not what it was when inhabited by the red deer and haunted by the outlaw. Yet patriarchal oaks stand like sentinels on the ancient domain of forest, and waving woods form a sylvan framework round the old historic walls, and seem to keep the spot with all its memories isolated from the turmoil of the world.

Of the situation of Newstead Abbey, the noble poet has himself drawn the best picture we can have in verse; it was composed in Italy, some years after he first saw Newstead, and when the ancestral seat was his own no more.

> It stood embosomed in a happy valley,
>   Crowned by high woodlands, where the Druid oak
> Stood like Caractacus,     *     *     *
> *     *     *     *     *
>
> And from beneath the boughs were seen to sally
>   The dappled foresters: as day awoke,
> The branching stag swept down with all his herd
> To quaff a brook which murmured like a bird.
>
> Before the mansion lay a lucid lake,
>   Broad as transparent, deep and freshly fed
> By a river, which its softened way did take
>   In currents through the calmer water spread
> Around: the wild fowl nestled in the brake
>   And sedges, brooding in their liquid bed:
> The woods sloped downward to its brink, and stood
> With their green faces fixed upon the flood.
> Its outlet dashed into a deep cascade
>   Sparkling with foam.     *     *     *

---

also), formerly, doubtless, used in the priory church, and thrown into the lake for concealment from Henry VIII.'s plundering " visitors." After remaining submerged for two centuries and a half, the eagle has found its way to the choir of the noble old collegiate church of Southwell. The hollow globe on which the figure of the bird stands was found to contain writings of the monastery. Two chests are said to have been seen when the lake was drained, but they were not raised, nor were they recovered (if they exist at all) when the water was again drained off after Colonel Wildman's purchase of Newstead.

And he thus describes the appearance of the buildings:

> A glorious remnant of the Gothic pile
> (While yet the church was Rome's) stood half apart
> In a grand arch, which once screened many an aisle;
> These last had disappeared—a loss to art.
> The mansion's self was vast and venerable,
> With more of the monastic than had been
> Elsewhere preserved; the cloisters still were stable,
> The cells, too, and refectory, I ween.
> An exquisite small chapel had been able,
> Still unimpaired, to decorate the scene;
> The rest had been reformed, replaced, or sunk,
> And spoke more of the baron than the monk.
> \* \* \* \* \*
> Huge halls, long galleries, spacious chambers joined
> By no quite lawful marriage of the arts,
> Might shock a connoisseur, \* \*
> Yet left a grand impression on the mind.

It was not Lord Byron's fate to see the domestic buildings of the monastery restored and preserved, as they have since been, or to leave many visible traces of his ownership at Newstead; but his genius has for ever surrounded the spot with poetic associations that will be more enduring than its walls. At Newstead, when

> The boy was sprung to manhood,

Lord Byron lived; here he wrote many of his lesser poems; near Newstead is the " gentle hill" on which, in his pathetic *Dream*, he

> Saw two beings in the hues of youth
> Standing;

and it was while living at Newstead that he beheld the face

> Which made
> The starlight of his boyhood;

for in the vicinity lived Mary Chaworth, the granddaughter of his predecessor's antagonist and victim. Even the grave of his favourite dog receives the honours of a place of pilgrimage, and " Boatswain " is quite one of the " dogs of history." The character of his monument among the ornamental trees that decorate the grassy site of the priory church, and its unfitness for such a spot, do not diminish the touching force of the epitaph written by Byron at Newstead on the 30th November, 1808, and engraved on the tablet in commemoration of his gentle and affectionate follower—

> The poor dog, in life the firmest friend,
> The first to welcome, foremost to defend.

One memorial of his boyhood's home at Newstead is still green and flourishing, namely, the oak which he planted near the house soon after his arrival. His name, too, has been attached to a spring that rises near a group of yews which were probably old before his ancestors had a name in history.

Byron, after long absence, took up his residence at Newstead in September, 1808, and there celebrated his coming of age (on the 22nd of the following January) by such festivities as his narrow means and limited society could furnish. Besides "the ritual roasting" of an ox, a ball was given in honour of the day. Nor were these the only revels of his "hours of idleness" at Newstead that startled the owls and woke the long silent echoes of the cloister. In the same year (1809), when contemplating a long absence from England, he assembled round him a party of young college-friends for a sort of festive farewell, and in a letter (written many years afterwards), in speaking of his friendship for Mr. Mathews, Byron himself describes their unhallowed doings:

"We went down to Newstead together, where I had got a famous cellar, and monks' dresses from a masquerade warehouse. We were a company of some seven or eight, with an occasional neighbour or so for visitors, and used to sit up late in our friars' dresses drinking Burgundy, claret, champagne, and what not, out of the skull-cup\* and all sorts of glasses, and buffooning all round the house in our conventual garments. Mathews always denominated me the abbot."

After returning in July, 1811, from his Eastern tour, Byron wrote thus in a letter to Moore: "The place is worth seeing as a ruin, and I can assure you there *was* some fun there even in my

---

\* The skull found in digging within the priory, which had been polished and mounted in silver for a drinking-cup, and is now among the few Byron relics preserved at Newstead. It is of a dark colour, mottled, and resembling tortoise-shell.

time, but that is past. The ghosts, however, and the gothics, and the waters, and the desolation, make it very lively still."

He peopled the gloomy and romantic pile with shadowy as well as substantial inhabitants, and it seems to have been during his visit to Newstead in 1814 that he actually fancied he saw the ghost of the Black Friar, which was said to have haunted the priory from the time of the Dissolution:

> A monk arrayed
> In cowl, and beads, and dusky garb, appeared,
> Now in the moonlight, and now lapsed in shade,
> With steps that trod as heavy, yet unheard:
>     \*    \*    \*    \*    \*
> He moved as shadowy as the sisters weird,
> But slowly.

This is the apparition that seems to have been regarded as a kind of evil genius of the Byrons:

> By the marriage-bed of their lords, 'tis said
> He flits on the bridal eve;
> And—'tis held as faith—to their bed of death
> He comes—but not to grieve:
>
> When an heir is born, he is heard to mourn;
> And when aught is to befall
> That ancient line, in the pale moonshine
> He walks from hall to hall.

The life and the brief dominion of the noble poet himself seem hardly less shadowy. He had not long attained twenty-one, when, writing to his mother, he said: "Newstead and I stand or fall together. I have now lived on the spot; I have fixed my heart upon it, and no pressure, present or future, shall induce me to barter the last vestige of our inheritance. I have that pride within me which will enable me to support difficulties. I can endure privations; but could I obtain, in exchange for Newstead Abbey, the first fortune in the country, I would reject the proposition."

This was written in 1809. In three years afterwards, Newstead was nevertheless put up for sale; but only 90,000*l.* being offered, a private contract for its sale at 140,000*l.* was afterwards made. The contract, however, was not completed, and in

September, 1814, Lord Byron wrote: " I have got back Newstead;" but in 1815 (on the 2nd January) his ill-fated marriage took place; and on the 25th April, 1816, at the age of twenty-eight, he left his native country for ever. In 1818 Newstead was purchased by Colonel Wildman; and his noble schoolfellow expressed to him his satisfaction that the place which had cost him " more than words to part with," had fallen into the hands of one who was likely to raise the venerable building to something like its former splendour. The purchase-money in 1818 is understood to have been about 100,000*l*.; and the much larger amount for which it was sold in the year 1861 marks the improvement which everything at Newstead underwent in the hands of the late owner, who not only planted largely, and increased the value of the estate generally, but evinced his good taste by care and improvement of the domestic buildings of this romantic old pile. In little more than eight years from his finally leaving Newstead the remains of Byron were brought from Greece to his last resting-place in the little village church of Hucknall, near Newstead, and deposited beside the remains of his mother. This was in July, 1824.

The rooms that the poet inhabited, and the furniture he used, were, at the time of Colonel Wildman's death, preserved as Byron left them—plain and sombre, but more attractive to the visitor who goes in retrospective mood, than the new and luxurious halls of Newstead in their modern splendour. The panelled room, now or lately the breakfast-room, is a chamber of great interest, not only from its seventeenth-century character, but because it was used as the dining-room by Lord Byron. His bed-room, too, was carefully preserved, furnished as he left it. His life-like portrait by Phillips adorns the drawing-room, and a few less important objects—personal relics, such as the little bronze candlesticks of his writing-table, and the collar of " Boatswain," his favourite dog, are still preserved upon the spot. The library is perhaps more in keeping with the historical shadows of Newstead Priory than any other room; and the books, which, after Colonel Wildman's death, were sold in bulk to the new owner of the estate, remain as they were in the Colonel's time; but in the collection none that appear to have belonged to

Byron are known. As far as regards pictures, Byron's description, in *Don Juan*, of the

> Gallery of a sombre hue,
> Long, furnished with old pictures of great worth
> Of knights and dames,

where

> The pale smile of beauties in the grave,
> The charms of other days, in starlight gleams,
> Glimmer on high—

has ceased to be applicable to Newstead. Heavy tapestries, old cabinets, and quaint portraits, collected from various sources and countries by Colonel Wildman, and carved ceilings of seventeenth-century date, give a very antique aspect to most of the bedrooms in the abbey, the names given to some of which—as " King Edward the Third's Room," " King Henry the Seventh's Lodgings," " King Charles the Second's Room," Prince Rupert's Room," &c.—are at least in keeping with the historical traditions of the spot, though it must not be supposed that the chambers themselves are of Gothic character, or their furniture of medieval date. The private apartments, as lately used by Colonel and Mrs. Wildman, enriched as they are by historical portraits and recent works of art, are of a more cheerful character; and in the stately and noble drawing-room, and equally fine dining-hall, into which the old refectory and dormitory have been respectively converted, one forgets the former destination of their walls amidst objects that certainly speak *more* of the baron than the monk.

The western front of the church, already mentioned, is the only fragment of ecclesiastical architecture that has been combined with the picturesque *façade* of the mansion; but it is a fragment remarkable for the elegance of its character and for its architectural value as a graceful work of the period when the early-English passed into that Decorated style which began to prevail late in the reign of Edward I. The enclosure, once beneath the vaulted roof of the church, is now an open lawn and shrubbery; but in the highest niche of the gable or western front, " alone and crowned,"

> Spared by some chance, when all beside was spoiled,

the statue of the blessed Virgin and infant Saviour holds its tutelary place,

And makes the earth below seem holy ground.

The pensive beauty of the scene is greatly enhanced when the calm and softening moonbeams fall on the ruins of human art, and the garden lies in pale lustre beyond the deep shadow of the ivied walls, and the cold uncertain light rests so tranquilly over the forgotten graves. Byron himself has pictured the scene when

—— the rising moon begins to climb
The topmost arch, and gently pauses there;
When the stars twinkle through the loops of time,
And the low night-breeze waves along the air.

"The sun of Newstead" is not likely again to shine, nor can it be supposed that "hours splendid as the past" will again be known; but it is a place that must ever be consecrated by historic memories as a mediæval shrine of worship and a modern home of genius.

# THE PERCY'S STRONGHOLD.

[*Morning Post*, August 1861.]

ALNWICK CASTLE, "the Windsor of the North," has for some time past attracted much public attention in consequence of the important works of renovation and embellishment which have been in progress for some years in that interesting old relic of feudal times, and are now approaching completion. It is not only the chief of the baronial castles of Northumberland, but is famous in English history, and quite foremost among England's monuments of the past; while it is of course celebrated in Border tale and song. As a building, it is remarkable architecturally, and for the mediæval character which, notwithstanding all the defacements of the Georgian era, it has retained; and its extent and picturesque grandeur are commensurate with its historic fame.

Before adverting to what has been going on inside the castle, we will briefly describe its situation and appearance. Alnwick Castle stands (as probably most of our readers know) on a high bank of the river Aln, about five miles above its junction with the sea, in a most fertile part of Northumberland, and midway between the Tyne and the Tweed. As the great north road passes through the thriving old county town that nestles beneath the castle walls, the castle commanded, by its situation, a highway which in the days of Border warfare was oftener traversed by armies than by peaceful travellers. The hills between Alnwick and the North-Eastern Railway intercept any view of the castle from the line; but no person who has seen it from the hill traversed by the north road, or has viewed from "the Lion-bridge" across the Aln the turrets rising above the wooded slopes that border the glassy stream, can forget the aspect of the picturesque and stately pile, with all its variety of towers, and with those strange warriors in stone that stand upon the merlons and are seen against the sky, as if some former garrison had been suddenly petrified and fixed in their attitudes of defence. But, indeed, the whole building preserves so antique an aspect, and seems so like a feudal castle that has remained spell-bound amidst all the changes of time, that many a spectator must have felt, on his first view, that it would scarcely have been surprising if he had seen the bowmen and helmed warders of the mighty Percy moving on the ramparts.

On the northern side, the castle, with its coronal of towers, proudly crowns the green declivity, at the foot of which the river flows, and from the terrace before the keep there is an enchanting view of the wooded scenery of the park, which stretches for miles over lands once held by the Carmelites of Hulne and the canons of Alnwick, under the protection of its martial lords. On the other sides, the keep and its great area are surrounded by curtain walls, partly of Norman masonry, but on which, towards the middle of the fourteenth century, strong towers were placed at intervals, each having its appropriate destination and name, as "The Constable's Tower," "The Armourer's Tower," "The Falconer's Tower," "The Postern Tower," and so on—defences that are characteristic of the time when they lodged the armed retainers of the lord of Alnwick, and when the spectator could not admire their commanding forms and picturesque variety of outline without the danger of receiving an arrow from their loop-holed walls. The chief entrance to the castle was then, as it is now, through a fortified gate tower, approached between high and massive walls, formerly strengthened by portcullis and double gates, and still retaining, with its fine barbacan—a work completed in 1315—much of its stern and feudal aspect.

The square keep-tower of the Norman lords which stood within this fortified area was succeeded early in the reign of Edward III., when the castle and barony had become the property of Henry de Percy, by a picturesque group of semicircular towers, built round an inner court, of polygonal form, to which a Norman gateway of immense strength gave entrance, and this noble archway is still perfect and undecayed. The Henry de Percy who defeated David King of Scots, at the battle of Neville's Cross,

K 2

and whose power in the realm seems to have made him hardly second in importance to Edward himself, was the lord of Alnwick who built this grand Edwardian castle—this Conway or Caernarvon of the Northumberland border; and his fortress, as completed shortly before the age of William of Wykeham, has stood to the present day, mutilated indeed, yet still

> Like veteran worn, but unsubdued.

His grandson, the first Earl of Northumberland of the Percy line, was the father of Hotspur, Shakespeare's hero, with whom the Lion of Northumberland fell in blood on the field of Shrewsbury. The earl's grandson, to whom the family honours were restored in 1414, repaired the castle, and fortified his town of Alnwick with four gate-towers, of which the " Bond-gate," on the entrance by the great north road, alone remains. He and his son, ever constant and loyal, were slain at Towton-moor; and so greatly did the Percy family suffer in the troubles which convulsed England during the century that followed the Wars of the Roses, that the castle had lost its ancient pride long before Thomas de Percy, who, in 1557, was created Earl of Northumberland, executed his works of building and repair. Alnwick Castle escaped destruction in the great rebellion and the civil wars of the seventeenth century, only to suffer neglect more wasting than the ancient sieges of Scottish kings. After another hundred years the honours of the family were revived, and the first Duke of Northumberland who held the princely possessions of the Percies undertook the repair and alteration of this old historic fortress, but in an evil hour employed Adam, the prolific builder, as his architect. When it is remembered that this was about 1780, when the military architecture of the middle ages was not understood, and Strawberry Hill, or Confectionery Gothic, was deemed the perfection of art, the result may be imagined.

The alterations made at this period afforded a warning example of the mischief which a presumptuous architect may perpetrate, who, without due reverence for a historical monument, dares ignorantly to raise his destructive hand against a building which the men of other days gave the best of their noble thoughts and constructive skill to fashion for future time. Alnwick Castle was deplorably debased, changed, and modernised, on the outside as well as in the interior. The towers clustered in the central keep were almost reconstructed internally, and little more was left than their outer shell. Even Percy's banquet hall was modernised, and its walls reduced to such a dangerous condition that the magnificent new dining room has had to be constructed on its site. Modernised reception rooms, a chapel and library (the only good room in the whole castle) were formed* and elaborately plastered with Gothic ornaments; and every part of the building underwent such a transformation that there was not a room of any historical or antiquarian interest left, or (excepting the library) a room of comfort or splendour acquired. The apartments remained isolated and inconvenient; and the liability of the patties and other artistic productions of the remote kitchen to be blown away in their passage through an open court used to be facetiously deplored. On the outside the imposing features of an ancient castle were mutilated; the aspect of the whole building became tame and level. The ditch or moat which had surrounded the keep was not only filled up, but the turf was heaped against the central towers; the characteristic pointed and mullioned lights of former days were altered. Here an incongruous quatrefoil was inserted; there, some travesty of the loopholes of a mediæval fortress. In short, few parts of the castle had not been altered, and whatever was altered was impaired.

About six years ago, therefore, the present Duke of Northumberland began to carry into effect a design the object of which is to restore to the exterior of the castle its mediæval grandeur; and, while retaining all the ancient architecture really worthy of preservation, to reconstruct a new and sumptuous interior, and to enrich it with decorations of the Renaissance period of Italian art.

These costly works have of course diffused some hundreds of pounds weekly in wages during many years past (more than 200 workmen have been employed upon the spot for six years, besides all the work in marble sculpture thas has been executed in Italy);

---

* The chapel was formerly over the second gateway, or middle ward of the castle, and was reached through the library, but the space which was occupied by these apartments is now converted into the private rooms of the noble duke and duchess.

and they have raised up at Alnwick quite a school of decorative art, with native workmen for the artists. But the importance of these works, and the exotic character of the style adopted for the decoration of the interior, has naturally led to much debate and no small difference of opinion as to the propriety of bringing Italian ornament to the great Border Castle of the martial Percies. On the one hand it is urged that, although Alnwick Castle has no longer to defend the Borders or repel besiegers, and its lords need no longer maintain it as a fortress, it is a historical monument so thoroughly mediæval in character and associations, that the interior cannot with any congruity or fitness be decorated in Renaissance style; that English decorative art of the time of Edward III. is a known reality, and can be modified to meet the requirements of modern luxury; that the renovation of Alnwick Castle afforded a rare opportunity for reviving this national style, and showing that it is as compatible with modern luxury as with architectural dignity ; that it is an error to regard tapestry and rushes as inseparable from a mediæval castle; and that a style of decoration founded on the noble works of art of our English forefathers in the fourteenth century can be adapted to the refinements and usages of the nineteenth. On the other hand, it is contended that such a style of decoration would be experimental, and would have to be reconstructed from illuminations in MSS. or studied from a variety of buildings of the period; whereas there was to be seen, in churches and patrician residences in Italy, ready to the hand, a system of decorative art—revived classic, certainly, but elaborated by great artists of the sixteenth century—in itself really beautiful, and recommended by very dignified associations; that its adoption for the interior of the castle need not affect the feudal simplicity or mediæval character of the structure externally, or sacrifice any architecture of Edwardian times; and that the stern character and associations of the castle he has inherited could not be a reason why the Duke of Northumberland should not surround himself with the richest productions that wealth and taste can command. Upon this controversy we do not intend to give any opinion, for our present purpose is only to describe what has been done.

As far as regards the exterior of the castle, the duke's noble idea of thorough renovation has been well carried out by his able architect, Mr. Salvin. It is a relief to find, after all the ominous suggestions by correspondents in daily newspapers, that no architecture of the Edwardian age has been destroyed for the present improvements, except two towers of the curtain wall, which, if we remember them aright, were not worthy of preservation; and the two damaged towers of the keep, which it was justifiable to sacrifice for the sake of obtaining so fine a feature as the new "Prudhoe Tower," by which not only a fitting entrance, vestibule, and staircase, and a spacious library are gained, but dignity and a culminating point to the grouping of the towers. The attempts made during the Georgian era to restore the castles of the middle ages in the style of their period were for the most part miserable failures, from Windsor Castle downwards; and equally offensive to good taste, although not also injurious to historical monuments, have been most of the pretentious adaptations of feudal architecture to modern mansions that aspired to swell into castles in the nineteenth century. But at this old stronghold of the Percies we have no mimic feudalism, and its noble owner is fast removing all the monstrosities of pseudo-Gothic. Even the range of stables, built in 1788, with their crockets and pinnacles of the period, are being swept away, and the new stables form at this moment the focus of building energy at Alnwick Castle, the spacious and magnificent kitchens, with their vaulted roof, having been completed. This new structure surpasses anything of the kind, and rivals the finest kitchens of the middle ages; indeed, the abbots of Glastonbury might covet such a building, replete as it is with all the appliances of modern art. Even the monastery of Alcobaca, of which Mr. Beckford gives such a glowing description, can hardly boast such a kitchen.

Alnwick Castle has retained, notwithstanding the weak and tasteless perpetrations of last century, so much of the grand simplicity of an Edwardian castle, that every Englishman who can value the historical monuments of his country is interested in the character of the works undertaken for its restoration. It has what Mr. Gilbert Scott has justly described as the requisites for a dignified building, inasmuch as it has a good and commanding position, actual extent, suitable material, and first-rate workmanship, and now, by the building of the " Prudhoe Tower," height, and due subordination of parts; and we have, moreover, at Alnwick a bold development of the features naturally arising from the exigencies of the building and adapted to its site.

As far as regards the interior of the castle, whatever view may be taken as to the fitness of the style of decoration adopted, it is at all events satisfactory that no sham, no machine-work has been admitted here: all the elaborate carvings have been executed by hand, and the carving (for example) for a door-panel in Italian walnut has alone occupied an artist for many months. The forms are classic and conventional it is true, and present none of the sculptured richness and variety of Gothic art, for in the works at Alnwick Castle the art workmen have not been sent—as those employed contemporaneously in the new Museum Buildings at Oxford have been sent—to study and arrange their designs from the works of nature, and copy actual foliage for the decoration of the marble arcades, so that

—— no herb or floweret glistened there
But was carved in the cloister arch as fair.

All, however, are characterised by beauty, richness of detail, and refined taste in colouring and combination. Wood carvings of fruit and foliage, refulgent in gilding, and framed on coloured panels, adorn the ceilings; painted friezes of classic design, and elaborate mouldings, enriched with gold and colour, decorate the walls; and these, moreover, are to receive panels of Genoa damask tissue.*

The gorgeous decorations above described are certainly of a character and designed in a style of art which the martial Percies never knew, and they glitter very unexpectedly before the visitor who enters the castle with the impressions which the stern simplicity of its exterior aspect can hardly fail to produce, and who passes under De Vesci's Norman gateway and Henry de Percy's grey feudal towers; but they transplant the decorative arts of Italy to remote Northumberland, and will form a sumptuous monument of the taste and splendour of a great English nobleman.

* Much still remains to be done in these state rooms, but the works are so far advanced that we understand fifty apartments are to be ready for use before the close of the present summer (1861).

# SUMMER DAYS IN SCOTLAND.

[*Bentley's Miscellany*, 1861.]

A GREAT charm of the ruined abbey of Melrose is the character of the scenery by which it is surrounded. Wooded acclivities adorn the landscape, and the silvery Tweed flows by green haughs bright with the golden flowers of " the bonny broom," by

—— waving fields and pastures green,
With gentle slopes and groves between,

in a region " where every field has its story and every rivulet its song," and where the natural features of the country derive a heightened charm from their historic memories. But the interest of association seems to culminate in " the ruined pride " of Melrose, which, with the Eildon's purple peaks on the one side and the bright river on the other, is set in a thoroughly Cistercian valley of wood and water.

That was a great day for Melrose and for Scotland which beheld a little colony of monks from Rievaux arrive, at the bidding of St. David, in this fair valley of the Tweed, to found a new abbey under those weird hills, and in the shadow of the great name of that older Melrose, which (originally deriving its faith from Iona) had been founded here in the seventh century by St. Aidan, the Celtic apostle of Northumberland, and was long a lamp of Christianity to the northern province. But the Cistercians, who came in David's reign to plant the light of the gospel among the rude and benighted natives of this part of the old Saxon kingdom of Northumbria,.chose for their abbey a different site to that of old Melrose, and reared its Norman walls upon a meadow sloping to the Tweed, where the triple peaks of Eildon rose above the adjacent hills of the royal forest in which the jolly abbots afterwards loved to chase their deer. But of this early fabric no portion remains. During the Wars of the Succession in Scotland, Melrose suffered in common with the other Border abbeys, and in 1326 the present edifice rose, under the care of King Robert Bruce, who marked his pious affection for the place by appointing his heart to be deposited within its walls. The architecture of the chief part of it shows that it was built before the close of the fourteenth century, and the graceful symmetry of its structure, the delicacy and profusion of its sculptured ornaments, render it the glory of Scottish ecclesiastical art.

It must be confessed that the reality falls short of the poetic ideal of Melrose; and certainly, on a first view, to see the grey and shattered ruins standing hardly apart from the little town, is to be disenchanted, for mean and unsightly dwellings have crept up to the walls of the church and deprived it of the romantic seclusion which generally characterises a Cistercian abbey, and always renders more impressive its " calm decay." But these incongruous surroundings may be forgotten when the spectator stands—not, indeed, by moonlight, but even in " the gay beams of lightsome day"—in the interior of the deserted pile. The nave is ruined and roofless, but the choir and transepts, which are in better preservation, retain much of their dignified beauty, and high aloft over the east end the fretted and sculptured stone roof remains. The

—— slender shafts of shapely stone
By foliaged tracery combined;

the capitals, the mouldings, the architectural enrichments and sculptured figures, are as sharp and perfect as when they were cut; and the east window and the south transept window retain their elegant tracery. The ruined central tower, with its curious parapet of quatrefoils, rises on lofty and massive pointed arches. The vaulting and quaint sculptured adornments of the range of chapels in the south aisle are still almost entire. On the outside most of the pinnacles, canopies, niches, statues, and strange goblin-looking heads that so profusely covered the building remain. But in every part of the abbey church that sacrilegious hands could reach, and in the total destruction of the monastic buildings, we see the barbarous ravages committed, first by the Earl of Hertford's army, in 1545, then by the reforming mobs of the hateful Knox, and afterwards by the fanatical rage of the Covenanters, in whose sight all architectural beauty was abomination. When more peaceable times arrived, the abbey became a convenient stone quarry for the buildings of the town.

Pursuing the journey to Edinburgh after seeing Melrose, and climbing "the steep where" Roslin's chapel "shines afar," it is curious to see the striking contrast presented between the Renaissance decorations of that unique and celebrated building and the Gothic graces of Melrose. Roslin chapel was built not long after the completion of the latest portions of that abbey church, for it was founded in 1446, but so exotic is its style, and so elaborately is it encrusted with decorations, that it seems a kind of architectural dream perpetuated in sculptured stone. The chapel has been restored for Anglican worship, but a fac-simile restoration of decayed parts has been attempted—a replacing which generally destroys all historical validity in a building, and is not restoration, but substitution. For the most part, however, what has been done is little more than renewal and repair, and the enrichments of the interior are brought out with almost their original freshness. It is exalted on a lofty ridge, from which there is a fine view of the picturesque Pentland hills and the distant range of the Lammermoors. The adjacent massive archway and tiers of strong vaults are the remains of the castle of its ancient lords—the stronghold " where erst St. Clairs held princely sway," and it is a fit scene for the most romantic legends. By supernatural aid the first Baron of Roslin is recorded to have won this lordship from Robert Bruce, and on the death of the lords of Roslin a supernatural illumination in the chapel is said to have been always witnessed.

It is pleasant to pass from the vaults of Roslin to the sunshine and exhilarating air—from the decaying monuments of human splendour to the ever-renewing beauties of nature in the adjacent scenery; and it would be hard to find a river glen where wood and rock and water are seen in more enchanting combination than in the deep dell which winds between Roslin and " the classic

Hawthornden." The mansion is built above caverned precipices, on a lofty cliff, round the base of which the North Esk river flows through a deep, luxuriantly wooded winding dell; and the house seems externally in much the same state as it was left when repaired, in 1638, by the poet and historian William Drummond, and when Ben Jonson made his pedestrian journey from London to visit him.

In those pre-locomotive days people were not so constantly admonished to "move on"—they enjoyed leisure to linger amidst caves and wooded rivers, and to turn aside from the crowded highways to visit monuments of religion and chivalry; but I was "to the Highlands bound," and a short ride exchanged these quiet old-world scenes for the metropolis of Scotland.

A nation's history seems to be displayed in the variety and multitude of picturesque objects which Edinburgh presents. Striking, indeed, is the contrast between the ancient and the modern city—between the squalid and narrow wynds of the former, with their tall dilapidated houses, and the broad and stately avenues of the new town. The change of times and manners can hardly be more strikingly displayed than it is in Edinburgh. Thus, the houses in the Cowgate—the hollow to the south of the central ridge on which the old High Street stands—which the Lowland nobility and judges inhabited before the extension of the city, are now abandoned to the poorest of the community; and many of the closes that diverge from the Canon (Kyning) gate, formerly inhabited by nobles and men of eminence, are now dark, dirty, and of unsavoury odour, and strangely unworthy of the noble appellations they retain.* All the historic scenes (of course) cluster in the storied line which ascends from Holyrood to the castle, and to mention them would be to write a book; whereas, the present paper is designed as a mere sketch of the archæological and the picturesque. The most ancient part of the palace is the north-

* Of this decadence, the large sombre mansion called Queensberry House, which encloses three sides of a court, affords an example. It was built chiefly by William, the first duke, was the frequent residence of his son James, the second duke (one of the chief promoters of the Union), and the birthplace of Charles, third duke, who, with his duchess—the " wild, witty, and beautiful " Catherine Hyde, commemorated by Prior, Pope, Gay, Swift, and Horace Walpole—here resided, but, the last duke having dismantled and sold the mansion, it has now become the " House of Refuge."

west angle, which was built in 1525 by James V.; the rooms shown as Queen Mary's are in a part of the building which is, perhaps, hardly older than the reign of Charles II. Of the ruined chapel (still, as in mockery, called the Chapel Royal), the oldest portion is a Romanesque door, which may belong to the age of the Augustine canons whom David, the royal founder of the abbey, brought hither in 1128—a time when, in the romantic wilds of what is now called the Queen's Park, the kings of Scotland chased the forest deer. The piers of the nave are of the middle of the thirteenth century, and the western front is of Transition date, but none of the windows seem much earlier than the time when Holyrood was the scene of the gay nuptial festivities held on the marriage of the English princess, Margaret, daughter of Henry VII., to James of Scotland. The so-called cathedral of St. Giles, the parish church of Edinburgh, contains some fine relics of Second Pointed architecture in the choir and in the piers of the tower. The modern façade of the buildings of the law courts in the Parliament Square does not prepare the visitor for such a sight as the spacious old Parliament chamber, with its open roof of dark oak timber—the Westminster Hall of Scotland; but the noblest monument that this Temple of Themis contains is the splendid library founded by Sir George Mackenzie, Lord Advocate. It is not rich in illuminated MSS. but among its 160,000 printed volumes are many rare works of literary as well as professional value.* From an instructive visit to the unique and well-arranged Museum of the Society of Antiquaries, and the silent relics of the Celtic and Scandinavian and mediæval inhabitants of the country, it is a striking transition to pass again into the region of daily life in the busy and splendid line of Prince's Street. From this point the most striking of the architectural and characteristic features of the city are seen in picturesque combination. Looking westward from that commanding terrace, considerable portions of the old town are beheld clustering on the ridge that terminates in the magnificent escarpments of the Castle rock, while a few steps in the opposite direction bring into view the new town of stately but monotonous streets, crescents,

* Amongst the curiosities are some poems from the press of Walter Chapman and Andrew Millar, who, in 1507, introduced printing into Scotland.

squares, and terraces with their pleasant gardens, which overspreads the declivities to the east. How different was the scene on which David I. looked down when he came to visit his castle of Edinburgh and his monks of Holyrood! In those days the country round was a wild forest tract, partly covered with native wood, and inhabited only by wild animals of chase. Probably the only existing edifice that was then standing in Edinburgh is Queen Margaret's chapel, on the highest ridge of the Castle rock, from whence, in the new gun-fire signal at one every afternoon, time is now electrically flashed from the Observatory clock on Calton Hill. What a wonderful view is beheld on these ramparts! The eye ranges from the grey slopes of Arthur's Seat, and the dusky grandeur of Holyrood, by clusters of cone-shaped turrets and tall gables, to the gleaming lines of the new town, and farther northward to the waters of the Forth and the distant shores of Fife; then, from the monumental heights of the Calton Hill, surveys the blue expanse of sea beyond, and the rocky wilds of Salisbury Crags, soaring darkly above the grey floating haze; and, while "the murmur of the city crowd" is wafted to the ear, beholds the silent landscape of the far-off hills, the wooded uplands, and yellow corn-fields lying in their "soft peacefulness of light." To the geologist, the rocky citadel itself, and its precipices of basaltic greenstone, carry back the thoughts to that remote prehistoric period when Edinburgh had no existence, and when glaciers or masses of ice probably traversed the Castle Hill and the Calton Hill, as well as the Castle Hill of Stirling, and left the striæ and marks of glacial action which have been traced upon these basaltic cliffs.

The traveller who wishes to make a rapid transition from the busy life and traffic and splendour of to-day, and to step back, as it were, into the decaying old-world scenes of former days, should stop on his way from Edinburgh to Glasgow at David's old royal burgh of Linlithgow (the chief industry of which appears to be that of the sons of Crispin), where the palace—the finest of Scottish regal buildings, the birth-place of Mary Queen of Scots, is, though in ruins, full of interest, architecturally as well as historically. The only other very noticeable building here is the adjacent church of St. Michael, the scene of the spectral pageant that warned James IV. against the campaign which ended so fatally for him on Flodden field.

It was not until a century ago, when the population of Glasgow had risen to about thirty-five thousand, that a regular conveyance for passengers between that city and Edinburgh was established, two previous attempts having proved abortive; and very deliberate was the pace, for with four horses the coach took twelve hours for the journey of forty-two miles, and for thirty years (as we learn from those entertaining "Domestic Annals of Scotland," for which the public is indebted to Mr. Robert Chambers) this was the only stage-coach upon the road. Yet Glasgow was described more than a hundred and thirty years ago as the emporium of the west of Scotland for its commerce and riches; but a carriage was unknown in Smollett's time, and Glasgow had not then seen the rise of the West Indian trade. The visitor, when he finds himself in the crowded thoroughfares, amidst the material, mechanical, and commercial activity of a vast manufacturing city with half a million of inhabitants, contrasts it with the time when "the tobacco princes" were the aristocracy of Glasgow, and might be seen on the plain-stanes daily with their scarlet cloaks, curled wigs, cocked hats, and gold-headed canes, the people reverently making way for them; or the earlier time when its antique burghers clustered under the shadow of its cathedral undisturbed by dreams of gigantic manufacture, and when the Blackfriars' Monastery and the University (founded late in the fifteenth century) were the chief foundations of St. Mungo's Town. And one loves to picture the solemn and stately procession of Masters, Licentiates, Bachelors, and Students of the Faculty of Arts, when (on the Sunday or festival next after the translation of St. Nicholas, 9th May) they rode forth from their college, bearing flowers and branches of trees, and traversed the streets from the upper part of the town to the cross, returning to the college to dinner, after which the Masters acted some interlude or show to rejoice the people. But Glasgow now retains few monuments of the past save the cathedral, once the metropolitan cathedral of the west, an edifice which has been justly described as the noblest unmutilated specimen of ecclesiastical art in Scotland. Here, again, we are on the footsteps of the good King David.

When his previous fabric rose, the population of the west of Scotland comprised descendants of the Britons of Strathclyde, among Saxon colonists, Norwegians, Celtic Highlanders, and men of Galloway; and with wonder must the rude natives have seen his Norman church rising in its Romanesque grandeur. The present edifice succeeded to it early in the thirteenth century, and very characteristic of the period are its massive clustered piers and graceful lancets, its long perspectives, its symmetrical and impressive crypt, and its pervading dignity; and much to the honour of the town and of the neighbouring contributors is the recent enrichment of this fine structure with stained glass, the work chiefly of Munich artists. Such architectural splendour presents a striking contrast to the sordid vulgarities of Presbyterian kirk-sessions; to see such a monument of the art and reverence of the past, and then to traverse the streets around it, is to realise the chasm between our days and the picturesque middle ages in which warriors and ecclesiastics raised Glasgow Cathedral! With a sense of relief and thankfulness I escaped from the dense, sunless atmosphere, the din and turmoil of Glasgow, and the muddy river crowded with the trade of nations and darkened by smoke, and ere long rejoiced in the wild freshness of the hills that lay in all the glory of sunshine beyond the bright rippling waters of the Firth of Clyde.

The tourist sees few spots of historical interest on the voyage between Glasgow and Loch Goil. The most conspicuous is the rocky citadel of Dunbarton, a curious isolated mount, which is said to have been the seat of royalty in the days of the British kingdom of Strathclyde, and was in the middle ages a strong castle "standing (as Froissart describes it) in the marches against the wild Scots." Geologically, this picturesque hill, with its double peak, is remarkable as a mass of trap-rock—a formation which composes some lesser eminences visible on the route; and the shores of the Clyde on either side present other objects of interest to the geologist, for sea-worn terraces or ancient beaches may be observed; there are boulders of ice-borne rock on the igneous range of Kilpatrick; the mica-schist mountains of Dunbarton and Argyll bound with serrated sky-line the distant landscape; and, below Gourock, the red sandstone is seen upon the shore.

After passing Helensburgh, the high but not mountainous shores of the Gareloch, with its promontories and rocky bays, and the white houses of its somewhat upstart sea-bathing villages, and the wooded peninsula of Roseneath, form a succession of pleasing objects; and then comes the grandeur of Loch Long, from whose clear deep water the blue hills rise in a picturesque variety of outline, their tints ever changing as the cloud-shadows traverse their wastes of rock and heather, every change in light and shade, and distance, and colour, presenting the landscape as a new picture. Then, past the silent glens, and under the dark, craggy hills that advance as if to bar the approach of man to the mountain fastnessess, the steam-boat speeds on through the still, cold depths, and seems a profane intruder on the solitude of nature. The mountainous shores of Loch Long have a grand breadth and massiveness, and, in their general forms and character, resemble the upper and finer parts of Loch Lomond; and the distant view of the "Alps of Arrochar," seen before diverging into Loch Goil, is one of wild sublimity. That mountain wilderness of rock and heather hears no voice but the wild bird's cry; and the occasional sound of a waterfall in some gorge or rocky channel which the melted snows have worn upon the mountain-side, seems to deepen our sense of the solemn stillness of the hills,

The work of God untouch'd by man.

The tourist on Loch Goil is not likely to forget the favourite lyric of which the "dark and stormy water" is the scene; and leaving behind—not pursuing foes, but—the cares of the busy world, he quits the boat at the head of the loch, and ascends the wild ravine called Hell's Glen (the name seems to be a memory of the Scandinavian goddess), where the great hills rise in magnificent walls of wild crag and natural wood. The steep road traverses a wilderness of mountainous wastes strewn with riven masses of rock, in such wild confusion, that this glen might seem part of the primæval realm of Chaos. On gaining the highest point of the road the gleaming water of Loch Fyne suddenly delights the eye, lying fringed by its wooded slopes, and surrounded by lofty hills, with the little town and the shipping of Inveraray sheltered in a pleasant bay, and the noble woods of the

L

Duke of Argyll's castle stretching to the distant heights of Glen Aray, and the mountainous forms around Glencroe rising in still and sunny heights amid depths of sombre shadow.

Arrived in the county town of Argyllshire, the antiquary does not find any object of interest save the Inveraray Cross—a fine specimen of those stone crosses which form the most perfect of the ecclesiastical remains of the diocese. It is said (but not historically known) to have been brought hither from Iona: the sculptured tombstones and stone crosses of Argyllshire are commonly, however, called "Iona Stones" and "Iona Crosses"—perhaps because they originated with the monks who, in rude and barbarous ages, cultivated art among the western waves, and colonised Argyll.* Foliage resembling vine-branches, with a kind of double leaf, is sculptured on this cross, with figures of animals, in the style of the Runic crosses, but the characters of the inscription it bears seem of the thirteenth century. The Argyll crosses are often rudely sculptured with a hunting scene or a mounted horseman, and the legs and tails whirl off in a strange way into intricate scroll-work and trails of wandering foliage which surround the stone. The art was probably of Scandinavian origin, like the one-masted galley with oars, which is borne as an heraldic device by certain families who had possessions on the coast, as, for example, the Earls of Arran, Orkney, and Caithness, and for the lordship of Lorn, and is quartered with the arms of several families in the west of Scotland; but is really a memorial of the times when the lords of Argyll and the Isles were pirates, and rude, independent princes.

But onward lies our route, through the magnificent woods of Inveraray Castle, where the graces of English park scenery and ornamental forest trees are bordered by wild alpine country. Here the tourist gladly exchanges the gloomy grandeur of barren crags and moorland wastes for luxuriantly wooded hills and an avenue of noble trees, stretching for more than two miles, and bordered by the sounding torrent of the Aray, which skirts a great part of the road to Loch Awe, and forms more than one

* Its original position seems to have been near the chapel in the old town, but until late years it was lying at the entrance of the great beech avenue, and is now erected near the edge of the loch at the end of the principal street of Inveraray.

beautiful waterfall in a rocky chasm, overhung by wood. When the plantations end, the road through Glen Aray becomes wild and hilly, and, as you ascend, the magnificent group of mountains which enclose Loch Awe come into view; and then the cheerful gleaming water is beheld, with its wooded promontories and its retreating bays (seen in its length, it seems a broad river rather than a loch); and, soaring beyond mountain slopes on its northwestern side, Ben Cruachan is seen, with the white mists floating below its peaks and filling its dark corries.

The shores of Loch Awe to the southward, though affording a thousand attractions to the artist, are tame and uninteresting compared with the northern end, where Glen Orchay opens to the lake, and where the scenery has a picturesque sublimity peculiar to itself, and affords a good example of that which is so great a charm of Highland landscape, viz. its infinite variety—the mingling of the beautiful and wild—the combination of sylvan beauty with rugged forms and mountain grandeur. The fair land-locked expanse is seen, bright as a burnished shield in the blaze of sunshine, set in a grand framework of bold, mountainous forms, melting in the distance into blue aërial tints; a softer beauty suffuses the scene when the roseate hue of evening glows upon the lake, or when the clouds, piled up in fleecy masses beyond the western sky, are bright with the orange tints of sunset, and throw a warm radiance on the glassy waters, its islets, and bay-indented shores; but it is in the soft lustre of moonlight that Loch Awe is a scene of unearthly beauty. And then, when only distant waterfalls break the silence of the summer night, the mind recalls the ancient association of these shores with the first apostles of Christianity in Argyll, the early religious sanctity of some of its shadowy islands, and the legends of which they are the scene. There is Fraoch Eilan, for example, which had its enchanted apples that were guarded by a dragon or great serpent, until it was slain by some mythic chieftain—strange, that this remote isle of heather should be the scene of what seems a Highland version of the Hesperian fable! Then, there is the Isle of Inishail (" the lovely isle "), where the inhabitants were more substantial, for it was the site of a Cistercian nunnery.

Crosses and sepulchral slabs of old chieftains of the hills mark this lonely island of the dead. The burial-ground is still a sacred spot, and in the chapel of the convent service was performed down to the time of George II., but now the chapel has disappeared.

Monuments of the feudal ages likewise remain on the shores of Loch Awe, and the chief of them is the famous Kilchurn, which, under the dark slopes of Ben Laoidh, appears to rise out of the water that nearly insulates the castle,

> Sole sitting by the shore of old romance.

It occupies the whole of a rock which seems to have been formerly an island at the mouth of the river Orchay; its aspect is well in keeping with its situation amidst the dark and solemn mountains, and it brings before us vividly the wild and picturesque life of its ancient lords. Although much ruined and very wild looking, it retains its massive strength, and has traces of ancient stateliness. And who can forget Kilchurn's well-known legend about Sir Colin Campbell (its owner in the time of our Henry V.), who, after long absence in the wars, returned hither, disguised as a mendicant, to find that his wife (a very strong-minded woman she must have been) had during his absence built this keep tower as a surprise for him, but, having given him up for dead, was, on the very day of his return, about to marry again, when he opportunely revealed himself at the wedding feast. Castle Kilchurn had ceased before 1551 to be the chief or even the usual dwelling of the lords of Glenorchy. On Fraoch Eilan are the ruins of the MacNaughtons' castle, with a great tree growing in what was the chieftain's hall.

The Orchay and Cladich rivers, and some lesser rills, fall into Loch Awe, but the river Awe is its only outlet, and within living memory the waters of the lake permanently submerged lands upon its shore, on which thriving plantations have risen since the channel of the river was artificially deepened. The Pass of Awe opens through very wild and impressive scenery. As the shores narrow towards its straits, the steep side of the mountain, covered to a great height by a thick wood of dwarf timber and coppice, leaves only a narrow strip of stony beach, above which the road from Oban to Dalmally has been formed; while the southern shore is almost a wall of steep and barren rock, rising precipitously from the water. This arm or outlet of the lake, after gradually contracting, ends at the rocks of Brandir, which approach so near that a tall mountain pine might reach across the strait, and, indeed, a rude bridge did probably exist at this spot in the days when great timber flourished in the forests of Glen Etive. From this outlet there is a gradual descent to the sea-loch of Etive, and the Awe rushes foaming over a bed strewn with the *débris* of the neighbouring heights. The defile where the mountains approach is dark and gloomy, and the ceaseless waterfall and the rushing torrent of the Awe fill the rocky pass with a sound like the roar of the sea. It was in this pass that the warlike clan of MacDougal of Lorn were nearly all destroyed by Robert Bruce. And by an old oak-tree—described by Scott as growing at the foot of a cliff from which a mountain stream leaps in a fall of sixty feet, near the bridge of Awe, on the left-hand side of the river as it descends, and where the rocks retain few remains of the wood that probably once clothed them—the superstitious believe that " the Woman of the Tree," Scott's Highland Widow, may still be seen seated, as was her wont.

Ben Cruachan, " one of the noblest of Scotland's mountain kings," is about the same height as Snowdon, but its base has a circumference of more than twenty miles, and, with its five wave-like peaks, it is conspicuous for its majestic outline as well as for its mass. The mountain seems to be composed of red and grey granite, with veins of porphyry, but clay slate and mica slate, veined with quartz, are found on its sides.

Some of the most beautiful scenery in the vicinity of Loch Awe is in Glen Nant, a pass which lies between it and Loch Etive, and Ben Cruachan forms a very grand object from the road. The rocky stream which traverses the glen is overhung in part by wild crags, and the other side of the ravine is covered with dense hanging woods of native oak, and birch, and hazel.

The scenery of Loch Etive derives a peculiar character from the granite hills that bound its shores, and from lying at the foot of the grand precipices and dark ridges of Ben Cruachan, while on the other side the deer forests rise steep from the water's edge in wild hills of grey crag and dark-green coppice, which are reflected in deepened colour in the still and tinted water. The head of Loch Etive presents one of the finest landscapes to be seen in the Western Highlands, for there the glen opens to Buachaille Etive and the other mountains which extend northward and eastward towards Glencoe. But Cruachan is the Giant of the Loch.

Loch Etive could boast at least one religious foundation—

<blockquote>Lone Ardchattan's abbey gray—</blockquote>

which was founded more than six centuries ago for Benedictine monks. Robert Bruce is said to have held a parliament here, the business of which was transacted in Gaelic. The buildings of the monastery are much dilapidated, but the basement walls of the church remain. This edifice and the prior's house appear to have faced the loch; the house is almost entire, and a green pasture ground adjacent is still called "the Monks' garden." One of the most beautiful scenes in Argyllshire seems here fitly consecrated to religious calmness.

At the head of this loch some of the large oak-trees, which appear to have abounded in this country in the time of Edward's wars, are, or lately were, remaining; and, though they stand in rocky soil, some of the trunks measure more than twenty feet in circumference. And near Inverawe, at the base of Cruachan, a group of noble and gigantic fir-trees, of great age, standing together, forms quite a dark and solemn grove.

Returning by the pass of Awe, I traversed the really noble vale of Glenorchy (from which the Marquis of Breadalbane takes a second title), one of the most attractive scenes in the Highlands. The grand mountainous forms of Glenorchy, rising one beyond another, compose landscapes which continually change as you advance; and from the peaceful village of Dalmally, whose English-looking white church-tower in the vale marks the site of Clachan Dysart—"the place of the High God"—the hills rise in many a grand unbroken sweep, and over their crests the white wings of the mists are floating, while rivulets here unheard, that only gleam like lines of quicksilver, are traversing their furrowed sides.

On a hill near Dalmally, commanding a fine view of his native glen, a monument in granite has lately been raised in honour of

Duncan Bane Macintyre, the bard of Glenorchy, who is stated to have served in the Argyll militia at the battle of Falkirk, and to have denounced in a poem (which led to his imprisonment) the vindictive attempts which were made by the government, after the rising of 1745, to crush the national spirit and the inborn loyalty of the Highlanders. Admirers of this native bard have ascribed to him the descriptive power of Thomson with the versatile genius of Burns. He could not himself have chosen a finer situation for his monument than the height on which it stands.

The vicinity of Tyndrum—a station at the head of Strathfillan between Dalmally and Loch Lomond, a vale in which St. Fillan had reverence of old—is wild and dreary, yet Strathfillan was probably not so desolate a tract when St. Fillan was the apostle of the vale. Lead mines are worked at Tyndrum, on the Breadalbane property.* At Crianlarich (where the Perthshire road diverges from that to Loch Lomond) the river takes the name of the Dochart, and a linn, called " the pool of St. Fillan," was in repute for the cure of insanity; but the process was a trying one, for the patient was immersed at sunset, and left bound in the ruins of St. Fillan's neighbouring church until the morning ! After traversing " the chilling deserts of Tyndrum," the wooded banks of Glenfalloch are quite refreshing to the eye, and the course of the river is diversified by more than one rocky cataract, and by scenes of grandeur as well as beauty when the glen opens to the mountains round the head of Loch Lomond.

It is not surprising that the palm of pre-eminence in beauty has been awarded to this charming lake. It would be the Mediterranean of the Highlands if it was an arm of the sea. Its shores are full of varied scenery; the grand and rugged mountainous forms that surround the upper or higher end of the lake are as remarkable for the picturesque character of their outlines as its shores and rocky promontories and islets are for their wooded beauty; while the majestic heights of Ben Lomond, which culminate above the wild mountains of its eastern shore, form a magnificent and distinguishing feature of its scenery ; and there the giant and

* The neighbourhood is one of great interest to the geologist, and presents one very remarkable feature, viz., a vein of quartz running for miles like a high wall over hill and vale.

master-presence of the Loch seems serenely looking down for ever on mountains and lakes and far-off western isles. In the lower part, where the lake expands into such a breadth that it seems an inland sea, it is crossed by a belt of wooded islets rich in picturesque beauty, and (many of them) distinguished by legendary associations, and marked by white villas now inhabited by "descendants of clansmen at enmity no more." The tourist is not likely to forget that it was chiefly in the mountains between Loch Lomond and Loch Katrine, then a Highland border country, that the ancestors of the Robin Hood of Scotland, popularly known as Rob Roy, had their abode. He appears to have held, and was perhaps entitled to hold, the domain of rock and forest called Crag Rostan, lying on the eastern side of Loch Lomond, where its bright waters are narrowed by the approach of the dark mountains of Glen Falloch, and here his cave, not far to the northward from Inversnaid, is shown. But to mention the spots with which his name is associated, would be to dwell too long on the Loch Lomond country.

A good road and the "Roderick Dhu" coach, and a steamboat on the lake, afford facilities for traversing Rob Roy's country, which, if they had existed in his days, would have deprived us of much of the attractive romance which surrounds his exploits.

Loch Katrine presents scenes of wondrous beauty, marked by features which, in many respects, give its scenery a character different from that of other lakes. Its waters are so tranquil, its shores of emerald green are so beautiful in form, they rise against a background of grey mountains so picturesque in character, its jutting peninsulas of rock and wood, and the islands that seem to rest on its unruffled waters, are so charmingly picturesque, and their graceful trees come down to the water's edge, and stand

With their green faces fixed upon the flood,

doubled in such magical clearness and beauty of tint, that the whole scene may appear a fit realm for Titania and a glimpse of fairyland. Then there are the beautiful declivities of Ben Venue, and there are the belts of natural wood hanging on the mountain's side, or marking the course of a waterfall in some deep chasm, and there are the softened tints of purple in which the regions of dark heather glow in the sunshine, and the changes of colour on the hills when the cloud-shadows sweep their distant slopes or darken their mysterious hollows; and there is the subjective and ideal charm which some of the most charming poetry in the English language has thrown over the scenery of Loch Katrine. I shall not attempt to describe that unique labyrinth the pass of the Trosachs—the " bristled territory "—where a narrow winding mountain-gorge or ravine is clothed almost to the grey crests of the wild rocks with luxuriant native wood, and every turn in the defile exhibits

These native bulwarks of the pass

under some new form of picturesque beauty. The waters were rippling in the morning light, and the feathery birch " that waves and weeps on Loch Achray " was bending to the breeze, when, with renewed love for the Highland hills, and with a pleasant recollection of the hospitalities of friends, of the salmon and mutton, and of the cream and butter of Highland farms, and the pure buoyant air, and the thousand scenes of beauty and grandeur, and the high-arched skies that spread above them, I quitted these realms, where Nature seems commissioned from Heaven to awaken the delight and gratitude of man, to return by the interesting valley of the Teith, between Loch Katrine and Callandar, to the more prosaic lowlands,

Where wrangling courts and stubborn law
To smoke and crowds and cities draw.

Dr. Buckland insisted that the ravines formerly covered, more or less, the valley of the Teith, from Loch Katrine to Callandar, and he regarded the lofty terraces which flank the valley from the last-named place to Doune, as formed by the ravines and modified by the great floods which followed the melting of the ice.

I have aimed at describing—not all that is worth seeing even on the route embraced in these notes, but—only what I saw in a few pleasant days in Scotland; and glad indeed shall I be if these pages shall recall to the reader pleasant recollections of places which have been to him also scenes of enjoyment.

# SCANDINAVIAN TRAVEL.*

*Bentley's Miscellany*, 1861.

DENMARK and JUTLAND are lands of legend and romance. Historic and even pre-historic monuments abound in them: barrows and tumuli are seen in almost every landscape, and the dreaded Vikings of old have left their mark upon the country. The manor-houses and castles of a later, yet ancient time, rise in every direction, and the memorials of bygone families linger on many a site. With so many visible monuments of former days around them, it is no wonder that the Danes live much in the past and cherish the memory of their own proud history.

The natural features of the Danish isles and Jutland are not less remarkable than the historical. Blue lakes and green woods diversify the wide plains in many parts of the country, and form a picturesque contrast to its tracts of moss and heather. The land is for the most part fertile; and the country generally (Lolland in particular) is famous for fair pleasure-grounds. The forests are gorgeous in their autumnal tints, but Denmark is especially the country of the spring. Most of the considerable towns (as Elsinore, for example) are adorned by charming walks; cheerful villages and country-houses enliven the shores of the Sound; distant objects of interest are seen on the horizon; and beyond a foreground of well kept gardens bright with flowers gleam the blue waters of the sea.

Then, too, everything in Denmark seems to have a well-to-do and prosperous air: the very *physique* of the people proclaims it, and eighteen stone, or thereabouts, is set down as the weight of

* A Residence in Jutland, the Danish Isles, and Copenhagen. By Horace Marryat. Two vols. London, Murray, 1860.

the full-grown Jutlander. Poverty is not seen; the lower classes are well-cared for and appear contented; and the inhabitants of the towns of Jutland, in conjunction with the authorities, do everything that can be done to make the towns desirable abodes for all classes, so that the poorest of the people enjoy advantages unknown in the overgrown manufacturing towns of England. Among the wild scenery of Hammershuus, in the remote island of Bornholm, more is done for the healthful dwelling and the out-of-door enjoyment of the people than is dreamed of in any of our wealthy centres of manufacturing industry, for in our English towns, too commonly, a sordid utilitarian aspect marks the culpable selfishness of the prosperous classes, the apathy of municipal bodies, and the absence of taste and public spirit.

Amongst the middle class of Danes, the author of the volumes before us sees, in their household arrangements, a refinement seldom to be met with in other countries; and in these " rambles beyond railways" he found civility and attention everywhere, and no illustrations of the old proverb that " Travellers find many inns, but few friends." The case may be otherwise some ten years hence, when the country comes to be intersected by railroads, and opened to wider intercourse with the rest of the world. When steamboats shall navigate the chain of lakes, upon whose placid waters the Vikings of bygone days bore the spoils of Gaul and England, and when Silkeborg shall have become the Birmingham of Jutland, simplicity of manners will probably disappear, together with the otter which now abounds in the streams, and with salmon—now so plentiful, that in Randers town (as formerly at Newcastle-upon-Tyne and some other places in England) the employer is prohibited from feeding his apprentice with it more than once a week. The improvement of agriculture, however, and the consequent enrichment of proprietors, only wait a better development of the natural resources of the country, and already mosses are beginning to be reclaimed and railways to be made.

The quiet old-world towns of Jutland must afford a striking contrast to the commercial activity of Hamburg, from which the writer of " A Residence in Jutland and the Danish Isles" started for his northern *séjour*, where the new streets, arcades, and buildings that have risen since the great fire, vie with Paris in their new-born magnificence. On his way to the sea-baths of Travemünde, he paced the shady walks, under fragrant limes, that are formed on the ancient ramparts of Lubec, whose tall unstraight church-spires, old gateways, and houses that threaten to topple over, are seen on the opposite side of the river Trave; and then, at the table d'hôte of Travemünde, he was waited on by buxom attendants, *décolletés*, under a summer sun, at two o'clock, and displaying feet, good, solid, and useful for common purposes, and capable of carrying them with ease even when they weigh sixteen stone.

Without following a given route, we may conveniently group together the châteaux of feudal ages and the historic sites that seem best deserving of notice.

The grim old castle of Sonderborg, once the residence of the Slesvig dukes, partakes in the decay of the capital of the ancient duchy; but, though fallen from its high estate, Slesvig is still memorable as the mother-town of early Christianity in this land. Another castle—that of Kolding, one of the most ancient in Jutland, called formerly Ornsborg (Eagle's Castle)—fell a prey to fire during the occupation of Bernadotte (every edifice in Denmark, royal or plebeian, seems fated to be destroyed, sooner or later, by fire), but the keep is remarkable for being still surmounted by two stone figures of warriors, resembling those found on some of the border towers of Scotland, and also at Alnwick Castle in Northumberland. The châteaux of the duchy of Holstein are substantial quadrangular buildings, surrounding a large court which has a green plot in the centre bordered by limes. The entrance is under a *porte-cochère*. In front is the large heavy schloss, with a huge portico supported by Corinthian or Ionic columns; and this is flanked by two stupendous buildings with high-pitched roofs, each as large as the abbey church of Malvern, which are used for storing the farm produce, implements, and stock. The live stock in cows on these domains is something enormous: *e.x. gr.*, the Countess Rantzau rejoices in four hundred and eighty cows, and in some of the great dairies hundreds of pounds of butter are produced in one forenoon. These useful animals, by the way, are called "cows" by the Jutland peasant; but this is not the only thing in sound and sight to remind the

English traveller of home: many expressions of the peasantry might pass for Yorkshire speech; the horses resemble the Yorkshire breed, and the sheep are the English "Southdown;" even the lofty stone monuments (dolmens) that are scattered over the country are called "Stonehenge" by the peasants. Some of the country residences are kept up, too, in a style that would not disgrace an English mansion. James Howell, writing from Hamburg, where he was on an embassy in 1632, says a Parliament was then sitting at Rheinsburg, where all the Younkers met, "and I put myself," he adds, "to mark the carriage of the Holstein gentlemen as they were going in and out at the Parliament House; and viewing well their physiognomies, their complexions, and gait, I thought verily I was in England, for they resemble the English more than either Welch or Scot (though cohabiting upon the same island), or any other people that ever I saw yet, which makes me verily believe that the English nation came first from this lower circuit of Saxony; and there is one thing that strengthens me in this belief, that there is an ancient town hard by, called Lunden, and an island called Angles, whence it may well be that our country came from Britannia to be Anglia."

Count Friis lives in Friisenborg, a château surrounded by a moat and horse-chesnuts of splendid growth—a quaint old building, flanked by antiquated towers. But the whole castle, excepting the stone foundation, is in a coat of whitewash, for the most respectable old red-brick is ruthlessly whitewashed in Denmark. At Katsholm we have the story of a Danish Whittington. An unjust man died, and his youngest son, on receiving his share, put his money to the water-ordeal, knowing that what was unjustly got would sink and the rest would float. A farthing only floated, and with it he bought a cat, which with her kittens he took to a foreign land where cats were unknown, and, with the fortune realised from the progeny of his cat, returned to Jutland, and built the castle of Katsholm. The castle of Kronborg has many a souvenir of interest to English readers. Here was celebrated the marriage by proxy of James VI. of Scotland with the youthful Princess Anne, daughter of Frederick II. of Denmark; and tales are current of the drinking-bouts of Prince Christian and the bridegroom. The ramparts of Kronborg are described as being *par excellence* the locality for Shakespeare's ghost-scene in "Hamlet," but the romance of Kronborg is over. A propos to "Hamlet," it may be mentioned that our author gives some illustrations of the story of the Prince of Denmark. A grassy mound that would be called in England a Danish camp goes by the name of Amleth's Castle, and he lies buried under a lofty tumulus that bears his name. At Rosenholm there are many memorials of the Rosenkrantz family. Amongst the portraits is one of Erik, the youthful ambassador at the pseudo-court of Cromwell, to whom he ought to have said, if he did not really say, when the ill-mannered "Protector" scoffed at a beardless minister, "If my sovereign had known it was a beard you required, he could have sent you a goat: at any rate, my beard is of older date than your Protectorate!"

Among the families ennobled are many of Scottish descent, whose ancestors settled in Denmark during the middle ages, but there is no trace of an Irish settler. The St. Clairs stand first on the list, and appear in councils of the kingdom in the fourteenth century. Near Helsingborg is "Hamilton House," the residence of Count Hamilton, a Swedish nobleman descended from one of the Scottish soldiers of fortune who joined the banner of Gustavus Adolphus, and at the end of the Thirty Years' War adopted Sweden. At Faareveile, by the tranquil waters of the fiord, on a little promontory jutting into the sea, we are at the burial-place of a Scottish nobleman of greater fame and darker fortunes; for within the walls of the little whitewashed gabled church are the mortal remains of the Earl of Bothwell, who died a prisoner in the castle of Draxholm (dragon's isle). This moated pile, which formerly belonged to the bishops of Rocskilde, later merged in the barony of Adelsborg. Bothwell's prison is now the wine-cellar of the castle. The mummy-like corpse of the earl is shown in the vault of Faareveile. He appears to have been of middle height, with a forehead not expansive, and head wide at the back of the skull, and his hair seems to have been red, mixed with grey; his cheek-bones high and prominent, nose somewhat hooked, and hands and feet well shaped and small. Had Bothwell in his stormy life selected a spot marked by quiet and repose in death, he could hardly have found in all Christendom a resting-place more calm and peaceful.

An English traveller in Denmark is struck by the large number of portraits of our royal Stuarts that are found in its portrait-galleries, but the fact that the mother of Charles I., the light-hearted Anne, was a Danish princess, of course sufficiently accounts for their presence. At the palace of Frederiksborg in particular, there is a most interesting series of portraits of the royal house of England. At Rosenborg the English visitor sees with great interest a princess of the present reigning family of England stand out brightly among the less refined specimens of German royalty. The portrait preserved in that castle of Queen Louisa, daughter of George II., and wife of Frederick V., must be a charming one.

Rostgaard, the only other castle we have room to mention, one of the most beautiful residences in the vicinity of Elsinore, derives some interest from the story of Kirstine, the Danish Penelope, the fair and youthful wife of Hans Rostgaard, who was lord of the castle in 1659. Becoming involved in a plot against the Swedes when their officers held Kronborg, he had to fly from his home, and deceived his enemies into the belief that he had been killed. The rich and pretty widow (for widow she was supposed to be) dared not reveal her husband's existence, and attracted the addresses of all the Swedish officers who were quartered at the manor-house, and who respected her property only because each of them hoped that it might in time become his own. When pressed by the most ardent of her suitors, she pleaded her recent widowhood, and, true to "The Wife's Secret," begged for time, and then coquetted so cleverly that each individual of the corps imagined himself to be the favoured man. At length a year elapsed, and peace was signed; she then made them a profound reverence, thanked them for the consideration they had shown to her goods and chattels, and reintroduced to them her resuscitated husband.

The churches of Denmark and Jutland have some peculiar features, and many of these edifices are of considerable antiquity, but the materials of which most of them are built—a mixture of granite, sandstone, and brickwork—does not give them an attractive appearance. Eight round churches are enumerated: the most perfect is that at Thorsager, built, it is said, upon the site of a temple of Thor, and the edifice appears to be of an earlier date than the twelfth century. The original part of the building is circular, and massive piers support the vaulted roof. At Veile, a city of ancient lineage, where some of the fairest scenery of the old Jutland province begins, the church had our Canute for its founder; and a figure, black like a statue carved in oak dug from the bogs of Hibernia, is shown 'as the body of Queen Gunhild, and is stated to have been translated thither from the morass in which she was buried. Her dress and hair are shown in the Museum of the Royal Society of Northern Antiquaries at Copenhagen, and eight centuries have not effaced from the woollen wrapper that enveloped the body the square pattern of a "shepherd's plaid" tartan. The Domkirk of Ribe, one of the most ancient cities of Jutland, is described not only as the great lion of the place, but as the finest church in the country. The interior presents some good architecture in what may be called the Norman style, but, in truth, the Romanesque of these northern churches is a style apart from that known in England, France, and Germany. The cathedral in the ancient city of Viborg is a sort of Westminster Abbey of the province, for the remains of many sovereigns repose in its round arched crypt. On the site of Viborg, the chief sacrifices to Odin were solemnised in pagan times, and here the Danish sovereigns were elected for the provinces of Jutland. In later times the city boasted as many churches as York, besides convents, friaries, and wondrous relics. The abbey church of Soro contains some interesting monuments, beginning with the sepulchral stone of Olaf, King of Norway and Denmark, and artistically culminating in the recumbent figures of Christian II. and his queen Euphemia. The king's effigy resembles that of Edward II. in Gloucester Cathedral: he is arrayed in royal robes, his hair flowing long, his beard pointed after the fashion of our early Plantagenets, and his head is encircled by the crown. There are also some interesting royal monuments in the cathedral church of Rocskilde, the time-honoured city which gives a patronymic to the Rothschild family, who, according to Mr. Marryat, emigrated from Denmark in the last century, and assumed as a surname the name of their ancestral birthplace. Here, too, is the monument of Queen Margaret, who first united under one sceptre the three Scandinavian kingdoms, and her effigy fitly represents the great queen recumbent, with eyes closed and hands meekly clasped, as if awaiting the day of judgment—a curious contrast to the martial gaze and impatient expression of Christian IV. in Thorwaldsen's bronze statue, a figure as little suited to a church as most of the statues of statesmen and heroes that crowd Westminster Abbey and St. Paul's.

The church *epitaphia* of the country must be curiosities. The oval medallion portrait common in the Duchies gives place at Rendsburg to a representation of scriptural subjects. One of these monuments was set up by a man whose three wives died before him, and as they had proved (as it would appear) no comfort to him, he has signalised at once his scriptural zeal and his marital resentment by a representation of the Last Judgment, in which they are placed among the condemned. The church of Eckernfiord is described as resembling an old curiosity-shop in its strange collection of all kinds of monuments, commemorating not only armed knights and high-born ladies but substantial burghers and their (too) fruitful spouses, and in its queer latticed pews, which are piled up anywhere and anyhow; some are like a sedan-chair, and made to contain one person; others are large enough to hold families as numerous as the family of Jacob; and the church keys are of such size and ponderosity, that the mace of the Lord Mayor and the state weapons of the Christ Church poker-bearers are ramrods in comparison.

"What families," exclaims Mr. Marryat, "people had in the days of these antiquated tombs! I may add, what a number of wives! If you closely examine the *epitaphia*, you may take as an average three to a family of sixteen children; sons ranged on one side behind the father, daughters behind the mother, and the babes who died in infancy spread out on cushions in front, done up in swaddling-clothes, the father and mother always dressed with the greatest decorum."*

Bornholm is remarkable for churches of blue marble; and in the church at Aarkirkeby one of the most remarkable sculptured fonts in Europe may be seen. At Nalborg, on the Liimfiord,

* The Danes wore armour later than other nations; hence the monument of the nobleman who, in 1740, was ambassador to the Empress Catherine, represents him in armour.

there is a circular antique font of sculptured granite. Mr. Marryat says the date 1166 is visible upon it, and that cherubim, with faces as broad as a Wiltshire cheese, are carved upon it; but in the twelfth century fonts were not dated, and the vulgarities familiarised to us by English churchwardenism and monumental masonry were not perpetrated in the middle ages.

But from silent churches and monuments let us pass to the picturesque and peopled city of Copenhagen (Merchants' Haven), and its beautiful environs, foremost among which is Lyngby—described as another Vale of Tempe—where, in early May, the peasants bring in baskets full of little nosegays, formed of the lilac flowers of the *primula farinosa;* and Marienlyst, where an English princess, Philippa, Queen of Denmark, sister of the hero of Agincourt, founded a Carmelite nunnery, to which a royal villa succeeded that has become a sort of Chelsea Hospital. The canals bring ships to the heart of Copenhagen. Its municipal privileges date from 1254, but not many houses of ancient date or historic interest remain in the city. It is pleasant to know, however, that the residence of Tycho Brahe—the northern luminary of his age—a heavy-looking, old, red-brick house, with massive stone window-copings, is still preserved. The palace of Christianborg, by which Frederic VI. replaced the edifice built by Queen Sophia Madalena, is not as useless as unsightly, for, besides the state apartments, it harbours the two chambers of parliament, the gallery of pictures, and the royal library.

The first idea of establishing the University of Copenhagen is attributed to Erik the Pomeranian, the royal spouse of Philippa, sister of our Henry V.\* Art and archæology, as well as literature, have their homes in Copenhagen: the Thorwaldsen Museum contains a most interesting collection of the works of the great Danish sculptor; and the Museum of the Royal Society of Northern Antiquaries, the formation of which has been achieved in little more than forty years, is not only a wonderful treasure-house, but fosters a national taste for the preservation of historical antiquities. The director of the museum happened to be able to give Mr. Marryat an example which could hardly have been anticipated. Seeing in the Ethnographical department three soldiers in blue,

\* See a drawing of her tombstone in 2 Arch. Æliana, 189.

who, catalogue in hand, were examining the collection, he remarked that twenty years ago no soldier would have thought of quitting his beershop to visit a collection of art, and oft' he went to explain the contents of the cabinet to his humble visitors.

The implements of the remote period known as the Age of Bronze, which are brought together in the Scandinavian collection, appear to belong to a period previous to the birth of Christ; and they are attributed to a nomadic oriental tribe, a small-limbed race, who settled in Denmark, but had no connection with their predecessors. And, *à propos* to this, it is curious to remark that in the island of Fano (nearly opposite the little sea-port of Hjerting, whence in summer a steamer bears beeves destined for the all-devouring London market) the young girls are described to have quite an oriental type of countenance, with long eyes and dark complexions; the women who tend the cows or work in the fields wear a black mask, and the place adheres to old customs and old habits, and is supposed to have remained stationary for a thousand years—things that are very suggestive of the people and customs of an eastern land. In this island, by the way, the womankind wear an indefinite number, from seven upwards, of substantial woollen petticoats of various colours—a bride once wore thirteen!

Even in the remote "Age of Bronze" the ladies appear to have possessed the requisites of the work-table, scissors excepted. The museum contains many needles in bone and in bronze, but some have the eye pierced in the centre. A pin or brooch for fastening the dress or plaid is described as precisely similar to the pins and brooches of the Scottish Highlands.

Among the antiquities of later periods preserved in this most interesting museum, drinking-horns of glass and of bone are found; and the collection formerly contained two golden horns, which were accidentally discovered—the one in 1639, and the other in 1737—in the same locality, and were valued respectively at 500*l*. and 450*l*.* The mosses, or morasses, and the tumuli of the country (the island of Samso alone is a very Kensal Green of

---

* These valuable objects were unfortunately stolen from the museum, and upon the event a funeral elegy was written, of so touching a character, as Mr. Marryat facetiously remarks, that it brought tears to the eyes of all antiquaries.

the early Scandinavian era), seem to hold golden treasures in their dark oblivion: thus, three gold armlets of beautiful workmanship, now in the museum—for in Denmark no pernicious law of treasure-trove consigns such treasures to the melting-pot—were found in an ancient grave at Buderupholm.

Accident has likewise disclosed many a hoard of coins. The Vikings who settled on the eastern shores of England in the ninth and tenth centuries coined money; but coin appears to have been first struck in Denmark in the reign of Svend, father of Canute, about the year 1000; and the first decent coinage Denmark ever possessed was that of Erik the Pomeranian. Large quantities of foreign coins have been discovered in various places—Cufic, Byzantine, Roman, German, and Anglo-Saxon, together with rings and bars of silver and gold, and beads and ornaments, gold-embossed, and apparently of Byzantine origin. Beads of glass, coloured and mosaic, probably likewise of eastern manufacture, are also found. Mr. Marryat does not attempt to explain the occurrence of such exotic objects in Denmark; but it is to be remembered that Northern Danes, Swedes, Norwegians, and even Angles, flocked by land through Russia to Constantinople in the tenth century, and took service in the imperial guard; and pure Old-Northern names occur in Byzantine writings. Northmen were ambassadors to the Greek emperors, and in those early times were much brought in contact with the East, which in ages still more remote had been the Northmen's home.

Their love of change and wandering seems afterwards to have lived in the old Viking spirit of the Danes, and now their descendants, no longer seeking adventures beyond the seas, and circumscribed in the area for their wanderings, indulge a last remnant of the native restlessness by frequently changing their abodes. The Copenhagen people are stated by Mr. Marryat to flit twice a year from one street of their capital to another! When ill, even the higher classes can rent rooms in the splendid hospital of Frederick V. and enjoy all the medical advantages of the establishment, without deranging or endangering their homes.

Under the fostering care of the Royal Society of Northern Antiquaries (which has the king himself for its president), the national antiquities are now so well cared for in Denmark, that one reads with astonishment of the highly disrespectful treatment of the public records in the archæologically dark age of Frederick V. That monarch, wishing to celebrate the marriage of Prince Christian by a grand display of fireworks, and paper for their fabrication not being accessible, is stated to have ordered all towns and conventual bodies to forward their archives to Copenhagen. Thereupon records arrived in cart-load after cart-load, obediently forwarded by their unsuspecting custodians, and were sacrificed in a holocaust of royal fireworks.

The folk-lore of the country and the ancient customs still observed are but incidentally noticed in Mr. Marryat's lively pages; but he mentions a few curious particulars. On one of the highest points of Zealand there is a blackened stone, on which the peasants light a bonfire on the eve of St. John—a relic (of course) of a very early Pagan custom. The sunset-bell always rings as the sun goes down, recalling the ancient Curfew of Normandy and England still rung in some cathedral towns. At Liselund, a place whose quiet and repose is seldom broken save by the little rural *fête* at harvest-home, the church bells "ring up the sun" (as the expression goes) and "ring it down" again; and, in the midst, nine distinct strokes are given, one for the Paternoster, seven for the seven separate petitions of the Lord's Prayer, and a loud booming ninth proclaims Amen. Nowhere are the good old Christmas customs more pleasantly observed than in Jutland. Even the little birds of the air are not forgotten, for a small wheatsheaf is laid in the garden over-night on Christmas-eve, in order that they also may eat and rejoice. The peasants believe that at midnight on Christmas-eve the cattle all rise together and stand upright; and, on that day, the cows and horses, and the watch-dog in particular, are fed with the best of everything by these reverent, simple-minded, tradition-loving people. From the 24th of December to the new year no one works, and all the young people dance; but the new year, at least in Bornholm, is not danced in—it is *shot* in, for every one who can obtain firearms discharges them at his neighbours' windows by way of wishing a happy new year. On the festival of the Three Kings, a candle of three wicks is burnt in every house.

Some of the superstitions, too, are noticeable. Second sight is as common in Jutland as in the Scottish Highlands, and is much believed in for the foretelling of fire. The huge black dog that haunts the ruined church of Skamm, quite recals the famous "spectre-hound of Man." Fairies, of course, and the much less amiable trolls, seem to stand beside you everywhere. The trolls, however, are not invariably mischievous beings, and fortunately they can transform themselves only into maimed animals: thus his satanic majesty himself affects the form of a rat, but never can grow any tail. Superstition thrives in Falster—witness the custom of casting a pail of water behind when a corpse leaves the door, so that no ghost may appear in the house.

There are relics of strange customs connected with church-going: e.v. gr. Christian V. placed "the yawning-stocks" at every church-door (the village stocks, though remaining in some places, are, as in this country, quite out of fashion), and in them the preacher's victims, when convicted of a second offence, had to stand with open mouth. Upon this, the people tried to protect themselves by going when the sermon was half over, for the early Lutheran clergy loved the sound of their own voices; but the authorities were a match for them, and placed the late comers in the stocks all the same. Then folks went early, and took refuge in sleep; but thereupon the churchwardens were charged to go round and stir them up continually. At length an hour-glass was fixed by the side of every pulpit. People go to christenings, at all events, merrily enough, for on a Sunday morning a stuhl-wagen may be seen to drive by, carrying a party of old-fashioned Jutlanders to the ceremony, and a musician with distended cheeks, playing vigorously on a flageolet, sits by the driver.

Carriages appear to have been considered a luxury in Denmark down to a date as late as the last half of the seventeenth century. It would seem that even in England the use of coaches cannot be carried more than a century farther back, that is to say, not beyond the time of Fitz-Alan, Earl of Arundel. Buckingham, King James's favourite, introduced sedan-chairs and the use of six horses for his coach—a novelty which then excited some wonder, and was taken as a mark of his extravagant pride. Such of the citizens of Copenhagen as could not afford to keep horses, were likewise carried about in sedan-chairs; and there was an Italian who contracted to supply the town with them.

This article has extended to so great a length, that we can only notice very briefly, in conclusion, some of the natural features of Jutland and the Danish isles. That the waters are retiring on the Liimfiord there can be no doubt: the names and the stranded appearance of such places as Tranders-holm and Engholm attest the fact; and the Mayor of Aalborg (Eel Castle) told Mr. Marryat that the bed of a little lake in which he used to fish eighteen years before was then cultivated land, although no process of draining had been resorted to. On the other hand, there are vast bogs, or mosses, the result of some ancient inundation of the sea, which have been reclaimed by draining, and in which the plough uncovers urns of black Jutland pottery with the zigzag ornament, and containing bones. The draining of the Sjorring Lake is looked forward to by antiquarians as that of a Jutland Tiber. Level lands so open to the sea are of course particularly liable to be overwhelmed by the sands and the salt waves. What is now a plain of driving sand, was in living memory one of the most fertile meadows in Jutland; and in many wild mosses, now inhabited only by the swarthy gypsy and the lapwing, ruins of cottages and remains of furnaces are found, and weapons are uncovered by the turf-cutters—memorials of a civilisation that the spot once knew, but which has long passed away.

The naturalist finds much to interest him in Jutland. Wolves do not exist there now, any more than in England, but they seem to have lingered in Jutland to a later period than they did even in Scotland, for, towards the middle of the last century, it was a common thing to hear of their destroying cattle and doing other damage. The last wolf is said to have been killed only fifty years ago. Christian V. signalised his energy against wild-boars no less than against yawning sermon-hearers, and is said to have killed sixteen of the former animals in one day's chase in 1671, but they are now quite extinct. In the manor of Asdal, great forests once stood, and lately the horns and bones of the wild buffalo and the elk, races long since extinct in Jutland, have been dug up. The storks arrive about old May-day (May 13). It must be curious to behold one of their gatherings before they take flight on the approach of winter. A friend of the author saw an assembly of four hundred perched on the eaves of farm-buildings in Zealand: the whole flock appeared to be mustered for inspection and review; and the aged and weakly being separated and pecked to death, the rest took their flight for Egypt. The birds are found to be quite right in their anticipation of summer, for vegetation suddenly breaks forth in a few days after their arrival. The larger falcon tribe abound. Everywhere in Denmark the swallow is a privileged bird; its nests are respected and preserved wheresoever built; and the reason given is, that the swallow was the most blessed of the three birds that came to our Saviour's cross. The Bohemian wax-wing (*Bombacilla garrula*), called in Denmark "silk-tail," a bird of sober plumage, with a beautiful little yellow tail, is stated to visit Denmark only once in seven years. It never lays its eggs farther south than Lapland.

When the birds of spring have collected, and rich verdure waves above the carpet of moss; when " the fresh green earth is strewed with the first flowers that lead the vernal dance," and the lily of the valley, the Solomon's-seal, the hepatica, and other wild flowers, gem the woods, the country must be charming, and as attractive to the lover of nature as its old historic sites must prove to the gatherer of history and legend.

# THE MEDITERRANEAN.*

[*Bentley's Miscellany*, July, 1858.]

THE Mediterranean Sea has always afforded a favourite and fertile theme to naturalists and geographers; its shores are pre-eminently lands of story and of song; and it has been the theatre of events that have employed the historian ever since history began. The beauty and grandeur of its natural features have suggested images for the loftiest poetry; they have furnished scenes of inexhaustible attraction to the artist; and the memories and monuments that linger on the Mediterranean shores give them an unrivalled interest for the architect, the antiquary, and the scholar.

By its eastern waters Art and Poetry, Eloquence and Philosophy, had their earliest seats, and events that occurred upon its coasts have affected the whole world and the destinies of the human race. Upon this splendid sea, "navigation," in the words of Admiral Smyth, "made its earliest efforts;" and it was the Mediterranean Sea that in ancient times brought Western Europe into communication with the lands that had long been the home of all civilisation. Almost every bay, every cape and noble promontory, from the Black Sea to the Ocean, from Neptune's watch-tower on Thracian Samos to the most southerly pharos-tower of the Levant, has its place in history or poetry; almost every river that falls into the Mediterranean is to this day made familiar to us by the classical associations of its coast; and undying memories of ancient genius and refinement give its shores attractions that are undiminished by time. By the Mediter-

* The Mediterranean: a Memoir, Physical, Historical, and Nautical. By Rear-Admiral W. H. Smyth, K.S.F., D.C.L., F.R.S. London: 1854.
Rambles of a Naturalist on the Coasts of France, Spain, and Sicily. By A. de Quatrefages, Member of the Institute, &c. Translated by E. C. Otté. Two Vols. 1857.

ranean Sea kingdoms that swayed the destinies of the world flourished and fell, and its coasts are haunted by the shades of ancient power. It gleams in the pages of sacred history and prophecy, for to the isolated Hebrew nation it was "the great," the unknown "sea," and its waters may be truly said to reflect the history of thirty centuries. By its shores the picturesque remote dynasties of Egypt ruled and accumulated their wondrous and colossal monuments; and upon the Mediterranean the Phœnician traders carried colonies and commerce to the limits of the known world. Amidst "Edens of the Eastern wave" flourished those republics of illustrious Greece—

> Immortal, though no more; though fallen, great—

which have left such imperishable remains of poetry, philosophy, and art. On Mediterranean shores rose Phœnician Carthage, and the later sway of that great empire which advanced, from a once-obscure town upon the Tiber, to the dominion of the world. And then the wonderful Arabian power, "offspring of the Koran and the sword," after subjugating the African coast of the Mediterranean and the richest part of Spain, reigned from Cordova to Mecca, and raised elaborate works of Saracenic architecture, to which princes of Western Europe were ere long to give a Christian dedication. Upon this southern sea Norman princes gained a kingdom and raised ecclesiastical edifices that at this day blend with Grecian temples on the hills of Sicily; and, finally, when more than a thousand years had elapsed since the events that had consecrated the land of Palestine, Christian powers established their dominion upon all the European coasts of the Mediterranean, and in its island fortresses the chivalrous brotherhoods of warrior-monks maintained the cause of Christendom.

But in the present article it is proposed to take a rapid survey of the geographical features and natural phenomena of the Mediterranean, rather than to indulge in historical retrospect. On looking at a map of this great inland sea, the most cursory observer must be struck by the remarkable character of its physical configuration. Opening from the Atlantic, its waters mingle at the entrance with those of the great ocean of the West; while their eastern extremity, two thousand five hundred miles distant, is divided by only a low, narrow isthmus from the ocean-inlets of another hemisphere, namely, the Red Sea and the Persian Gulf. Its land-locked area; its immense expanse between the great continents (its total periphery, following the shores of its principal gulfs, is more than 13,000 miles, and its area in square miles is 760,000); the innumerable bays which deeply penetrate its shores;* its mountainous and volcanic islands; and its straits and inner seas—for the Black Sea, the Sea of Azof, and the Sea of Marmora, may be regarded as inner basins of the Mediterranean—are not less striking features of its outline. Channels, in some respects as remarkable as the straits of Gibraltar, connect the Mediterranean with these inner seas, which bring its waters to the foot of the Caucasian chain and the steppes of Russia; and they flow between shores memorably connected with the history of former times, and conspicuous for the unchanged grandeur of their scenery. The archipelago of mountainous islands and lofty coasts, which those straits and channels penetrate, display physical features of the most extraordinary and romantic character.

But the lofty mountain chains which, for the most part, surround the Mediterranean, and the mountain-isles which stud its surface, constitute its grandest scenery. The entrance to the sea is fitly guarded by that stupendous monument of some distant geological convulsion, the rock of Gibraltar—a mass of oolitic limestone, rising to a height of more than fourteen hundred feet, and forming a narrow peninsula of nearly three miles in circuit, joined to the continent by a low, sandy neck of land. Then rise the stupendous mountain ranges of Spain, many of whose snowy peaks exceed ten thousand feet in height; the Maritime Alps; the "marble-crested Apennines" (which run in parallel ridges through the centre of Italy to Calabria, there dividing into two branches after a course of eight hundred miles); the mountainous ranges on the eastern side of the Adriatic; the long line of capes, headlands, and mountainous coasts of Asia Minor and Syria; and, loftier than these, the ranges of African mountains, which are divided from the waters of the Mediterranean by

* Thus, Sicily, though in surface actually smaller than Sardinia, has a coast so diversified by bays that its circuit, following the indentations of its shores, measures 550 miles.

―――a dry unfathomed deep
Of sands, that lie in lifeless sleep
Save when the scorching whirlwinds heap
Their waves in rude alarm.

The Black Sea is equally bordered by precipitous cliffs, and is girt on its eastern side by that vast rampart of the Caucasus, which seems as if intended to divide two different races of men, and rises everywhere to a height of ten thousand feet, with glacier-filled valleys and gigantic peaks of snow. Besides these mighty barrier-ranges, a hundred mountains and promontories, celebrated in classic story, diversify the Mediterranean coasts, or rise as islands amidst its waves, from the mighty rock-fortress of Gibraltar at its entrance, to those marvellous straits—the Dardanelles and the Bosphorus—where the promontories and palaces of Europe and Asia border the same great stream.

First and fairest of Mediterranean isles is mountainous Sicily, with its woody heights and sunny bays; its lovely Castellamare, the dark blue waters of whose bay are enclosed on one side by a crescent of olive woods rising from the sea towards the distant mountains, and on the other by precipices of bare grey rock that rise abruptly from the water's edge; its beautiful Palermo, whose domes and spires give the town an almost Oriental aspect as it spreads between hills clad with verdure and encircled by a framework of lofty mountains; its rich valley of the Concha d'Oro, where the vegetation is quite southern and African in its character, and where the eye ranges over forests of citron and orange; its mountain scenery, and its monarch Etna—Sicily, where Doric temples blend majestic relics of Greek art with Italian beauty, on sites around which Nature again reigns in loveliness, alone, and retains an impress of beauty that has resisted time, "as if Venus still continued to shed her favours on the land that was once consecrated to her worship."

And here we are tempted, in passing, to glance from the physical geography of the Mediterranean to those picturesque combinations of the characteristic features of the East and the West which meet us in many parts of Sicily, and on other shores of this wondrous sea. At Palermo, for example, edifices raised by Norman princes blend with Moorish palaces that look like the fabric of Aladdin's genii. The palaces and ecclesiastical buildings of the city are adorned with marbles, malachites, and lapis-lazuli, and one may traverse churches and cloisters that are enriched with wondrous carvings. Their Moorish builders have encrusted the walls with mosaics wrought in porcelain and delicate plaster of variegated tints; and roofs that rest on palm-like pillars of marble are pierced as with lacework, and are bright with colour and gold. In other parts of the island, as if in contrast to this Arabian splendour, one may stand beneath a weather-stained and stately monument of severe classic art, rising on its rocky plateau, amidst the mountain scenery which entranced the sight of Æneas, in a solitude that might seem to have escaped all contact with human industry. In such a desert situation the temple of Segesta stands, the solitary monument of a once proud and opulent city, the rival of Syracuse and Agrigentum. Time has not " rounded with consuming power " the cornice-stones of this noble edifice, nor overthrown one of its thirty-six columns.

In features of natural grandeur, Sardinia, and Corsica—island of mountains and forests—are likewise conspicuous amongst the islands of the Mediterranean, and seem to belong to the mountain system of the Maritime Alps. Then, as we glance from the volcanic islands of the Calabrian Gulf towards the wood-environed heights of Corfu, and the multitudinous isles of Greece, we must not unobservant

──────── pass Calypso's isles,
The sister-tenants of the middle deep;

for the island citadel of Malta has not only been surrounded with illustrious memories by the Knights Hospitallers who there maintained the cause of Christendom so proudly, but is unrivalled for exhibiting the alliance of the finest and most strongly fortified of harbours with the greatest of maritime powers.

The coasts of Greece are remarkable for their bold mountainous frontage to the waters. Some of the chasms by which its mountain-chains are torn form gulfs of the sea, whilst the valleys are for the most part basin-shaped hollows, enclosed by lofty walls of rock which look as if they had been filled by lakes in some remote geological epoch. The shores of the Ægean, serrated by bays and islets, and abounding in phenomena produced by former volcanic agency, proclaim the ancient power of those forces of upheaval which have raised mountains and continents of the globe. There is not, perhaps, in these waters so conspicuous an example as the giant height of lonely Athos—the " Holy Mountain " of the modern Greek monks—that stupendous promontory whose precipices of greyish-white marble are piled magnificently to a height of six thousand feet above the sea, whilst in the wooded region below the monastic mountaineers thickly cluster —the only populous government in the world where there is not a woman or child! In like manner, but on a comparatively miniature scale, most of the Lipari Islands present steep cliffy fronts on the western side, which plunge into deep water, sloping on the eastern side, and shelving to a regular gradation of soundings.

In the bay of Cattaro, below the natural citadel of Montenegro, is presented the spectacle of a line of gigantic docks hewn from the mountains by the hand of nature. Three vast basins communicate with each other by narrow channels, termed "mouths" (*bocche*), which the Austrian Government, bent on making Cattaro the Sebastopol of the Adriatic, is now strongly fortifying, Cattaro being an Austrian frontier-town situated at the inner extremity of that beautiful inlet of the sea—the Rhizonic gulf of antiquity, now known as the Bocche di Cattaro. So great is the expanse of water that the united fleets of Europe could find safe and commodious shelter in each of these harbours, and their depth would allow the largest ships of war to be moored close to the shore. As the traveller proceeds through the winding gulf from the entrance of the Bocche to the town, a shifting panorama of views recalls the soft beauty of the Lake of Como mingled with the sterner scenery of the Lake of Lucerne. The craggy mountains rise abruptly on either side with a majestic sweep, barely allowing room for the succession of villages which fringe the shore at their feet, and whose gay Italian towers and steeples, surrounded with gardens and vineyards, and embowered in groves of olive and cypress, are mirrored in the deep still water.\*

The volcanoes, which are still active in different areas of the

\* Edin. Rev. Ap. 1859. " Montenegro."

Mediterranean, are significant of the gigantic forces which determined the configuration of this wondrous Valley of Waters and raised its majestic eminences. A volcanic zone is found to extend from the Caspian to the Azores, and the Mediterranean has been aptly described as undermined by fire. Dark, igneous rocks pervade islands of the Ionian Sea; trachytic and trap-rocks border the Bosphorus, and are scattered over Asia Minor and Greece, where volcanic districts are found that resemble in their structure those of Central France. Parts of Italy abound in extinct craters, evidently, at some remote period, centres of volcanic action, now no longer exerted in those particular areas of the country. Of the continued energy of volcanic forces in the area of the Calabrian and Sicilian shores, Mount Vesuvius, the ever-fiery crater of Stromboli, the active volcanoes of the Lipari Islands, and the monarch cone of Etna, afford, of course, the most terrible and conspicuous proofs; and to those ancient and gigantic volcanoes may be added the isolated craters that have suddenly risen amidst the waters, and, after a brief reign of terror, as suddenly disappeared.*

But igneous rocks, and lava-streams ancient or recent, and craters extinct or still burning, are not the only phenomena resulting from the energy of subterranean forces. The mountain chains and towering land-marks that now stand so steadfast in their "sublime repose," are the more stupendous monuments of volcanic forces, but of forces which Nature no longer employs on the same gigantic scale. To their action, however, although in a greatly modified form, we must attribute that gradual upheaval of some coasts and gradual depression of other coasts, which we may at this day witness on many parts of the Mediterranean shores.

In many places on the western coast of Italy the sea has steadily advanced upon the land, and some tracts have been submerged even within historic times. Thus, Astura, an island about six miles from Antium, the favourite retreat of Cicero, and

* The reader need not be reminded of that wondrous island which arose in the year 1831 in the midst of the sea, beween Sicily and Pantellaria, and threw from its crater columns of burning cinders and lava, amid flames and fumes of sulphur, and which soon afterwards sank again beneath the waves.

the place where he appears to have erected a memorial-temple for his daughter Tullia, is partly submerged, and all traces of his villa and temple have been swallowed by the sea. The coast of the bay of Baiæ, on the northern shore of the gulf of Naples, has undergone great changes since the time when its baths and villas were resorted to by the Romans. Their ruins may now be seen many feet below the surface of the pellucid sea, just as the ruins of Greek towns are seen on the submerged eastern coast of Candia. Neptune has taken into his embraces the temple which the Romans dedicated in his honour, and the adjacent Temple of the Nymphs besides. And the ruins of the once-stately Temple of Jupiter Serapis, near Puzzuoli, afford a celebrated example of oscillations in this tract of land. It is supposed that the temple must have actually sunk, and long remained below the level of the Mediterranean at some unknown period; and, as it afterwards rose again, and has again become depressed, it is continually a matter of interest to learn what may be its actual state, and to speculate on what may next happen to it. When, in the year 1750, its columns and basement-walls, then standing twelve feet above the sea-level, were excavated from the mixed deposit which covered them, the three erect marble columns then and now standing were found to have been perforated by a marine shell-fish, whose habit it is to make its cell in calcareous rock, and it was evident that the sea had once covered the ruins to the depth of fifteen feet. The architecture of the temple appears to assign it to the time of the Emperor Augustus. In 1814, the pavement was dry, but was only a little above the sea-level. In 1822 it was covered with salt-water to the depth of two inches; and, twenty-three years later, the water sometimes stood two feet above its floor, having gained at the rate of three-quarters of an inch yearly. From observations made in 1852, it was inferred that the subsidence of the land had ceased. But all that part of the coast appears to be in a state of instability. At Caligula's bridge the land must have risen, for there are indications in the piers that the water formerly stood four feet higher than its present level; and elsewhere in the vicinity are ancient beaches, from the position of which it has been inferred that the land has risen many feet. In other parts of the Mediterranean, a gradual rising of the coast and retirement of the sea has taken place even within the historic period. In some instances, land formerly isolated is now far from the sea; in others, land that was overflowed by it a century ago is now clothed with vineyards, and some places that were anciently seaports are now far from the coast. Thus, in the walls of a castle of the Saracens, from which the sea is now a mile and a half distant, on the gulf of Iskanderun (the extreme eastern point of the Mediterranean), are the rings to which ships were formerly moored. So, too, if we pass to the sites of the earliest of the Greek colonies, we find that the ports of the once-powerful city of Cyrene, and of other members of the Pentapolis, have shared the fate of some of the English cinque-ports. Again, the very ancient city of Adria, which is supposed to have given its name to the Adriatic Sea, and which was a station for the Roman fleet, is now many miles inland. The present city stands on the ruins of two earlier towns, the fragments of the oldest and lowest of which appear to be Etruscan. And it is not only at the ancient Adria that we have an instance of the retrocession of the sea upon the western shore of the Adriatic. Ravenna, formerly built on piles and surrounded by lagoons communicating with the sea, is now in the midst of gardens and meadows; Ragusa, which has been called the Paris of the Adriatic, was once a powerful maritime city; and between that New Tyre—the once potent city of Venice—and the Adriatic we see a long if not final divorce. Ostia, the ancient port of Rome, affords in another part of Italy a similar instance of this kind of change.

On some other parts of the Mediterranean shores similar changes have been produced by a different cause—namely, the accumulation of sedimentary deposit at the mouths of rivers. Thus, Aiguesmort, near a mouth of the Rhône, was a port five hundred years ago, and remarkable as the place from which St. Louis embarked on his crusade, but it is now five miles from the sea. According to M. Tessier, the sea is slowly retiring from the southern coast of France, leaving behind new land or muddy deposits, whilst on the coast of Normandy the ocean is encroaching. The Castle of Iskanderun is not the only instance of the retirement of the sea from eastern shores of the Mediterranean.

Thus, the Isle of Lada, where the Athenian fleet rode in the days of Thucydides, is now a hill in the midst of a plain of alluvial deposit of the Mœander; the once flourishing town of Miletus, having lost its harbour, has become a heap of ruins; the port of Ephesus is converted into a stagnant pool; and the *delta* of the Hermus has been described by Mr. Strickland as threatening to destroy eventually the harbour of the prosperous city of Smyrna. But in mentioning these changes we have made a digression, for they, of course, are not brought forward as examples of the continued action of subterranean forces in altering the relative level of sea and land.

Of the activity of those subterranean forces, we have more terrible and more impressive results in the earthquakes by which the coasts of the Mediterranean, especially in its central and eastern portion, have been shaken; and which have been especially felt throughout the whole of that line which begins at the Euganean hills, and, extending through the region of extinct volcanoes in the Roman States, is continued in that submarine barrier or ridge of elevation which separates the Mediterranean into two great basins, and which is marked by its active volcanoes. To earthquakes the Mediterranean shores have been subject from very early historic times, and Roman historians have described, as the reader will remember, the devastation sustained from this cause in their days.

Of the forces that shook the Sicilian and Calabrian shores two thousand years ago, the country to the south of Naples has lately sustained a terrific manifestation; so, too, the eastern basin of the Mediterranean, and the Ionian Islands in particular, have repeatedly felt these disturbing forces, which have fatally shaken Corinth during the present year. Still, the intensity of subterranean force seems to have diminished in certain parts of the volcanic zone already mentioned; and Sicily, which seems to have been formerly a centre of disturbance, has not for some time sustained the volcanic paroxysms that formerly shook the land.

But the great volcano which entombed the Roman towns of Pompeii and Herculaneum, and the monarch Etna, of whose eruptions in the days of the Roman Empire we possess such memorable notices, still throw the light of their lurid fires on the blue waters of the Mediterranean, and display occasionally the impressive phenomena of volcanic force. Books have been devoted to the wonders of Vesuvius; to the lofty cone of Stomboli, two thousand feet in height, whose constant fires have given to it the title of the Lighthouse of the Mediterranean; to the volcanic phenomena of the Lipari Islands; and to the enduring Etna, towering ten thousand feet above the sea, girdled round by lavas older than the pyramids, and to this day occasionally spreading around the terrors of its active fires.

But it is time that we should pass to the hydrographical division of our subject, and briefly indicate some of the very interesting phenomena it embraces.

Amongst the prominent wonders of the Mediterranean are the vast river-floods which it receives. Let it be remembered that nearly half of all the running water of Europe falls into the Black Sea; and that, besides the Don, the Dnieper, and the Danube, not to mention innumerable lesser streams of Europe, the mighty floods of the Rhône and the Nile fall into this great land-locked sea, bringing to it the melted snows of the greatest mountain ranges of the south of Europe and Asia Minor. A body of water two hundred and fifty times greater than that of the Thames is brought down annually by the Nile—the wondrous Nile—which, coming from unknown fountains, and flowing twelve hundred miles through Nubia and Egypt without a tributary, divides sterile sand from profuse vegetation, and has fertilised for four thousand years a country which, but for its waters, would have been a desert. The constancy in the rise and fall of its periodic flood, which has probably been nearly uniform for that time, is not the least wondrous of its phenomena. Flowing into a sea that has been for ages the centre of commerce and civilisation, the Nile has a place in history from the earliest times, and marvellous monuments of science and empire dignify its banks. It was the connecting link between Africa and the civilized world, and was the highway of the earliest merchants in times when the western portion of the Mediterranean was the *Mare tenebrosum*, dreaded and unknown. Upon its spreading waters was formerly borne that eastern commerce to which Thebes and

Memphis are thought to have owed their ancient splendour, for the Indian produce which Arabian navigators of the Red Sea brought in early ages from the distant East was introduced to Mediterranean shores by the merchants of Tyre and Sidon, and was conducted upon the Nile to the magnificent cities that were once reflected on its stream. It is now gradually entombing their ruins under its alluvial deposits, as Etna is covering its ancient eminences under recent lavas; and the "sceptered isle," which was unknown to the civilised world of Egypt in the days when Phœnician merchants imported the produce of the tin mines of Britain, finds its pathway to Indian empire among the ruins of Egyptian power.

Seeing, then, what river-floods descend to the Mediterranean, and remembering that a volume of water sets in from the ocean, while no perceptible current sets out to the Atlantic, the constancy in the level of this great land-locked sea has long been regarded as one of its marvels, and as a phenomenon most difficult of explanation. Admiral Smyth does not adopt the evaporation theory of Halley, who sought to explain the phenomenon by assuming the weight of water raised in evaporation to equal the influx from rivers ; and, upon the whole, it seems to be probable that an under-current sets outward, at the Straits of Gibraltar, to an amount more than equivalent to the volume setting in from the ocean. In some other parts of the globe counter-currents do exist ; and there is this remarkable fact, that, within the Straits, the waters of the Mediterranean increase in specific gravity with the depth. But, whatever the true explanation may be, there is no doubt that the surface of the Mediterranean has been maintained at nearly the same level for at all events two thousand years. This is apparent from many considerations into which we need not enter, and from the evidence afforded by old marine works, as, for example, at Civita Vecchia, Genoa, and Marseilles, where no subterranean movements have affected the relative level.

The profound depth of the Mediterranean in many parts of its area, and its general submarine configuration, are most interesting features of its physical geography. It has the aspect of a sunken basin, which the long peninsula of Italy and the Island of Sicily

—approached within eighty miles by the projection of the African continent at Cape Bona—divides into two great though unequal portions. Upon the land, this barrier-line is marked by the lofty ridge of the Apennines, which stretch to the extremity of the peninsula, and reappear in the Pelorian—or, as they were formerly called, Neptunian—mountains of Sicily; and beneath the sea it is marked by a bar, or submarine ridge, which stretches between that island and the continent, separating the profound depths that lie on either side. A similar bar, or submarine ridge, may be regarded as dividing the Mediterranean from the ocean at the Strait of Gibraltar. At its narrowest part the depth of the mid-channel is nine hundred feet; but the water deepens rapidly on each side, insomuch that, between Gibraltar and Ceuta, a plummet carried out six thousand feet of line, and a little farther to the eastward no sounding was obtained. So, too, at Nice, within a small distance from the shore, the depth exceeds four thousand feet. This remarkable submarine configuration, and the near approach of the opposing shores,

> Where Europe and Afric on each other gaze,

affords some countenance to the tradition of antiquity, that a barrier once existed between the Mediterranean and the Atlantic; and the whole scenery of the coast suggests great movements and changes in a remote epoch, appreciable by the geologist but antecedent to human tradition. These deep soundings on each side of the ridge or bar in the Straits, and on each side of that submarine ridge stretching between Sicily and Africa which divides the Mediterranean into an eastern and a western basin, are thought to indicate depths in this sea equal to the average height of the mountains that surround it. In recently laying down the telegraph cable, the profundity opposite Mount Etna was found to be immense, and the depth very great in the direct course between Malta and Corfu. Between Cyprus and Egypt six thousand feet of sounding line were run out without the plummet reaching the bottom; in a sounding taken between Alexandria and Rhodes the depth was unfathomed by nearly ten thousand feet of line; and the

> Isles that crown the Ægean deep

are, probably, only the highest portions of a mountainous region now submerged. The eastern basin of the Mediterranean slopes to these unfathomed depths of the Levant, many of whose ancient historic promontories rise sheer from immense depths, in walls of rock, to twice the height of our giant Skiddaw. There are, probably, in many parts of this sea depths even more profound. At about ninety miles to the east of Malta there is an abyss equal to the height of Mont Blanc, for fifteen thousand feet of line were run out without reaching the sea-bed. The vertical distance is not, perhaps, far short of twenty thousand feet from the submarine abyss near Mount Etna to the summit of that majestic mountain; and it is even greater when the submarine depth is compared with the crests of the Atlas range, which attain heights greatly exceeding the height of Mount Etna itself. It would seem that on the coast of Syria the average depth is about equivalent to the average height of the mountains of Lebanon. Mount Casius, with which that celebrated range may be said to begin, rises abruptly from the Mediterranean, near the mouth of the Orontes, a few miles northward from the city of Old Tyre, to the height of seven thousand feet. From this promontory the range, it will be remembered, runs in a southerly direction parallel to the seashore in a continuous line of peaks and precipices, to the sources of the Jordan. The whole valley of that river, to the Gulf of Akaba on the Red Sea, is the most remarkable instance of depression known. At the sea of Galilee the river is six hundred and thirty feet below the level of the Mediterranean, and the Dead Sea is thirteen hundred and twenty feet below it. That mysterious sea being about two thousand feet in depth, its basin is, consequently, no less than three thousand six hundred feet below the surface of the Mediterranean!

Very interesting phenomena are connected with the currents, colour, and luminosity, as well as depth, of this great inland sea. Facts do not warrant the common belief that it is tideless. From its peculiar configuration it does not exhibit the phenomena of the ocean tides; but a rise and fall of the tide is witnessed on many parts of the Mediterranean coast, as, for instance, in the gulf of Venice, where the tide rises nearly three feet. On the Mediterranean shores of France, and round the shores of Italy, the tides are smaller, a rise of only one, or at most two, feet having been observed. The tidal influence is, however, so modified by local peculiarities that in many parts of the Mediterranean there is not any perceptible tide; while in others, as, for example, in the narrow strait dividing Euboea from the mainland of Greece (now known as Negropont), the tides were said, as the reader will remember, to flow and ebb seven times a day—a phenomenon of reciprocated motion, of which Aristotle vainly endeavoured to discover the cause. In serene weather the flow appears to be as regularly alternate from north to south, and *vice versâ*, as the tides of the Ocean, but during storms the apparent flow and ebb in this narrow strait is disturbed and variable. As the maritime knowledge of the Greeks and Macedonians did not extend beyond the Mediterranean, Alexander and his army might well view with astonishment the rise and fall of the tide of the Indian Ocean when they first beheld this great phenomenon; and it was viewed with similar wonder and alarm by the Roman legions who left their native coasts of Greece and Asia Minor to carry the victorious arms of Rome to countries on the Atlantic coast.

Their blue tint has been observed from early times as a distinguishing characteristic of the Mediterranean waters. Here, as in the Ocean, an emerald colour of different degrees marks shallow water, and the indigo colour marks the depths. The pure, intense, and beautiful blue is especially observable when the water is seen by transmitted light (as, on looking into it from the side of a ship); and it is not affected by the circumstance of the sky being covered by masses of grey clouds. The water is described, however, as bright and colourless when drawn up for examination.

The occasional luminosity of the Mediterranean waters is a most remarkable and beautiful phenomenon. That it is due to microscopic animals seems now beyond a doubt. It is an effect which must be seen to be properly appreciated; but the author of the " Rambles of a Naturalist " gives a good idea of it in the following description:

" For more than an hour," he says, " the waters around us seemed to be kindled into a blaze of light. The waves, as they broke along the rocky shore (of Sicily), encircled it with a glowing band of light, while every projecting cliff seemed circled at its base by a wreath of fire. Our boat opened for itself a passage as through some fused and glowing liquid, and left in its wake a long track of light, each stroke from the oar brightening the surface with a broad silver gleam. Water taken up presented the appearance of molten lead as we slowly poured it back into the sea. Everywhere, over this brilliant surface of calm light, myriads of dazzling green sparks and globes of fire were flashing, quivering, and dying amidst the undulations of the waves."

Another recent voyager, who observed the luminous appearance of the waves during a December gale, says:

" From the bow, two broad streams of greenish light passed along the ship's sides, and a similar stream followed in the wake of the rudder, extending fifty yards or more. This light was also diffused over adjacent waves, and at times the sea appeared almost covered with it when the crests of the waves were broken into foam. This green pathway of light was studded with sparkles of greater brightness which appeared for a few moments while gliding by, and then disappeared. At times, there were only a few of these stars, at others shoals of them."

The beautiful scintillations thus described arise from myriads of living creatures—microscopic animals belonging to the crustacean annelids and medusæ. They acquire, at certain times of the year, the property of emitting light at each muscular contraction, and hence every movement is made apparent by a luminous flash. On the coast of Sicily, ophiuræ—radiated animals allied to the asteridæ—are found, whose long and slender arms exhibit the singular property of emitting bright sparks when the animal moves. The eunice, too, under the microscope emits prismatic flashes of light when it moves; and the marine animalculæ, which Mr. Edwin Clarke examined, emitted light when violently pressed. The abundance of these singular forms of animal life in the Mediterranean waters has been attributed to certain peculiarities of this great inland sea, for, it being highly saline, contiguous to subterranean heat, and subject to few currents, its recesses have been thought favourable to their development. And as regards the saltness of the sea, it is a remarkable fact that it is more saline and of greater density than the water of the ocean. This peculiarity has been attributed to excessive evaporation; but, whatever the cause may be, water taken from a depth of four thousand feet, at about fifty miles eastward from the strait of Gibraltar, was ascertained to be more dense than ocean water, and to contain four times its proportion of salt.

The marvellous translucency of the Mediterranean waters contributes, of course, to heighten the beauty of its shores, and to surround its islands with charming illusions of sight that are, in many instances, quite in keeping with their fabled associations. M. de Quatrefages has well described how enchanting it is to float, as in an atmosphere, above the picturesque submarine world, and watch, as it flits beneath the boat, a vision of hills and vales, some clothed with the *flora* of the sea, others having bare and rugged sides, or being dotted with tufts of brownish verdure; and to see moving over the sandy ridges of the marine bed, or gliding past the edges of the rocks, or revealed amongst tufts of brightly-coloured weed and glossy, waving fronds, the strangely-formed and often richly-hued creatures that harbour in these marine retreats. To the hue and brightness of the Mediterranean water is, of course, attributable much of the enchantment which seems to be thrown over the marine grottos and other objects of coast scenery which tourists visit and writers celebrate, as well as many of those atmospheric effects which heighten the charms of form and colour in the rocky shore. In the work of M. de Quatrefages we find many scenes of natural beauty described with quite a poetic colouring; and as his coasting voyage in Sicily was made in an open boat, he was rewarded by many sights that would have been lost to any voyager who was not so borne upon the blue translucent wave. He describes, for example, the fantastic scenery of the coast to the westward of Castello di Molo, where the beach is formed of limestone, so highly porous that the force of the waves has undermined and broken it up into a perfect labyrinth of grottos, opening under semi-arches, garlanded by the cactus and other shrubs.

" In these submarine grottos," says our naturalist, " we saw a marvellous admixture of forms, colours, and effects. Irregular porticos with strangely-contorted pillars seemed cut out of colossal agates, and the most different colours were blended together, varied and contrasted in the most striking way. The narrow and deep fissures, in which the waves had only just rippled over the arches at the water's edge, were engulfed amidst the strangest and wildest sounds. The slight ripple caused by the boat sufficed to raise these singular voices of the shore."

But we must not linger on the coasts of Sicily to hear these wild syrens, for the limits of the present article forbid more than the very general and rapid glance we have now taken of some principal features in the physical geography of the Mediterranean, and we must not attempt to describe the picturesque scenery of its shores. Each sheltering bay

And glittering theatre of town,

each mountain height and ancient promontory that diversifies those unrivalled coasts from the caverned rock of Gibraltar to the historic capes of Greece, presents some memorable, beautiful, or noble object. What a succession of pictures rise to the mind's eye as we follow on a map the Mediterranean coast, and what striking contrasts do many of those portraits present! A few miles' breadth of sea separates continents utterly dissimilar in their inhabitants, aspects, and character; and the remains of Moorish dominion fill with most striking architectural contrasts many picturesque cities on the European shores of the Mediterranean, especially on the Andalusian coast,

Whose dark sierras rise in craggy pride.

It has been truly said that the East meets the West at the straits of Gibraltar, the European side of the picture being made up of its red-coated sentinels pacing their measured beat, its coal-wharves for English steam-vessels, its British diversions, and the appearance of Barclay and Perkins; and the Eastern side being formed by the African produce in its shops, its esplanade, where cannon-balls are piled among tufts of green palmetto, and the mixture in its population, of the Eastern Jew and the turbaned Moor. In memory, though not in a similar personal presence of its representatives, the West also meets the East at Ceuta, on the opposite shore, for that place recals the victory gained over the Moors by that illustrious prince, Henry of Portugal (son of Philippa of Lancaster, the sister of Henry IV.), who gave so great an impulse to maritime discovery on the Atlantic coast of Africa shortly before the voyages of Columbus, and who, in his retreat near Cape St. Vincent, drew around him men eminent in science and in Arabian learning. At Algiers, still more startling opposites are combined. There " the most lively of European nations " is seen in picturesque contrast with the stern, unbending Mohammedanism of the East; and to the contrasted figures of the French soldier and dusky Arab are added Moors and Turks, Jews and negroes, Maltese boatmen and German traders. There the banana and the English hawthorn grow side by side, and the honeysuckle may be gathered among the prickly aloes. Algiers —once the warlike, "the pirate's daughter"—is, happily, no longer the metropolis of piracy, for it has long been the resort of painters rather than pirates, and has been selected by the French for the formation of a noble harbour. It has been described as rising like a triangular town of chalk upon green hills, backed by the high and distant ridges of Atlas. Flat roofs, low minarets and cupolas, thinly interspersed with palm-trees, seem to proclaim the repose of an Eastern city; but the shipping in the bay, the lighthouse, and the French barracks, all tell of the activity of Europe; and, accordingly, the lower part of the town is full of busy life, whilst the upper part is in the impassive state of Oriental calmness. Algerine interiors, too, afford some striking contrasts. As far as regards mixture of races, Oriental features are likewise brought into startling juxtaposition with their opposites at Malta. But the architecture of bygone Arabian power, the horse-shoe arches and wreathed marble shafts, the open courts paved with porcelain and cooled by fountains, which are so characteristic of Moorish luxury, nowhere stand in more striking contrast to the edifices of Christian civilisation than in cities to be found upon the shores of Spain and in Sicily. If Venice preserves, in the Byzantine arches and bright mosaics of St. Mark's, the monuments of a migration from the Christian East that preceded the establishment of the Arabian power, some characteristics of Western architecture are henceforth to be prominent in Constantinople itself, for there—

   'Mid cypress thickets of perennial green,
   With minaret and golden dome between—

the early-English style of the British Memorial Church (which is to be adapted from the model of the church of St. Andrew at Vercelli) will permanently oppose the Crescent by the Cross. The characteristics of the West have also obtained a very decided footing in Corfu, and even amongst the ruins of august Athens. Only castles that crumble on the distant shores of the Euxine and the Levant remain to tell of the ancient maritime glories of the Genoese, whose harbour formerly bore such mighty armaments in days before Columbus opened the career of modern discovery, but now so peacefully reposes before "the superb" city in its crescent theatre of hills, its palaces and convents—so purely European in aspect—gay with terraced gardens, and crowned by forts and ramparts.

If space permitted, it would be tempting to bring together some more of the picturesque contrasts between the West and the East, and to linger amidst the natural scenery of the coasts that stretch from the gulf of Genoa to the bay where Naples rises circled by its panorama of mountains, its high romantic capes, and the serrated peaks of the Calabrian shore; to enter the bright portals of the East and glance at islands of purple Greece; to recal the train of historical recollections that dignify the wooded hills and towering castles of Corfu; or to trace, with Mr. Hamilton, amid the sands of tawny Africa and the mountains of Cyrene, the sites of the earliest of Greek colonies. All these places, and a hundred others on the Mediterranean shores, afford scenes of picturesque beauty and memories of undying interest to the Christian, the patriot, and the scholar; and it is not one of the least merits of Admiral Smyth's excellent work that these memories are everywhere kept in view with the physical features with which they are associated, and which are described by the gallant officer with so much scientific accuracy and professional knowledge.

# DIVISION II.

## ESSAYS, SCIENTIFIC AND MISCELLANEOUS.

# SCIENCE AND ROYALTY UNDER HIGHLAND SKIES.

[*Bentley's Miscellany*, Nov. 1859.]

THE British Association, which keeps the light of science burning like the Persian fire upon the hill-tops, has this year carried it towards the Highlands of Scotland, and in the prosperous seaport of Aberdeen it has lately sat enthroned, receiving the homage of a royal devotee, and attracting votaries from afar.

Founded twenty-nine years ago, for the purpose of giving a stronger impulse and more systematic direction to scientific inquiry, promoting the intercourse of its cultivators, obtaining a more general attention to its objects, and facilitating its progress, the British Association encourages an army of philosophers to go forth into the great realm of knowledge, following the various inductive sciences in their divergent roads, each division taking its own special science, but all working for the common object of discovering the laws of nature, and as pilgrims to the Holy Land of Truth.

In this age the philosopher is no longer a member of some exclusive fraternity jealously guarding the mysteries of science, but the cultivator of his special branch of inductive philosophy for the general use of man, labouring in a spirit of profound humility, and knowing that, though he should devote a life to his pursuit, he must still be a learner. For, as the Prince Consort in his appropriate and modest address at the Aberdeen meeting remarked, the boundlessness of the universe, whose confines appear ever to retreat and enlarge as we advance, strikes our finite mind with awe, no less when new worlds are revealed to us in the starry crowd of heaven by every improvement in the telescope, than when in the drop of water or particle of rock the microscope discloses new worlds of life, or the remains of such as have passed away. By the intercourse of the cultivators, the comparison, discussion, and publication of their labours, the knowledge acquired by the philosopher in his seclusion, and by the traveller in his journey, is made available for future students and for the advancement of knowledge. The geologist is aided by the chemist, the geographer by the naturalist, the astronomer by the student of physical laws and applied mathematics; and, instead of one mind being occupied with the thoughtful acquisitions of the past, as in the science of our youth, new thought is produced by the contact of many minds, and new relations are established between the various departments of philosophy. In one department, for example, that of " Zoology and Botany," a satisfactory proof was mentioned at the Aberdeen meeting of the more extended attention which has been given to the laws and phenomena of natural organisation since the first meeting of the Association twenty-nine years ago: zoology and botany were then represented by only five members and one paper, whereas no fewer than seven hundred and nineteen papers and reports in this department alone were read down to the close of the Leeds meeting in 1858. It is satisfactory to see this increasing recognition of the importance of animal and vegetable products to the use of man; such investigations, moreover, are full of interest and information, and continually illustrative of the power and beneficent design of the Creator. This is especially the age in which discoveries in applied science, or, in other words, the practical results of knowledge accumulated by scientific investigations, have been made of surpassing interest to mankind; but (as Lord Rosse remarked in his presidential address to the section of Mathematical and Physical Science) the gradual development of scientific discoveries, the steady flow of knowledge into the world, increasing like a stream as it proceeds in depth and breadth, serves more noble purposes than merely ministering to the physical wants of man, and their increase with the progress of civilisation. Even in the mechanical sciences, where principles are applied to practice, the results have often become stepping-stones for further progress. Again, in electricity, " every new fact opens a new field of research; and the power which we apply to our lightning-conductors, our telegraphs, and our lighthouses, promises to elucidate molecular attraction. This continual springing up of new discoveries in endless procession brings the rewards of industry to the encouragement of scientific labour, quickens the faculties of man, and inspires him with hope, teaches him to look both to the future and the past, and exercises on his thoughts the discipline of a moral training."

In Aberdeenshire the philosophers met nature in her wild and primitive form. They stood face to face with the stern, bare hills of crystalline rock, the crag and foaming fall, the wild forests in which the red deer roam, the wastes where only moor-fowl dwell amongst the heather, the dark mountain and the silent tarn, the wave-worn sea-coast and the sounding surge. They saw descendants of Celtic, Gothic, and Scandinavian races, of the ancient inhabitants of Caledonia—the people and the scenes that have ever formed a theme for poetry; and might put in contrast with the days when fleets of Vikings destroyed the infant civilisation of Apardion, and left memory of their ravages in *sagas* of the hardy Norsemen, the now populous and flourishing condition of the granite city at the mouth of the Dee. *Old* Aberdeen, once the city of scholars and salmon, if now deserted by the latter, and become a kind of old-world suburb to its modern rival, can still boast its university, whose characteristic coronal spire and mitred insignia fitly mark its ancient pride in the royalty and episcopacy of Scotland, and some remains of its still older cathedral. But the old town is quite eclipsed by the fine streets and the public and collegiate buildings of Aberdeen, which have been raised for the most part since the granite trade to London was begun by the brothers Adam in 1764, and since the development of the manufactories in which science unknown to the founders of the old university is applied to the use of man. The town is finely situated, and its buildings display the taste and public spirit, as well as the prosperity, of the inhabitants, and mark their pride in their fair and flourishing metropolis. Manufactories of linen, cotton, paper, quills, and combs, besides shipbuilding, and works for polishing the many-tinted granites of the district, were seen by the learned visitors; and Mr. Bothwell, in a paper " On the Manufactures and Trade of Aberdeen," gave some striking illustrations of the rapid development of its manufacturing industry, and mentioned some "things not generally known." It was at the linen factory established in the latter half of the last century at Grandholm on the Don that chlorine was first employed in Great Britain as a bleaching agent; and its introduction, according to Mr. Bothwell, was due to Professor Copland, of Marischal College, who, when travelling in France with Alexander Duke of Gordon, learned, on visiting the laboratory of Berthollet the French chemist, the effect of chlorine on vegetable colours. At Mr. Stewart's great comb manufactory (established in 1830), steam power was first employed at Aberdeen. From two thousand five hundred to three thousand different kinds and sizes of combs are made, and such is the effect of the application of machinery, that one thousand two hundred gross are produced weekly, and the combs which, thirty years ago, were sold for three shillings and six pence a dozen, now bring only half-a-crown a gross! Then there are the paper works of Pirie and Sons, where the manufacture of envelopes was first introduced into the North of Scotland, and where the machinery can now produce three millions a-week: and, appropriately enough, a quill manufactory besides; but, since the days of the penny postage, so many more people write, it is computed that all the geese in the world could not supply the unfeathered bipeds; and, but for the introduction of metallic pens, multitudes of people would have no pens to write with.

But the philosophers did not go to Aberdeen to buy combs, or only study the industry of the inhabitants: the physical peculiarities of the region were more interesting to *savans* the proper object of whose study is nature; and, accordingly, there was abundance of information as to its mountains, sea-coasts, and rivers, its *flora* and *fauna*, soil and climate, meteorological phenomena, and mineral productions. This, the first meeting of the British Association held north of the Grampians, had, moreover, the distinguishing feature, that, while the philosophers came to meet Nature, Royalty came to meet them. Probably all our readers have already perused the becoming and graceful address which the Prince Consort read to the general meeting on the evening of the 16th September, which inaugurated the business of the week—an assembly that, even to the Prince's eye, must have appeared brilliant and imposing. The presidency of his royal highness was a recognition of the high place which science occupies; an expression on behalf of all the British public of its interest in the labours of scientific men, and a sort of royal proclamation in favour of the British Association; and nothing could be better than that emphatic conclusion of the address, in which, after declaring that philosophers are no vain theorists, selfish pedants, or presumptuous unbelievers, the prince admonished them to humility amid all their achievements, by contrasting the humble limits of human discovery with the infinitude of Omnipotence. On the following day, when the royal president visited the different sections, it seemed as if the General Recreation Society had been at work and the whole population were making holiday. The sunshine was brilliant, and the people crowded the streets to view the strangers of the day. Within Marischal College, where the sectional meetings were held, the scene was curious; the prince's presence in any room gave a sudden attraction to the paper that was being read there, and even the ladies—the diligent votaries of geology and geography throughout the meeting—deserted those attractive departments for the time:—

> But O for the touch of a vanish'd hand,
> And the sound of a voice that is still!

The sections have been truly said to present in their external aspect a curious study, nearly all having their several peculiarities. The section of " Mathematical and Physical Science " and that of " Mechanical Science " are mostly composed of middle-aged and elderly men, calm, hard-headed, practical, and seldom having a lady to decorate their sittings. In the " Statistical " section you see a number of plain, slow men—sometimes a Quaker or two amongst them—men of self-denying tastes, gravely interested in prisons and reformatories, relishing arithmetical matters for their own sake, yet sometimes falling out much more amongst themselves than one would expect numerical matters to give occasion for. The " Geography and Ethnology " section generally has a large miscellaneous attendance, including a profusion of ladies, though seldom in these respects equalling " Geology," which is obviously, for the present, the favourite of all the sciences. The geological section (as a northern newspaper remarked), " being surest of a large audience, had the hall of the college assigned to it—a fine room hung with the portraits of old professors, ancient patrons, and eminent *alumni*, and now and for once a perfect flower-bed of beauty and fashion."

But to come to the business of the meeting. Not, however, that it is designed to make this article any report of the scientific business of the week, or even a *résumé* of the most noticeable of its features as regards scientific results; it is intended only to give an outline of the matters most likely to interest the general reader.

As to the Aberdeenshire of pre-historic times, some interesting particulars were stated by Professor Nicol. The formations of Scotland range under three geological divisions:—1. the southern district, forming the old Border-land, a region of mountain and dale, composed chiefly of the Cambrian and Lower Silurian formations, identified by *Trilobites* and fossils of the Llandeilo series; 2. the central region, composed of old red sandstone, igneous rocks, and carboniferous formations, and constituting a sixth of the whole area of Scotland, but supporting fully two-thirds of its population, and comprising the principal seats of its mineral wealth and manufactures; and 3. the northern region, composed of old crystalline rock, traversed by granite, and surrounded by a framework of later deposits, a region constituting two-thirds of the area of Scotland, but supporting only a quarter of the population of that kingdom. The granite forms not only some of the highest mountains of Aberdeenshire, but also the wild plains of Buchan. The mountains are for the most part massive and dome-shaped, are often bounded by lofty precipices, and enclose deep, black mountain tarns; and cairns of cyclopean masonry are found piled on the sterile slopes, now the sheltering places of the red deer and the ptarmigan. The pass on Mount Keen (about thirty-eight miles from Aberdeen) is two thousand four hundred feet above the sea, and in a section of ten miles from east to west there is a steady increase in the height of the mountains until a zone is reached in which few eminences are lower than from two to three thousand feet, while some exceed four thousand feet, the culminating point being Ben Muich Dhu (mountain of the black boar), which attains 4,320 feet, and is second in Britain to Ben Nevis only. It is characteristic of this region of mountainous heights, that the river Muich, in a course of ten miles from the lake of that name, in which it has its source, to its confluence with the Dee at Ballater, descends gradually five hundred feet. The dislocations produced in Aberdeenshire by the upheaval of these mountainous masses of granite, and the intrusion of other igneous rocks amongst the sedimentary strata, render it impossible at present to define the order and superposition of its formations. Professor Nicol maintains that the granite, though the nucleus of all this region, is not the oldest of its rocks, it having here, as in many parts of the Grampians, clearly intruded on the old sedimentary formations. A fine coast-section of the granite is seen in the cliffs south of Peterhead, which are fissured by long narrow gullies and deep recesses, ever resounding to the restless waves. The whole coast-line of eighteen miles, from Aberdeen to Dunnottar Castle (near Stonehaven), is also most interesting to the geologist: there may be seen cliffs of porphyries, and strangely contorted gneiss, and stratified rock tilted up by intruded wedges of granite; and Carron Point (where magnetic iron ore resembling that of Sweden is worked) is a study in itself. To the lover of the picturesque few objects are more attractive than Dunnottar Castle, that rude and ruined fortress on the great sea's edge, its rocky precipices still crowned by the old battlemented towers of the grim Earls-marshal of Scotland, their deserted chambers open to the sea-birds and the ocean spray, their vacant windows looking out upon the wide sweep of headlands where the surges "leap and fall." The diversity in the mineral character of the granite rocks, and the fact that they are sometimes traversed by veins of a different granite (as may be seen in the Rubislaw quarries near Aberdeen), show that granite is not all of one period or contemporaneous formation. The coarse-grained rock is regarded as having been formed at less pressure than the fine-grained granite, the pressure on which is estimated (by Mr. Sorby) as equivalent to seventy-eight thousand feet of depth. The gneiss rock has a wide extension in Aberdeenshire; it is generally found surrounding the granite, and sometimes forming the hills, while the valleys are of granite. In the hills north of Ballater it is seen side by side with the granite. The quartz rocks are found chiefly in parallel masses, and for the most part in the north of the county. The green-sand formation and the chalk flints, which are scattered over the rising country from Peterhead to Cruden, seem to have been once *in situ*, perhaps when all but the eminences of Aberdeenshire was below the sea. The beds of the Lower Boulder clay constitute another remarkable formation of this district: they were evidently deposited in an Arctic sea, round the shores of an ice-clad sinking land, when glaciers descended from the mountains and icebergs floated on the waters. In the peat-bogs also found in this region we have the remains of a more recent yet still pre-historic period, and in these formations have been found skulls with gigantic horns—the remains of the great fossil ox, which inhabited the forests of Caledonia, the *Bos primigenius*, which was probably seen living in the wild forests of Britain by Julius Cæsar, and in those of Germany when they were penetrated by the Roman legions—days when, according to Professor Owen, we may have had our own British lion!

Professor Nicol's subject forms only part of the larger province on which Sir Roderick Murchison—the veteran campaigner in the fields of Scottish geology—entered when he introduced to the listening senate of philosophers and fair ladies, who crowded the large Music Hall of Aberdeen, his Reform Bill for the reclassification of Highland rocks. Thirty-two years have elapsed since this eminent man, who had some time before quitted the army, entered on the examination of the rocks of his native Highlands, in conjunction with Professor Sedgwick; and very interesting it was to see at the Aberdeen meeting those eminent geologists as ardent as they ever were in their former fields, and to hear the Cambridge professor describe with all his wonted animation those stupendous dislocations amongst the rocks of Cumberland and Westmoreland which indicate such a wondrous intensity of action. So, too, in Scotland, by an intruded band of igneous rock, the ancient conglomerates and sandstones forming the base of the old red sandstone group have been thrown into vertical and mural forms on a great line of fracture across the country, in the direction south-south-west to north-north-east, marked by the great depressions filled by lochs which the Caledonian Canal has united. Without attempting to give any *résumé* of Sir Roderick

Murchison's discourse, which occupied a whole evening, and was elucidated by diagrams, we may mention a few points of general interest. The foundation-stone of Scottish geology, according to Sir Roderick, is gneiss, contorted, crystalline, and massive; and the Scottish lion must have been flattered by hearing that there is no rock in all this hemisphere so ancient as the gneiss of old Scotland; it beats the Cambrian hollow! The Cambrian formations, the oldest known rocks south of Scotland, are second in order of antiquity in the north-western Highlands. The pyramidal masses of dark red rocks which rise so picturesquely on the north-west Sutherlandshire coast (one of these weird hills towers two thousand five hundred feet above the silent loch) are rocks on which the Silurian formations rest—those old Silurian beds of crystalline limestone and stratified rock which contain *cephalopoda* and other organic forms, the remains of marine creatures in whose days not a vertebrate animal had been created. We understand Sir Roderick to be of opinion that these fossiliferous limestones of the west of Sutherland, though containing lower Silurian forms of life, may belong to the carboniferous epoch. Above them come the mica-schists of the Sutherland moors, and these are overlaid in geological succession by the flagstone conglomerates, which in Caithness are so bituminous from the remains of fishes that petroleum might be derived from them.* In the

* In the year following the Aberdeen meeting, Sir Roderick resumed his survey of the geological structure of the Highlands, and examined the west coast and some of the adjacent islands, including Isla and Jura, with the coast of Argyle, Inverness, and Ross, which, with the assistance of Mr. Geikie, one of his staff of the Geological Survey, he compared with his typical tracts of Duirness, Eriboll, and Assynt, in Sutherland. The general result of the labours of Sir Roderick in 1860 were the complete confirmation of his views, as embodied in a small geological map already published, and the correctness of which (great as are the changes upon all former maps which it indicates) has been testified to by Professors Ramsay and Harkness, as well as by Mr. Geikie. These changes are—1. That the gneiss of the west coast and of the Lewis is the oldest rock in the British isles, and is entirely distinct and widely separated from the lower gneiss of the central and eastern Highlands; 2. That this old gneiss is surmounted by red and brown sandstones, formerly mistaken for old red sandstones, but which are of the remote Cambrian age; 3. That the superjacent quartz rocks and limestones are of Silurian age and contain Silurian fossils; 4. That the great masses of gneiss, mica-schist, clay-slate, &c., of the central and eastern parts of the Highlands are the youngest of all these crystalline rocks; and, 5. That the old red sandstone of the east coast rests upon all these anterior formations.

Elgin district, a mass of white and yellow sandstones of marine origin are found, which have lately excited much attention from containing not only fishes, but reptilian remains. The first reptilian fossil discovered in these rocks was the air-breathing lizard, named *Telerpeton Elginense*, and more recently in the white Elgin sandstone several reptilian forms of high organisation have been found, and amongst them a reptile of crocodilian affinities, which formed during the Aberdeen meeting the subject of a very interesting discourse by Professor Huxley, who, after reconstructing a portrait of this formidable creature, introduced it by the descriptive name of *Hyperodapedon Gordoni*. If these reptilian beds are nevertheless still to be classed with the old red sandstone formations, the age of reptile life upon the globe must be carried back to a much more remote era than has been hitherto assigned to it. Land plants of great size, of which, until the recent discovery of a *Lepidodendron*, no traces had been recognised in Silurian rocks, begin to appear in the old red or Devonian epoch, and amidst these plants reptilian *amphibia* lived. After that epoch the Grampians and adjacent mountains probably formed an island, and on its southern shores grew the tropical flora out of which the coal-fields of Glasgow and Fife have been elaborated.

From a valuable paper read by Professor Owen, "On the Orders of Fossil and Recent Reptilia, and their Distribution in Time," it appears that late researches into the forms that have become extinct have shown how artificial is the boundary between the class Fishes and the class Reptilia of modern zoological systems, and that there are characters which indicate one natural group blending fishes and reptiles. The *Archegosaurus*, or primeval lizard (discovered, we believe, some years ago in the Bavarian coal-fields), had aquatic habits; and the characters of this representative of the oldest known order of reptiles assign it a low position in the class, and an affinity to the ganoid fishes of the Devonian series. The *Plesiosaurus*—an old acquaintance, a reptile with Lacertian affinities not in the head only—was better organised for occasional progression on the land, notwithstanding its turtle-like paddles. It is curious to see how in the *Pterodactyle*, or flying lizard of the Lias formations, the whole osseous system became modified to the possession of wings expanding twenty feet; but this strange creature must have moved upon the ground like a bat. The most gigantic of Crocodilians was the *Cetiosaurus longus*, caudal vertebræ of which have been found in the Portland-stone formations at Garsington measuring seven inches in length. Crocodilians with "cup-and-ball" vertebræ, like those of living species, are first found in Europe in the Tertiary strata: these lived in rivers flowing over what now forms the south coast of England. An enormous species of turtle, the skull of which is a foot in breadth, lived at that period at Sheppey, where its remains are found in the Eocene clay. There should have been also aldermanic giants on the earth in those days— veritable prototypes of Gog and Magog!

But more interesting than these curious traces of extinct *amphibia* was the statement of Sir Charles Lyell, in his address as President of the Geological Section, touching some recent discoveries in France, which affect the question whether man really was contemporary with the great tropical *carnivora* now extinct in Europe. The occurrence of weapons of human workmanship in association with remains of those extinct animals in cave *breccia* in certain localities in England, seemed to indicate that the era of man must be carried back much beyond the date hitherto assigned to the human period. A new piece of evidence, supposed to have the same tendency, was discovered in 1844, in a volcanic *breccia* in Auvergne: it was, the occurrence of parts of two human skeletons, embedded in the *breccia* in the environs of Le Puy en Velay. Sir Charles Lyell in the summer of 1858 examined the human fossils and their alleged site, and came to the conclusion that they afford no proof of man having witnessed the last volcanic eruptions of Central France ; had he done so, the human race would be older than the Siberian mammoth. Another piece of evidence has been more recently adduced from Abbeville and Amiens, in the north of France, viz. the discovery of flint implements associated in undisturbed gravel with the bones of elephants, as to which remains a clear statement was laid before the Royal Society by Mr. Prestwich, in the year 1859. Two of the worked flints were discovered—the one at the depth of ten, and the other of seventeen, feet below the surface—at the time of Sir Charles Lyell's visit, but not in his own presence. M. Pouchet, of Rouen, author of a work on the " Races of Man," has, however, since extracted one of these implements with his own hands, as Mr. Prestwich had done before him. The stratified gravel in which they were found is a fluviatile and post-glacial formation, and the area over which similar hatchets, spear-heads, and wedges have been found exceeds fifteen miles in length. Sir Charles believes the antiquity of these flint instruments to be great indeed, if compared to the times of history or tradition; and the disappearance of the elephant and rhinoceros (some bones of rhinoceros were found over the bed containing the flints) implies, in his opinion, a vast lapse of ages separating the era in which these implements were formed and the Roman invasion of Gaul.

In the discussion which followed, Professor Phillips disclaimed on the part of geologists any attempt to fix the duration of that interval, and pointed out that the contemporaneousness of the human remains with certain animals now extinct in the locality was all that these discoveries established.

So much for the department of geology. A paper contributed by Mr. John Stuart, of Edinburgh, Secretary of the Scottish Antiquarian Society and of the Spalding Club (which Aberdeen had the honour of instituting), " On the Sculptured Stones of Scotland," called attention to a class of antiquities which have lately excited much curiosity, viz. the rude pillars covered with symbols found in the district between the Dee and the Spey, and the sculptured crosses found from the Forth to Caithness, and especially in Forfarshire; and the former of which class of monuments, although not dating from pre-historic times, are, perhaps, the earliest existing works of art of the former inhabitants of Caledonia. The sculptured stones of Scotland form two classes; the one bearing symbols of a rude and simple character, such as the double disc, the crescent, &c., some of which are common to the Celtic races of the South of Europe and to the Caledonians, and others of which are found among sculptures in the cave-temples of India; the other class belonging to Christian times and resembling crosses, many of which are adorned with interlaced work, and some of which bear the ruder symbols found on the earlier sculptured stones. It is remarkable that the subjects sculptured on these upright stones in Scotland are secular, whereas the crosses of Wales and Ireland represent scriptural subjects. On those remaining in Scotland we have horsemen in armour, processions, a hunt in which an antlered animal is represented, and a centaur bearing a bough, which is a figure delineated on tombs in Etruria, and on some Etruscan vases. Fish also, and the serpent, are represented. Many of the symbols sculptured on these early stones occur in illuminations of the celebrated Book of the Gospels which was written and illuminated for St. Cuthbert, probably by Scottish monks, in the monastery of Lindisfarne. As to the unsculptured standing stones of Scotland, Mr. Stuart attributes them to the ancient Caledonians, who were overcome by the Scoti from Hibernia. The paper was appropriately followed by Colonel Forbes's Discourse on the Ethnology and Hieroglyphics of the Caledonians, whom he regards as an Indo-Highland people allied to the Celtic races whose monuments are found from the shores of India to those of Brittany, of many of which monuments he exhibited his beautiful drawings.

A most remarkable collection of objects of antiquity, illustrative as well of the Pictish, or stone period, as of later Scottish history, were brought together during the meeting at Aberdeen. The relics exhibited ranged from the stone weapons of the aboriginal inhabitants, through the weapons and objects of decorative art belonging to the Middle Ages down to the arms borne by the followers of "the Pretender." The collection of celts, hatchets, arrow- and spear-heads, hammers, and flint implements, seemed to bring the spectator in contact with the ancient inhabitants of Scotland, with the chieftain of pre-historic days clad in his skins or ox-hide, armed with his flint-barbed arrows, his stone axe, or his flint-headed spear, who felled trees and chased the deer in forests that have sunk into mosses or been cleared for the towns and trodden streets of men. Urns, exhibiting various degrees of progress in the art of pottery, were also exhibited; and, coming to the bronze period, which in Scotland, as in Scandinavia, is supposed to have extended over six centuries, a large collection of works of Promethean art was shown, including swords, spears, and battle-axes, gold armlets, and other personal ornaments. An early excellence has been claimed for Scottish art in the fabrication of metals. The weapons exhibited a remarkable uniformity of type; so, too, through the bronze armlets there runs a noticeable similarity of design—for example, that peculiar snake-form which has been regarded as especially belonging to the races of Northern Europe. There was a complete and interesting collection of brooches; some were Scandinavian, of elegant form, which were found in Caithness and Sutherland; and there were Highland brooches of every age and shape, but marked by that uniformity of style which characterises Celtic art. There was also a fine collection of old silver armlets; conspicuous amongst those of mediæval date was the jewelled silver armlet of the Campbells of Glenlyon, a work of rude yet sumptuous art, bearing the names of the three kings enshrined at Cologne; and there was the lord of Glenlyon's walking-stick, mounted with a beautiful relic of Roman art—a pair of eagle's wings. In mediæval weapons there were arms of every period, ranging from the old double-headed sword that might have been wielded against the Norsemen, through Lochaber axes, dirks, and daggers, rude cross-bows, and the later transitional forms of arquebuss, matchlock, and musket. One could not look upon these relics without recalling the state of Scotland especially in the sixteenth century, when the usages of polished life had but recently penetrated into the Scottish Highlands, and the population still retained the unlettered simplicity and the rude manners of mediæval days; when commercial towns were of no importance, the people generally vassals of feudal lords, and often at war amongst themselves; when sanguinary feud and Border warfare disturbed the land, and the Reformation mingled the elements of religious discord with civil turbulence. To the archæological curiosities of the collection were added a most interesting and unexampled series of Jacobite relics, miniatures, seals, rings, lockets, and other memorials of the royal house of Stuart, from Darnley's seal and Queen Mary's watch to relics of the last princes of that ill-fated line. Then, the wonderful collection of portraits which adorned the walls of the temporary museum during the meeting, brought before us most of the leading actors in events memorable in Scottish history: there were maids of honour to the Scottish queen, and historical beauties with the light of old romance about them; military leaders in troubled periods of the national annals; bishops and statesmen; the sourest of Covenanters and the most chivalrous of Royalists. To this collection of portraits were added some interesting autographs collected with a view to illustrate the civil and literary history of the country by the handwriting of men celebrated in her annals. It contained a complete series of the signatures and letters of sovereigns of Scotland from James IV. to Queen Anne; several letters of princes and princesses of the House of Stuart; and autographs of most of the statesmen and divines distinguished in the great rebellion.

And, while the archæological museum thus contained the relics of extinct dynasties, the visitor might examine in the fine geological museum, opened in Marischal College, the relics of extinct creations and pre-Adamite conditions of the globe.

But we must pass from these memorials of other days to some matters relating to our own, which were discussed in the sections. None of the subjects brought before the Geography section were more attractive than those which directed attention to the East. A very animated and agreeable description of Arab character and customs was given by M. Ameuney, a native of Mount Lebanon (who speaks English fluently, and pleased his hearers by mentioning that he had learned it in order to read the poetry of Sir Walter Scott), and who has come to Europe for the purpose of arousing sympathy and obtaining aid towards the social regeneration of the native Christians of his race. He maintains that Arabic was the original of Hebrew—at all events, that the children of Israel spoke Arabic when they went into Egypt, lost its purity during their sojourn, adopted many Egyptian words, and, after their return to Judæa, wrote their language in the form known to us as Hebrew. After adverting to our obligations to the Arab race for much of the learning preserved in the Middle Ages, and for the introduction of paper into Europe, he gave many traits of Arab life and character, representing them as a spiritual-minded people; he described their hospitality, honour, and brotherhood, and their love of poetry; he gave examples of its amplitude in the language of the lover, and stated that the production of sixty verses is deemed sufficient for the lifetime of a great poet.

A paper on the Russian trade in Central Asia led to some interesting statements. Russia, which had formerly a monopoly of the inland trade with China, has lately made treaties with that empire, and acquired vast territory in Chinese Tartary. The trade is a system of barter, and, to keep up the high price for Muscovite woollen manufactures, they put enormously high prices on Chinese productions, and pay three times the price for tea that we do. Russia has found an outlet for her fleet into the Great Southern Ocean by passing down the Amoor. Cities are being established and commerce fostered, and colonies of settlers are drawn from inhospitable Siberia to the Land of the Rising Sun. Sir John Bowring, who was present at the reading of the paper, expressed his opinion that Russia cannot compete with England in the Chinese markets; and, as regards tea, gave some idea of its enormous production in the Chinese Empire, by stating that a hundred and twenty millions of pounds are exported annually, notwithstanding that in every Chinese household tea is drunk five times a day, and the population has reached four hundred and twelve millions.

Mr. Lawrence Oliphant, in his "Notes on Japan," awarded to the Japanese people a high place among the nations of the East for civilisation and good government; he described them as sufficiently enlightened to appreciate a policy founded on higher considerations than commercial gain, and admonished the British people, that, having now opened to the world this prosperous and happy community, they deserve our care to win their confidence and respect. He gave a pleasing picture of the great natural beauty of the amphitheatre in which lies the port of Nagasaki—a name now for the first time made so familiar to English readers; the swelling hills around, terraced with rice-fields, the valleys clothed with wood and watered by gushing mountain streams, the projecting points crowned by temples amid sacred groves approached by rock-cut steps, cottages deep in foliage, and tasteful gardens bright with flowers. He estimates the population of Nagasaki at fifty thousand, and that of Yedo, the capital city of the empire, at two millions. The citadel or residence of the temporal emperor is more than five miles in circumference: elsewhere in Japan, the spiritual emperor passes a sub-celestial existence, reminded of his humanity only by his twelve wives, who are not spiritual. Some of the streets are lined with peach- and plum-trees; and there is a bridge of enormous length, which is the Hyde Park Corner of Japan, distances through the empire being measured from it.

In a discussion on changes of deviation of the compass on board iron ships, Professor W. Thomson urged the necessity for constant determinations of the error of the compass, and, as the only way of using the compass safely on board iron ships, recommended masters never to trust to it alone. Referring to the wreck of the Tayleur (a new iron ship), which disaster the late Dr. Scoresby attributed to a change in the magnetism of the ship, produced in consequence of the vessel being tossed about in a gale soon after leaving Liverpool, the Professor remarked, that this case appeared to corroborate the opinion now expressed by the Astronomer Royal, that new iron ships are liable to sudden and great changes of magnetism on being knocked about by rough weather at sea.

At the second of the two evening meetings of the Association, a crowded audience assembled to hear the reverend and eloquent Dr. Robinson, of the Armagh Observatory, lecture " On electrical discharges in rarefied media." How strikingly does our present knowledge of electricity, and its various ministrations to the use of man, contrast with the little that was known when the Greek mind was given to some electrical phenomena two thousand years ago ! Even after Volta's invention, sixty years since, of the potent instrument that bears his name, how wonderful has been our advancement! The brilliant experiments by which the discourse was illustrated were made by means of the induction coil machine, in which, as is well known, a length equal to six miles of wire is coiled in helix form round a bar of magnetic iron. The stream thus produced would probably pass through eighty yards of rarefied media as well as it did through the exhausted seven feet glass tube, in which the lecturer showed a brilliant auroral discharge of rose-coloured light *in vacuo*, which became surrounded, after a few moments, by a blue light of amethyst tint. The electrical current appears to differ remarkably from the solar ray in not having chemical power; but letters on a sheet of paper, the forms of which had been traced by a chemical solution, and which were invisible by the light of the room, started into brilliance in the electric light. In some beautiful experiments made with M. Becquerel's vacuum-tubes, from which hydrogen, oxygen, nitrogen, and atmospheric air, respectively, had been exhausted, different tints were produced, and a fine wavy stratification was shown. In another tube, a current rotatory *in vacuo* round a magnetic bar was shown, and the stratified light was deflected by the magnet.

At the evening assemblies, addressed by Dr. Robinson and Sir Roderick Murchison, and more particularly on the evening when the Prince Consort inaugurated this meeting, there was a brilliant and intellectual-looking assemblage; but the animated picture seen on these occasions, and on the two *conversazioni* of the Association, wanted the splendid framework of the Victoria Hall at Leeds (where, it will be remembered, the association met in 1858), the spacious new Music Hall of Aberdeen being almost destitute of ornament and colour. But it is a building well adapted to its purpose, and a great credit to the town.

The scientific labours of this busy week having been brought to a happy close, and Her Majesty having graciously invited that distinguished but somewhat numerous body, the general committee of the Association, to a luncheon at Balmoral, it was pleasant to see that they could shut up their books like any schoolboy, forget their learned convocations, and eagerly set forth with the sunrise on a bright September morning, to be the guests of their sovereign in her Highland home, and the spectators of Highland sports in the shadow of the mountains. Perplexed by "the hypothesis of Berkeley," wearied by "Chinese genealogical tables," escaped from a debate on "Indian finance," or some other Slough of Despond and Dulness; bored by "the classification of the salmonidæ," or by a Scotch missionary's history of some hill-tribe in India, or sickened by "the composition of Thames water," they doubtless thought "a system of moving bodies" was best studied in the progress of two hundred philosophers to a royal luncheon; that "the organs of the senses and the mental perceptive faculties" would be better understood amidst mountain scenery than in a crowded lecture-room; and that the distribution of *savans* over the slopes of Balmoral would be a refreshing contrast to studying " the distribution of heat over the surface of the sun," or " the connection between the solar spots and magnetic disturbances"—subjects discussed during the week.

> By Heaven! it was a glorious sight,
> When the sun started from the sea,
> And in the vivid morning light
> The long blue waves were rolling free.

This is not the place to expatiate on the picturesque beauty or historic interest of the country traversed between Aberdeen and Balmoral: suffice it to say, that Nature presented a very beautiful aspect to her votaries on that bright morning. The foliage had begun to be touched with the gorgeous tints of autumn; red and pale yellow charmingly contrasted with the sombre hues of the forest and the dark green foliage of the pine and larch woods. The steep, bare sides of mighty hills, grey with the stony *débris* of ages, were purpled by the heath-flower; and the shadows that chased one another over their expanse continually presented some new charm of light and shade, while in the blue distance the giant mountains reared their dark grey forms. Such a cavalcade of philosophers had never before been seen in these mountain solitudes; and great was the sensation when they alighted amongst the wondering inhabitants on changing horses at Ballater and Aboyne, and when, from the omnibuses of arkite dimensions, strange figures descended, some wearing hooded cloaks that seemed fit to cover some philosophic mystery, and all attired in anything but courtly costume. There were Oxford professors and Indian officers, grave divines and German *savans*, Scotch mathematicians and lively Irishmen; there were men who had grown grey in patient investigation of nature—inheritors of elder wisdom—scientific leaders who had won European fame; and they were going amidst the rude, unlettered mountaineers, and amidst the representatives of a patriarchal and unlearned state of society. Chiefs in science were to meet clans marching under Highland chieftains; victors in intellectual conflict were to see men competing for the prizes of strength and agility in the games and wild costume and to the primitive music of the ancient inhabitants of Caledonia. Yet many a master in science, gifted with the power to view unrolled the stores hidden from grosser eyes, and learned in the laws that hold the planets in their courses, may that day have envied those rude clansmen their health, and their freedom from smoke and crowds and cities, from ambition, and from wearing toil; and when they thought of the labours of the week in studying mathematical formulæ and applied mechanics— papers "On the Application of Quaternions to the Geometry of Fresnel's Wave-surface," on "The Theory of Numbers," on the "Theory of Light," on "The Dynamical Theory of Gases," or "The Mechanical Theory of Electricity," on "The Genetic Cycle in Organic Nature," or the "Statistics of Vaccination," may have been ready to exclaim,

> O! that I were a mountaineer,
>   To dwell among the Highland hills!
> To tread the heath, to watch the deer,
>   Beside the fountains of the rills—
> To wander by the lonely lake
>   All silent in the evening's glow,
> When, like a phantom, from the brake
>   Comes gliding past the stealthy roe.

At times the cavalcade was seen winding round the base of massive rock-strewn hills, now crossing a wide heathery moor, then mounting a height above the "rushing Dee," or skirting vast hill-side plantations of dark evergreen, and passing under avenues of the graceful weeping birch.

The Queen's mountain château, as the reader probably knows, stands on a mountain plain, skirted by the Dee, and is a building of varied outline in Scotch baronial style, built of a beautiful greyish white granite, dressed in ashlar work, with chaste and effective ornament, and presenting the bold aspect of an ancient stronghold in a tower eighty feet high, which gives dignity of outline to the structure, and from which the royal standard of England was floating to the breeze. It was a pretty sight to see this picturesque edifice glistening in the sunshine like a castle of romance; and, surrounded as it is by giant hills and far from any towns, it struck the eye with all the unexpected charm of palatial elegance in the midst of mountain solitude. The terrace and slopes on the west of the castle command a green meadow, on which the games and dances of the day came off; and beyond a beautiful mountain pass

> The steep, frowning glories of dark Loch-na-gar

close in the scene. On the southern side rises a vast hill clothed with wood, already tinted with gorgeous hues. On the north-west, a blue mountain range soars beyond the wooded hills that form the middle distance; and the valley between them was often filled during the day by driving mists, which the sun turned to golden haze as it declined. On the level greensward to the west, the clans were gathered under their respective banners in every variety of picturesque grouping: there were the Duffs (who carried warlike-looking spears), the Farquharsons, and the Forbes' men; various tents surrounded the square, and beyond stood the peasantry of the country round. The scene reminded one of the games provided by Menelaüs for his honoured guest, and the poet's description by a slight alteration applies to it:—

> Meanwhile, 'neath Loch-na-gar the Highland powers
> In active games divide the jovial hours;
> On verdant meadows with athletic art
> Some whirl the disc, and some the javelin dart;
> Aside, sequestered from the vast resort,
> VICTORIA sat, spectator of the sport.

Many tartans and military uniforms were mingled in the picturesque group of courtiers and visitors which surrounded her Majesty and the royal family on the grassy slopes of the castle terrace, to view the foot-races, games, and dances; and these characteristic features of Highland life, the old-world character of the games themselves, and the presence of the peaceful and learned Englishmen amid such sights, all placed the present time in striking contrast with the by-gone days, " when English lords and Scottish chiefs were foes." Nothing could be more picturesque and suggestive than the whole scene.

The philosophers, no doubt, acknowledged all its poetical

interest, but also showed great capacity to enjoy the good things to which they were invited; and when the time came to drive homeward amidst the mountains, lighted by the silent stars, they were again in the presence of Nature in one of her most impressive aspects; nightfall hid the sterility of the rocky wastes, and only the grand soaring forms of the everlasting hills and the dark woods were seen, with here and there a light twinkling from some hill-side shieling. And so returned the guests to Aberdeen, and so ended one of the most successful meetings the British Association has known.

# THE BRITISH ASSOCIATION AT OXFORD.

[*Bentley's Miscellany*, Sept. 1860.]

> I roamed
> Delighted through the motley spectacle;—
> Gowns grave or gaudy, doctors, students, streets,
> Courts, cloisters, flocks of churches, gateways, towers.

THE British Association for the Advancement of Science, which held at Oxford, in June, 1832, the first annual congress after its birth at York, returned in June, 1860, to that venerable seat of learning, in full maturity of vigour, to hold its thirtieth annual meeting. The cultivators of natural science, whose motto is " Progress," again met in the time-honoured University, whose traditions are so peculiarly classic, ecclesiastical, and retrospective, and whose genius, while looking to the future, seems ever mindful of the past. The students of nature assembled not only amidst objects of natural beauty, amidst libraries, museums, and collections illustrative of natural history, and among professors and scholars, but were surrounded by such buildings of historic grandeur, such objects of artistic grace, and such treasures of fine art, as can be found only in the queen of English cities. And the Oxford meeting had the added charm of contrast and variety, inasmuch as the Association met last year beyond the Grampians, in the remote capital of northern Scotland. Aberdeen has likewise, as everybody knows, its University and its High Street to boast, and it rejoices in those lions of the modern town, if it is not so proud as it ought to be of the religious and regal memories that cluster round the quaint half-deserted adjacent town of Old Aberdeen, once famous for scholars and salmon, and still dignified by the remains of the cathedral and the buildings of King's College, with their unique coronal spire. But the characteristic features of the past have yielded to the prosaic sights and sounds

of commercial industry in the granite city of the Dee, whereas
at Oxford the romantic character of the middle ages seems even
now to pervade the buildings which have there "been sheltered
under the wings of Time," and, lingering amidst the graceful
monuments of pious zeal and religious learning, still to throw
upon them all the dignity of age. In the aspect of the great city
of Aberdeen there is nothing distinctly academical: Marischal
College certainly cannot be called collegiate in its aspect; and,
instead of the grey pinnacles of shapely stone that have been
raised at Oxford amidst venerable trees, "into the midst of sailing
birds and silent air," the modern pile is closely surrounded by
the buildings of a busy and prosperous seaport. The High Street
of Aberdeen may undoubtedly boast the impressiveness of two
very long parallel lines of granite houses, grey, cold, and uniform;
but the High Street of Oxford presents a matchless variety of
architecture, and a succession of buildings adorned with the
graces of art and dignified by the witness of history; all differing
in form and character, but all picturesque and beautiful, and presenting a *tout ensemble* which has no parallel in the world. Father
Lacordaire, in recounting his impressions of a visit (in 1852), well
described in the following eulogium some of the aspects of this
ancient seat of learning:

" How calm and beautiful is Oxford! Fancy, in a plain, surrounded by uplands, and bathed by two rivers, a mass of monuments, Gothic and Greek; churches, colleges, quadrangles, por-
ticoes, all distributed profusely, but most gracefully, in quiet
streets terminating in trees and meadows. All those buildings,
consecrated to letters and science, have their gates open. The
stranger enters as he would enter his own home, because they are
the asylums of the beautiful to all who are endowed with feeling.
As you traverse these noiseless quadrangles you meet here and
there with young men in cap and gown, but no crowding, no
din. There is a solemnity in the very atmosphere, as on walls
darkened by ages, for it seems to me that nothing here is repaired, for fear of committing a crime against antiquity; and yet
you have the most exquisite neatness in all these buildings, from
the base to the summit. I have nowhere seen such an appearance of ruin with so much of preservation. In Italy the build

ings breathe of youth; in Oxford it is Time which shows itself, but Time without decay, and with all its majesty. The town itself is small, but even this does not take from the grandeur of the place; the monuments serve for houses, and give it an air of vastness."

Towers and spires and domes rising amidst clusters of foliage, seem (as Dr. Waagen, the art-critic of Berlin, observes) to proclaim from afar the Gothic glories of Oxford; and a first view of its buildings undoubtedly produces, as he has remarked, an impression that is ineffaceable. The preponderance and profusion of artistic beauty and sumptuous architecture give to its aspect such a peculiar character that the spirit of the middle ages might well seem to dwell spell-bound there, and to be still a living power.

We propose to give a *résumé* of the pleasant week which began with the speech of the Prince Consort, and closed under the presidency of Lord Wrottesley; and to any readers unacquainted with Oxford, it may be acceptable if we introduce our sketch of the scientific business of the meeting by glancing at the collegiate and other antiquities which brought the votaries of science in the year 1860 face to face, as it were, with the art, and learning, and piety of the past. And perhaps no monument of former days at Oxford can place the past in more striking contrast with the present, than that chief, if not sole, relic of what Oxford's noble Chancellor might call "pre-scientific" times, the old royal castle, which dates from the reign of William Rufus. "The massive arches broad and round" that remain in what was probably the crypt of the great hall, are characteristic of Anglo-Norman days; and from the existing tower—remarkable for its rude construction and peculiar form—the Empress Matilda is said to have escaped when besieged by Stephen; but the mound on which the castle stands is perhaps as old as the days of the Mercian kings. The adjacent locality of Beaumont, however, was the seat of royalty down to the time of the Plantagenets, and in it Richard Cœur de Lion was born, but no fragment of the palace remains. So likewise have disappeared the various other buildings once enclosed by the walls of Oxford Castle; among the historic associations of which it is memorable that in 1258 the barons here exacted from Henry III. those celebrated "Provisions," which, however objectionable on the score of abuse of power by the nobles and unconstitutional encroachment on royal prerogative, ultimately extended the constitutional liberties of England; and that in a parliament held (probably in the great hall of this castle) in 1264, the custom originated of choosing knights of the shire by assent of the county instead of the nomination of the Crown. It is characteristic of the times, that in one of the earliest parliaments (or councils of the realm) held at Oxford (A.D. 1189),* advantage was taken of the presence of the King and several bishops to disinter the remains of St. Frideswide, "the fair and perhaps fabled" inhabitant of the bowers of Woodstock in days of Mercian rule, and translate them to a shrine in the then new priory church, now the cathedral. In remembrance of what befel the Saxon prince who pursued the saint herself into Oxford, it had been for centuries forbidden for any monarch to approach her relics, and the humiliation of Henry III. by the barons at Lewes was superstitiously attributed to his indiscreet devotion in approaching the shrine.

But the latter part of Henry's reign saw at Oxford the rise of buildings and the establishment of societies that were destined to survive the edifices of feudal power, and to enshrine there for all future time the light of religion and learning. The latter half of the thirteenth century was an age of great activity and zeal in the foundation of halls of learning at Oxford, and saw the beginning of the great and venerable institution which has been for centuries so famous throughout the world. Most of the halls established at the period referred to had monastic bodies for their founders, who maintained there the scholars of the parent house sent to prosecute their studies at the university. And accordingly, while the realm was distracted by political strife, many a white line of cloistered wall was rising at Oxford amidst its wooded glades; but, although some of these monastic edifices appear to have had such architectural pretensions as to make their destruction in the sixteenth century a loss to art, they were very different in their constitution and extent from the stately and independent

* Oxford was the scene of a still earlier parliament, viz. in 1189, when the king was present.

collegiate foundations that to this day gem the university coronal. Probably they too gained by the taste for pictorial decoration which had so greatly extended in England at that time, and which adorned "the great chamber of the King" at Woodstock, "the private chapel of the Queen" in Oxford castle, and other royal palaces, as well as the religious houses, with artistic decorations in a style of which we have an example in the Painted Chamber at Westminster, and of which we can still form some idea from the contemporary specimens remaining in the Chapter House of the Abbey.

The representatives of the philosophical nineteenth century, when looking at the fragments which here and there remain of those first houses of the university, or at the building (near the bridge) which bears the appellation of "Roger Bacon's Tower," might think with allowable pride of the pebbles that have been gathered on the shore of the great ocean of truth since the days when the learned friar studied by the rippling Isis, and when Aristotle was the sun of doctrine to the university. From the present 'vantage ground of science, the attainments of the profoundest philosopher in the days of the Plantagenets may undoubtedly seem very small; yet we must not forget that an enlightened zeal for knowledge is then seen humanising an age of political strife, and that its architects brought, to honour the abodes of learning and grace the houses of God, a decorative art, which we are but humbly emulating in these days of scientific advancement.

A description of the colleges of Oxford would, of course, be foreign to the scope of the present article, and, indeed, a book might be written on many a college separately, so beautiful externally, so interesting in associations, and so rich in literary and artistic treasures, are those noble foundations; yet their more prominent features of general interest to a stranger may be brought together in a brief view. As several parts of Merton College are the most ancient academical buildings in the university, so, as regards antiquity of foundation, it would seem to have priority over the other colleges, for Walter de Merton, Bishop of Rochester and Chancellor of England, its founder, gave its first statutes in 1264. The grand old chapel, which consists of choir, transepts, and tower, the nave and aisles never having been completed, is a peculiarly dignified and beautiful structure; the choir, which has seven windows on each side, of fine Decorated work, was completed before 1277; the transepts were finished by Cardinal Archbishop Kempe, and the glorious tower was completed about 1424. Amongst the chapels of colleges, it is not, perhaps, too much to assign to the chapel of Merton the first place; and, à propos of the recent decoration of its roof and walls, Dr. Waagen says (and an accomplished foreigner's remark on such a subject is worth quoting), " I the more rejoiced to see such a work in progress [it was in 1850], as showing that the unfortunate prejudice which has banished art from the service of the Church, whereby all cultivation of genuine monumental art has been hindered in England, is now at last giving way." The buildings of Merton are remarkable for presenting some interesting specimens of early domestic architecture. At University College, a nearly coeval foundation (its statutes date from 1280), the want of ancient architecture is very disappointing, as this society claims King Alfred himself for its original founder, and has celebrated the six hundredth anniversary from its second foundation by the learned and munificent William of Durham, afterwards Archbishop of Rouen. It was not, however, until nearly a century later that the society became established on the present site, and the Edwardian buildings seem to have been in decay in the seventeenth century. Whosoever founded the first University Hall, University College has vindicated its right to the privileges of a royal foundation. It has always had a traditional connection with the north of England, and the library had for its first known benefactor Walter Skirlaw, Bishop of Durham. This part of the college is much indebted for its present creditable state to the judicious care and taste of the Rev. Dr. Plumptre, the present Master; and a new library in the Decorated style is now in course of erection from the design of Mr. Scott, much to the credit of the college authorities.

Neither do we find many actual remains of the old buildings of Balliol College, which had for its founder that great martial baron John de Balliol, whose widow the lady Devorgilla gave the original statutes in 1282; but there is a fine tower gateway of the time of Henry VII. The dignified though piquant-looking chapel of Balliol, as rebuilt by Mr. Butterfield, in which coloured materials are introduced externally as well as in the interior with good and original effect, adds a new work of beauty to Oxford itself. Then, at Exeter College, founded by that worthy prelate-architect Walter de Stapledon, who became Bishop of Exeter in 1307, few of the buildings have any interest for the antiquarian visitor; but its long stately front, with oriel windows and tower gateway, is worthy of this eminent foundation, and quite an ornament to the university. The new chapel recently built by Mr. Scott (at the cost, as it is understood, of 16,000*l.*) is the chief architectural ornament of Exeter College, and a splendid addition to the glories of Oxford. It is a lofty and dignified apsidal building, imitating, but with English features, the Sainte-Chapelle, in which pointed architecture seems to have culminated in France. The new chapel is a really noble monument of the *renaissance* of Gothic architecture at Oxford ; and its erection is another proof of the attachment felt by her sons for the foundations they inherit from elder days, and that her colleges are still animated by the spirit which in the middle ages adorned the university with the best achievements of art. The hall of Exeter likewise attracted many visitors during the meeting, it being a good specimen of a college dining-hall of the early part of the seventeenth century. Queen's College—the next in time of foundation—is architecturally remarkable only for the façade which forms so conspicuous an object among the palatial ornaments of the High-street ; but no parts of the college building date from the time of Robert de Eglesfield, the worthy chaplain of Queen Philippa, who, in her honour, designated his foundation here " the hall of the Queen's Scholars." At New College, however—that noble monument of the munificence and skill of William of Wykeham, Bishop of Winchester, its founder in 1380—the buildings remain, for the most part, as erected in his time and upon his plan. The chapel, which has been pronounced the pride of the whole university, the hall, cloisters, groined gateways, and many windows in different parts of the college buildings remain nearly as they came from the hands of the illustrious founder; and the feudal-looking tower, still adorned with its three canopied figures, is thought to have been his latest work. Probably (as Dr. Ingram suggested) it is because this foundation introduced the collegiate as distinguished from the aularian system, and thus marked a new era in college annals, that it is still called " New College "—a designation which does not prepare the stranger to witness the thoroughly medieval character of the best of its buildings. Magdalen College, which had for its founder another great prelate-architect, William of Waynflete, Bishop of Winchester, and Lord Chancellor in the reign of Henry VI. was meditated by him in 1457; but he saw the union of the Red and the White Roses before his work could be completed. The graceful belfry-tower, finished in 1505, combines with the western front to form an architectural group of most striking beauty. Considering the reforming rage of the sixteenth century, the foul atrocities with which Cromwell repaid the hospitality of the college in 1649, and that his myrmidons tore down and trampled on the stained glass from the chapel windows, and committed every outrage that fanatical hatred of religious and scholastic learning could dictate, it is wonderful that so much of the old building has escaped destruction. The quadrangle, containing the hall, chapel, and cloisters, is ancient, and there is a fine coeval entrance-tower; the west door of the chapel is rich and elegant, and the interior has been very successfully restored; but the most distinguishing feature of this great college is the lofty and wondrously beautiful tower, whose melodious bells are

> Still wont to usher in delightful May.

Contemporary with Magdalen College and the munificent founder's great works at Eton and Windsor, is the richly decorated and interesting edifice known as the Divinity School, built soon after 1480, in the time of Humphrey Duke of Gloucester, where, during the meeting of the Association, the section of " Geography and Ethnology" assembled to meet travellers from countries that were undiscovered, and to consider subjects that were not studied at Oxford, in the days when loving hands were encrusting these walls with a thousand forms of beauty. It is difficult to believe that this once gorgeous work can have been reduced to such a state after the Reformation, that nettles and

brambles grew about its walls. The architectural defects of
"the schools' quadrangle" and its strange eclectic gateway are
forgotten when we consider that it encloses one of the most
celebrated libraries of Europe (the Bodleian), and that in one of
the old schools, on the basement story, are some of the marbles
collected by the great Thomas Howard, Earl of Arundel.

The reign of Henry VII. was a time of great architectural
activity at Oxford, and to that period belongs also the whole of
the fine church of St. Mary, except the tower and spire and a
portion eastward of the tower. The original foundation of this
remarkable church is referred by tradition to King Alfred himself: at all events, its royal origin is made probable by the fact
that the patronage has belonged to the Crown from the earliest
times, and that St. Mary's has always been peculiarly the church
of the university. The beautiful spire, " thick set with pinnacles,"
a work of the Decorated period, was built under the care of Adam
de Brome, the first founder of Oriel College and almoner of
Eleanor of Castile, but the whole body of the church fell into a
ruinous condition in the time of Edward IV. and was, in 1492,
rebuilt by benefactions from all England. The incongruous
though picturesque south porch, with its well-known twisted
columns, is a seventeenth century addition. There are not any
old buildings at Oriel College (said to have taken its name from
L'Orielle, the building that was the first home of the society),
which was originally founded by De Brome,—Edward II., the
reputed founder, being but its foster-father. In Corpus Christi
College—the next house in order of foundation—the munificent
and learned Fox, bishop successively of Exeter, Bath, Durham,
and Winchester, nobly commemorated the devotion of his latter
days and his wealth to the service of God and the benefit of
future ages. Architecturally, the hall—a well-proportioned specimen of late Perpendicular work—is the most interesting part of
the college buildings, but the whole quadrangle is remarkable for
what has been called its genuine and characteristic aspect. No
member of the British Association could forget, amongst the
modern memories of these walls, that Dr. Buckland resided here
before his preferment. Then comes Archbishop Chichelé's magnificent foundation of All Souls' College, the long façade of which

forms so picturesque an addition to the beauties of High-street. The gateway and first quadrangle are contemporary and interesting specimens of Perpendicular work of the founder's time. His connexion with the earlier history of Saint John's College is not generally remembered. In 1437, about a hundred and seventeen years before the foundation of St. John's, Chichelé selected its site for a college, but he appropriated it to a body of Cistercian monks, whom he brought there to cultivate philosophical learning, and he founded All Souls' on another site. The tower of St. John's and its gateway—a conspicuous ornament of the picturesque entrance to Oxford from the north (St. Giles's Street), which, with its fine trees, resembles a Parisian boulevard—belong to the time of Chichelé's silent but not inactive Cistercians, and the effigy of their holy patron, St. Bernard, is still in its original niche; the hall (though modernised in windows and interior) was their refectory, and below it is the original crypt.* Of course, the good Archbishop's foundation, being, as it was, semi-monastic, shared the fate of non-collegiate establishments at the dissolution; but, in 1554, Sir Thomas White, the first London alderman and mayor who ever founded a college, bought the site and lands, and endowed a college under invocation of St. John the Baptist, to which he afterwards added the lands of the old Benedictine house called Gloucester Hall. But the founder lived in days of persecution; his president and fellows were scattered by Queen Elizabeth, and the college languished until the time of William Laud, afterwards Archbishop of Canterbury, who became its president in 1611. He

* While the more costly monuments of All Souls' and St. John's Oxford, and "the Oxford Tower" at Canterbury, tell of Chichelé's regard for his university and his diocess, the church, the college, the school, and the bede-house, which remain to give character to the little, faded borough of Higham Ferrers, speak no less plainly of the love he bore to his native birthplace. The church of Higham is invested with interest on account of its builder. It was in a neighbouring field that Henry Chichelé was found by William of Wykeham, as Giotto by Cimabue, tending his father's flock; and the prelate-architect and the painter each led his pupil to follow worthily in his patron's footsteps. Rising peacefully above the civil brawls of the fifteenth century, few calmer and nobler figures appear than that of Archbishop Chichelé's, who, in a boisterous age, with one hand laid the foundation of so many noble institutions of learning and charity, while with the other he manfully resisted the papal encroachments on the liberties of the Anglican Church. (Q. Rev. Jan. 1857, art. on Northamptonshire.)

employed Inigo Jones to build the inner quadrangle (the first quadrangle dates from White's time); and at this day the eastern (or garden) front of the library, which was built at the cost of the illustrious president, is one of the most picturesque of all the University buildings. Here, on the 30th August, 1636, Laud, then Chancellor of Oxford, entertained the King and Queen, Prince Rupert and the court, all of whom afterwards witnessed a play in the college hall. What a picturesque scene must have been presented at St. John's, when the gay costumes of the cavaliers, their lace collars, buff coats, and crimson scarfs, their broad plumed hats and flowing hair, mingled with the black academic gowns in these grey cloisters! Although the contents of the Ashmolean Museum were more interesting to physiologically inclined members of the British Association than historic memories and ecclesiastical relics, visitors to St. John's did not forget that to the chapel of his beloved college—successfully restored some years since by Mr. Blore—the remains of Laud were translated from the church of All Hallows by the Tower, and that here also repose the bones of the founder, and of Archbishop Juxon. Books with Laud's autograph, the stick with which he walked to his execution, and his portrait by Vandyck, are likewise treasured at St. John's. Lincoln College has some features of fifteenth-century architecture, but is chiefly interesting as a monument of the days when Oxford was in the diocese of Lincoln, this college having been founded by Thomas Rotherham, Bishop of Lincoln, afterwards Archbishop of York, and chancellor of the last Plantagenet king. Its chapel is a curious specimen of the Jacobean Gothic of Inigo Jones.

Then, passing to the colleges that were founded after the dissolution of monasteries, we come to the partly academical and partly cathedral establishment of Christ Church, that splendid monument of Wolsey's magnificent spirit, the most imposing of all the colleges in architectural extent, and whose long street façade, dignified by Wren's picturesque and well-known gateway tower, the home of deep-voiced "Tom of Oxford," is so prominent among the lions of the university. The kitchen, which remains nearly as built by the mighty cardinal, is said to have been the first building that was finished in the college—a significant recognition, certainly, of what Sydney Smith called the roast-beef basis of our English strength. There is not a more stately refectory in this country than the noble and beautifully proportioned hall of Christ Church (built in 1529); and the staircase, although built ninety years later, is remarkable for preserving Gothic forms, and for the lightness and richness of its fantracery vault, which springs from a central pillar like some tall palm-tree. The open timber-roof of the hall is one of its finest features; and the portraits that cover its walls are remarkable, not only as historical works of art, but for the long array they present of distinguished Englishmen who have been on the foundation of this unrivalled college. Historical memories alone remain of the priory of St. Frideswide, and of the twenty-two other foundations which were absorbed into Wolsey's new college; but the Norman church, which he altered for the collegiate chapel, placing on the choir its curious and beautiful vaulted roof with rich pendants, is the present cathedral. But very unworthy it is, architecturally, to be the mother church of such a diocese, for the choir and transepts only remain; the choir is narrow, it has no carved stalls or side-screens, and the whole interior is much wanting in dignity. Some of its singular architectural features led to the supposition that it was a Saxon building heightened and enlarged in Norman days, but no part is older than the latter half of the twelfth century. The Norman tower and early spire are remarkable, and the chapter-house (which has an enriched Norman door-way from the cloister), though small, presents some of the finest early-English work in the kingdom.* Proceeding to the other colleges of post-Reformation date, Trinity College is historically remarkable as the first house of learning founded after the dissolution of monasteries, and as the successor of that old college of the Benedictines which was connected from very early times with the great see of Durham, one of whose bishops—the celebrated Richard de Bury, the tutor and friend of Edward III.—bequeathed to it such an unrivalled collection of MSS. as led to his being regarded as the first founder of the university library. The picturesque and quaint buildings of the president's lodgings group with the fine yew-trees of the garden to form a picture

* The dedication stone of Wolsey's intended college of Ipswich is here preserved.

characteristic of the Oxford of other days, when her benefactors took such care that the serious pursuits of learning should not be without the cheerful solace of natural beauty and the adornments of art. At Brasenose (brasen-huis), founded in the time of Henry VIII., the tower gateway and hall retain their original character, but the chapel is a strange specimen of what has been called the unhallowed union of the Grecian and Gothic styles. Its materials, however, are worthy of respect, for they were derived from the chapel of the Augustine canonry of St. Mary, where Erasmus studied, and which occupied the site of "Frewen's Hall," the house lately selected as the residence of the Prince of Wales while pursuing his studies at the university. At Wadham College, which was completed in 1613, and succeeded to an old Augustine priory of which no portion remains, the windows of the chapel are in such good taste and style as to have been mistaken for monastic work, and the hall has a timber roof and fine oak screen. The college which commemorates the name of William Earl of Pembroke rose, like some other colleges, on the ruins of an earlier academical foundation. Pembroke College dates from 1614, but none of the buildings seem as old even as the time of the Restoration. The hall, however, should not be forgotten in this retrospect, for a distinguished circle was there received by the Vice-Chancellor, and Pembroke was the only college at which any general reception took place during the meeting. Lastly, as the most modern of the nineteen colleges and five halls of Oxford, comes Worcester College, which was founded at the close of the reign of Queen Anne, upon the site of Gloucester Hall, one of the earliest foundations for religious learning, and is remarkable for the beauty of its gardens rather than its edifices.

But we must not detain the reader any longer amongst these academic buildings: Oxford is accustomed to look to the past, and it is hardly possible to mention the colleges amongst which the members of the British Association met in 1860, without falling into the retrospective mood. Our brief survey of their chief architectural features cannot, however, be concluded without deploring that so many examples of the debased architecture of later times deface the mediæval beauty of Oxford, and that its buildings have suffered, not only from the abortive attempt made after the restoration of Charles II. to revive Gothic forms, but from the tasteless, ignorant, and presumptuous attempts that were made during the Georgian period—that long dark age of architectural debasement. Nevertheless, the eighteenth century did add to the ancient buildings of Oxford two of its most remarkable and important edifices, viz. the stately Sheldonian Theatre and the spacious Radcliffe Library—a building of imposing style and dimensions, the more remarkable for the contrast a circular temple in the classic style of architecture presents to all that here surrounds it. But as a perishable free-stone was unfortunately used for the rebuilding, enlargement, or repair of many of the colleges in the seventeenth and eighteenth centuries, the masonry of most of the buildings is in a state of ruinous decay and discoloration, and the destructive hand of Wyatt, in his so-called restorations in more recent days, has done more mischief than that of Time. Yet, although the forms of the university buildings may thus have changed, the great institution itself happily remains in its original character and force, exercising its privileges, bestowing its honours, and fulfilling the high purposes of its mission.

Of course a volume might be devoted to describing only the more remarkable of the literary treasures in the college libraries. Most of them contain ancient manuscripts, and many a volume is adorned with illuminated drawings and miniatures of great value in the history of art—productions that occupied perhaps a lifetime, and commanded in former days as high prices as are now given for fine pictures. And while, in the college libraries of Oxford, books place her students in familiar intercourse with the master spirits of the past, so from many a college hall the worthies of former generations, whose portraits adorn the walls, seem to be looking upon the votaries of learning; and as in the streets of Rome the country's gods were everywhere set up to remind her citizens of moral obligations, so at Oxford illustrious men seem ever encouraging her students to follow their good example. Then, too, there are the university galleries of paintings and antique sculpture, and that wonderful domain of books, the Bodleian Library, with the celebrated manuscript and other treasures of whose lengthened galleries the exclusive devotion of the whole week would not have sufficed to acquaint a visitor. To the capacious archives of Bodley's Library, by the way, the whole Ashmolean collection of MSS. has lately been transferred.

More attractive, however, than the architecture, the libraries, the old plate,* or the other historical relics of the colleges of Oxford, were those sequestered gardens which constitute their distinguishing charm, and are never seen to such advantage as in Commemoration week, or on a gathering like the present, when the cool glade and the "shadow-chequered lawn" are lighted up with many a bright glow of colour, and animated by many a graceful form. The delicious gardens of the colleges set the antique, time-worn, edifices amidst the ever-renewing loveliness

* Few of the college treasures are more attractive than the old plate, but it is of course only shown as a matter of favour. In this particular, the university suffered in succession from both parties in the contest between Charles I. and his parliament. After the battle of Edge Hill, the king established his court at Oxford and his mint at New Inn Hall, whither, in January, 1643, the loyal but reluctant colleges and halls brought their plate to be coined into money "for his Majesties use," and an enormous quantity in the aggregate must have been obtained. Thus, Wadham College alone gave up a hundred pounds' weight of silver plate, and twenty-three pounds of gilt plate. There had not been such spoliation since the days of Henry VIII., when that royal miscreant despoiled the monasteries. Some of the colleges managed, however, to preserve a few relics, now highly prized, and celebrated as specimens of mediæval goldsmith's work. At their respective foundations of New College and Corpus Christi are preserved the magnificent pastoral staves of Wykeham and Fox ; the former is especially remarkable for its elaborate canopy-work, enamelling, and jewelled ornaments. Amongst the sacramental plate at All Souls' are two silver-gilt flagons, the covers formed of a swan's head and neck—the heraldic cognizance attributed to Archbishop Chichelé; and here, too, is his silver-gilt and crystal salt-cellar. At Corpus are the silver-gilt salt-cellars and cups of the founder (whose device of a pelican is repeated on one of them), and other cups and tankards, older than any of the college buildings, besides a fine pyx, and a beautiful chalice of silver-gilt, the founder's gift. At Trinity College is preserved a fine fifteenth-century chalice, saved (by the founder) from the spoils of St. Alban's Abbey. The buffalo horn, mounted with silver-gilt bands, preserved at Queen's College, and said to have been the gift of Queen Philippa herself, is thought to have been originally employed for convening the members of the foundation (who by the statutes are to be called together by sound of horn), but it is used as a drinking-horn on days of festivity. At New College are several silver-gilt cups of elaborate work, and a chased silver-gilt salt-cellar, given in 1493, besides the silver seal which was engraved in Wykeham's time; and at Oriel there is a silver-gilt cup attributed to Edward II., though not of so early a date, and a cocoa-nut cup set in silver, given by Bishop Carpenter, provost, in 1470.

of nature, and relieve with bright verdure and noble trees the grey lines and angular forms of the buildings. After sedulously attending the scientific discourses in the sections, and witnessing the intellectual conflicts that occasionally animated the proceedings, it was especially refreshing to seek the college gardens; to wander beneath the leafy arcades of Magdalen, or view the pleasing landscape, varying at every step, in Christ Church meadows, on the banks of Isis and Cherwell; or see from the beautiful and tastefully disposed gardens of St. John's, where the stately chestnut trees wave above the shady lawn, the many picturesque views of college buildings, round which memories cluster as thickly as their ivy; or seek the meditative seclusion of Wadham, or the gardens that surround Wykeham's graceful architecture with perennial beauty; or wander where the bright lake ripples on its green margin in the ornamental grounds of Worcester.

Such, then, are the historic and suggestive scenes amidst which the representatives of natural science assembled. But a new and most attractive building of another kind, and of peculiar interest to the members of the British Association, has lately risen under the tutelage of the university—we mean the OXFORD MUSEUM; and we must briefly glance at its structure and purpose. This ambitious building proclaims both the revival in Gothic architecture and the resolution of the university that from henceforth the knowledge of natural phenomena and of the laws which govern the constitution of the earth and its inhabitants shall be engrafted on Oxford studies.* The building, which has been erected on Mr. Woodward's prize design, is quadrangular, enclosing a great central area. Externally it presents on the chief front a long façade of windows in Italianising Gothic style, in two tiers, pointed roofs, and central high-capped tower. Inside, the area is lighted by a glass roof, and surrounded on the basement and on the upper story by a pointed arcade, opening to corridors on each side of the square, and they give access to lecture-rooms and professors' apartments, in which utility and fitness seem to have been judiciously studied. This area is destined for the display of various collections in Physiology

---

* The introduction of geological studies into the university of Oxford is due to the lectures delivered between 1805 and 1810 by Dr. Kidd, Professor of Chemistry.

and Natural History; à propos to which, we are glad to see that the promoters desire to bring into conjunction with them a library of books on medicine and physical science. This part of the structure presents a bold and novel attempt to combine the iron-work of this materialistic nineteenth century with the graceful stone architecture of the middle ages; for we have here wrought-iron banded shafts for the piers and iron arches and spandrils, so that the spacious Exchange-like area presents a forest of slender pillars, expanding, far above, into interwoven branches, with leaf, and flower, and fruit boldly and truthfully wrought in the same material. The selection and arrangement of the British marbles which form the shafts in the two tiers of open arcades, is an instructive as well as striking feature of this building, and here science and art have been—as was fitting—most happily combined. Thus, on the western side of the arcade, the shafts are of various granitic rocks; on the south, of our native British marbles (still too little known); on the east, of trap rocks; and on the north, of Devonian and Irish mountain limestones; so that this part of the building is itself a systematic exhibition of natural objects. Then, in the sculptured decorations, it is full of beauty and promise, the style of ornamentation selected being less conventional than founded on natural forms and produced by the workman's imitative powers as exercised on objects gathered from Nature; yet there is in some of the details too little of conventional restraint, or, in other words, of the spirit in which Gothic architects expressed natural form. The capitals and bases, too, are peculiar, inasmuch as they represent groups of plants and animals of various epochs and climates, arranged according to their natural orders. The statues of illustrious discoverers or cultivators of the various branches of natural science to which the edifice is dedicated, which have been contributed by her Majesty and by the friends of the undertaking, and are placed on brackets in front of several of the arcade piers, add greatly to the animated and pleasing effect of the interior, and fitly associate the sister arts of architecture and sculpture. The design of this building is undoubtedly lofty and original, the execution is in the highest degree meritorious, and the outlay upon it has been very great, the cost of the fabric and fittings being understood to amount to 65,000*l.*; yet it is unfortunately marked by a rigidly restrained economy in many parts where expenditure was essential to effect and grandeur, and the long façade presents an unpleasing flatness, which, however, would be greatly relieved by a bold central porch. The Oxford Museum nobly inaugurates the new order of things in university education, and, whatever the success of that change may be, presents at all events a splendid proof of Oxford's good will to the important studies connected with Natural History.

In the days of the founders and benefactors of her colleges, physical science had no especial schools, professors, or students, and university education did not profess to aid the learner—as he is henceforth to be aided—"in acquiring a general view of the planet on which we live, of its constituent parts, and of its relations, as a world amongst worlds; and in studying in the most scientific manner, and with a view to any pursuit, any detailed portion which his powers qualify him to grasp." As Professor Faraday has observed, education in science teaches us, first by tutors and books to learn that which is already known to others, and then by the light and methods which belong to science to learn for ourselves and for others—to render fruitful for men in the future that which has been obtained from the men of the present or the past; and the promoters of the Oxford Museum exemplify the principle taught by Lord Bacon, that the scientific student ought not to be as the ant, who gathers merely, nor as the spider, who only spins, but rather as the bee, who both gathers and produces. On this meeting of the British Association the building afforded ample accommodation for the natural history sections, and was an object of novel attraction to the visitors who thronged it, as well in the daytime as in the evenings when it was opened for general receptions or conversazioni. On the last of those meetings there was a perfect feast of microscopes, and it seemed as if there had been a general levy of these instruments throughout England.

The meeting was inaugurated by an admirable address from Lord Wrottesley, as president, delivered to a brilliant and crowded audience in the Sheldonian Theatre, and we shall endeavour to give an outline of its principal topics. He opened his address by placing in striking contrast with the present condition of science the state and teaching of science in the university in 1814, when he was a pupil at Oxford, remarking that he regarded the School of Physical Science lately instituted, and the prizes now founded for encouraging its cultivation, as full of hope for the future. The noble President adverted to the progress of astronomy, and to the labours of the private observers—voluntary rivals of the public observatories—whose labours have been chiefly devoted, first, to the stars—those "landmarks of the universe," other than the brighter stars, about a hundred in number, whose places it is the province of the public observer to establish, and to mapping the smaller stars; secondly, to the positions and relative distances of double or multiple stars; thirdly, to the nebulæ; fourthly, to the minor planets; fifthly, to comets; sixthly, to observations of the sun's spots and other solar phenomena; and seventhly, occultations of stars by the moon, eclipses, &c. The observations and cataloguing of the smaller stars, and the comparison of the results obtained at different and distant periods, have revealed the wondrous fact that the sun itself does not occupy one fixed spot in the universe, but is constantly moving (at the supposed rate of eighteen thousand miles an hour) towards a point in the constellation Hercules, carrying with it the whole planetary and cometary system. Many of the double or multiple stars, appearing single to the naked eye, are in fact suns, and probably systems. As regards the cataloguing and mapping of the stars, it may be mentioned that Dr. Robinson's catalogue gives the places of more than five thousand stars, whereas the catalogue of Flamsteed, first Astronomer Royal at Greenwich, contained about three thousand only. Still more than even these distant and distinguishable bodies, do the nebulæ—those mysterious starry clouds of light—afford an overwhelming view of the infinitude of space. The noble president referred to the unrivalled instrument erected by Lord Rosse, and the curious discovery that some of these nebulæ are arrayed in a spiral form, and mentioned the powerful instrument just finished by Mr. W. Lassell, the discoverer of Neptune's satellite. He then passed to the observations of comets, and mentioned that the important and unexpected fact that at each successive approach the comet of Enckè arrives at its perihelion sooner and sooner, has led to the supposition that space is pervaded by a rarefied atmosphere or ether, which does not exercise a perceptible effect on the solid planets, but influences the more attenuated bodies moving with great velocity, the effect of the resistance being to allow the attractive force of gravity to draw the comet nearer to the sun, and thus to continually contract the dimensions of its orbit and augment its velocity, as if, said the President, the comet, circling like a celestial moth round the great luminary, were destined to be mercilessly consumed. We could not but think of the ancient (astronomical) fable of the phœnix, which, after a wandering life of fourteen hundred and eighty-one years, was to return to die, consumed by the rays of the sun in the Temple of Heliopolis. Lord Wrottesley mentioned the suggestion of Professor W. Thomson, that the heat and light of the sun may be from time to time replenished by the absorption, not only of comets, but of the countless meteors which circulate round it. Herschel, it is known, regarded the zodiacal light as "a tornado of stones." The phenomenon witnessed in September 1859 by Mr. Carrington and Mr. Hodgson would seem to show that the process of feeding the sun by the fall of meteoric matter was actually then beheld. The next astronomical topics of general interest adverted to were the recent observations of the spots and peculiar appearances on the sun's disc, and the indications of a connexion between magnetic phenomena on the earth, and events taking place upon the surface of the sun; and the remarkable fact was mentioned that a moderate but marked magnetic disturbance occurred at the time of the apparent absorption by the sun of two bright meteors, as witnessed by Mr. Carrington and Mr. Hodgson.

Then, from wandering on the dim confines of the unknown, the President, after referring to the means of rendering more conducive to science the government expenditure of 1000*l.* a year for scientific objects, passed to chemical science, and mentioned the activity which had been displayed, especially in the organic department of chemistry. Among its practical applications, he instanced the beautiful dyes now extracted from aniline, an organic base formerly obtained as a chemical curiosity from products of the distillation of coal-tar, but now manufactured as an article of commerce, in consequence of the demand for "mauve," "Magenta," and "Solferino," which are prepared by the action of oxidising agents (as bichromate of potash, corrosive sublimate, and iodide of mercury) upon aniline. We are sorry to say, that, in a paper read by Professor Voelcker in the Chemical Science section, a very different application of chemical agents was described—viz. the employment in some of the dairies of Gloucester and Wilts of sulphate of copper or sulphate of zinc in the making of cheese. In Geology, the principal topic discussed in the President's address was the bearing of recent discoveries in the valley of the Somme, in Picardy, on the question of the high antiquity of man. Rude flint implements, unquestionably of human workmanship, have been found (at Abbeville and Amiens) in such a position in old fluviatile formations as to show that these weapons are at least as ancient as a great mass of alluvial gravel which stretches between those cities, and sometimes contains, and sometimes occurs under beds containing, fresh-water shells and remains of a foreign and extinct *fauna*, beside bones of the mammoth, an extinct species of rhinoceros, and an extinct species of deer, probably the contemporaries of the deposit of these flints. Their high antiquity is also inferred from the changes which the physical geography of the country has subsequently undergone, and which are of such a character as to testify a slow lapse of geological time. Moreover, the accumulation of those deposits of peat in the valley of the Somme which belong to pre-historic times, and contain monuments of the Celtic period, has been subsequent to the formation of the uppermost of the alluvial beds overlying the gravel. In connection with this subject, Lord Wrottesley referred to the flint implements observed by Dr. Falconer in caves at Brixham and at Palermo, associated in such a manner with bones of extinct mammalia as to indicate that man co-existed with certain lost species of quadrupeds. The Amiens flints were described and exhibited at the Aberdeen meeting, but their discovery did not form at Oxford, as it did at Aberdeen, the subject of more than incidental discussion in the sections. Similar flint implements have been found on a Mediterranean shore, and also in Terra del Fuego, as Admiral Fitzroy took occasion to remark in the Geography and Ethnology section. Another topic of general interest adverted to in the address was, the more extended and successful application of chemistry, physics, and collateral sciences to the study of the animal and vegetable economy, and the progress made in scrutinising animal structures by the microscope, and in extending our knowledge of the functions of the nervous system. Well might such a survey be concluded by the remark, that the secret forces which retain the planets in their course, the boundless extent of space, the means by which light and heat are conveyed through unfathomable distances, the subtle agencies of electricity, the beauties and prodigies of contrivance displayed by all animals and plants, and the geological changes of our planet, all present such marvels and mysteries as must ever task the highest efforts of the mind!

The scientific business of the week thus inaugurated was, of course, for the most part transacted in the sections, but was also marked by an admirable discourse from Professor Walker on the present state of our knowledge of the sun, addressed to a brilliant assemblage that again crowded the Sheldonian Theatre, and by an interesting discourse by Captain Sherard Osborn on Arctic discovery. In such a paper as the present it is impossible to give any outline that could convey a just idea of Professor Walker's discourse; it must suffice to say, that it presented a masterly view of what is known of the sun. Perhaps no parts of the discourse were more interesting than those in which the Professor adverted to the still unresolved questions whether comets are the aliment of the sun, whether aërolites and meteoric stones do fall into it, and by what means its light and heat are uniformly maintained; and in which he treated of those dark shallows or cavities in the phosphorescent atmosphere of the sun called spots, and of their now ascertained periodicity, or, in other words, their decennial cycle of maximum development—a phenomenon of periodicity with which magnetic disturbances remarkably coincide. The sun's action on the needle is unconnected with heat, but, as regards the meteorological influence of the spots, it is remarkable that a year of greater spots appears also to be one of greater moisture. In describing the appearance and magnitude of the solar spots, the professor stated that one of them seemed to be a cavity large enough to hold the earth. He gave a good idea of the attractive force exerted by the enormous bulk of the sun by stating that upon the solar surface a man would weigh two tons! The attendance in the sections, throughout the meeting, showed that they also exert a great attractive force: these constitutional chambers of the association were sedulously attended, as at former meetings, not only by the habitual votaries of science, but by the ladies, for it is the pleasantest feature of these gatherings that we always find "beauty ministering to philosophy."

We cannot here attempt anything like a report of the scientific business of the week. We can only select, and for very brief notice, those papers which afforded matter of general interest. In the "Mathematical and Physical Science" section, some of the most scientific papers read were on such subjects that no idea of the contents could be conveyed in a popular sketch, and the same remark applies to the sections of "Chemical Science," "Mechanical Science," and "Zoology and Botany."

Two papers relating to atmospheric phenomena that were read in the first-mentioned section may however be mentioned. The one was the Report on Observations of Luminous Meteors by the late able Professor of Geometry Professor Baden Powell, continued by Mr. J. Glashier, in which he considered the three current modes of accounting for the luminosity of meteors. These, as stated by Mr. R. P. Greg, are, first, the supposition that they are opaque bodies illuminated by the sun's light after emerging from the earth's shadow, a theory to which there are grave objections; second, that they are self-luminous, an opinion now almost abandoned; and, third, that they become incandescent in the earth's atmosphere. A considerable portion of the report was devoted to the large meteor seen in sunlight over a considerable portion of the United States on the 15th November 1859, which seems to have had a velocity of at least thirty miles a second. The other was a paper by Admiral Fitzroy, " On Storms on the British Coast," in treating of which he described the gale of the 25th and 26th October 1859, (in which the *Royal Charter* was lost), and its attendant phenomena of cyclonic commotion, and referred to diagrams representing, as it were, soundings in the atmosphere, and showing that the pressure was exerted over large areas rather than particular lines. In that fatal storm the wind attained a maximum velocity of from sixty to a hundred miles an hour! He adverted to the power of the mountain-ranges of Wales and Scotland to alter the direction, and probably the velocity, of the wind; and, on a review of the investigations of Dr. Lloyd and Mr. William Stevenson, deduced that storms which come from the west and north come on gradually, but that those from the south and east begin suddenly, and often with extraordinary force. Of these the barometer does not give notice, but the thermometer affords some indications. Amongst the signs which preceded that particular gale, were great electric or magnetic storms in the atmosphere. The gallant admiral referred to the recent extraordinary storm near Calne, which transcended the supposed feats of the spiritualists with tables, for it lifted a broad-wheeled waggon from the road over a hedge into the next field; and he explained in detail the arrangement by which, under government authority, warning of storms will be communicated by telegraph from one part of the country to another, and the mode in which the signals will be visibly repeated along the coast, by which means, it is hoped, the shipwrecks that too often strew our coasts may be diminished.

In the " Zoology and Botany" section a crowded audience was attracted, and a lively debate was led to, by a paper in which the startling theories of Mr. Darwin, as to the development of species by what he calls " natural selection," came into discussion. It was a paper by a Dr. Draper of New York, " On the Intellectual Development of Europe;" and the author, referring to the views of Mr. Darwin and others, that the progression of organisms is determined by law, attempted to draw a parallel between the intellectual progress of man and the physical development of the lower animals. Mr. Darwin's theories were eloquently and vigorously opposed by the Bishop of Oxford, who was supported by the views expressed by Professor Owen himself, and by Sir Benjamin Brodie and other eminent naturalists. Dr. Hooker explained that Mr. Darwin's theory does not assert the transmutation of existing species one into another, which is quite a different thing from the successive development of species by variation and natural selection, an hypothesis which he considered to be strongly countenanced by the characteristics of the vegetable kingdom, but Dr. Hooker reserved liberty to resume his allegiance to the doctrine with which he said he had begun the study of natural science, that species are original creations. A paper " On the Final Causes of the Sexuality of Plants," particularly referring to Mr. Darwin's work, led to a debate, in the course of which Professor Owen remarked that there are facts from which a conclusion may be formed as to the probabilities of the truth of Mr. Darwin's theory. In the course of his remarks he adverted to the deficiencies in cerebral structure of the gorilla as compared with man, and described them as immense (the intelligence of some tribes of the Quadrumana had been mentioned, and Dr. Wright had instanced a gorilla which took its young to the sea-shore to feed them on oysters, which they broke with great facility); but Professor Huxley denied that the deficiencies are so great as represented by Professor Owen, and contended that the great attribute which distinguishes man from the monkey is the gift of speech.

In the Geology section, Professor Phillips's paper " On the Geology of the Vicinity of Oxford" attracted (as might be expected) a large and much interested audience. The fossil contents of the " three square yards of Triassic drift" (near Frome) were described by Mr. Moore, who exhibited a series of organic remains, almost sufficient to set up a museum, including teeth and vertebræ belonging to three or four genera of mammalia, supposed, therefore, to have inhabited the adjacent dry land from which the drift came. In the course of Dr. Daubeny's " Remarks on the Elevation Theory of Volcanoes," he pointed out several volcanic formations, the phenomena of which could not, he thought, be ascribed (according to the theory held by the Greeks) to the scoriæ and lava flowing from a vent, or crater, having accumulated in the conical mass of a volcanic mountain. There are many places in which the fluid lava seems to have been horizontally spread over a subjacent and submarine granite bed, and to have then been raised up, in some cases broken through, from below by a mass which has formed a cone and crater. The paper led to a discussion, in which Sir Charles Lyell spoke on these theories with his accustomed animation, the venerable President, Professor Sedgwick, protesting against our thoughts on this subject being macadamised, and, as it were, constantly turned over by a new pickaxe.

Several papers of a most interesting character were read in the Geography section. Dr. Livingstone's letter (dated River Shiré, 4th Nov. 1859) on the latest discoveries in South Central Africa attracted a large audience. Describing the course of the Shiré, he mentioned a table-land three thousand feet above the sea, with mountains, some of which are from seven thousand to eight thousand feet high, a region well watered by springs and clear, cool, gushing mountain rills. He describes many of the natives as intelligent-looking, with high foreheads and well-shaped heads; but, nevertheless, they wear copper, brass, and iron rings on their arms and legs, and the women (for beauty) wear a ring through the upper lip. They wear goatskins, prepared bark, and a cloth of strong cotton. It is a great cotton-growing country. He describes the country as healthy, well timbered, and having water communication all the way to England, except thirty miles. Large quantities of what is called beer are drunk, and the people often get tipsy; but notwithstanding this, and that they never wash themselves, they attain a great age in the high lands. An old man said he remembered having washed once when a boy, but he never repeated it; and a man was threatened, as a severe punishment, to be taken to the river and washed. They believe in witchcraft, and try by ordeal accusations of its practice. A badge of mourning consists of narrow bands of palmyra leaf worn as armlets. The people have the idea of a Supreme Being and a future state. " Sometimes," said a chief, "the dead come back again; they appear in dreams, but they never tell where they have gone to."

An interesting letter to the noble President from Captain Maury, of the United States navy, was read, in which that scientific officer urges the exploration of the unknown regions (eight millions of square miles) in the Antarctic regions.

The lost Polar expedition, and the possible recovery of its scientific documents, was the subject of an interesting address by Captain Parker Snow, whose proposal to take the command of an expedition with that view received some cordial and liberal support.

Dr. Rae gave a highly interesting description of the aborigines of the Arctic regions with whom he had come in contact. He corroborated the statements as to the Mongolian type of the Esquimaux, described their life, habits, and character, but spoke of them favourably, describing, for example, their affection to parents. Some of their superstitions are curious: they look on the stars as spirits of the dead, and, when they see meteors or falling stars, say the spirits are visiting each other. They make propitiatory offerings to a supposed spirit of evil, deeming the Almighty too benevolent to will anything but good. Such is the sterility of their country, that the undigested grass and moss in the stomach of the migrating deer are frozen and often used as vegetable food. Sir Edward Belcher exhibited to the section some of their stone hatchets, tools, and arrow-heads, of native manufacture.

Captain Sherard Osborn, in a paper read to the Geography section "On the formation of Oceanic Ice in the Arctic Regions," described the enormous extent of some of the glacial regions, and helped us to appreciate what the English climate owes to the coast of Labrador. Captain Osborn saw a floating iceberg as large as the new palace at Westminster, and gave some notion of what a battle of the bergs must be in those latitudes.

From these sterile regions it was refreshing to glance with M. Pierre de Tchihatcheff at the luxuriant flora of the mountains in Asia Minor. His paper was on the geographical distribution of plants in those regions, and he described it as distinguished by a remarkable localisation or isolation of the tribes growing on the mountains. On five mountains of Armenia are found more than all the kinds of plants known in Great Britain. In Asia Minor the birch-tree lives at a height of seven thousand feet, and the remarkable atmospheric dryness of the climate is shown by the great height at which the grape flourishes. How strange it is that a mountainous region, which may well be called the Almighty's masterpiece in natural grandeur and fertility, should be politically a scene of desolation!

Mr. Ball (of the Alpine Club) mentioned, at the close of the paper, the remarkable resemblance in the flora of Anatolian mountains to that localised in a mountainous region of Spain, and its pre-eminent richness in kinds.

In a paper on microscopic vision, and on some optical illusions connected with the inversion of perspective, some interesting theoretic views were brought forward by Sir David Brewster, who also exhibited some beautiful drawings by the Hon. Mrs. Ward, explanatory of the phenomena in common and in polarised light, which are exhibited by the specimens of decomposed glass found at Nineveh, Rome, &c., on which specimens he had read a paper at the Aberdeen meeting. The rock-crystal lens found by Mr. Layard at Nineveh is as perfect as it was many thousand years ago, whereas the Assyrian glass that had surrendered to time was found much altered. The optical phenomena exhibited by films of pure glass from these specimens were minutely described, and the curious question they raise as to atomic forces was discussed. As regards the optics of the photographic art, an interesting paper was read by M. Claudet on Woodward's solar camera, an improvement which he deems capable of producing results of the greatest beauty. It decides the difficult question as to the right position of the focus of the condensing lens, and by its means small negatives may produce pictures that can be magnified to any extent.

So much for the sections. The mental strain of all this scientific business was pleasantly relieved throughout the meeting by the hospitalities of Oxford (Dr. Waagen enthusiastically declares its roast beef unequalled); there was, as already mentioned, a select evening reception at Pembroke, and there was another by Dr. Daubeny in the charming Botanical Gardens; there was an excursion to Shotover by a party of geologists, and less ardently scientific visitors formed parties innumerable to the splendid grounds and galleries of Blenheim. The Association has never met at a place better suited to such a gathering than Oxford. The reader has seen what architectural lions the university can boast; and to the lovers of architecture few localities are richer in objects of interest than its vicinity. There are the monastic sites of Godstow and Abingdon, the picturesque and pleasant village of Ewelme, with the quaint and curious old buildings (in moulded brickwork and wood tracery) of the hospital known as "God's House," and the parish church, remarkable in the annals of revived ecclesiastical taste as the first church in which open benches were substituted for pews, and for its enriched south aisle, containing the fine monuments of the Duchess of Suffolk and Sir Thomas Chaucer. Then there is Dorchester (where in Saxon times was the bishop's see, before William the Conqueror transferred it to Lincoln)—a noble old church, partly Norman, full of architectural interest, and enriched with brasses, stained glass, and ancient monuments, among which is the recumbent effigy of Chief Justice John de Stonor, who died in 1348. Near Dorchester, too, are the remains of the earthworks of a British town and Roman camp. Nearer Oxford there is the Norman church at Sandford, where once the Templars had their preceptory, and the interesting church of Iffley, over the older parts of which seven centuries have passed:—the tower-arches, groined chancel, and early-English work of the latter edifice are well worthy of attention.

Thus, on the steepled plain of Oxford, the cultivators of natural science ever found themselves amid scenes hallowed by historic memories, and nobly marked by the patriotism and the devotion of our forefathers; scenes upon which (as has been truly said) it is impossible we can ever look coldly, for they seem to reanimate the life of former days, and to detain the fleeting shadows of the past, to link its noble examples with the greater refinement and more advanced knowledge of the nineteenth century, and to surround with "the impressive grandeur of historic recollections" the academic pursuits and the scientific labours of the present time.

# MINERAL SPRINGS:

## THEIR MEDICINE AND MYTHOLOGY.

[The substance of the following Paper appeared in *Household Words*, Mar. 19, 1859.]

O ye Wells, bless ye the Lord: praise Him and magnify Him for ever.

THE springs and fountains that are perpetually rising to the surface of the earth seem to be the providentially-appointed nourishers of organic life, the messengers of health and renovation to mankind. They not only restore to the service of animated nature the waters that have fallen from the atmosphere, but, after traversing dark veins and caverns of the earth, they bring to the surface medicinal ingredients derived from nature's laboratories, deep hidden in the hills. The varied characters and properties of mineral springs are attributes not less wonderful than their chemical permanence, their constancy and abundance. Welling forth unfailingly through ages to bear health and life and beauty in their course, their value to mankind is unspeakable, and it was natural that, in the simplicity of early times, a kind of worship should be paid to the waters that sprang—

As a banquet from the friendly rock,
Furnished by the King of Kings.

Many of the mineral waters—wines we may call them, from the cellarage of mother earth—

Springing through the veins of the mountains,

come up tolerably well iced, others froth over at various degrees of heat, up to the temperature even of boiling water; some springs are bright and sparkling; others, like "fruity port," are deeply tinged with alkaline and earthy matter. "It is sufficient," says a physician who has lately written on mineral springs, "for water to dissolve a little oxygen or a little carbonic acid, a trace of phosphoric and nitric acids, to act upon substances which might seem the farthest removed from its action. By these simple means it dis-aggregates by slowly decomposing the constituents of the granites, porphyries, basalts, and crystalline rocks; it extracts the silicic acids, the alkalies, and earthy bases, and, holding these materials in various combinations, our mineral springs offer them everywhere to organic life."

Thus, the gaseous and the saline contents which have been absorbed by the water during its course through the channels of the rocks, give to mineral springs their diversity of character and their various remedial powers; and the earthy substances they hold in solution give them, as Humboldt has pointed out, another kind of action—at once formative and metamorphic; in other words, the waters transport saline and earthy substances from one kind of rock to the fissures of another, and issue from the earth charged with ingredients derived from deep and distant formations, so that many springs exert in their passage a formative, a metamorphic, or a destructive action.

The gaseous constituents of mineral waters are generally nitrogen, oxygen, carbonic acid, and sulphuretted hydrogen. The alkaline, earthy, and metallic constituents are, most commonly, the muriates and sulphates of potash, soda, baryta, alumina, and lime. The active mineral principles of waters are, the sulphates of soda and magnesia, the hydrochlorides of soda and lime, the muriates of lime and of soda, the chlorides of sodium and magnesium, the carbonates of soda, magnesia, and iron, and the sulphurets of sodium and calcium. Other salts occur in some few springs, but the constituents just enumerated are the most common and important. Of the sulphated saline springs, one class comprises sulphates of soda (Glauber's salts); another, sulphates of magnesia (Epsom salts); another, as, for example, the Bath waters and some other thermal springs, sulphates of lime; and a fourth, as at Cheltenham and Leamington, sulphates of iron, but most ferruginous springs owe their character to carbonate of iron held in solution by excess of carbonic acid. The greatest quantities of saline constituents are generally found in those springs which rise in low situations, while the springs which rise from primitive rocks are generally the most pure.

Mineral springs, therefore, present a surprising variety of medicated contents, insomuch that it would seem as if the earth was an apothecary's shop. The druggist must acknowledge that the mixtures are made up with a wondrous accuracy in the subterranean establishment, and may well marvel that each stream or spring should absorb its definite proportion of solid or gaseous constituents, unchangingly as far as we can observe, through all time, so as to present always, like the ocean or the atmosphere, the identical character which constitutes its settled value. Here the prescriptions are, indeed, carefully prepared, and from Nature's laboratory mankind from generation to generation has been freely supplied with medicine. Well may their physical and medicinal properties have procured popular reverence for the health-giving waters from early times, and made the spring the object of rustic gratitude and honour!

Many a votive altar erected at the spot where a stream first issues to the day, remains in England, as well as in the south of Europe, to testify the grateful appreciation of the Romans; and the beautiful ceremony of well-flowering, which still takes place annually in some few English parishes, is the expression of a simple love and gratitude which has proved as perennial as the spring itself. The emblematic flowers and songs bestowed on certain wells in this pleasing custom of our English ancestors represent the earlier rites of worship that were observed at wells and fountains. According to pagan ideas, nymphs exclusively presided over wells; and it is perhaps for this reason that in Christian times so few springs and fountains came to be dedicated to male saints. An old Roman writer tells us that "all waters had their particular nymphs presiding over them." Everybody has heard of Egeria and her fountain, not left unsung by Ovid:

Egeria est quæ præbet aquas dea gratu Camœnis<br>
Illa Numæ conjunx consiliumque fuit—

and the remains of this celebrated spring, once sacred to the nymph and the muses, are, or lately were, existing, in a romantic spot in the valley of Egeria.* It is through this valley that the Rio di Appio runs—the Aqua Mercurii, with which the Roman

---

* In his *Notes on Italy*, 1859, Lord Broughton discusses the question as to the locality of this fountain.

shopkeepers blessed their goods, and which seems to have been sacred to Cybele.

Mythical as the gentle deities of the fountain may seem, there is, at all events, one instance on record in which the presiding nymph condescended to appear in person. About eight miles from Rome, on the Via Collatina, near to Salone, is the Aqua Virginis, a spring which, according to Fontinus, took its name from the apparition there of a virgin, who pointed out the well to a body of soldiers. Those thirsty souls, in return for her favour, built an Ædicula, or small temple, to the nymph of the well, and honoured her as a divinity.

It was not in Italy only that the Romans recognised a nymph as the presiding genius of a well.

At Bagnères, which has been a favourite summer retreat from the age of the Cæsars of old to the hour of the Cæsars of to-day, there are votive tablets of the Roman era, which were dedicated to the nymphs presiding over streams, and they manifest a gratitude for health restored which modern refinement, it has been justly said, would do well to imitate, only in a different manner. So, too, at Bourbonne-les-bains, a votive tablet was raised by a Roman consul to the goddess Vorvonna (honoured by the Gauls as presiding over mineral springs) for the cure of his daughter Cocilla; and, indeed, so numerous are the mineral springs in the Bourbonnais, that this goddess is supposed to have even given name to the province, and thus to the royal family of France.

Again, to come to our own country, two instances may be given from Yorkshire, namely, the inscription that was found on the banks of the river Greta, near Bowes (the Roman Lavatræ) being a votive offering by two Roman ladies, in honour of the nymph Elaune, perhaps, as Professor Phillips has suggested, the river Lune; and the votive altar dedicated at Ilkley, the Roman Olicana, to Verbeia, the nymph or goddess of the fair impetuous Wharfe. Nor (as Whitaker in his *History of Craven* remarks) was this an idle homage: Verbeia was dangerous as well as fair, the Roman Trajectus was a deep and stony ford; and the Prefect Claudius Fronto having unwarily plunged into that deceitful torrent might vow an altar in the moment of distress, and absolve his obligation in the grateful season of safety.

To the intuitive scent of the prætors and legionaries of Rome for mineral and thermal waters we probably owe the knowledge of many springs which have given importance in modern times to a whole district and still draw strangers from afar; and it is curious to see how large a proportion of the mineral waters known to us were known to the ancients, and particularly to the Romans. The warm springs of Thermopylæ still attest the origin of a name which has been consecrated by the history of the spot. In ancient times these springs were sacred to Hercules, and bathing establishments once stood near to them.* These are not the only remarkable mineral waters in Greece. Adjacent to Thermopylæ are the muriated sulphurous springs of Hypate. At the foot of Hymettus are muriated waters which are resorted to for diseases of the eye. At Ædepsos in Eubœa there are thermal waters resembling those of Wiesbaden; and many sulphurous thermal springs are found in the Archipelagus,† the formation of which is altogether volcanic.

It would seem, from the testimony of Aristotle, that the Greeks were the first to use mineral waters as remedies in disease. Most of the thermal springs in which Greece abounds were sacred to Hercules, and Herculean baths existed of old in all parts of Greece, Sicily, and Italy. The temples erected to the god of medicine were adjacent to mineral springs, and such temples were connected as well with medical schools as with places of amusement. The most fabulous effects were ascribed to some of the mineral waters of Greece—*ex. gr.*, there were not only the springs of Lethe and Mnemosyne (the one of which gave oblivion and the other memory), but also a spring, mentioned by Herodotus, which enabled those who bathed in it to live beyond 120 years. There was a healing spring at Patras to which a prophetic power was ascribed, as appears from Pausanias, whose description of the spot has enabled Mr. Clark, a recent traveller in the Peloponnesus, to identify it with a well, which has been covered with Byzantine masonry, and dedicated to St. Andrew—so permanent is a tradition connected with a stream or fountain.

---

* The springs of Thermopylæ have an incrustating quality and a temperature of 110°. The soil in the neighbourhood of them gives a hollow sound to the tread.

† Dr. Althaus' *Spas of Europe*, p. 261.

A famous bath in the ancient country of the Edomites was known to the Greeks as Calirrhoe (beautiful spring): the great virtue of these thermal waters in restoring health was known to the Romans, and is spoken of by Pliny. At the springs of Tiberias the Romans erected baths, as they did at other springs in Palestine besides these.

The Phœnicians bathed in the hot vapours of the grottoes of Monte Calogero in Sicily, where the baths are still used for the relief of gout, rheumatism, and even paralysis. The Carthaginians first, and afterwards the Romans, used the sulphurous springs of Termini (Thermæ Himerenses) in the same island, and there too, from very early times, the sulphurous springs of Segesta (Aquæ Segestanæ) which have a temperature of 165°, and the sulphurous baths of Selinunte, by the sea, which are of various degrees of heat, were in high repute. Other sulphurous springs rise at Santa Vennera near the foot of Etna.

The most famous of the mineral springs in which the Neapolitan States abound, and many of which are thermal, were the springs of Baiæ, the centre of fashion and luxury in the time of the Roman emperors; even now, some remains of Nero's baths exist. At the Acqua di Bagni a temple of Serapis formerly existed.

Then, in the Papal States, there is the sulphurous Aqua Albula, near Tivoli, to which Augustus resorted, and whose praises have been sung by Virgil. The Aquæ Stygianæ, now Bagni di Stigliano, were still more important, for their temperature is higher, and they contain iodine as well as sulphur.

While, however, these once famous springs became for a long time (to use the language of Dr. Erhardt) abandoned to archæology, the cold acidulous chalybeate and the warm sulphurous waters of Viterbo have never ceased to be esteemed. In Trajan's villa, near Civita Vecchia, where the sulphur spring is hot enough to boil an egg, the old bath may be seen in which the emperor of the world reclined. Near Padua, the Fontes Patavini of the Romans, many thermal springs issue from the Euganean hills. But the most ancient bath on record in Italy seems to be that of the grotto of Cumæ, in which the sibyl gave her oracles.

The discovery of many of the most important thermal waters of Europe was probably made by the Romans, and the legions were often stationed near hot springs in the course of the Roman campaigns. Even at the edge of the desert of Sahara, in the oasis of El Kantara, the ruins of a Roman town and Roman baths are near a thermal spring.

Many of the thermal waters still deemed the most important were undoubtedly known to the Romans. It is sufficient to mention Acqui, Baden (Thermæ Helveticæ), Wiesbaden (the waters of which place are mentioned by Pliny as being used for the cure of rheumatism), Aix-la-Chapelle, Spa in Belgium (Aquæ ad civitatem Tungriam), Aix in Provence; and in the Pyrenees, Bagnères du Luchon (Thermæ Luxovienses), and Bagnères de Bigorre. The handsome modern temple of the springs of Plombières is on the site of ancient Roman baths; and Aix-les-Bains, in the newly annexed province of Savoy, was the seat of an immense thermal establishment in the days of the Romans; even now the principal spring is called after the Pro-Consul Sextius, whose name is preserved by an inscription in the great baths he reconstructed. At Luxeuil, too, an inscription remains, from which we learn that soon after the conquest of that eastern part of Gaul, one of the first acts of the conqueror was to repair the fountains of Lixovium. A long-forgotten warm sulphur spring, surrounded by remains of Roman baths and Roman pottery, has lately been discovered at a place called Thermes, between Paris and Neuilly. And, to come nearer home, we find that the Romans duly honoured the hot springs of Buxton and of Bath, where the waters still well forth from the sources which gave them the name of Aquæ Calidæ in the time of Ptolemy. The use of mineral springs seems to have diminished with the decay of the Empire; but, as far as regarded thermal waters in Germany, the example of Charlemagne did much to revive their use.

When Christianity prevailed, springs and mineral waters that had been famed for healing powers became "Holy Wells," and acquired a new sanctity from consecration to some tutelary saint. A holy well is connected with some of the oldest ecclesiastical sites in Great Britain, and the waters have a reputation derived either from the character of the patron saint and the miraculous legends connected with them, or from the medicinal virtues they have been found to possess. Many

> a crystal stream
> Which from a sacred fountaine wellèd forth alwaye

gleams in one's memory as seen overshadowed by some rural ancient church, or rising in its rocky basin by the remains of some lowly hermitage, or laving its verdant margin in the garden of some deserted religious house—a holy well,

> Whose clear wave brimmed
> A hollow basin in a living rock,
> But never flowed or ebbed, though winter rains
> Or summer suns might gush or glare around:
>     \*       \*       \*
> O'er the gray rock's sheer ledge
> The lady-fern hung lovingly; its sides
> Were all aglow with lichen: earliest there
> The primrose and the violet bloomed, and there
> Flowers latest lingered when the year grew old;
> And it was said a spirit loved the well
> And had breathed virtue in it and around it.

In the history of ancient churches, especially in Cornwall, Wales, and Ireland, mention frequently occurs of wells which are reputed holy, and are associated with the history of old Cornish, British, or Irish saints, whose names, if they do not belong to an obsolete language, at all events now sound outlandish in the places where they used to dwell. Many of such wells appear to have been places of baptism from very early times. A tradition of this kind is attached, for example, to the clear spring at East Dereham, which rises near an ancient baptistery, and appears to have been hallowed in the days of St. Augustine's mission. In many parts of Ireland pilgrimages to wells reputed holy are still common, and the customs observed are believed by the peasantry—as they were believed in the early days of Christianity—to be preservatives against spells of the fairies and sorceries of the Druids. A visitor is expected at this day at many wells to throw in a crooked pin; and it is worthy of remark that this act is noticed by some Persian travellers as an oriental custom. It seems to be intended as a propitiatory offering to the tutelary spirit of the well. Equally remote, but less seemly, and also Persian (it recals to mind the theory of the close kindred between Erin and Iran), is the custom of hanging rags round the inclosure of a well in repute for healing properties, as at the famous holy well of St. Winifred in Flintshire, at Madron Well near Penzance, and other places. Sometimes the well itself has disappeared along with its tutelary saint and all holy influences. Of this, a sufficiently notorious and homely example is found in Holywell-street, near the Strand, in London. In other countries, springs of bright water still retain the names of St. Paul, St. Dionysius, St. Donatus, or St. Francis; but the lively faith of olden times in their healing virtue does not always now prevail. An instance is mentioned by Mr. Marryat in his Travels in Jutland. The Koldekilde in Bornholm was once a celebrated spring whose waters, if quaffed on St. John's Eve, cured all sorts of maladies, and the taste of it is said in old books (written, one must suppose, by enthusiastic water drinkers) to be at all times of the year equal to brandy; but the water, or at least its fame, has changed with the times, and now, at the horse-fair, for every farmer who drank of the limpid fountain, ninety-nine take a draught from the brandy bottle itself! St. Bride's well, of the metropolis, has had a harder fate than that of many other such springs, for its name, having been first transferred to a neighbouring church, next descended from church to state; and served to designate a palace, which in due course of time became a workhouse, and ultimately a prison, and even throughout the kingdom the name Bridewell has come to denote a prison, though neither saint nor spring has anything to do with the building.*

But, whatever may have been the merits of the saint, the well seems, in most cases, to owe its fame to medicinal virtues, or sometimes to a mysterious property attributed to its waters. In the case of the celebrated well of St. Keyne, or Saint Kevin, near Liskeard, such faith is still reposed in its power to confer domestic authority that a good cellarage full of Keyne water under the Divorce Court might be worth trying as a means of settling matrimonial causes and abating litigation. The well lies down a

* Edin. Rev. April, 1860, p. 382, in article on English Local Nomenclature.

green lane, a good run from the church dedicated to the old British saint; and the bride or bridegroom who first drinks the water gains the mastery, as we have all read in Southey's ballad, where the newly-married man relates how he was outwitted:—

> I hasten'd, as soon as the wedding was o'er,
> And stole from my bride in the porch:
> But the daughter of Eve had been wiser than I,
> For she took a bottle to church!

The reputed virtues of the saint's well near Polperro have survived the edifice which enclosed it. People suffering from inflamed eyes and some other ailments still resort to it, but not without observing certain ceremonies. Saint Augustine's well, another spring also reputed good for sore eyes, rises in the western suburb of Leicester, near the old Roman road; and in Carmarthenshire, six miles from Llandilo Fawr, an out-of-the-way well is resorted to for the same complaint. So also is the spring known as Holy Well, or Cefyn Bryn; and the well by the chapel or hermitage of Saint Goven, on the coast of Pembrokeshire, in a small bay between Tenby and Milford Haven, below which there is another spring, reached by a descent of fifty-two steps, which is visited from distant parts of Wales for the cure of scrofula, and even paralysis. The saint is said to have been buried under the primitive altar in the building which incloses this collyrium.

Some of the most favourite and celebrated mineral springs in England and on the continent are, however, of comparatively recent discovery, and rise in some instances in places which were remote solitudes, and which are connected with no saintly legend. The instinct of birds, it is said, first led to the discovery of the Spa of Cheltenham. It was noticed in the year 1716 that flocks of pigeons daily resorted to the head of a small stream in a meadow near the town, for the purpose of feeding on some white saline particles deposited there by evaporation of the water. The same kind of birds have been seen to resort to the mineral spring at Inverleithen (the Saint Ronan's Well of Scott) before it acquired any celebrity. The discovery of the healing waters of Schlangenbad, in the Duchy of Nassau, is attributed to the conduct of a cow,—the animal, which, it will be remembered, led the monks to Durham, as we read in the legend of Saint Cuthbert. In

Nassau, the story runs that there was a heifer which wasted away and was given over, but which, after having been absent for some weeks, re-appeared amongst the herd in re-established health; whereupon the herdsman took notice, and observed that this animal, every evening, made its way into the forest until it reached a spring, not previously known, and drank from it. A young lady, sometime afterwards, exhibiting symptoms of the heifer's malady, was prevailed upon to try the heifer's remedy, and became one of the stoutest and comeliest of the daughters of the duchy.

In like manner Bagnoles, in the department of the Orne, owes the discovery of the virtue of its waters to a horse. An old animal suffering from disease of the skin and covered with sores was turned into a valley surrounded by rocks, and abandoned to its fate. Two months afterwards, on its master passing the end of the valley, a fat and healthy horse came trotting towards him familiarly, and turned out to be his once sick old servant. He thereupon watched its proceedings, and presently saw it roll in mud intermingled with green marshy vegetation. On draining the marsh, springs of hot water, limpid and abundant, were revealed.

So, the thermal sulphurous springs of Barèges are said to have been discovered through a sheep having been seen to traverse the snows every morning to the springs. The anecdote of the discovery of Karlsbad has been often told:—A stag, flying before the Emperor Charles the Fourth and his huntsmen, plunged through a thin crust into thermal waters, which were afterwards made baths for the Emperor, and restored him to health.

Before glancing at the chief of the continental spas of Europe, the mineral waters of England may be briefly enumerated. The chief of them are the muriatic gypsum springs of Bath, and the waters of Buxton and Bristol, at all which places the water is thermal; the brine springs of Droitwich, Kingswood, and Ashby-de-la-Zouch; the iodine and bromine springs of Purton in Wilts, the calcareous bitter water of Epsom, the muriatic springs of Harrogate, the alkalines of Malvern, the muriatic alkalines of Leamington, the muriatic salines and chalybeates of Cheltenham, and the alkaline chalybeate of Scarborough.

As to the characteristics of the mineral waters of this country, there is, as Dr. Glover has pointed out, a decided difference in the character of the northern and southern mineral springs of England. In the north, sulphur-waters prevail; in the south, the sulphated saline waters are more common. But chalybeate and saline springs are to be found in all parts of England. The opposition shop delivers its goods, carriage free, all over the country, and yet has not so much as a boy to pay for carrying a basket. Patients, however, may find the devil to pay if they drink those waters without due advice. Such waters, being for the most part highly medicated in Nature's laboratory, may prove really dangerous to persons who take them under the vague idea that the draught cannot prove otherwise than wholesome—that "the well" is a specific for every sort of disease.

The most northerly of the English spas is Gilsland, which is situated on the river Irthing, near the opening of high, barren moorlands upon the cultivated vale of Eden. Adjacent to the line of the Roman wall, it is near to scenes famed in Border story, and to a country of historical, as well as picturesque, attractions: it was at Naworth, near this spot, that Lord William Howard, the Belted Will of Marmion, had his stronghold, and, ruling there, he crushed the moss-troopers in their last retreat. Burdoswald, too, a fine specimen of a Roman camp, is near Gilsland; and the place has received in recent times more gentle associations; for here, as the reader will remember, Scott first met the lady who became his bride; and near Gilsland, scenes in The Bridal of Triermain, and a portion of Guy Mannering are accordingly laid. Sulphur in the form of sulphuret of sodium exists in this spa—an ingredient to the existence of which in mineral waters of the Pyrenees great importance has been attached.

Scarborough, fondly called the Northern Brighton and the Queen of English spas, has predominant advantages in its situation, sheltered as it is by high cliffs overlooking a fine bay, and surrounded by noble marine scenery. It is, moreover, adjacent to a beautiful country full of interest to the naturalist and the historian. The medicinal properties of the Scarborough waters, which are valuable saline chalybeates, seem to have been discovered in 1621.

At Filey, too, the rising and attractive neighbour of Scarborough, there is a water highly charged with alterative salts.

As Scarborough, Brighton, Hastings, and some less famous marine localities, first made attractive by their mineral spring, have become since its discovery favourite places of resort for sea-bathing, the advantages of the health-giving wells are more widely diffused every year; and the condition of Scarborough and other towns of popular resort contrasts curiously enough with the present condition of places that were once famous for their mineral waters, but where fashion no longer courts the genii of the well.

Of inland spas, Harrogate is not surpassed in the whole island for the power and variety of its mineral waters, which have the additional advantage of rising in a healthy and interesting country. The strength of Low Harrogate is in the sulphur wells, the discovery of which dates from the year 1561 (at which time this now fashionable place was a remote hamlet in the forest of Knaresborough); and it also affords an almost pure muriated water, which has sulphuretted hydrogen for its most active ingredient.

As Professor Phillips has remarked, the many wells of Low Harrogate may have their local origin determined mainly by the anticlinal axis of strata which may be traced in the higher ground west of Harrogate, between the millstone-grit ranges of Rigton and Birkscrag, which dip in opposite directions. The existence of chalybeate waters is, of course, common enough; but the sulphuretted water of Harrogate, loaded with common salt, indicates a deep seated spring rising under peculiar circumstances. The Old Well is, in fact, a salt spring with traces of iodine and bromine, as in sea-water. The difference between it and adjacent springs in the proportion of sulphates especially, seems to be attributable to the different channels through which they reach the surface. The only deficiency of the Harrogate waters is, that they are not thermal, nor are they aërated by much carbonic acid.

Leamington now so populous and splendid, was in 1811 a village, containing only sixty houses, yet the saline waters—which are aperient and alterative—were known more than two centuries ago.

The powerful saline springs of Cheltenham, which likewise are aperient and alterative, became famous after the cure of George the Third by the water of the Royal Old Wells. Cheltenham waters have been pronounced by medical authority to be preeminent in the treatment of diseases induced by hot climates. If Cheltenham has lost any of its reputation as a spa, the loss is, it seems, to be attributed—as in the case of Bath—to its extension as a city, and to the aggregation of splendid dwellings, which invite gay visitors rather than the invalid. Seated in the rich valleys of Evesham and Gloucester, natural scenery and historical monuments combine to surround with attractive objects these health-giving wells.

Other saline springs are at Woodhall, Tenbury, Ashby, Stratford, and Kilburn, which latter place, though now so nearly in the stony embrace of London, was quite a rural resort even late in the last century. The medicinal virtues of the water were probably known to the monastic recluses, but they do not seem to have been publicly announced until the year 1742. Kilburn wells, however, became famous early in the reign of George the Third, when it was fashionable to resort to them; and an enthusiastic singer (which must surely have been their own water when boiled fortuitously in a tea-kettle,) thus addressed the spa:—

> O, were thy virtues but as fairly known
> As universal as their good foretells,
> How should we hail thee, Pyrmont of our own,
> And bid adieu to all the foreign wells!

But, alas! their glory has departed, and of the three wells which were formerly celebrated only one is now known, and that last well of Kilburn, left gushing alone, is in a stable to the north of the railway. Kilburn spa seems to have been only one in a numerous cluster of suburban wells which were formerly resorted to by Londoners. Epsom spa had acquired earlier celebrity, namely, at the beginning of the eighteenth century, when Prince George of Denmark drank the water: and we are told that, under the stimulating influence of the South Sea Scheme, this spa became frequented like a fair, and was crowded by alchemists,

Dutchmen, Germans, and Jews,—motley votaries, who, it is to be feared, were not attracted thither by the waters only.

Shadwell, too, was in great esteem for years; and so was "Anne's Well" in Hyde Park, called after Queen Anne, who had faith in its efficacy, but is believed, nevertheless, to have qualified the water by the addition of *eau de vie*.

In those days Hampstead was celebrated for its chalybeate spring, which seems to have been known in the reign of Charles the Second, when, indeed, spas were much in vogue. It was then that Scarborough, Harrogate, Tunbridge, and Epsom started into fame; it was then that the reputation of Bath extended, and that the new Islington spa was discovered. The Islington wells were also called " Sadler's Wells," from a spring of mineral water discovered by a man named Sadler, in 1683, in the garden of a house which he had opened as a public music room, and called " Sadler's Music house." A pamphlet was published in 1684 in praise of the water, which is said to be of ferruginous quality, much resembling the water of Tunbridge Wells:—

> People may talk of Epsom wells,
> Of Tunbridge springs, which most excels ;
> I'll tell you by my ten years' practice
> Plainly what the matter of fact is :
> These are but good for *one* disease,
> To *all* distempers *this* gives ease.*

The fame of the Hampstead water has departed, but the Wells Tavern and the pump room—now a chapel—remain to tell of its whereabouts. The holy spring of Saint John, at Clerkenwell, and that on the site of Holywell Street, seem to have owed their fame to an early reputation for sanctity and brightness, rather than to any mineral virtues. A pump now covers St. Clement's Well. Fitzstephen, in his description of London in the reign of Henry II., informs us "that round the city again, and towards the north, arise certain excellent springs at a small distance, whose waters are sweet, salubrious, and clear, and whose runnels murmur over the shining stones. Among these, Holywell, Clerkenwell, and St. Clement's Well, may be esteemed the principal, as being the most frequented both by the scholars from the school (West-

---

* A Morning Ramble, or Islington Wells Burlesqt. Lond. 1684.

minster) and the youth from the city, when in a summer's evening they are disposed to take an airing." The last-named well was also much resorted to, because it was supposed to be of peculiar efficacy in the cure of cutaneous disease and other disorders. At the end of Old Street Road is a famous spring dedicated to St. Agnes, which, from the transparency and salubrity of its waters, is denominated St. Agnes la Clair. It has claims to antiquity, for it appears that in the reign of Henry VIII. it was thus named:— "*Fons voc' Dame Agnes a Clere;*" and has been described as belonging to "Charles Stuart, late king of England." This spring is 18 feet deep. It is said to be of great efficacy in all rheumatic and nervous cases, headache, &c. The spring was divided into two baths. In a six-acre field facing the great wall of Aldgate House gardens, but on the other side of the high road to Bow, a fine spring of excellent water was dedicated as early as the year 1160 to St. Winifrid. The water was conveyed to adjacent houses by copper pipes underground, and to the villages, monasteries, and other religious foundations in the neighbourhood. Dudley, third Lord North, who succeeded to that title in 1600, writes: "the use of Tunbridge and Epsom waters, for health and cure, I first made known to London and the king's people." James the First considered he was cured by the Tunbridge water. These chalybeate wells are still resorted to: those of Brighton, Sandrock, and Hastings, are of more modern though not less deserved celebrity. Brighton, however, owes its splendour and extension more to its convenience as a marine bathing-place, than to the qualities of its chalybeate water. Situation and associations seem to be the chief causes of the pre-eminence of Tunbridge amongst English chalybeates; the place, moreover, presents more of the attractive villa-like English houses than other spas. Some iron springs are even more tonic than sea-water when used as baths, and such is the water of Sandrock—the most powerful iron spring in English territory. The climate of that part of the Isle of Wight has been thought superior for equability even to the climate of Madeira.

The thermal springs of England are at Bath, Clifton, and Buxton. The Romans early availed themselves of the thermal waters of Bath. Extensive remains of their baths were found twenty feet below the level of the street; and these buildings showed the importance of the establishment that was maintained here. In the days of the Romans the hot springs of Bath (*aquæ Sulis*) appear to have been held sacred to the god Sul or Sol, who was probably worshipped in the adjacent temple. In mediæval times, the friars and monks, whose church rose on the site of the Roman fane, were bound to keep the baths in repair, to be in readiness for the King's use. The brethren seem to have been caught napping in this respect in the year 1235, for a sum of thirteen pounds, eleven shillings, was then levied upon them to repair the King's houses and the King's bath. Queen Elizabeth vested the baths in the corporation. When Anne of Denmark, queen of James the First, was bathing here, her Majesty was frightened by a sudden evolution from the water of phosphuretted hydrogen in the form of a flame. The waters were always in favour with royalty: Catherine of Braganza came to them, and so, in 1687, did Mary of Modena; and the history of Bath in the eighteenth century exhibits constant increase of prosperity. The spring that supplies the King's Bath rises at the temperature of a hundred and sixteen degrees. The Bath waters have stimulant properties, and are beneficial in nervous and paralytic as well as gouty and rheumatic affections, and diseases of the skin.

The Clifton waters are inferior to those of Bath in strength of saline ingredients and also in temperature, for their heat does not exceed seventy-six degrees. As a spa, Clifton is now of little importance; and the qualities of the place as a healthy residence, combined with its romantic scenery, are thought to constitute its real advantages.

Buxton, the only mountain-spa in England,—its elevation is a thousand feet above the the sea—is of course much indebted to its situation amidst the wondrous scenery of the Peak, and to its interesting vicinity and bracing air. Buxton, like Bath, retains many traces of the regard paid by the Romans to good mineral springs; but one such monument, namely, the wall of Roman bricks round the well of Anne the Saint, was destroyed in the reign of Anne the Queen. The water is still chiefly used externally. In the reign of Henry the Eighth it was customary for sick people to resort to Buxton, who, not having the fear of Thomas Cromwell before their eyes, superstitiously hung, as in old times accustomed, their votive offerings upon the walls of Saint Anne's chapel; and, what was worse, the poor men among the votaries used to beg—offences which the Tudor Parliament took care to interdict. Mary Queen of Scots appears to have resorted often to Buxton under the stern escort of the Earl of Shrewsbury, who erected that building at the well in which registers of cures were for many years preserved amongst rows of crutches left by the cured. The Buxton water is remarkable not only for its thermal temperature: its medicinal qualities are not (as Dr. Glover has remarked) sufficiently accounted for by the nitrogen gas which issues with the water from its native rock. All thermal springs that are at all of atmospheric derivation contain nitrogen, but some—for example, the waters of Pfeffers—are in other respects absolutely pure; whereas some thermal springs—those of Luxueil and Gastein, for example, hold in solution from eight to twelve solid or gaseous bodies.

No warm springs whatever occur in Scotland. It has many sulphurous waters—the spas of Strathpeffer and Moffat are examples, —and some saline and chalybeate springs. The Well of Moffat was discovered in 1653, and extolled shortly afterwards in a Latin pamphlet. The water rises from two springs in one of the beds of shale and anthracite that occur amongst the greywacke rocks. It is beautifully clear and sparkling, but the sulphuretted hydrogen makes the draught at first somewhat unpleasant. The water is said to be useful in chronic rheumatism, gout, and dyspepsia, and some forms of liver-disease. Moffat has also a chalybeate spring in a valley near the base of Hartfell: it contains sulphates of iron, aluminum, lime, and magnesia, and is therefore used as a tonic, and in diseases accompanied with debility and deficiency of blood.*

---

* The mineral waters of various parts of England have had a literature of their own. A Collection of Tracts relating to them, in twelve thick octavo volumes (!) published between 1587 and 1773, is offered by a London bookseller. Many of them are of great scarcity, *ex. gr.* "A briefe Discours of certaine Bathes of medicinal Waters in the Countie of Warwicke, neere unto a village called Newman Regis, 1587." This most rare book appears to have been printed for private circulation. "Fons Sanitatis, or the Healing Spring at Willowbridge, Staffordshire, found out by the Lady Jane Gerrard, Baroness of Bramley; published for the common good by Samuel Gilbert, Rector of Quat, 1676." "The Queene's Welles, that is, a Treatise of the Nature and

It is now time to glance at some of the chief springs in Germany and France. Here the traveller leaves the comparatively tame scenery of most of the English spas to imbibe the mineral waters under mountainous heights and first experience the sparkling qualities imparted by carbonic acid gas. And, out of England, mention must first be made of Spa, that great mineral spring of Belgium, which is so renowned that its name has been given to all mineral waters. The copious escape of carbonic acid gas gives a kind of life to this water, and aids its remedial efficacy.

The spas of Germany, however, have for the most part become so well known in England that I shall say very little about them. From the hills of Nassau mineral waters of various descriptions spring; and besides the Selters water, which is drunk as a luxury in every quarter of the globe, bright sparkling remedies are said to be found for almost every disorder. As Sir Francis Head observes, the consumptive or dyspeptic patient is sent to Ems; the worn invalid in search of tonic and strengthening agents to Langen Schwalbach (the swallow's stream); if the brain requires calming, the nerves soothing, and the skin softening, he goes to Schlangenbad (the serpents' bath); and if he be rheumatic he may lose his aches in the hot springs of Wiesbaden. The effect of the iron springs of Schwalbach has been compared to that of a tan-pit; and in the same category we find the mud-baths for which Franzenbad is celebrated. The peaty mud there used is diluted with mineral water, and the mixture is compared to a soft poultice of bread steeped in ink. Such a remedy was known to the ancients, and was revived in a modified manner at the close of the last century, when a certain Doctor Graham went about recommending earth-baths. He was accompanied by a nymph whom he styled the Goddess of Health, and the doctor and his goddess might be seen separately buried up to the neck, he with

Vertues of Tunbridge Water, by Lodowick Rowzee, Dr. of Physicke, practising at Ashford in Kent, 1632." "Treatise of Metal and Mineral Waters, viz.: those of the Spaw, Bathe, Epsom, Northall, Barnet, Tunbridge, and the New Wells at Islington, by E. P[ratt], M.D., 1684."

The Bath waters seem to have been known to Dr. William Turner, who in 1562 published "A Booke of the Nature and Properties as well of the Bathes in England as of other Bathes in Germanye and Italie."

his powdered head and pigtail just above the ground. His patients, when induced to put themselves in this helpless situation, are said to have been made the objects of a refined cruelty, the doctor having permitted a zealous preacher to come and lecture them while undergoing their sentence in the earth-baths. Much more agreeable are those mud-baths at Saint Arnaud in France, in which the patients play at cards and receive visits. But no charlatanrie detracts from the opaque mud-baths of Franzenbad, or the sparkling flow of the cold iron-waters of Schwalbach, although (if sentenced to such a life) most people would deem it melancholy beyond endurance to crawl and fret—as many hundred quiet people may be observed crawling and fretting—at the rate of a mile and a half an hour through that narrow portion of their existence which lies between one glass of cold iron-water and another. There is, however, no habit (as the author of *Bubbles from the Brunnen* has remarked) which fashion cannot gild or custom sweeten. On the other hand,—

" How delightful it is on a balmy morning of June to start from your couch ere yet the heat of the day has begun, and, after a cold ablution, to wend your way through paths lined with flowering shrubs to the fountain, where the attendant nymphs dispense the sparkling element. No wretched pumping apparatus, like those exhibited on the counters of the gin-palaces, is there: through a basement of polished pebbles the beautiful clear water bubbles up into the basin, and in the glass it shines and sparkles like diamonds dissolved into dew. Drink it, wasted and weary man!—drink it with a grateful heart, and render thanks and praise to HIM who is the giver of all good things!"*

But—

> Devoid of care approach this spot
> That you may part devoid of sickness;
> There is no cure for those who care."†

Of the bath of Langen Schwalbach no inviting account can be given. The mixture is best described as resembling a horse-

---

\* Blackwood's Magazine, Oct. 1861.

† Curæ vacuus hunc adeas locum,
Ut morborum vacuus abire queas;
Non enim hic curatur, qui curat."

pond, and being about the colour of mulligatawny soup. It is so deeply tinged with the red oxide of iron that the body is invisible three inches below the surface. The temperature strikes the bather as neither hot nor cold, but the water is felt to be of a bracing strengthening nature. Its solitary virtue of strengthening the stomach has been declared to be the secret of its power in almost every disorder of body and mind, for every malady is said to be either by highways or byways connected with the stomach. In the time of the Romans, Schwalbach, then in a forest, was known for the medicinal effects of its sulphurous and other fountains, and a small street sprang up adjacent to the well.

The mineral springs of Carlsbad contain a considerable quantity of silver, and have the property of converting into a hard red-coloured stone anything that is immersed in them for some days. At the Exhibition in 1862, various little statuettes and other objects formed in soft clay thus hardened and coloured formed very peculiar and pleasing objects.

A fact in the history of Pyrmont in Westphalia shows the influence of fashion upon spas. Three hundred years ago those celebrated chalybeate waters were so renowned that people flocked to them from all parts. More than ten thousand persons are said to have come in a month, and a camp was formed for their accommodation as the surrounding villages could not hold them. But the spa has now lost much of its once unrivalled fame, probably because so many other valuable springs have been made known.

So too, the modern Romans had at the close of last century quite abandoned the waters of the sulphurous lake—the Solfatara (anciently Aquae Albulae mentioned by Pliny in his Natural History), which were much resorted to in former times. In the south of France, however, the springs that the ancient Romans valued are for the most part still in repute.

Of the springs in the Pyrenees those of Barèges and Cauterets are the most important. The springs at Barèges rise at a spot about sixteen miles from Luz, and on the left bank of the impetuous torrent of the Bastan in wild and savage scenery at a height of four thousand feet above the sea. From the granite and clay-slate rocks of this high narrow valley eight thermal springs have their source. Winter avalanches often fall on the site of the wooden barracks that are erected each summer down the one long street that forms the village. Its modern fame dates from the visit of Madame de Maintenon with the young Prince of Maine in 1675. La Raillère is a celebrated spring in Cauterets,—a district three thousand feet above the sea. Every year horses afflicted by chronic bronchitis and leanness are brought here from Tarbes and Pau, and they drink with instinctive avidity and recover.

The mineral waters of the Pyrenees are for the most part sulphurous, some are merely saline, others are chalybeate. The sulphurous springs rise generally in granitic or transition rock, and they are eminently thermal, for their temperature varies from 53° to 172°. The saline springs, on the contrary, issue from the upper limestone series or the adjacent alluvial formation. In the Pyrenean waters great importance has been attached to the existence of sulphur in the form of sulphuret of an alkali or earthy base. Sulphuretted hydrogen is probably held in solution in waters which do not contain any carbonate of soda, but in others, as for example in springs of Aix-la-Chapelle, no sulphuretted hydrogen has been found. The sulphurous springs of the Pyrenees appear to have peculiarities which distinguish them from all others. Throughout the Pyrenees these medicated fountains issue from the granitic formation at varying degrees of heat.

Bagnères de Bigorre is the chief seat of the thermal springs, of which there are seventy-two, varying from 81 to 124 degrees of temperature, and owing their saline properties to salts of lime, soda, and magnesia. The whole town is pierced by thermal springs. Some of these which contain more or less iron and issue at a high temperature are stimulating; others are sedative, and the temperature of these does not exceed 90 degrees. They rise amidst splendid scenery and in a sheltered climate at a height of one thousand seven hundred and forty feet above the sea. Persons weakened by sedentary pursuits find a remedy in the stimulating waters of Bagnères; and sufferers from other causes find in one or other of its saline and thermal springs a remedy combining tonic and alterative agents.

Bagnères de Luchon—known to the Romans as Aquæ Balneariæ Luxonienses—is situated near the Spanish frontier, at an elevation of nearly two thousand feet above the sea, in a magnificent valley, in which thirty-eight springs rise from the granite and limestone rocks.

Fifty-six miles from Pau, in a little green hollow of the Pyrenees, at the stupenduous elevation of eight thousand feet, are the three springs of Penticosa—one of the most remarkable of Spanish watering-places. The baths of Penticosa lie in the heart of a vast stony *cirque* or amphitheatre, formed by a lofty range of mountains rising abruptly round it. The waters are considered of unparalleled efficacy for all complaints of the liver. The place is really one of surpassing wildness and grandeur, though not without a certain cast of gloom from the impression of profound solitude it creates. It is about nine thousand feet above the level of the sea, and yet the boundless range of mountains seems as if it stretched still upwards for another thousand. In fact you stand in the centre of an enclosure of steep barren precipices seamed by torrents, scarred by fissures, and patched by snow-drifts. The granite around is in immense masses. The springs generally issue between or near the junction of the limestone and granite. It is one of those wild and secluded spots to which mere fashion could never suffice to bring votaries; the real virtues of the healing fountain could alone induce sufferers to resort to Penticosa. The Spanish ladies take the waters apparently in solitude, and any Englishman who chances to catch glimpses of them will probably for days carry with him the memory of the haunting beauty of their eyes, for the fame of the baths and the coolness of the mountains often bring Spaniards here even from Andalusia or Castile.*

The hot springs of Fuente Caliente in Valencia are also famous. Twelve hundred mineral springs have been enumerated in Spain; they are for the most part of sulphurous thermal water.

A spring much resembling Bath water, except that it has a lower temperature, rises at the foot of an immense precipice, amidst highly picturesque scenery, on the border of the Ariege, a few leagues from Foix, the water of which is sedative, and

* Wayside Sketches in South of France and Spanish Pyrenees. 1859.

valuable in neuralgic affections and disorders induced by over study or anxiety.

It would extend the present sketch beyond its destined limits to add anything more about the waters of the Pyrenees than that their reputation is increasing: a fame which they are thought to owe to the character of the sulphur springs especially; and that the new roads and handsome houses that have risen at some of the Pyrenean springs contrast strikingly enough with the rude huts of the time when they were resorted to by the kings of Navarre. After all, these and other celebrated spas owe much to the fine scenery which has always been recognised as such an important adjunct in the administration of mineral waters. Fine country and pleasant climate are the most potent of the attractions of the baths of Lucca, to which many nervous and rheumatic patients resort; and the beautiful regions in the vicinity of the Pyrenees and the Alps present that aiding charm of scenery in perfection. It pleases the mind, and withdraws it from former scenes of anxiety or pain, while the mountain air exhilarates the animal spirits and excites to active recreation. Happy the man who can visit the clear fountains of health amid such advantages!

Nearly a thousand springs are enumerated in France; but the mineral waters of that great country are less known in England than the spas of Germany. The establishment at the German spa is generally a matter of government, and often a large part of a grand duke's revenues is drawn from a well. In France, on the contrary, many medicinal springs are the property of a commune, and therefore suffer under as sordid and grasping a spirit as if they belonged to a reformed municipality of England. Some improvement, however, is noticeable, and access is becoming more easy; so that when the extreme value of many of the springs and the grandeur of the scenery in which they rise, as well as their advantages of climate, become better known, many of the waters of France and Savoy will probably be as freely resorted to by our countrymen, if sufficient accommodation is provided.

The mineral waters of Central France are chiefly situated in the old province of Auvergne and in the Bourbonnais, which are chiefly composed of vast granitic formations, with porphyries and volcanic rocks. The temperature of some of the springs approaches the boiling point. The waters of this Terra del Fuego are saline: they contain sulphates, bicarbonates, chlorides, and silicates, and abound in carbonic acid gas. The springs of Bourbonne les Bains are muriated, and rise in granite rocks at a height of eight hundred and seventy feet above the sea: the waters resemble those of Baden. The Spa of Vichy is unlike any other alkaline water, and unites rare and valuable qualities. The bicarbonate of soda so predominates in all the eight springs of Vichy that it is regarded as the essential element in their mode of action. The alkaline springs generally contain the carbonate of soda, sometimes the carbonate of lime or of magnesia, and often other salts. Such springs are generally found near volcanic rocks.

The predominating element in the waters of the east of France is common salt. Its presence is sufficiently explained by the abundance of sea-salt in the formations of marl from which these springs proceed. The mountains amidst which they rise, unlike the volcanic mountains of Auvergne, are covered with umbrageous woods. The temperature of these springs, too, is less elevated than that of the springs in the volcanic districts of Central France. To this eastern division also belong the much frequented springs of Plombières, the most peaceful part of France. The spring of Bourbon l'Arch-ambault, in the department of Allier, is the place to which Madame de Montespan retreated to end her life in repentance and devotion; and here it was that on the night of her death a cavalier dismounted at her door, and, hastily entering her chamber, withdrew the clothes which covered her breast, and tore away a key that was suspended at her neck; then, taking a casket from a drawer, he, without having spoken, remounted his horse and pursued his way to Paris. It was her son, the Duke of Antin; but what mystery the casket concealed was never known.

Tuscany affords a comparatively larger number of mineral springs than any other country. Two hundred and thirty have been enumerated.

Piedmont possesses powerful thermal springs of sulphurous water at Acqui near Genoa—the hottest of these has a temperature of 167°.

The spas of Switzerland are chiefly in the canton of Berne, and they rise at heights varying from two thousand to four thousand feet above the sea. Remarkable variations of temperature are witnessed in some of them, for example, in the thermal springs of Lavey in the canton of Vaud.

In Germany and Austria there are more than two thousand mineral waters, some of which are hot springs. Many of the German waters have been adverted to above, and it will be sufficient to add that the mineral waters of Germany are in their medical properties unequalled by those of any other country, and they are declared by Dr. Althaus to include every mineral water of any importance in the treatment of disease.

The hot springs of the Arctic province are not within the category of mineral waters that have therapeutic powers, but they present—the Geysers in Iceland especially—more astonishing phenomena than any other hot springs. Such phenomena might have been thought, from their very nature, the subjects of unceasing change, yet the numerous and extraordinary hot springs of Reykolt were found recently by Capt. Forbes, on his visit to the island, to be much as they were described by Mackenzie fifty years before. At Yakutsk in Siberia hot springs rise up through the frozen soil from a greater depth even than six hundred feet.

The mineral waters of Sweden and Norway are not thermal: observers have connected the issue of hot springs with an alternation of crystalline and sedimentary formations, which is not found in those countries.

Asia and several islands of the Eastern Archipelago contain many sulphurous, acidulous springs, both cold and thermal. There is hardly a station between Mecca and Medina without thermal waters. The spas of Erzeroum in Armenia, and of Tiflis in Georgia, have long been celebrated, and on the Steppes, north east of the Caspian, springs containing soda and magnesia abound.

So too, in Africa: at the Cape, and in the oasis of the African desert, as well as along the northern coast, various mineral springs are found. There are many mineral waters in Algeria, and here, also, remains left by the Romans testify to the curative qualities of the springs. The most important of them is said to be the Hamman Miskoutin, the largest sulphurous spring known, and it is moreover a hot spring, its temperature being 96°. It led the French to found there a military hospital, and the waters are found potent in the cure of confirmed rheumatism and of old wounds, insomuch that patients and tourists from Europe are expected to be attracted thither.

From mountain-chains of both North and South America, in Mexico, and in the West Indian Islands, hot mineral springs are likewise found, and on the Atlantic coast of the Western Continent there are many mineral, but not thermal, springs.

So much for the universality of mineral waters in point of geographical distribution.

A few words remain to be said on another branch of the subject, viz. the temperature of springs, and the supposed volcanic source of those mineral waters which are thermal. Edward Hallmann (whose thermometric measurements were made on the banks of the Rhine and around Rome) distinguishes three classes:—1st, pure meteorological springs, whose mean temperature is not raised by the internal temperature of the earth; 2nd, meteorolo-geological springs, which, being independent of the distribution of rain and warmer than the atmosphere, are changed only by the ground through which they issue; and 3rd, abnormally cold springs, in which the low temperature is brought down from great heights. To this class belongs the famous Styx—a rill or river even now of evil renown amongst the inhabitants of Arcadia. An enterprising traveller recently succeeded in reaching the rocky precipice from which the water trickles down just as indicated by Homer, Hesiod, and Herodotus; and, not being as credulous as Aristotle was with regard to its poisonous qualities, he drank of the cold, pure water. But it is on the temperature of *thermal* springs that I wish to add a few words in conclusion of the present essay. Wholly due, as many of their characteristics seem to be, to processes of deep-seated volcanic activity (to use the language of Humboldt), what a striking contrast to the transitory and tumultuous phenomena of volcanic emissions is nevertheless presented by the vast and tranquil system of springs which we see flowing so permanently, clear, calm, and bright, from the bosom of the earth!\* Four theories have been pro-

* Humboldt's Cosmos, Sabine's edit. 1853, vol. iv. p. 292.

posed in order to account for thermal springs, 1st, the Artesian, or that which attributes their temperature to the internal heat of the earth; 2nd, the volcanic, the supporters of which urge the frequent occurrence of thermal springs in volcanic districts, the fact that their constituents are in many respects such as volcanoes evolve, and the alteration, modification, or augmentation of waters after earthquakes; 3rd, the chemical theory which is based on the evolution of heat in chemical action; and 4th, the electrical theory, which regards certain rocks that form the crust of the earth, as a kind of voltaic pile, and depends upon the power of certain magnetic rocks to evolve continually those electrical currents which we know can produce heat and chemical decomposition. The electrical theory is certainly in harmony with the general constancy of action seen in thermal springs, with the occasional interruption of that action by earthquakes, with their thermality, if not with their variety of temperature, and with their chemical constitution; and has been suggested, moreover as a possible explanation of that medicinal action in which they so greatly differ from and exceed the action of ordinary springs. To the theory of their volcanic origin it is objected that some thermal springs, as for example those which rise in the lias and the oolites of Bath, seem unconnected with volcanic rocks; and that, if a thermal spring depended on that agency, it would not be regular in its flow or uniform in its temperature. As regards the chemical theory, it has been pointed out that there is no connection between the amount of contents held in solution by thermal waters and their thermality. There are undoubtedly many volcanic districts like Broussa, for example, where the connection between hot springs and volcanic action seems irresistible. At that place amidst mountains often torn by earthquakes, a fountain which has a temperature of a hundred and ninety-eight degrees was known in the early ages of Christianity; and, according to the legend, was made the instrument in the martyrdom of St. Patricius, who, for refusing to sacrifice to the gods, was thrown into the reservoir which receives that scalding water. The phenomena of thermal springs, of saline springs, and the effervescence of carbonic acid gas, may be due to a deep-seated volcanic action, but they are witnessed in springs that are connected with the sedimentary as well as with the volcanic rocks. It is observable, however, that, in the north of Germany, at many of the carbonic acid springs of water and gas, the actual dislocation of the strata and the character of the valleys in which the springs rise suggest volcanic action. As regards the heat of the earth, no doubt the temperature of the solid crust of the globe, as far as it is known to us, does increase with the depth. Artesian wells with absolute depths varying from 750 to 2,000 feet, have shown an increase of temperature at the rate of a degree of Fahrenheit for a mean descent of fifty-six feet; but the temperature of such mountain-springs as are permanent decreases unequally with increasing elevation. The difference between the temperature of the air and the spring increases with the elevation, but the phenomena of disturbing causes are very intricate, and the question is altogether one that could not be adequately discussed here.

After so much water, it is pleasant to turn one's thoughts to the roast mutton and potatoes which Sydney Smith deemed the only satisfactory basis on which human ills could be encountered; and the good sense is unquestionable of Sir Francis Head's remark, that if our countrymen, instead of breaking up their English homes to seek health and cheapness of living on the continent, would have sense enough, or rather courage enough, to live as economically and as rationally at home as foreign princes and people of rank live throughout the rest of Europe, much health and real happiness would be the result. At all events an Englishman has an additional cause for thankfulness in the reflection that when unhappily driven to seek medicinal agents, he may find in his own country healing fountains that have for centuries proved waters of mercy to mankind:—

   Felix qui potuit boni fontem vivere lucidum!

# RIVERS, AND THEIR ASSOCIATIONS.

[*Bentley's Miscellany*, July 1860.]

—— See the rivers; how they run
Through woods and meads in shade and sun,
Sometimes swift, sometimes slow,
Wave succeeding wave, they go
A various journey to the deep—
Like human life, to endless sleep!

SOUTHEY has remarked that rivers may be considered

> Physically, geographically, and mathematically;
> Politically and commercially;
> Historically;
> Poetically and pictorially;
> Morally, and even religiously.

Were we to say all that might be said on these various heads, our readers (if any should remain) would be provided with enough fluviatile reading to last for a voyage up the Rhine, or the Nile itself; but although we propose to glance at rivers under these several aspects, we intend to do so within the compass of a short article, and to suggest rather than to discuss some considerations presented by rivers. First, then,

PHYSICALLY and GEOGRAPHICALLY. In the earth's structure, rivers have been aptly enough called its veins, just as the mountains and the mighty masses of granite represent its bones, and, like mountain-chains, rivers mark out Nature's kingdoms and provinces, and are the physical dividers and sub-dividers of continents. Some of the most picturesque features of natural scenery are obviously due to the action of rivers; and in many a mountain-gorge and rocky valley we see them still exerting their plastic force in wearing down solid rock, and carrying the *débris* towards the sea. In mountainous countries some of the grandest scenery of glens and ravines is due to a river having forced its way between the rocky walls that now compress its current; and many a rich and beautiful river-valley seems to have been once either stony wilderness or ancient lake. Rome would not have crowned her seven hills if the waters of the ancient lake of the Roman plain had not found an outlet in some pre-historic age through the gorge in which the Tiber flows. The flowery vale of Tempè is said to have been inundated before Ossa and Olympus were separated, as Pliny says, " by divine agency," and gave an outlet to the river Peneus; but we need not go so far as Thessaly for instances where a river flows between approximating precipices which seem to have been riven asunder by an earthquake, or a cataclysm.

The geologist sees in rivers " the faithful and continuous chronologers of the earth," the recorders of ages anterior to human records, and even to the existence of man, for by their uniform and endless flow they register in visible characters in their channels and valleys successive changes of bygone time. He is, indeed, led to startling conclusions with regard to the lapse of pre-historic ages, and the antiquity of the existing continents, by studying the action of great rivers. For instance (but it is, perhaps, the grandest example that could be given) the seven hundred thousand tons of water which rush over the precipice at the Falls of Niagara every minute, are estimated to carry away a foot of the cliff yearly, and the cataract having evidently once been at Queenstown, four miles below, it is concluded—assuming this rate of destruction to have been uniform—that the fall has been twenty thousand years in receding to its present site. Again, we see immense deposits accumulating at the mouths of great rivers, and tracts of new land in course of formation—as, for example, at the mouth of the Rhône—by the *débris* and shingle carried by the river towards the sea; and in the extent of those formations we have, in many instances, proof of the lapse of immense periods of time; thus, it has been calculated that the " delta " of the Mississippi, which is fourteen thousand square miles in extent, cannot have been formed in less than sixty thousand years. But this is not the place to pursue geological arguments, or to treat of what rivers have done in modifying the surface of the globe, for an essay might be devoted to that subject alone.

The quantity of water which they are continually pouring into the seas and oceans, is, perhaps the most astonishing of river phenomena. It is computed that eighty thousand cubic feet of water flow every minute into the tideway of the Thames at Teddington; but the Ganges receives in its course of sixteen hundred and eighty miles (by the windings) eleven tributaries, some of which are as large as the Rhine, and none smaller than the Thames; and the Nile brings down annually a body of water two hundred and fifty times greater than our metropolitan river. *A propos* to the Nile, it is a peculiar attribute of that wonderful stream that he has no tributaries. After having advanced eight hundred miles up his course, you naturally expect, as in the Rhine, that when you have tracked him to his mountain-bed, and are approaching to his veiled sources, you will find the vast volume of water shrink, but, on the contrary, the breadth and strength below are found to have been all his own, and throughout that long descent no tributary augments his flood; so that (as Canon Stanley remarks) you have the strange sight of a majestic river flowing like an arm of the sea in the Highlands, as calm and as broad amidst those wild Nubian hills as in the plain of Egypt.* The remarkable fact that the period of its annual rising was the same four thousand years ago as it is at the present day, affords another proof of that uniformity of physical conditions, during a long series of ages, of which science in modern times has furnished so many examples. The hopes of the shepherd and husbandman, which depended on the annual rising of the Nile, were thus connected with the fall of periodical rains on the melting of collected snows in a far-off region of unknown mountains.

Although most large rivers have their origin, like the Nile, in mountainous ranges or tracts of table-land, some of the largest rivers have a hardly perceptible fall. Thus the Volga, the largest stream of Europe, which has a course of two thousand miles, rises in a district little more than a thousand feet above the sea, and the still greater Mississippi rises in a tract of country of little higher elevation. Generally, the sources of the English rivers, likewise, are only a few hundred feet higher than the mouth. What a striking contrast between a rushing mountain torrent that descends perhaps two or three thousand feet in a few miles, and the sullen river of the plains

——where hardly flows
The frozen Tanais through a waste of snows!

* Sinai and Palestine, Introduction, p 50.

Some idea of the enormous quantity of water that is perpetually flowing into the oceans of the globe is derived from the extent of its chief river-basins. The Rhône, for example, drains the waters from an area of 7000 square miles of country; the Rhine, which has a length exceeding 600 miles by its windings, drains the waters from a country of twice that area; and the Danube from 55,000 square miles of surface; but the waters from an area of 300,000 square miles fall into the St. Lawrence, and those from 1,000,000 of square miles into the Mississippi, which, by its windings, has a length of 3560 miles. It is estimated that 1,800,000,000 of tons of water flow daily into the Mediterranean, which, besides the great rivers that fall into it, receives more than twenty secondary rivers and innumerable smaller streams. More than a fourth of the river-water of all Europe falls into the Black Sea.

If it was our present object to give a complete physical description of any river, we should have to go somewhat deeply into the science which Southey hailed as "Potamology." We must consider its basin, comprising the entire tract drained by the chief stream and all its branches; the features of its channel; its direct length from the source to the sea, and its length with windings (that of the Thames is stated at 220 miles, or double its direct length);* the height of its sources, and of different points

* The following table shows the length in miles of the principal rivers of the world:—

| River | Length | Outflow | River | Length | Outflow |
|---|---|---|---|---|---|
| Missouri | 2310 | To the Mississippi. | Euphrates | 1716 | Persian Gulf. |
|  | 4096 | To the sea. | Orinoco | 1556 | Atlantic Ocean. |
| Amazon or Maranon | 3545 | Atlantic Ocean. | Columbia | 1565 | Pacific Ocean. |
|  |  |  | Dnieper | 1243 | Euxine Sea. |
| Yangtsekiang | 3314 | Pacific Ocean. | Don | 1104 | Sea of Azof. |
| Volga | 2762 | Caspian Sea. | Tigris | 1010 | To Euphrates river. |
| Amur | 2739 | Sea of Japan. |  | 1100 | To the sea. |
| Obi | 2670 | Gulf of Obi, Arctic Ocean. | Weser | 922 |  |
|  |  |  | Rhine | 690 | To German Ocean. |
| Nile | 2578 | Mediterranean Sea. | Rhone | 644 | Gulf of Lyons. |
| La Plata | 2210 | Atlantic Ocean. | Loire | 598 | Bay of Biscay. |
| St. Lawrence | 2072 | Gulf of St. Lawrence. | Tagus | 552 | Atlantic. |
|  |  |  | Neva | 506 | Gulf of Finland. |
| Indus | 2256 | Arabian Sea. | Po | 405 | Adriatic Sea. |
| Ganges | 1933 | Bay of Bengal. | Seine | 391 | British Channel. |
| Jumna | 780 | To Ganges. | Guadalquiver | 299 | Atlantic. |
|  | 1550 | To sea. | Severn | 240 |  |
| Mississippi | 1930 | Gulf of Mexico. | Thames | 220 | British Channel. |
| Danube | 1722 | Euxine Sea. | Forth | 120 | German Ocean. |

in its course, above the level of the sea (as regards the Thames, the fall in its navigable distance from Lechlade to London is 258 feet, or 21 inches per mile); the rapidity of its current as a mean quantity, and in different places (the mean velocity of the Thames is 2 miles an hour); its depth under similar conditions; the quantity of water it contains and conveys as estimated from these particulars; the variation in the quantity at different seasons; the extent of river navigation; the proportion of earthy matters the stream brings down, and the extent and place of their deposit; the manner of its termination in the sea, and the influence of tides ascending the channel. Suffice it to say, that, whether we dwell on such physical details as regards any one great river, or view rivers collectively, we cannot fail to see how essential they are to the great scheme of circulation for the waters of the earth, to maintaining the purity of the atmosphere and the health of mankind. Everywhere we find rivers ministering to beauty and fertility as they flow, and giving commerce and communication to lands that would be otherwise inaccessible deserts.

We have alluded to some of the mightier rivers of the globe, but the importance of a river is not, of course, in proportion to the extent of country drained by it, the magnitude of its flood, or the length of its windings. The Tiber, which has been justly called the most illustrious of rivers, is little more than fifty yards in width where it is girded by the double line of buildings through which it flows; and above and below the city, where it has more scope to wander and expand, it does not generally exceed eighty or a hundred. Though it sweeps along with great power and concentrated energy, it is only (as a traveller has remarked) from its historic associations that it can excite enthusiasm or even command admiration. Considered merely in its physical aspect, how different is this comparatively diminutive but classic river from the majestic flood of the Father of Waters of the New World! But what native of the banks of Isis—what Englishman—can forget that the Thames " diffuses more of power and activity over the whole earth than all other European rivers conjoined?" The father of British floods becomingly asserts his dignity when he says, amidst the tributary rivers assembled round him by the poet,

 Though Tiber's streams immortal Rome behold,
 Though foaming Hermus swells with tides of gold,

From Heaven itself though sevenfold Nilus flows,
And harvests on a hundred realms bestows;
These now no more shall be the Muses' themes—
Lost in my fame as in the sea their streams.
Let Volga's banks with iron squadrons shine,
And groves of lances glitter on the Rhine;
Let barb'rous Ganges arm a servile train—
Be mine the blessings of a peaceful reign.

\* \* \* \* \*

The time shall come when, free as seas or wind,
Unbounded Thames shall flow for all mankind,
Whole nations enter with each swelling tide,
And seas but join the regions they divide.

And this brings us to consider rivers POLITICALLY and COMMERCIALLY. Upon the banks of the Euphrates, which was distinguished emphatically in Asia as THE RIVER, shapeless mounds of ruin mark the earliest cities of mankind. Upon the banks of the Nile, which might well be called the "fertilising nurse of Egypt," are the mightiest and most magnificent monuments of ancient genius and power that the world can show; and to the commercial riches borne by the Arabian merchants upon the spreading waters of the Nile, Thebes and Memphis have been thought to owe their former splendour. Thus, in one part of Africa, the Nile, flowing into the frequented waters of the Mediterranean, has raised upon its banks imperishable monuments of early civilisation, and has become renowned by historians sacred and profane; while on the Niger, flowing into the lonely and long unknown Atlantic, the natives of its shores remain in their original state of barbarism. Again, upon the four rivers which flow from the mountain-chain of Lebanon sprang up successively the four ruling powers of that portion of Asia: the northern river—the Orontes—is the river of the Greek kingdom of Antioch and Seleucia, and, rising from the fork of the two ranges of Lebanon and anti-Lebanon, it forms the channel of life and civilisation in those highlands of Syria which are interposed between the great plains of Assyria and the Mediterranean shores; the western river—the Leontes—is the river of Phœnicia, and, rising from the same water-shed between the two ranges, near Baalbec, it falls into the sea close to Tyre; the eastern river—the modern Barada (the Abana or Pharphar of the Old

Testament)—is the river of the Syrian kingdom of Damascus; and the southern river—the Jordan—which rises at the point where Hermon divides into its two parallel ranges, is emphatically " the river of Palestine "—a river which, as is well known, is the artery of the whole country, and which, in the deep depression of its valley and in its extraordinary physical features, is unique on the surface of the globe.* The first-mentioned of these four very remarkable rivers—the Orontes—presented (says Canon Stanley) the chief point of contact between this corner of Asia and the Western World. Near the turning-point of its course rose the Greek city of Antioch, to which, on one side, the river formed a natural moat; by the beauty of this new capital all the cities in Palestine were eclipsed: here the disciples " were first called Christians;" and here, on the banks of the Orontes, was (as it were) the halting-place of Christianity before it left its Asiatic home for the banks of the Tiber and the Western World.

In like manner the foundation, no less than the prosperity, of many another city of renown, as well in ancient as in modern times, has been connected with a river. But we will not lengthen our paper by dwelling on this part of the subject. To turn from rivers gleaming with the Eastern light to nearer and more homely streams, the reader need not be reminded that to the falls of its rivers South Lancashire owes the establishment of those mills driven by water-power which have exercised so important an influence in the developement of British industry. The tract of country lying between the Ribble and the Mersey is surrounded on the east and north by high ranges of hills, from which numerous streams descend rapidly towards the level country on the west; along these valleys hundreds of mills were erected, and the water (as a contemporary writer remarks) was made to pay a tribute in power to each as it passed. But here we find ourselves in a region where intensely utilitarian views of rivers would naturally be taken, just as in the view of Brindley, the engineer, rivers were only made by the Creator in order to feed navigable canals, or, perhaps, in the view of an epicure, have their most interesting associations in the fish they furnish to cookery. By

* Stanley : Sinai and Palestine (5th edition), p. 110.

Southey nobler uses are ascribed to rivers. " They welcome," he says, " the bold discoverer into the heart of the country to whose coast the sea has borne his adventurous barque; the richest freights have floated on their bosoms: and while by their mechanical power they move the wheels of cotton-mills, and afford transit for the goods of the merchant, they furnish the most profound philosophy with illustration and example." And so, reminding the reader that it was upon rivers that the gigantic power of steam now governing the ocean first began its sway, we pass from the political and commercial aspects of our subject to consider rivers

HISTORICALLY. Great natural objects, such as rivers and mountains, retain their original or ancient names longer than anything around them; they survive human revolutions; and while they enjoy, as it were, a perpetual youth, the names they received from the first settlers on their shores have very commonly passed untranslated into the speech of the modern inhabitants. No natural features more permanently fix, and, as some writer has said, endear, the classical associations of a land than its rivers. The primeval names of many rivers have thus been transmitted, little changed, from age to age, and they often preserve the remains of ancient language. Most rivers of France retain the names by which the Romans knew them. In caves by many a river side Celtic colonists of Britain made their dwellings, and at the present day we find many of our native rivers that retain their old British names—*e. g.* Thames and Tamar, Avon and Severn, Isis (Ouse) and Derwent, Aire and Calder, Wye and Lune, Yare or Gar, Ure and Irwell (Ir-gwili, as in Abergwili); indeed, Celtic is the prevailing element in the river names of Europe. The Cymric word *aber*, found in so many local names in Wales, denotes the mouth of a river, and where found on the eastern coast in Scotland indicates the former presence there of the Cymric race. In their language and in Celtic the word *abhain*, and in Sanscrit the word *ab*, denotes a river; the same word in Hebrew, and *aba* or *abhar* in Irish, is " father," or " cause;" thus the Nile is said by Bruce to be called in its higher regions *abay*, or father. It is worthy of remark, that *au* is a most ancient appellation of water in Gaulish and British speech, and from the simple form *abh*, (found in obsolete gaelic) we have probably derived many ancient compound words relating to water, as Avernus, Avignon, Aar, Awe, and Avren (in Scotland), and Alaunus, (in Northumberland,) mentioned by Ptolemy; and, the *b* and *u* being promiscuously sounded in some ancient languages, *aber* is probably related to it.* It has also been traced by an ingenious philologist even in America, in the names of Niagara and Kanawha, attributed to Sanscrit. So that traces of a lost speech seem to survive in rivers just as those natural fountains which still freshen the flowers of Helicon and are so celebrated in classic legend, point (as the Sanscrit Helikonda does) to a forgotten worship of the sun upon that Heliconian mount. The names of most of the rivers of North Germany are Gothic, and related to the Scythian and Indian dialects: thus, Elbe is probably derived from the Sanscrit *al*, to move; Oder, from the Sanscrit *udra*, water; Vistula, from the Sanscrit *dwis*, to separate; Rhine is the swift water; and Danube (Danawa or Tanais) the broad water, from the Sanscrit root *tan*, to spread.†

But we must not lead the reader among the "mazy waters" of etymology. Whatever traces of the descriptive language of our forefathers may survive in the names of rivers, we find that from a river many a name "familiar as household words" has been derived. Even in the arid page of those old laws of the Franks, which have an historical existence from the time of Clovis (the Salic laws), we seem to behold the river Sala flowing by the old Palatium Salæ, where Saltzburg stands. If we sometimes find a sort of fossil history in the name of a river, much more exciting associations are often connected with its shores. Some of the most memorable battles of the world have been fought upon the banks of rivers; some of the richest monuments of the arts of peace are reflected in their waters. Their boundaries are enduring landmarks of history; and, as regards most of the rivers that fall into the Mediterranean, the classical associations which seem inseparable from them render those streams familiar to us at the present day,

* Rowland's Mona Antiqua.

† We can often recognise the ancient names as fitting and descriptive of the particular river, just as it was with some rivers of Palestine that are mentioned in Scripture; thus the Kedron, "the black," is a stream which western nations might call the Black-water; the Kishon is winding, the Arnon noisy, the Pharphar rapid.

and people them with the forms and memories of their old renown. And this brings us to consider rivers

POETICALLY and PICTORIALLY. Ancient nations were accustomed to personify rivers and recognise in them a mysterious presence. To the Greeks, a river was in some measure a local seat of deity: by its waters the productive spirit diffused its influence, and attributes of the universal divinity were ascribed to the river; hence rivers became personified as of the immortal progeny of Jupiter, the guardians to mortal man, and objects of his reverence and invocation. In the Homeric times, the nymphs seem to have been considered as the guardian spirits or local deities of the springs and rivers, the companions of the river-gods, who were accounted the male progeny of the Ocean, though the mystic system gave them a more exalted genealogy. Next to the host of heaven, rivers seem from ancient times to have attracted a sort of grateful worship in the adjacent lands. Even in northern climates, the gushing of a fresh stream seems like the presence of a living power, and the water is, as it were, the very soul of the landscape; but in Syria and the East the life-giving power of running water is yet more strongly felt. To the Hebrews, springs were "the eyes"—the bright glistening eyes—of the thirsty land; a sort of personality was given to the stream: it had its "right hand," the estuary its "lip," the bay its "tongue." On many a river in a sterile, mountainous region of Palestine, the spectator (as an eminent author, writing of the Barada on its course towards Damascus, has remarked) literally stands between the living and the dead; for, bursting forth from a cleft in the rocky hills between two precipitous cliffs, the river, as if in a moment, scatters life and foliage over the plain, and the rushing flood of crystal water, overhung by willow, poplar, hawthorn, and walnut, carries a belt of verdure through a framework of barren and desert hills.

> Noble the mountain stream
> Bursting in grandeur from its vantage ground;
> Glory is in its gleam
> Of brightness—thunder in its deafening sound.
> Yet lovelier in my view
> The streamlet flowing silently serene,

> Traced by the brighter hue
> And livelier growth it gives, itself unseen.
> It flows through flowery meads,
> Gladdening the herds which on its margin browse;
> Its quiet beauty feeds
> The alders that o'ershade it with their boughs.

The stream, flowing from its spring, rising, as it were, out of the midst of gloom, comes forth sparkling to the sun. Its waters carry life and beauty on their course as on they flow through lights and shadows and depths and shallows. Like the youth springing to manhood, how it deepens as it goes, involving larger interests and wider aims, but still retaining its pure living waters! How it visits every region! The long unlovely street, pleasant villages where the sheep-bells tinkle on the breezy downs, the waste and lonely wilderness, or the umbrageous wood; now within hearing of the minster clock, now of the college bells and the vague hum of the crowded city; and overhead through all its course, the mighty heaven with its clouds, its sun and moon and stars; but always and in all places declaring its source, and at length mingling with the sea, like thoughts that wander through eternity.*

The old Greeks, in their fertile climate, had not the same reason that the inhabitants of Syria had for (as it were) personifying a river, and treating it as a living power entitled to their grateful worship; but in giving to each river a semi-human personality, a river-god of its own, they showed, as has been truly said, their deep insight into Nature. It is hardly necessary to refer to Homer's mention of

> ——Scamander's worshipped stream,
> His earthly honours and immortal name;

or to Achilles offering his hair to

> ———Sperchius' honoured flood.†

Among the Greeks, rivers were commonly honoured with offerings of hair. Their deities were thought to have a title to this respect, perhaps (as Archbishop Potter suggests), because some

---
* Dr. Brown, Horæ Subsec. 1st series, p. 297.
† Iliad, v. 140.

philosophers taught that all things had been produced out of water.

Such great rivers of the earth as the Nile, the Ganges, and the Indus preserve to this time the adoration of the inhabitants of the fruitful countries through which they flow, and their waters are still held sacred. On some East Indian rivers an offering to the deity of the stream takes at this day the picturesque form of tiny rafts, bearing lights, which maidens launch in the still night, and many a dark-fringed eye is said to watch the trembling flame as it floats onward, and to regard its long burning as a happy augury. The Chinese offer sacrifices to the spirit of the river; and Hornemann, in his "Travels in the Interior of Africa," mentions the custom to have been not long before observed at Bornou, of throwing a girl richly-dressed into the Niger, as an offering to the river—a custom which certainly cannot be said to be honoured in the observance. It reminded that traveller of the similar sacrifice to the Nile which is stated to have been annually made at Cairo. Whatever their form of sacrifice was, the Egyptians undoubtedly paid divine honours to the Nile.* So did the ancient Persians to their rivers and fountains; but, in fact, the sentiment seems to have been almost universal in the ancient world. As we read in the Vedas of three thousand years ago of the wayfarers supplicating the spirit of the stream for safe passage, so we read in the newspapers of to-day of the pilgrims, as the train rattled over the iron bridge, casting their propitiatory offerings into the river below.†

The point of the junction or union of streams and rivers seems to have been selected for ancient rites. Such junctions are still mysterious or poetical amongst the Hindus, the junction of three rivers being pre-eminently so. Thus, where the Ganges, the sacred river Yamuna ("Daughter of the Sun"),‡ and the Sarasvati unite, is Allahabad ("Residence of the Most High"); and where

---

\* Osiris being with the Egyptians "god of the waters," in the same sense that Bacchus was among the Greeks, all rivers when personified were represented under the form or symbol of the Bull. On the coins of some Greek cities of Sicily and Italy, rivers appear thus personified.

† Ferguson's River Names of Europe, p. 21.

‡ Sir W. Jones: Asiatic Researches, 29.

the three sister-streams of Ireland unite, is Kilkenny.* These conjoined river-goddesses of Ireland number Spenser among their tuneful admirers:

> The first, the gentle *Shure*, that, making way
> By sweet Clonmell, adorns rich Waterford;
> The next, the stubborn *Newre*, whose waters gray
> By fair Kilkenny and Roseponte board;
> The third, the goodly *Barrow*, which doth hoard
> Great heaps of salmon in her deep bosome;
> All which, long sundred, do at last accord
> To join in one, ere to the sea they roam:
> So, flowing all from one, all one at last become.

*A propos* to the disposition of some ancient nations and of the Greek poets to attribute a semi-human personality to rivers, the following reasons are fancifully given by the Rev. Charles Kingsley for regarding a river as a living power. "It may be," he says, "but a collection of everchanging atoms of water—what is the human body but a collection of atoms decaying and renewing every moment? And is not the river, too, a person—a live thing? It has an individual countenance which you love, which you would recognise again anywhere; it marks the whole landscape; it determines, probably, the geography and the society of a whole district. It draws you to itself, moreover, as by an indefinable magnetic attraction. If you stop in a strange place, the first instinct of the idle half-hour is to lounge by the river. It is a person to you;—how do you know that the river has not a spirit as well as yourself?"

Thus, at the present day, the great rivers of Scotland, as Sir Walter Scott has remarked, are often spoken of with a certain respect, and an almost personal character is attributed to them. So, too, in Devonshire, the rivers that have their sources on Dartmoor still retain something of the reverence with which they were anciently regarded. Dart, especially, has been said to bear traces of his former distinction. The "cry of Dart"—as the moor-men call that louder sound which rises from all mountain-streams towards nightfall—is ominous, and a sure warning of approaching evil when heard at an unusual distance.†

* Moor's Oriental Fragments, 412.
† Article, "Devonshire," in *Quarterly Rev.* April, 1859.

"Blessed things," says Bulwer, "are those remote and unchanging streams—they fill us with the same love as if they were living creatures."

The sanctity attributed of old to rivers, and the association of a tutelary god of its own with each river and fountain, was, doubtless, the origin of many of the strange old superstitions connected with rivers; and it was probably for this reason, too, that to step over any of the tributary streams of Clitumnus was accounted an indignity, which rendered the offender infamous.* Thus, nearer home and to this day, it is in many places an article of popular faith that a running stream destroys a spell or enchantment; if you can interpose a brook between you and witches, spectres, or even fiends, you are safe—a superstition of which, as the reader will remember, Burns has availed himself in "Tam o' Shanter."

Its unchanging character and perpetuity are some of the most poetical attributes of a river:

>    No check, no stay, the streamlet fears;
>    How merrily it goes!
>    'Twill murmur on a thousand years,
>    And flow as now it flows.

So likewise the brook, which is the miniature of the river in its natural characters and aspects, partakes of its poetry of life and ceaseless motion; the little streamlet knows no sleep, no pause; the great frame of Nature may repose, but the spirit of the waters rests not for a moment.†

"No haunting tone of music," says Bulwer, "ever so recalled a rushing host of memories and associations as that simple, restless, everlasting sound—the murmur of the sunny rivulet fretting over each little obstacle in its current, the merry child of Nature. Everlasting! all else may have changed, yet with the same

---

* Pliny, b. viii. 8.

† Horace's journey to Brundusium being mentioned at a dinner-party at which Dr. Johnson was present, he observed that the brook which Horace describes is to be seen now exactly as at that time; and that he had often wondered how it happened that small brooks such as this kept the same situation for ages, notwithstanding earthquakes by which even mountains had been changed, and notwithstanding agriculture which produced such variation in the surface of the earth. Thus, while most of the solid structures of Rome are perished, the Tiber remains the same.—Boswell's Johnson, vii. p. 83.

exulting bound and happy voice the streamlet leaps along its way." But alas!—

> Unlike the tide of human time,
> Which, though it change in ceaseless flow,
> Retains each grief, retains each crime,
> Its earliest course was doomed to know;
> And darker as it downward bears,
> Is stained with past and present tears.*

The permanence of the stream, and the evanescence of man, are well contrasted by Sir Charles Bell, the eminent physiologist, in the following passage inscribed in one of his daily monologues, on returning from a fishing-party:—

" Whoever has sat on a sunny stone in the midst of a stream, and played with the osier twigs and running waters, must, if he have a soul, remember the day should he live a hundred years; and to return to such a spot after twenty years of a struggling life in the great world of man's invention—to come back thus to Nature in her simple guise, again to look up to the same dark hill, again to the same trees still in their youth and freshness, the same clear running waters,—if he can do this and think himself better than a cork floating on the stream, he has more conceit than I."

"Rivers," says the Rev. John Eagles, in one of the pleasant papers published under the title of ' The Sketcher,' " are always poetical; they move, or glide, or break into fall and rapid through their courses, as if they were full of life, and were on Nature's mysterious errands. The sunbeams gleam upon them with messages from the heavens; trees bend to them, and receiving freshness and fragrance grow beside their waters, flowers kiss them, love haunts them, silence keeps awake in their caverns and sequestered nooks, and there the nightingale sings to her; the bright and many-coloured bow arches their falls, and the blessed and blessing moon shines upon them and gifts them with magic. Let the lover of landscape follow some of our sweet rivers from their sources in mountain or moor, through dell, dingle, ravine, and more open valley over which the clouds loiter; and if the mind of the sketcher does not drink poetry

* Lay of the Last Minstrel, canto iv. st. 1.

through his eye, and convey it to his portfolio, he may be sure neither Nature nor Art intended him to be painter or sketcher."

But, to multiply the testimony of writers to the poetical and picturesque charms of rivers would be a work of supererogation, like that of the worthy divine mentioned by Washington Irving in the "Sketch Book," who astonished his rural congregation at Christmas by a learned array of quotations from old Fathers of the Church in favour of a joyful observance of the season; the worthy preacher having, as afterwards appeared, entangled himself in his reading amongst the Puritan controversies of the seventeenth century, and having conjured up a host of ideal adversaries to contend with in the pulpit. Where is the lover of Nature who does not acknowledge with Southey the "endless interest which rivers excite?" Where is the artist or the poet whose soul has not drawn inspiration from their picturesque beauty? Where is the Christian who does not regard them with something of the religious honour given to them by the heathen from the earliest times, but with the purer love and reverence due to the revealed Creator, and recognise the sublimest of their associations in the scenes which hallowed the banks of Jordan, and in the fact that rivers form part of the scenery of Paradise in the Revelations of St. John?

And now, in conclusion, let us briefly glance at rivers considered MORALLY. Southey's remark, that "rivers enforce the maxims of the moralist," is aptly illustrated by the old moralising of Pliny, who has pointed out the resemblances that rivers bear to the life of man. The river (he says) springs from the earth, but its origin is in Heaven. Its beginnings are small and its infancy frivolous; it plays among the flowers of a meadow, waters a garden, or turns a little mill. Gathering strength in its youth, it becomes wild, impetuous, and impatient of restraints; it is restless and fretful, quick in its turnings, and unsteady in its course; sometimes turbulent and headlong in progress, and sometimes sullen in repose, it leaves behind what it has swept along, and, quitting its retirement for cultivated fields, yields to circumstances, and winds round the obstacles that oppose its current. It passes through the populous cities and the busy haunts of men, tendering its services on every side, and becoming the support of the country. Now increased by alliances and advanced in its career, it becomes grave and stately, loves peace and quiet, and flowing on, at length in silence mingles with the ocean depth.

"Your mighty world's river rises in high and lonely places among the everlasting hills; amidst clouds or inaccessible clearness. On he moves, gathering to himself all waters; refreshing, cheering all lands. Here a cataract, there a rapid; now lingering in some corner of beauty, as if loth to go. Now shallow and wide, rippling and laughing in his glee; now deep, silent, and slow, and not to be meddled with incautiously. Now in the open country, not so clear, for other waters have come in upon him, and he is becoming useful,—no longer turbulent, but travelling more contentedly; now he is navigable, craft of all kinds coming and going upon his surface for ever; and then, deep and smooth, he pays his last tribute to the sea, his power and volume bearing him out fresh into the main for many a league."

Considerable rivers possess attributes essential to greatness: they have breadth, depth, clearness, rapidity, strength. Calm and majestic, an image at once of power and peace, well might Denham address to the Thames the well-known apostrophe:

  Oh! could I flow like thee, and make thy stream
  My great example as it is my theme:
  Though deep, yet clear; though gentle, yet not dull;
  Strong without rage; without o'erflowing full.

Truly, indeed, may it be said that rivers feed with pleasing images the fancy of the poet, and yield illustration and example to the teachings of philosophy. But, although there is no end to the reflections that rivers excite in the contemplative mind, we must now bring to an end our remarks about them. If the constant, everlasting flow recals a host of memories, so, whether we listen to the many-murmuring voice " of some rejoicing stream " gliding smoothly under arching shade, or to the thunder of the rolling flood, our fancies wander to the unknown and to the future, seeming

  —— to rehearse
  Our little life.

In the river's onward course we are ever admonished to

> Let the turbid waters brighten as they run;

and ever see a familiar image of the stream of life and time flowing onward to the ocean of eternity.

> Oft have I thought, and thinking, sigh'd—
> How like to thee, thou restless tide,
> May be the lot, the life of him
> Who roams along thy waters' brim;
> Through what alternate shades of woe
> And flowers of joy my path may go!
> How many a humble, still retreat
> May rise to court my weary feet,
> While still pursuing, still unblest,
> I wander on, nor dare to rest.
> But, urgent as the doom that calls
> Thy waters to their destined falls,
> I see the world's bewildering force
> Hurry my heart's devoted course
> From lapse to lapse, till life be done,
> And the lost current cease to run!

# HAILSTORMS AND THEIR PHENOMENA.

[*Bentley's Miscellany*, May, 1861.]

FEW occurences in all the range of atmospherical phenomena are more calculated to excite terror and awaken curiosity than hailstorms. The dazzling and infrequent meteor and aërolite derives an interest of its own from its brief splendour, the mystery of its origin, and the wonder with which the inhabitants of the earth naturally regard bodies that seem to be fragments of other worlds. But hail—a phenomenon of the terrestrial atmosphere, like the thunder and the wind—is not the less remarkable for being familiar: the whirlwind may uproot the oaks that have stood for centuries, and scatter branches like autumn leaves, but a hailstorm is often more sweeping in its desolation. It is as fatal as the hurricane, and as awful as the thunderstorm, and often more destructive to life; and it is frequently attended by circumstances very surprising in their nature, and exceedingly difficult of explanation.

In the Bible, hail is frequently mentioned, with circumstances of terror, as an instrument of divine vengeance. We have not only the plague of hail that smote the land of Egypt in the days of Pharaoh,* but in the flight of the Amorites we read that—

"The Lord cast down great stones" (*magnos grandinis lapides*) "from heaven upon them unto Azekah, and they died: they were more which died with hailstones than they whom the children of Israel slew with the sword."†

In the prophetic, as well as in the historical books, hail is frequently mentioned; and it is alluded to in many places by the Royal Psalmist; *ex. gr.*:

"The Lord also thundered in the heavens, and the Highest gave his voice; hailstones and coals of fire."‡

* Exodus ix. 25.     † Joshua x. 11.     ‡ Ps. xviii. 13.

"He gave up their cattle also to the hail, and their flocks to hot thunderbolts."*

"He gave them hail for rain, and flaming fire in their land."†

But the terrors and the destructive power of the hailstorm do not need illustration from Scripture or from history.

Although hail, destructive to animals and vegetation, is rarely seen in climates not bordering on the tropics, its power to destroy life is frequently witnessed in India to the present day. There is something peculiarly terrific in the character of the tropical hailstorms, and in British India the average size of the hailstones and the masses of ice that have occasionally fallen greatly exceed anything known in Europe.

The phenomena of hailstorms are manifested with peculiar frequency and magnificence in the East Indies. Dr. George Buist, of Bombay, who gave much attention to this curious subject, prepared an historical list of sixty-one remarkable hailstorms, observed from the year 1781 to 1850, which was communicated by Colonel Sykes to the British Association.‡ Notices of many hailstorms are preserved in the *Asiatic Journal* from 1816 to 1842, and a paper on hailstorms in India from 1851 to 1855, was subsequently contributed by Dr. Buist to the proceedings of the British Association.§

From a review of these Indian observations it is deduced that the average *maxima* of hailstones is from eight to ten inches in circumference, and from two to four ounces in weight; and in the majority of cases the hail exceeds the size of filberts, whereas in Europe it does not often exceed that of peas. But in the Indian hailstorms the stones are more frequently accretions of ice than what we know as hailstones. In 1822, at Bangalore, bullocks were killed by the hailstones, which the natives declared to be as large as pumpkins; and although it was in the scorching month of April, some of the hailstones remained on the third day after they fell, and then measured three inches and a half in thickness. At Rangpore, in May 1851, the stones that fell were

---

\* Ps. lxxviii. 48.

† Ps. cv. 32. The words "hægle," "hagol-stan," from which (it is hardly necessary to say) the English words are derived, occur in the Anglo-Saxon Psalter given by the great Earl of Arundel to the Royal Society.

‡ Report of Edinburgh Meeting, 1851, p. 43.

§ Report of Glasgow Meeting, 1855, p. 31.

as large as ducks' eggs. So too, iu Bengal, various officers, in describing hailstorms which they saw, declare that the stones were as large as turkeys' eggs. At Calcutta, in April 1829, in a hailstorm which killed several natives, the hail fell in angular fragments of ice. In the Himalayas, north of the Peshawur, in a storm on the 12th May 1853, the ice masses were globular and compact, and many were upwards of three inches in diameter, while some were nearly a foot in circumference. And in what might be described as an ice-storm, which fell in the Lower Himalaya on the 11th May 1855, the hail increased from stones of the size of pigeons' eggs to that of cricket-balls.

But what is more extraordinary, masses of ice exceeding a hundred weight are recorded to have fallen on four occasions in India. Dr. Buist* sees no reason to doubt that a mass of ice which fell at Seringapatam in the time of Tippoo Sultan was, as stated by Dr. Hyne,† as large as an elephant, and took three days to melt! That a mass of hailstones may have been violently swept together and congealed into such an enormous block is conceivable enough, but it is hardly credible that such an aggregation can have been formed in the air and have actually fallen, unless, indeed, a body of water like that of a waterspout can have become frozen in its fall. Yet it seems authenticated that in April 1838, a mass of hailstones, cemented in one block measuring twenty feet fell at Dharwar; that immediately after another hailstorm in that locality, a mass described as an immense block of ice, consisting of hailstones frozen together, was found; and that in 1826 a mass of ice actually fell in Candeish which must have been nearly a cubic yard in bulk.‡ Astonishing as it is that such ponderous masses can have been formed in the air, it is certainly conceivable that falling hailstones may have been swept into a mass by violent whirlwinds or eddies. Hailstones of great size, but more moderate bulk, have often been found to be aggregations. Dr. Buist accounts for the larger concretions of ice by supposing that a whirlwind at a great height swept the hailstones together,

---

* See his communication on Indian Hailstorms in Report of Brit. Assoc. for 1851, p. 43.
† In his Tracts, published in 1814.
‡ Dr. Buist's communication in Report of Brit. Assoc. for 1852, p. 32.

and that they became immensely enlarged before escaping from that influence and falling on the earth.

Neither in magnitude nor in frequency of occurrence can the cognate phenomena in temperate climates be paralleled with these marvels.

In only one instance on record has any similar mass of ice or aggregation of hailstones fallen in Great Britain: in Ross-shire, in August 1849, a huge mass of ice, twenty feet in circumference, is described to have fallen like an aërolite during a thunderstorm. But there are cases in which it would seem that the ice masses of India might really have been paralleled in Britain if a whirlwind, or the kind of agency which produces the waterspout, had accompanied the hailstorm. For example, on the 24th July 1818,* in a storm which passed over the Orkneys, and was twenty miles in length and a mile and a half in breadth, ice covered the ground to the depth of nine inches in as many minutes.

On the afternoon of 31st Aug. 1862 Corfu was visited by a brief but terrible hailstorm. It was limited to a belt of a mile wide across the island, but not in a direct line. On the following morning the hailstones lay a foot deep in the ditches, and were of the size of hens' eggs. This was sixteen hours after they had fallen. In the evening of the day after the hailstorm the narrator brought home blocks of hailstones six inches thick, though the sun had shone unclouded all day, and the thermometer had marked 85° in the shade. From the sheltered watercourses blocks of ice were carted away for the ice-shops in the town.

And, to come nearer home, a shower of ice-stones, which might really be described as a *hail-spout*, fell about three years ago on a spot among the hills near Eslington Park, the Northumberland seat of Lord Ravensworth. Trustworthy persons living near the *locus in quo* declared that hailstones and fragments of ice of various shapes fell in a great heap, and they were seen in a mass sufficient to fill many baskets upon the spot shortly afterwards.

So, too, in the terrific hailstorm which devastated several districts of France on 22nd June 1861, the hailstones lay so thick on the ground at Sainte-Seine and the neighbourhood, that a trustworthy witness asserts that he saw *a bed of hailstones three feet*

* Dr. Thomson's Meteorology, p. 175.

*thick* on the road between Sainte-Seine and Vaux Saules.* And in a tremendous storm which visited Lavington in Wiltshire in 1862, hailstones covered the ground to the depth of seven feet in half an hour!

But the largest hailstones that are recorded to have fallen in Great Britain or in any part of Europe have very seldom reached dimensions that can be compared with those of hailstones witnessed in British India. In a storm of hail on the Norfolk and Suffolk coast, on the 17th July 1666, hailstones were taken up some of which were as large as turkeys' eggs, others measured eight inches, nine inches, and a foot in circumference, and one weighed two ounces and a half. On the 17th May 1685, in a great thunderstorm at Bishop Auckland in the county of Durham, hailstones five inches in circumference fell. The hailstones that fell in a storm on the Denbighshire coast in 1697 were so heavy they not only ploughed up the earth, but killed lambs and a mastiff, as well as poultry and the birds. Some of these accretions of ice weighed five ounces, and the force with which they fell showed that they came from a great height. At Hitchin, on the 4th May 1797, after a thunderstorm, a black cloud suddenly arose in the south-west, opposite to the wind, and was immediately followed by a shower of hailstones, some of which measured from seven to fourteen inches in circumference. At Offley, near the extremity of the storm, a young man was killed by the hailstones, which bruised his body and beat out one of his eyes; and these formidable missiles tore up the ground, split trees, and destroyed the crops. On the 29th June 1820, a shower of ice-stones, accompanied by a thunderstorm, fell in the south-east part of the county of Mayo. The breadth of the hailstorm did not exceed half a mile, but it left that breadth of country a ruin. Some of the stones were flat, heavy, and as large as a watch; the greater part were larger than pigeons' eggs in size, and of a similar shape. The bog-turf was penetrated by them as if by shot.†
A hailstorm occurred in North Staffordshire on the 22nd July 1857, in which masses of ice fell that were an inch and a half in diameter.‡ This storm continued for half an hour, and was

* Paris Correspondent in the *Times*, 4 July 1861.
† Blackw. Edinb. Mag. vol. vii. p. 688.
‡ Report of Brit. Assoc. Cheltenham Meeting, 1857, p. 39.

attended by gusts of wind and by thunder. At the distance of four miles a violent wind blew from the opposite quarter about the same time, but no rain or hail fell there. Hailstones as large as pigeons' eggs, and some of two and even three inches diameter, fell in a severe storm at Augsburg in Aug. 1862. Authentic instances might be given in which masses of ice have fallen in hailstorms in Britain weighing from four to nine ounces, and measuring from a foot to fifteen inches in circumference.* Again, at Lille, on the 25th May 1686, hailstones fell which weighed from four ounces to a pound. But it is needless to multiply instances; those above given seem to be the most remark- that have been recorded.

The different forms and the structure of hailstones invite curious inquiry not less than their occasional magnitude.

The forms of hailstones are very irregular. Hail in Europe is generally pear-shaped; but the forms vary. Thus, in the storm in 1797, some of the hailstones were round, others oval, others angular, others flat; and in the Denbighshire storm some were round and others semi-spherical. In the East Indies, too, the forms of the hailstones are very irregular. Some hailstones of angular form and others of oval form have fallen in the same storm, as in 1822 at Bangalore; in another storm they were compact and spherical; while in the storm at Calcutta already mentioned the hailstones are described to have been angular masses of ice, in every variety of form, but quite irregular. Sometimes the hailstones have assumed the form of convex lenses.† It has been already mentioned that in the shower of ice which fell in Mayo in 1820 some of the stones were as flat, large, and heavy as a watch.

The structure or constitution of the hailstones differs like their form and size, but in almost all cases there is a kernel or nucleus, white and opaque, which often appears to be a mere floculc of snow. When the hailstone is large, it is generally found to consist of a nucleus of frozen snow coated with ice, and sometimes with alternate layers of ice and snow,‡ but always with an icy transparent surface. In the storm on the Denbighshire coast,

---

* Prof. J. F. Daniell's Elem. of Meteorol. i. 24.      † Ibid. 25.
‡ Somerv., Phys. Geography, ii. 62.

some of the hailstones were smooth, others embossed and crenated, and the ice was very hard and transparent. The hailstones that fell in the storm in North Staffordshire are described to have had nodulated nuclei containing particles of air, and externally to these were formed irregular conglomerations of ice, looking like a mass of imperfect but transparent crystals. In the storm on the Norfolk and Suffolk coast the hailstones were white, smooth on the surface, and shining within. The concentric strata round the opaque nucleus have generally all the transparency of common ice. In the hailstones that fell at Serampore, which were larger than hens' eggs, the nucleus was observed to be whiter than the exterior. Almost all very large hailstones that have fallen in India were found to enclose a nucleus which appeared to be of snow, or what resembled a small opaque hailstone was in the centre, surrounded by several distinct and very distinguishable layers of transparent ice, these concentric coverings surrounding the nucleus like the coats of an onion, as if the first concretion had been a small one, and the ice had accumulated in its descent.

Colonel Sykes describes a still more remarkable formation— viz. globular masses of clear ice, in which a central star of many points of diaphanous ice, resembling ground glass, was enclosed in the transparent covering.*

Amongst the remarkable phenomena of hailstorms are the amazing rapidity of their motion, and the comparatively narrow breadth to which they are limited.

In Europe hailstorms usually travel in straight bands of great length but small breadth, and travel very rapidly. The storm that passed over the Orkneys in 1818 was twenty miles in length and a mile and a half in breadth, and travelled at the rate of a mile in a minute and a half†—the speed of a race-horse. Showers of hail are generally limited to a locality or line of country, and extend over it in long narrow bands. A hailstorm which fell on July 13th 1788, on the Continent, began in the morning in the south-west of France, and reached Holland in a few hours, destroying a narrow line of country in its course. It moved in

---

\* Philos. Trans. 1835. Colonel Sykes also mentions the fall of masses of clear ice exceeding an inch in diameter during hailstorms.

† Thomson, Meteorol. 175.

two columns twelve miles apart, the one on the west ten miles broad, and the other five miles broad, the one extending nearly five hundred and the other four hundred and forty miles. Again, the main body of the hailstorm which visited the Denbighshire coast, as before mentioned, appears to have fallen in Lancashire in a right line from Ormskirk to Blackburn on the Yorkshire frontier, and the breadth of the storm-cloud was estimated at two miles. How enormous must have been the mass of watery vapour which became congealed in hail over such long tracts of country!

The Indian hailstorms appear to fall in limited patches, as if affected by configuration of the country or other local circumstances. They frequently occur simultaneously at remote places, but nearly in straight lines, like a string of beads stretched across the land.

In all climates local circumstances appear to affect the formation of hail: thus, it occurs—at least in Europe and America—more frequently in countries at a little distance from mountains than in those close to them. But, whereas, in temperate climates it rarely falls among the mountains, the case is otherwise in India. Dr. Buist compiled a table of localities in which the hailstorms observed during seventy years had fallen, from which table it appears that most of them occur in the delta of the Ganges down to the sea—a plain, the humid warm atmosphere of which contrasts strikingly with the pure, crisp, vapourless air of the mountains; but hail is nearly unknown in corresponding latitudes and heights on the Malabar coast, although appearing in abundance to the north-west along the shores of Cutch and Scinde, and to the eastward (as at Sattara), and over the Deccan, at heights of fifteen hundred feet above the sea.* The case of the

---

* The quantity of rain which falls on the delta of the Ganges amounts to hardly one-third of that which descends on the low country of Arracan, for the moisture is discharged on a tract of comparatively small extent, when (as in this case) the winds blow on a coast-line at a right angle, and are arrested by high and precipitous mountain masses. On the coast of Malabar the phenomena are remarkable on the setting in of the south-west monsoon. In February, the low country from the sea to the base of the Ghaut mountains becomes very hot, and the air becomes saturated with vapours. These, during March and April, in which months the heat increases, remain suspended in the air, sometimes rising to the altitude of the mountain-range, where they

valley of the Ganges seems anomalous, for elsewhere hail is rare in the tropical plains, and often altogether unknown, although common at heights exceeding seventeen hundred feet above them. According to the above-mentioned report on Indian hailstorms, the largest number occur in the month of April, and the next largest number in March, which in British India is also one of the driest months. In the coldest months hail is very seldom seen. In the interior of Europe, too, one-half the hailstorms occur in summer, and where the period of the day has been recorded it is found to have been generally during the hours of greatest heat. It appears that in the climate of Britain hailstorms usually occur about the hours when the daily temperature is highest.

Hailstones sometimes fall with a velocity which Professor Leslie computes at seventy feet in a second, or fifty miles an hour. From their destructive power, and the depth to which they have been known to penetrate the earth, we may infer their impetus as well as weight. To the instances already mentioned of the destructive force of hailstones may be added the curious fact that the hailstones are so violent on the elevated plateau called the Grand Coteau de Missouri, that the stones have been known to penetrate the buffalo-skin tents of the Indians who hunt on that territory. The prairies sometimes retain for many weeks the marks of the occurrence of the hailstorms which during the summer months are not unfrequent in Rupert's Land.*

Hail often precedes heavy rain-showers: it seldom follows them. The large drops of rain which often precede a thunderstorm are supposed to be hail which has become melted in its passage through a lower stratum of warm air.

To the investigator of hailstorms hardly any of their phenomena are more interesting than those which seem connected with the action of electricity. Hailstorms, indeed, are always accompanied by electrical action; thunder is frequently heard, and the electrometer manifests rapid changes in electric intensity. Very often a hailstorm is preceded by a rustling noise in the air, but in

become checked by the cold, and then, descending, are rarefied before reaching the earth. The violent winds, attended by thunder, which accompany the setting in of the monsoon, condense these vapours into rain, but for the first two months they remain suspended in the heated air, as above described.

* Hind's Narr. of Canadian Expl. Exped., ii. 363.

the tropical hailstorms this manifestation of electric disturbance is greatly augmented. These symptoms of an approaching hailstorm will remind the reader of the fine passage in Virgil:

> Continuo ventis surgentibus, aut freta ponti
> Incipiunt agitata tumescere, et *aridus* altis
> Montibus *audiri fragor;* aut resonantia longe
> Litora misceri, et nemorum *increbrescere murmur.*\*

Thus, in the hailstorm of the 11th May 1855, in the Lower Himalaya, an eye-witness, stated to be a person of intelligence and information, says it was heralded by a noise as if thousands of bags of walnuts were being emptied in the air. There cannot be any doubt that electricity, quite as much as cold, is an active agent in hailstorms. The clouds from which hail falls are often extremely dense: they generally exhibit a sort of bronze colour, and the edges are irregular. In the memorable "Whit-Monday storm" of (28th May) 1860, that swept over Yorkshire, a remarkable hissing sound is stated by an observer at Pickering to have accompanied the large dense cloud that gathered in the north-west, and moved before the furious gale.

From the following passage in Lucretius, De Rerum Naturâ,† it would seem that the poet, like Pliny,‡ had imagined that the clouds could contain and support the hailstones, or frozen vapour:

> Principio, tonitru quatiuntur cærula cœli,
> Propterea quia concurrunt sublime volantes
> Ætheriæ nubes contra pugnantibus ventis:
> Nec fit enim sonitus cœli de parte serena,
> Verum ubicunque magis denso sunt agmine nubes,
> Tam magis hinc magno fremitus fit murmure sæpe.

---

\* Georg., i. line 355 *seqq.*     † Lib. vi. 120 *seqq.*

‡ Historia Naturalis, ii. 43. Pliny states the drink from melted hail to be most insalubrious. "Pestilentissimum potum en grandinibus," for which he gives the strange reason that all the softer lighter elements of the frozen liquid have been eliminated by congelation!

It is curious and worthy of remark, that a correspondent of the *Gentleman's Magazine*, in 1764, in describing the sheep and sheep-walks of Spain, says the shepherd takes especial care never to let the sheep approach a rivulet or pond after a shower of hail, believing that if they should drink *hail-water* the whole tribe would become unhealthy, fast pine away, and die, as had often happened! Hail-water, he adds, is deemed so pernicious to men in this climate, that the people of Molina will not drink the river-water after a violent shower of hail: however muddy after rain, they drink it without fear.

Præterea, neque tam condenso corpore nubes
Esse queunt, quam sunt lapides ac tigna: neque autem
Tam tenues, quam sunt nebulæ, fumique volantes:
Nam cadere aut bruto deberent pondere pressæ,
Ut lapides; aut, ut fumus, constare nequirent,
Nec cohibere niveis gelidas, et grandinis imbreis.*

It is surprising that fleecy masses of coherent mists could have been supposed capable of sustaining congealed bodies of such density and gravity, and quite inconceivable that solid aggregations of ice, or of hailstones of even the moderate size which we are accustomed to see, could be developed in the clouds from which they fall, or sustained in the form of clouds at all.

The condensation of the crystalline particles of floating vapours which ensues upon electrical action, must be followed by precipitation. That hailstones are drops of rain frozen during their descent through the air can hardly be doubted. If the air is very cold throughout the greater part of the stratum through which hail falls, the hailstone is probably increased in size during its descent; and there seems little reason to doubt that a progressive concretion takes place, the result of a gradual congealing, and that this process is entirely performed between the region of clouds and the earth. The fact that the hailstones and drops of rain that fall on high mountains are smaller than those that fall on the plains seems to strengthen this view.

The rarer phenomenon of the fall of masses of ice appears to

---

* Thus rendered into English by Dr. Busby:
    When lofty clouds, by adverse winds impelled,
    Meet, strike, and furiously dispute the field;
    Spread thick around their louring, shaggy forms,
    And fly, disordered, on the wings of storms:
    Then Heaven's blue arch tremendous thunder shakes,
    And earth, affrighted, to her centre quakes.
      No thunders roll through clear and smiling skies,
    From congregated clouds alone they rise,
    And, as those blend and blacken, fiercer lightning flies.
    Of wood's nor marble's texture clouds consist,
    Nor are so rare as fleeting smoke or mist,
    Or to the ground, like stones, they quick would fall,
    Or fly, dispersed, like melting vapours all;
    Aloft no chilling mass of snow would keep,
    Nor magazines of hail within their frame would sleep.

have engaged the attention of Descartes, who thought that the aqueous clouds might sometimes fall in masses or streams of water, and that these might become frozen in their descent. But whether the drops of rain or aqueous particles congeal in hailstones or become aggregated in the more singular masses and blocks already described, the phenomenon can only be attributed to instantaneous and intense cold in upper strata of the atmosphere; and to what extent atmospheric electricity affects these extraordinary operations of nature cannot be satisfactorily ascertained in the present state of our knowledge.

An hypothesis to explain the formation of hail and rain was submitted by Mr. Howell to the British Association in 1847, and appears to be as follows:—Electricity having no weight, and diffusing itself equally on the surface of bodies, the minute particles of water, even in their most condensed state, are enveloped, as it were, in the natural coating of electricity, and occupy, together with that envelope, nearly the space of an equal weight of air. They are thus rendered buoyant; but, when by heat their specific gravity is lessened, and their capacity for electricity enlarged by their superficial extension, they rise in the atmosphere. When they become condensed, the electricity being in excess escapes to the earth; but, where the particles are above the earth's electrical action, they mutually attract and form clouds, which, under certain circumstances, condense in rain, which becomes frozen, and falls as hail if it passes through a colder stratum of air.*

Beccaria found that the density of the spherules of hail decreases as the parts recede from the centre; and he therefore supposes that the electrical action—to which, by the way, he also attributes the formation of hail—is more intense in the regions in which the concretion of the aqueous particles into ice begins.

Volta's theory, as modified by M. Peltier, is as follows:—When two clouds in opposite electrical states are placed one above the other the mutual attraction is considerable; the strata approach without any signal electric discharge, but the one acts on the

* By this theory, the fall in very short times of extraordinary depths of rain is sought to be explained, and the occurrence of irregular winds is attributed to the partial vacuum thus occasioned.

other by induction, and the electricities are exchanged. This, however, does not happen without vaporising the water contained in the clouds, and hence the temperature is immediately lowered. If the temperature of the one stratum be near *zero*, the portions not vaporised must be congealed, and they are transformed into flakes of snow, which become quickly surrounded by ice, and fall as hail.

That difficult problem in meteorology—the electric formation of hail in summer—receives some illustration from the facts narrated in the following description of a storm which visited Wakefield on the 7th May 1862:—

" The day has been excessively hot for this locality, and the air nearly saturated with moisture; hardly any wind, and the little there was veering about to nearly all points of the compass. Shortly after four o'clock dense banks of black clouds in the south-west betokened an approaching storm, and by 6.30 the storm-clouds so obscured the town that lights were required to enable persons to read or write. A strong wind suddenly sprang up, and at 6.41 a very heavy fall of hail and rain descended. The rain was continuous throughout the storm, but the hail fell in pulses with the increase of the wind. The hailstones, till 6.51, were of transparent ice with an opaque nucleus; their form being that of segments of spheres. During this interval of time I saw no other form, nor were any of the hailstones without the opaque nucleus. The flashes of lightning coincided with the pulses of wind and hail. A short lull followed, during which no hail fell; but at 6.52 fresh hail descended. This coincided in time with the lightning and wind, as the former did, but the hailstones were of all kinds of irregular figures, and all opaque. They resembled lumps of frosted silver. The rain and hail ceased here at 6.58, but the lightning and thunder continued for about a quarter of an hour longer, and while I write a fresh wind from the south-west is blowing. The hail and cold rain beat against my study-window, and so chilled the glass that it became covered with moisture on the inside, deposited from the air of the room."

Upon the whole, it appears that the phenomena of hailstorms are closely connected with electric agency, if they are not in all cases due to it.

# IMPRESSIONS OF THE INTERNATIONAL EXHIBITION.

[*Bentley's Miscellany*, Aug. 1862.]

As if to show the Commissioners' lofty disregard for the æsthetic sympathies of our foreign visitors and for the architectural honour of our country, Captain Fowke's great building for the "World's Fair" resembles on the outside only an overgrown railway terminus; and to make it the more unlike anything that has ever been constructed, two gigantic glass domes, each as high and broad as the dome of St. Peter's, "shine afar;" but they have no relation to the character of the building, nor are they in harmony with it, and they only proclaim that the contriver of this enormous structure has, like Martin in painting, aimed at the production of effect by magnitude, and has resolved to show how greatly he at all events is above architecture and the laws of composition.

But the interior presents a scene which affords to the eye an unexpected pleasure, yet one which is due more to the harmonious colouring of the structure than to any beauty of form or proportion that it can boast, for the plan and materials of the building, and the opaque roof and want of picturesque character in the long monotonous nave (as it is called), give irredeemable heaviness to the interior. The popular structure at Sydenham is a palace of grace and beauty compared with the Exhibition building; and the visitor who enters here should abandon his remembrances of the memorable structure that rose in 1851 in Hyde Park; of its sunny, spacious interior, the airy lucidity of the crystal vault that spanned it, "the bright hues of heaven" that fell upon its well-grouped forms of grace and beauty; the trees, the flowers, the fountains, the statues, and the rainbow-tints, that gave such variety and animation to its bright vistas and its long arcades. During the month of May, at all events, and some part of June, the visitor also missed the music that used to float so pleasantly through the Hyde Park building; but there has been subsequently a too liberal supply, especially from the great organs.

The view from the raised platforms under the eastern and the western dome, though gaudy and bewildering, is striking, and those graceful objects the majolica fountain and the noble choir screen for Hereford Cathedral seem to stand there as conspicuous indications that decorative art has found high place in the industrial display. But the "trophies" with which "blatant advertisers" have been allowed to fill the nave, although they now occupy less obstructive positions than at first, do not contribute to the picturesque character of the scene; and the visitor only too soon discovers that the Exhibition is for the most part composed of objects brought together more for business purposes than for the illustration of progress in the industrial arts. Still, one cannot attentively survey its multitudinous contents without acknowledging that a very wonderful, if not unrivalled, collection of beautiful, costly, artistic, and instructive objects has been here brought together. All countries of the globe seem to have sent tribute to Great Britain; and things upon the earth, things under the earth, productions of nature and achievements of human intellect, are here contributed, to help on our knowledge of the world and its inhabitants. But the things really worthy of attention, and illustrative of the progress of nations in art and manufacture, are to be sought out amidst the acres of egregious shop-fronts, Lowther-arcade stalls, black bottles, and wax-candles, which are seen in every direction, and display only the advertising faculties of enterprising tradesmen.

But when the productions of Great Britain are compared with those of foreign countries in arts and manufactures, the Englishman may look with pride on the results of the Exhibition, for his own country not only still holds her superiority in manufactures and in those applications of science which contribute to material prosperity and power, but has no reason to fear the competition of foreign artists even in artistic productions. Thus, even in the French display of ceramic works, there is nothing equal to the best of the English porcelain. In this beautiful branch of art-manufacture, the most costly, ornate, and artistic works exhibit a wonderful finish and refinement, an admirable delicacy in colouring and grace in outline. Perhaps among all the beautiful porcelain shown by English manufacturers none better exhibits the perfection they have attained than the group of jewelled and Limoges ware in Copeland's stall, or (to instance a different branch of the art) the dessert service with landscape subjects from Turner's views of rivers in France. The imitations of old Limoges and of Sèvres ware now displayed are marvellous. In other kinds of earthenware an equally creditable display is made in Minton's court. His works in majolica, and Wedgwood's majolica, are admirable naturalisations of an exotic style. But, although the superiority of English manufacturers is not more conspicuous in any department of art-manufacture than it is in porcelain, the Saxon china from Dresden seems the very perfection of its style, and is especially commendable for its subdued and delicate tints and general good taste. A majolica vase and candelabra in porcelain may be particularly mentioned. There is also a small but very remarkable collection of porcelain from Copenhagen: the subjects and design are for the most part classical, but buildings and landscape scenery are also represented. The Romanoff set and other groups in porcelain are sent from Russia: Berlin, Austria, and Hungary likewise contribute productions in earthenware.

It is not only in this branch of art-manufacture that British proficiency in the application of correct principles of design and ornamentation is shown: a great improvement on the productions of former years is apparent in metal-work, in carving, in furniture, and in woven fabrics. But we see few departments in which the French applications of design to art-manufacture have kept pace with their progress in England. There are indications, however, that the French exhibitors more correctly appreciated the true purpose of the "World's Fair" than many of the British exhibitors appear to have done, for, instead of admitting everything sent in, and turning the Exhibition into a collection of shop-windows, the best articles in each class would seem to have been selected.

Next to the matchless collection of pictures—the chief glory of the Exhibition—the display of jewelry and plate is perhaps its most attractive feature; and in this department purity of design and true artistic character are for the most part as remarkable as the splendour and intrinsic value of the objects displayed. One of the finest collections is the display of rare corals in Phillips's case, where corals of every tint have been brought together. Here, too, are reproductions of Egyptian, Etruscan, and Greek jewelry, which rival M. Castellani's famous specimens. The enormous value of the diamonds, rubies, and pearls exhibited in the cases of some of the great jewellers may well astonish foreigners. In Hancock's display there is a diamond necklace the price of which is 85,000 guineas, and near it are the Devonshire gems, as valuable perhaps as the Koh-i-noor itself. Even this large diamond in its newly-acquired splendour is less attractive than the graceful and magnificent ornaments that sparkle in its vicinity.* In the French jewelry there is much that is spirited and striking in design and fanciful in form, but it has almost a distinct nationality; and, excepting the more costly and artistic specimens of the traditional taste of French jewellers, it seems to place what is only showy and glittering in unfavourable contrast with the splendour and intrinsic value of the best part of the English display. There is too much of the Palais Royal, and (what is worse) too much in the style of the false and despicable produc-

* The diamond in itself is without a history; it is never old in the common decay of ordinary matter; its lustre represents an eternal youth without one reminiscence of the past—a perpetual newness, though it has been in wear for hundreds of years. There is no possibility of affirming—the past is wholly lost in the refracted light of the present. It is certainly true that there are some few stones which possess a history, but the interest here is no higher than the interest which is attached to the lowest order of historic value—mere relic interest. In this matter the poor onyx stone holds its own triumphantly against the diamond; it is elevated to such a value by the hand of man that it has been deemed worthy of the choicest setting—a setting in which diamonds are only used as auxiliaries to its beauty—its beauty, the genius of fine workers in past times. When the dazzle of the diamonds has satisfied the eye, examine, at Hancock's stall, the Devonshire gems (cameos and intaglios) which were mounted for the late Lady Granville to wear at the coronation of the Emperor of Russia. Every stone enshrines some artistic creation, it tells some tale of the art and faith or incidents of classic times; perhaps perpetuating, as a reduced copy, some great work of sculpture long ago destroyed—appealing at once to the lover of art, the antiquary, and the historian by its intrinsic beauty and its high historic value.—*Once a Week*.

x

tions in which, unfortunately, Birmingham has rivals. The jewelry of Marret, Beaugrand, and Mellerio, a coronet and jewelry exhibited by Rouvenat, the Swiss enamelled watches of Rossel, and Castellani's selection of old jewels, are, however, most deserving of honourable mention. In precious metal-work, and particularly in plate, our artists and silversmiths have put forth their strength since the Exhibition in 1851, and have produced works generally remarkable for grace of design and careful execution. Hunt and Roskell's display of English race-prizes, won since the first international display, is a unique and most remarkable series of costly and artistic works. Even to people who estimate gold and silver work only by size and weight, the silversmiths' work displayed in the present Exhibition must appear surpassingly magnificent; but it not only affords what must be to many of our foreign visitors a striking picture of our domestic luxury, it shows also a gratifying improvement in correct artistic taste as well as workmanship. The Kean testimonial, although one of the most ambitious, seems to us one of the least commendable, of the works displayed in this department; and the great silver table and candelabra, the wedding presents of the Berlin silversmiths to the Prince and Princess Royal of Prussia, are, we must own, disappointing. But the enamelled metal-work displayed is generally of the highest character. Elkington's table-service, enamelled with arabesque patterns, are admirable works, as are a vase and candelabra at the same stall; and Her Majesty has specially lent some examples of their gold and silver work. Foreign countries also contribute some curious enamelled metal-work: *ex. gr.* there are vases and ewers from Russia; and Denmark, whose peat-mosses seem so rich in the golden treasure of other days, sends in this department likewise some very noticeable work, particularly a gold horn inlaid, and a silver tazza. The Spanish damascened and Indian enamelled work repay inspection. There is also a display of church plate, which exhibits very high artistic merit; and with the ecclesiastical gold and silver work of Hardman and Keith we are enabled to compare foreign productions, for there is a Russian gold-enamelled altar-service, a Belgian shrine by Chaudronnier, and an enamelled shrine by Rudolphi, besides ecclesiastical candelabra, and episcopal staves enamelled by Troullier. These we fear will have still less honour from the visitor who has fresh in his remembrance Wykeham's pastoral staff from New College, Oxford, and Fox's pastoral staff, and the other matchless specimens of mediæval art which are to be seen in the adjacent collection of works on loan in the South Kensington Museum. There is also a very fine display of ecclesiastical work in metals not precious, and foremost in merit as well as in size are Skidmore's magnificent choir screen and corona for Hereford Cathedral—works worthy of the best period of decorative art in England. It is an instance of the abominable arrangements of the Exhibition that the display of church metal-work, instead of being grouped with the mediæval court, is to be sought out in another part of the building, where it is eclipsed by a large display of Birmingham manufacture.

*Apropos* to this mention of ecclesiastical art, we must acknowledge the highly interesting character of the mediæval court undertaken by the Ecclesiological Society. It shows how successfully the revival of church architecture and the study of mediæval art has carried some of our artists backward into the spirit and the forms of the middle ages. Amongst the beautiful sculpture for architectural decoration displayed in this court the recumbent effigy of Dr. Mill, the reredos for Waltham Abbey church, and Mr. Street's rich pulpit for Bournemouth, are particularly noticeable. The applications of coloured marbles to architectural ornamentation are also very striking, and the carved oak slabs and pavement for Chichester cathedral are worthy of their destination; and we should rejoice to see the incised pavement for Lichfield brought into general use. Some remarkable furniture in antique style is also displayed in this court; particularly Gray and Davison's organ with Westlake's illuminated panels, and Seddon's library case for prints and maps, and library chair. It is to be regretted, however, that some furniture, needlessly rude and ugly, should have been exhibited as mediæval, as if rudeness and ugliness were characteristic of mediæval art. The church furniture is really good, especially in altar embroideries and textile fabrics.

The furniture courts contain some really noble works of art, especially in cabinets and sideboards, but, by allowing the British furniture court to be cut up by partitions, the officials have done their best to mar the effect of the finest collection of cabinet work that has ever been displayed. It is remarkable that, whereas in 1851 British manufacturers exhibited little that was worthy of notice in this department, they now bring to the " World's Fair " many works exhibiting proficiency in the tasteful application of decorative art to furniture, and achieving beauty of form, fitness of ornament, and excellence in carving and execution. English makers in this department unquestionably take the chief honours, but foreign countries have sent very creditable and artistic works; the Italian inlaid ivory cabinets, the ebony cabinets of Fournier and Fourdinois, Marchand's enamelled slate chimney-piece, the Russian pietradura cabinet and flower-stand, and the very beautiful and novel works in the onyx marble of Algeria, are all remarkable and meritorious. In the Austrian court very little of the furniture can be praised for design or taste, but the bronze-gilt fenders and great bronze-gilt chandelier from Vienna are fine and meritorious, and the ornamental wood-work in the form of jewel-cases and cabinets inlaid with malachite and coloured marbles exhibits a great advance.

Porphyry vases, fine mosaics, and bronzes are the boast of the Russian collection; and here, if we miss the unique yet tasteless works in malachite that drew so much attention in 1851, we have some new and interesting specimens of the little known Russian plumbago. But Russia shows no progress.

For pure and uncoloured cut and engraved glass, nothing in the foreign division at all equals the productions of English manufacturers, which, indeed, form a collection of objects as much to be admired and coveted as any in the Exhibition. The cut table-glass shown by Pellatt, Dobson and Pearce, Powell, Phillips, and Copeland, exhibits what seems to be the very perfection of this fine branch of art manufacture; and the pure and brilliant radiance of these gems forms a remarkable contrast to the dazzling and many-hued ornamental glass of the Continent, Bohemia especially, and to the gold and white jewelled ware of Austria.

The stained glass has been, for the most part, placed in such unsuitable situations, that it is perhaps hardly fair to judge of its merits; we will therefore, from this hasty glance at productions in the arts which decorate our homes, pass to the fabrics employed for dress.

And first in elegance and costliness, if not in utility, comes the exquisite display of lace. The specimens which are shown (in the south gallery) by English and Irish manufacturers evince a wonderful advance since 1851. France well maintains here its ancient eminence, and by its "point d'Alençon" rivals the most costly Brussels lace. Of the whole industrial display from Belgium, the Brussels lace in the present Exhibition may well constitute the chief glory, and in such works as the deep white flounce shown by Julie Everaert, Brussels point seems to have attained its perfection. But such specimens as the Honiton lace dress exhibited by Howell and James, and the Irish lace by Forrest and Allen, show that our manufacturers have at least kept pace with their foreign rivals, pre-eminent as the latter still continue in regard to design.

The British silk trade makes an admirable show, and likewise exhibits honourable progress. Of foreign collections of silks, the Austrian exhibition is, perhaps, the most successful in its class.

The cotton fabrics from Ghent and Bruges, and the woollen cloths from Verviers, show that the countries from which England first derived her skilled workmen and these branches of manufacture can still hold their own. The cotton manufactures of Great Britain, however, make no remarkable display in the present Exhibition, for, while it presents everywhere successful applications of mechanical and chemical science to the natural productions with which God has surrounded us, the "cotton interest" has done nothing in these ten years to secure sources of future cotton supply that shall be independent of the American Slave States and of American disruption.

The Scotch and the Belfast damasks and the Norwich shawls exhibit creditable progress. In embroidery work, save as applied to altar frontals and other church furniture, Vienna appears to send the best specimens; but Spain and Italy both contribute tissues and embroidery of considerable merit. For muslins worked in gold and silver we of course look to Turkey, and a very fine display of embroidered tissues the Turkish court contains. The gold embroidery from the Ionian Islands forms also a characteristic and beautiful collection, and the contributions from India are in this department also of a most interesting kind. The collections from Japan present us with interesting specimens of its non-progressive and grotesque civilisation—the more curious from contrast with the advance of Western nations. We looked in vain for the waxed-paper great-coats at eighteenpence, which would surely have found a ready sale in this rainy summer!

The designs for carpets, so far as regards British manufacturers, have greatly improved in taste, and show that a carpet is now recognised as having a different purpose from a hanging or decoration for a wall. The French carpets, on the other hand, though they may have improved in texture, are stationary in design and objectionable in taste.

But the International Exhibition is not merely devoted to the industrial arts, for sculpture, architecture, painting, and music are all represented. The picture-galleries contain, perhaps, the real glory of the whole display, and to the works in sculpture and painting we must briefly advert; but we must first halt on the threshold of the fine arts; and, looking back on the multifarious contributions of nations in industrial art, the impression which is, perhaps, uppermost in the mind of the visitor is, that the industry of all nations has remarkably developed since 1851. We have said nothing about the wondrous collection of machinery displayed, nor about the processes of manufacture which are illustrated in action in the "annexes" of this vast building, nor about the magnificent display made by the British Colonies, which is really one of the most impressive features of the "World's Fair" in 1862. Twenty acres are devoted to machinery, raw materials, and manufactures: the western "annexe," with its stupendous marine engines and its attractive miniature models, is, indeed, a wondrous world of brass and iron; but it needs more than an ordinary intelligence, and a doubling of the length of days, to appreciate the works displayed. It must suffice to say, that all these departments strengthen the conviction that the great show is altogether one which may fairly make an Englishman proud of his country. It is a suggestive fact, that, of the twenty-five thousand exhibitors of all nations, seven thousand receive medals, and five thousand receive certificates of honour—whatever the worth of such awards may be; and we believe the council of juries do no more than justice when they observe that the state of industry as displayed in the Exhibition evinces a healthy progress throughout the world. It is a gratifying and hopeful sign, that, while we find new productions of nature sought for and rendered useful to man, and while the machinery employed to adapt them to his use has visibly improved, attention has been successfully given to the arts which gratify our taste and minister to our sense of beauty.

And here let us say that the many tasteful works in painting, sculpture, and metal-work displayed not only in the mediæval court, but throughout the Exhibition, encourage the hope that ere long the fine arts will be again employed, as they were in the middle ages, in the interior adornment of our buildings. We have already adverted to the mediæval court, the protégé of the Ecclesiological Society; certainly the recent endeavours of that association to show how painting, sculpture, and metal-work may be used in architectural decoration, receive in the present Exhibition a very hopeful response. The court devoted to those objects in 1851 was an isolated, and as it were exotic, production; but now it has in a manner spread itself over most parts of the building, and it seems to show that the movement which has done so much for architecture is extending to the other decorative arts of the middle ages. At all events, it is a great fact that architecture and painting, to which no place was appropriated in 1851, are in 1862 not only represented, but more attractive than the Industrial Show itself.

It seems, indeed, as if a great art congress of nations had assembled in these spacious halls, and brought the best of their works to show the state of art in their respective countries, and, as it were, give back the light that genius has thrown on other lands. Perhaps there is nothing more striking and suggestive than the vividness with which the decay of old Rome is brought by the photographs of Roman ruins exhibited in the Roman court into contrast with the vitality of her arts, as shown in the statues and the mosaics and other fine-art collections from Italy, the work of living artists.

Sculpture can hardly be said to be adequately represented in the present Exhibition. Perhaps it was foreseen that the uncultured visitors from the country, and " the million " whose shillings seem to have been the especial care of the commissioners, would only yawn before the cold, inanimate representatives of Greek and Roman mythology—those modern imitations of the antique which are but the spectres of a " dead yet sceptred " past. Much of the sculpture in the Exhibition is good, but it affords very few works of commanding excellence. There are many failures, which we cannot regret, in the false conventional school of allegory and in monumental sculpture; there are some fine and careful works in imaginative or ideal art; and, to go to actual life, there are some honourable successes in the art of portraiture in marble. The piece of sculpture which is, perhaps, the most observed in the Exhibition is Gibson's tinted " Venus;" but the effect of the head and hair is hardly such as to convert observers to the expediency of so colouring statues; it is, however, a graceful and piquant representation of the female form, though expressionless and wanting in vitality. We do not know that Wyatt's " Girl Bathing " is not a more charming work. Of the male figure in repose, a more beautiful specimen is not exhibited than the " Mercury " of Thorwaldsen. Of draped statues, Story's figures in the Roman court are much to be commended: perhaps the most dignified of these works are the " Sibyl " and " Cleopatra." Cavelier's " Cornelia," too, is a fine piece of statuary. Behnes's " Cupid " (in the English picture gallery) is a natural, poetical, and beautifully executed work, and Woolner's " Constance and Arthur " (near to it) is full of imaginative power, and admirable for its delicacy and truth. In portrait sculpture, we see no works that more finely render the expression and character of the originals than the bust of " Tennyson " by the same artist, and Behnes's " Lyndhurst " and " Clarkson."

The intelligent and harmonious arrangement of the treasures displayed in the charming picture-galleries—the only portions of this vast Exhibition that one can visit with unalloyed satisfaction and delight—cannot be too highly praised. The British gallery is the more attractive, as it is really the only department that is free from the commercial spirit which has been the curse of this Exhibition; yet art, separated from manufactures, was hardly within its scope. The Exhibition comprises in all about seven thousand pictures, sculptures, drawings, and engravings, no fewer than four thousand one hundred of which belong to the English division. The British pictures comprise—it is now hardly necessary to say—only selected works of the last hundred years, and there is scarcely a bad picture in the whole collection. Here it is not only living artists whose works compete with those of foreign schools, but celebrated pictures by all the great artists who have made the British school of painting what it is, and who have flourished within the last hundred years, have been brought together in this unrivalled collection. It has no relation to the great industrial display below and around—the

> Wide hall, with earth's inventions stored,
> Where science, art, and labour have outpoured
> Their myriad horns of plenty at our feet—

it asks no awards of juries; and it seems to place the spectator in a purer air and a region more serene. It must gratify thousands of visitors to behold face to face pictures already familiarised to them by engravings, pictures that have acquired a place in history, and are celebrated gems of collections which are not easily accessible by the public. Not to mention the works of Hogarth, the great English humourist on canvas, there are the most famous of Gainsborough's works, most of Reynolds's celebrated portraits, and such a collection as the world has never seen of the best works of more recent and living artists, including Landseer's glorious pictures of deer and wild Highland hill-sides, and specimens of the best English landscape painters; but few historical subjects compared with the number in the foreign galleries. Nor are many portraits exhibited in the British division; Grant's " Lord Clyde," " Mrs. Markham " by the same artist, and Watts's " Tennyson," are perhaps the most noticeable. The foreign schools are for the most part well represented, and there are even Norwegian and Swedish pictures so masterly and true that they awaken surprise as well as pleasure. There are enough pictures in each national school to afford an instructive study of foreign art, and to enable an English student to compare foreign schools with his own. As regards the French division, the landscape painters appear to us to suffer by comparison with those of our own country; but in the drawing of the human form it must be confessed that the artists of the French, Belgian, and German schools excel. In pictures taken from rustic life, and which invest "common things" with an eloquent poetry, the artists of France likewise show conspicuous merit. The collection of works brought together in the French gallery is altogether one which must impress beholders with the genius, the learning, and the skill of her living artists. But the galleries of the Louvre and the Luxembourg must contribute their best works of modern painters before the national school can be as fairly represented as the British. The chief masters in France are, indeed, very inadequately represented, or wholly absent. Of all the pleasing portraits that are in the foreign schools, Schrotsberg's "Empress of Austria" is the most charming. It would be impossible, however, to mention particularly the works of art best worthy of attention in these delightful galleries without devoting a separate essay to the subject.

The Exhibition shows upon the whole that, in the decade, arts and manufactures have made a great advance; but our countrymen must not rest complacently satisfied with the honours they have taken. The Englishman has only to look to his public edifices, his national "monuments," and the inferiority of his countrymen to their continental rivals as regards design, to see how much remains to be done, and how needful it is to advance the education of the people in the principles of art. One would have thought a Department which professes to advance them, would have taken care that the Exhibition building itself should emphatically mark the progress of constructive art and taste in England.

# ART TREASURES
# AT SOUTH KENSINGTON.

[*Bentley's Miscellany,* Oct. 1862.]

THE objects of art and *virtù* lent for exhibition, and now collected in the new court of the South Kensington Museum, instructively display the skilful handiwork of former ages side by side with the artistic achievements of modern days shown in the International Exhibition. Some of the choicest treasures of private and public collections have been here brought together, and the intention of "the Science and Art Department" in forming such a collection, and opening it during the continuance of the International Exhibition, has probably been to enable comparison to be made, in certain definite lines, between the art of former days and the modern objects of artistic manufacture accumulated in the World's Fair—perhaps also to teach exhibitors modesty, and to admonish all modern aspirants by bidding them look at the work of the great artists of bygone times.

So valuable an exhibition, however, deserves a London season to itself, and justice is not done to it in adding such a display to the multitudinous attractions and distractions of the summer of 1862; its unobtrusive worth is, indeed, likely to be overshadowed by its imposing and all-absorbing neighbour, and to be recognised only by the connoisseur.

Within its special limits the collection is the most important that has ever been brought together, and, unlike the bewildering contents of the International Exhibition, it presents only what is of high artistic as well as money value. It is really a national display, and one which England alone could furnish. The richest productions of art that any country has afforded are well known to have been attracted to these realms; and this magnificent show gives a good idea of the richness of our private collections. It affords the visitor the rare privilege of seeing the choicest ornaments of many a collection not easily accessible by the public, and of comparing productions of the same kind borrowed from different depositories and here ranged side by side.

The dingy galleries of the South Kensington Museum through which it is approached have an educational character which does not prepare one for the holiday splendour of this exhibition: they are filled by the models which are destined by schools of design to educate art students and guide the artistic workmen of the future; but the treasures of the new hall appeal to the connoisseur in objects of luxury and to the educated student of mediæval art. The exhibition is altogether one that takes the visitor by surprise, and not the less for being collected in a great hall now opened for the first time, and which, although it is the work of the indefatigable Captain Fowke, has considerable pretensions to architectural merit. It forms the only finished part of a new building destined for a permanent art-gallery—a building of brick walls, ornamented by arches, pilasters, and bays, and roofed with glass and iron, like the new museum at Oxford. The lighting and the ventilation seem to be all that can be desired, and the collections may be viewed with ease as well as profit. Here, too, as in the picture-galleries of the adjacent International Exhibition, the commercial element has not intruded: everything is to be seen, and nothing to be sold. The only drawback was the want of a catalogue (the instalments first published embracing only part of the twenty-three classes of objects displayed); and people naturally thought that a little of the energy which certain busybodies of "the Department" have been discreditably expending as officers of the Society of Arts on officious interference in the Prince Consort's Memorial, might have been much better employed in providing a catalogue of the treasures so liberally confided to their care.

Nearly all the considerable collections in England have contributed to this exhibition, but the objects collected are less remarkable for number than value. From her Majesty to the City companies, from colleges to municipal corporations, most liberal contributions have been obtained. We have the rarest porcelain, and the finest work of the best periods of English art in the precious metals; articles of decorative plate that might have graced the banquets of the Medici, and works of ecclesiastical art from the rudest Christian enamels to the most elaborate ornaments of the time of the Plantagenets; wonderful carvings in ivory, ranging from the consular diptychs to the finest works of the fifteenth century; jewels, antique gems, and work of the lapidary, rich cabinets, rare glass, art-bronzes, book-covers, embroidery, illuminated manuscripts, and rare historical miniatures. We have even some specimens of the art of pre-historic times—of Egyptian as well as of Greek and Roman art—which, disentombed from the keeping of the dead, here again glitter before the eyes of the living: thus, Signor Castellani sent a set of golden ornaments brought from an Alexandrian tomb of the time of the Ptolemies, and the Royal Irish Academy contributes golden torques and brooches worn by the primitive Celts of Ireland, and some of those remarkable monuments of ancient Irish art, the shrines overlaid with interlaced lacertine patterns in metal-work, which were fabricated for her early bishops.

A chronological or a classified arrangement of these various objects, though much to be desired, has not been attempted, and was, perhaps, impracticable; besides, some of the exhibitors preferred to keep their collections separate. All the objects shown are tastefully arranged in glass cases.

The collection does not embrace the Fine Art of Painting, and in this respect is unlike that which made the memorable exhibition at Manchester a complete epitome of art. But, except as to painting, the visitor seems to have before him at one view, in this magnificent collection at South Kensington, the thoughts and works of the artists of sixteen centuries, and to be enabled to look back upon all Mediæval Art; he may see behind it in a remoter distance some of the waifs and strays of classic ages left by the stream of Time—sculpture from the old city of the Cæsars, and ivory carvings contemporary with the empire of the East; may look upon objects which reflected the dawn of Christian art, and upon treasures of its culminating glory; may trace its progress and decline, and may see what the Romantic and the Renaissance schools could do to supply its place. How striking is the contrast, when we pass from the whirl of revolving wheels, the ponderous masses of metal set in motion by steam, and all the marvellous automata of engineering skill that are displayed in the machinery pandemonium of the adjacent exhibition, to see in this more tranquil atmosphere how the artist's mind and the labour of a life can spiritualise material, can transform iron into delicate filigree more precious than gold, give priceless value to fragile pottery, and make a little slab of carved ivory more valuable than many tons of metal.

We wish more specimens of illuminated manuscripts could have been collected, for it is very desirable to bring together materials for illustrating that branch of native pictorial art—an art which was as much naturalised in England as architecture, and for which we must look to manuscripts alone. Like our religion and earliest learning, it seems to have been originally derived by Great Britain from Ireland. In mediæval illuminations we often see portrayed the habits and characteristic aspects of the age; they often exhibit much feeling for the higher departments of pictorial art; are frequently marked by the humour of some Hogarth of the cloister, and in their delineation of popular occupations exhibit the English as the cheerful and poetic people indicated by Shakspeare.

So much for the general aspects of the exhibition. A separate essay would be necessary in order to do justice to any one of the classes of objects it contains, but we will nevertheless throw together some brief remarks on its more conspicuous features.

The ivory carvings form a very fine display of objects at once remarkable for antiquity, tasteful design, and delicate workmanship. The collection includes specimens of various styles and ages: there are carvings of the time of Justinian, and carvings of the time of Charlemagne, and a fine series of devotional tablets in ivory of the thirteenth, fourteenth, and fifteenth centuries, chiefly from the collection lent by Mr. Webb. Of that different but very ancient and remarkable class of objects, the carved tenure and other horns in ivory, Lord Northampton contributes a well-known specimen—the horn of the clan Clephane, probably a Carlovingian work of the ninth century. Here, too, are the chessmen carved in walrus tusk which were discovered in 1831 in the Isle of Lewis in the Hebrides, Scandinavian works probably of the twelfth century, which have formed the subject of a learned dissertation by Sir Frederic Madden. Among the carvings in ivory, the head of a pastoral staff or crosier of rich fourteenth-century work, the property of Mr. Howard of Corby, deserves particular notice. " The Grace-Cup " of St. Thomas of Canterbury is, as an historical relic, one of the most celebrated and interesting objects in the whole collection of ivory cups and tankards. It was left by Sir Edward Howard, the high admiral and standard-bearer of Henry VIII., to Katharine of Aragon, and was for some time in the Arundel collection, whence it came to Bernard Edward, Duke of Norfolk, by whom it was given to the father of the present Mr. Howard of Corby, its worthy possessor. It is a plain ivory cup mounted in gold, and is conjectured to have been presented to the Archbishop by Eleanor of Aquitaine, consort of Henry II., but a more modern aspect has been given to it by the jewelled ornamentation of its mounting and cover, which are of cinque-cento style. A fine basin, elaborately carved with hunting subjects, a work of German seventeenth-century art, is sent by Mr. Beresford Hope, and Baron Rothschild's collection contains some splendid ivory cups and tankards of most exquisite workmanship.

In metal-work, as well secular as for ecclesiastical use, the show is especially rich. The colleges of the universities have sent maces, and pastoral staves, and crosiers (the matchless enamelled pastoral staff of William of Wykeham, Bishop of Winchester, is sent by New College, and the staff of Bishop Fox by Corpus College); and there are such salt-cellars, and salvers, and grace-cups, and goblets, as only the colleges of our universities can boast. City companies and various municipal corporations have likewise sent fine specimens of goldsmiths' work: if they are generally of less antiquity, and have less illustrious associations than the college plate, many of the contributions are remarkably fine and interesting. In the gold and silver plate, the capacious grace-cups, and the maces and municipal " regalia" preserved by the City companies, and shown in this unrivalled exhibition, we behold a striking proof of the vitality amongst us of old-world ways and objects. Not only colleges of learning, but municipal corporations, shorn as they have been of their splendour, and identified as they are with the trading classes, show how strongly rooted amongst Englishmen is the love of tradition, and the good habit of looking to former ages. Indeed, this exhibition, as a whole, affords another and a noble proof of the attachment to the Past which survives in England. When one thinks of the ravages of "reforming" visitors and the destructive storms of the sixteenth and seventeenth centuries, one must look with grateful wonder on the quantity and antiquity of the beautiful church and college plate that has come down to our more happy days. Several noblemen and private collectors have lent fine works of mediæval goldsmiths and costly productions of a more modern school. Conspicuous amongst the latter, for imposing weight of precious metal though not for any beauty of design, are some "centre-pieces," and the ponderous wine-coolers belonging to the Duke of Rutland and Earl Spencer. Besides these, there are the golden ice-pails given by Queen Anne to the Duke of Marlborough, the cost of which, if it had been accumulated at compound interest, would now, it is said, represent a fortune of between two and three millions. What western nation but the English could let such treasure remain unproductive in articles of mere luxury? We must not omit to mention, amongst the wondrous collection of metal-work, the famous Cellini shield, contributed by her Majesty, and that wonderful steel chair (sent by Lord Folkestone) which was executed in 1577, and presented by the city of Augsburg to Rudolph II., which has been described as a museum of delicately-modelled and gracefully-arranged figures, the subject being no less ambitious than an allegory of the history of the world.

The rare jewelry and personal ornaments, intaglios, cut crystals, cameos, and engraved gems, form a very interesting feature of the exhibition: the objects displayed are, however, such that the historic or sentimental interest in most instances surpasses the artistic beauty; and it is well that, in an exhibition in which the Fine Art of Painting does not appeal to the feelings, the cold lustre and passionless dignity of the collection should be set-off by deriving historic interest from the associations connected with many of its contents. Thus, there is the rosary of embossed gold beads, formerly enamelled in blue, with pendent crucifix and drop-pearls, which, by the tradition of the Howard family, is the chain of beads worn by Mary Queen of Scots at her girdle on the morning of her death, and sent through Melville to the Earl or the Countess of Arundel as the last token of her affection. It formed part of the collection of Thomas the famous Earl of Arundel, and came to Charles Duke of Norfolk, from whom it was acquired by the father of the present Mr. Howard of Corby, its owner. Many other personal relics might be mentioned—*ex. gr.* the pectoral cross of the Abbot of Colchester, one of the victims of Henry VIII. Mr. Waterton sends his wonderful collection of rings and gems, almost every one of which has some romantic or historical association with the fair, the noble, and the great of other days. Among the gems and historic jewels sent from Corby Castle is the signet-ring of Sir Edward Howard the high admiral, bearing his initials and the blanch-lion of Mowbray engraved on an old Roman gem. The collection of personal ornaments belonging to the remote period of ancient Irish and of Anglo-Saxon art is very remarkable. The torques and other gold ornaments sent by the Royal Irish Academy and by Lord Londesborough form a most interesting collection. The last-named nobleman also contributes some ancient brooches of Celtic work; and there are some rare jewelled and enamelled ornaments of the Anglo-Saxon period, chiefly from the Ashmolean Museum.

The enamels collected in the exhibition display the art from the early Byzantine work to the exquisite grey enamels of Limoges.

Among the vases and other objects in rock crystal, sardonyx, &c., one of the most noticeable is Mr. Beresford Hope's enamelled sardonyx vase, attributed to Benvenuto Cellini, and worthy of that artist for its delicacy of design and execution. But one of the most ancient, and in many respects most remarkable, objects in the whole exhibition is the glass cup or vase covered with figures—a work of the period of the Lower Empire. Except for its iridescent hue one could hardly believe the material to be glass. It is well known, however, that vessels of glass coloured to imitate precious stone, or of glass resembling rock crystal, and intended for cutting by the lathe, in the style of cameos, in relief,

Y

had in the time of Nero almost superseded cups of gold among the Romans, who seem to have originally procured their glass from the artists of Alexandria. *Apropos* to glass, we must not forget the choice collection which is here brought together of the fragile achievements of Venetian art. The most extraordinary feature of the exhibition is, however, the splendid collection of ceramic works, from the precious porcelain of Limoges, the rare and curious pottery known as Faïence de Henri Deux, the Majolica ware with its bright tints of green and orange, Bernard Palissy's naturalistic productions, old Dresden, and the most alluring Sèvres, to Wedgewood-ware and some of the comparatively little known porcelain of the old English manufactories. The manufacture of porcelain in France does not appear to be older than the seventeenth century. Palissy, three centuries ago, produced the first enamelled pottery made in France, and porcelain was first manufactured at St. Cloud in 1695; but within fifty years porcelain of the greatest delicacy was produced at Sèvres, where now a new manufactory is being constructed by order of the Emperor.

The Henri Deux ware has a romantic interest beyond its artistic curiosity, from its unknown origin, its traditional connection with the name of that sovereign and the celebrated Diana of Poitiers, and from having been a favourite object with royal and noble personages in a brilliant epoch of French history. Half Oriental as its aspect is, it was probably produced somewhere in France between 1540 and 1560, but it is not known where or by whom it was manufactured. Its characteristic ornaments are finely-modelled raised rosettes, Medusa masks, and shells in forms of the Renaissance period, and engraved arabesques; some of the patterns are incised, and resemble the inlaying of niello-work. Some of the pieces bear the double D or H and double C of the king; whether the interlaced crescents or Cs were or were not adopted in compliment to Diana of Poitiers, the badge seems to be in reality the monogram of Henry II. and his queen Catherine de Médicis, inasmuch as it occurs in the façade of the Louvre. At all events, it is curious that the initials which he loved to link with his own on royal palaces have come down to us in combination on these fragile works. Several of the pieces bear also the arms of royal or noble French personages of the period. All the pieces of this ware known to exist are carefully enumerated, and, of the fifty-five known specimens, twenty-three (the whole number contained in English collections) may now be seen at South Kensington. They consist of cups, candlesticks, and other articles: a salt-cellar, or some other small piece, cost 700*l*., and the twenty-three pieces are estimated by enthusiastic virtuosi to be worth thirty thousand pounds! The large and unique ewer from Mr. Magniac's collection may be taken as the finest specimen of this ware, and perhaps the most original and interesting types of it are the candlesticks from the collection of Sir Anthony de Rothschild and Mr. Fountaine.

The matchless Sèvres contributed by Her Majesty is the finest collection ever seen by the public. Some perfect and brilliant specimens of old Sèvres, inlaid in cabinets and tables, are amongst the furniture displayed. The work-table and music-table presented by Queen Marie Antoinette to Lady Auckland, at the period of Lord Auckland's embassy, have associations which enhance their artistic value.

But, for interest derived from historical association and for artistic beauty, there is no class of objects in all this wonderful collection of art treasures that is better deserving of study than the numerous and valuable portrait miniatures; but we must not yield to the temptation to mention any of these relics more particularly.

We have said that, with one or two exceptions, painting is not (and was not intended to be) represented in this exhibition, neither are there many representatives of the sister fine-art of sculpture. The works in marble and terra-cotta are few, but include some fine specimens of sixteenth-century Florentine work. The only piece of sculpture we noticed on a subject connected with English history is the life-sized head in marble which is said to be a portrait of Henry VII. by Torregiano, and is contributed by the Duke of Northumberland—a nobleman who has signalised his taste, munificence, and love for art, by surrounding himself with such works and collections, artistic and archæological, as a nation might be proud to possess.

Upon the whole, then, it may be affirmed that this exhibition contains a most valuable and systematic collection of art treasures, remarkable as well for the historic interest as for the artistic beauty of most of the objects displayed, and that within its limits a finer collection has never been brought together for the gratification and instruction of the public. One cannot help regretting its necessary dispersion at no distant time, but it will long be remembered as a bright vision, and is, we hope, destined to leave beneficial results behind.

# DIVISION III.

## BIOGRAPHICAL AND HISTORICAL ESSAYS, REVIEWS, AND LECTURES.

# AUGUSTUS CÆSAR:
## HIS COURT AND COMPANIONS.

[*Bentley's Miscellany*, January 1861.]

A FORTNIGHT after the assassination of Julius Cæsar, a delicate and sickly-looking youth, the dictator's grand-nephew and adopted heir, appeared in Rome, at the critical moment when the murder of Cæsar had spread terror and confusion, and when Antony had roused the Roman people to indignation against the conspirators. Landing from Apollonia, an adventurer, Caius Octavius—for it is of him we speak—had not long arrived in Rome when he became a hero; gained statesmen and officers to his interest, and divided with Antony, the consul, the favour of the people; and entered on that marvellous career which, after long years of civil war, and tyranny, and bloodshed, ended in the dissolution of the republic itself, and in his being hailed by the grateful senate and people of Rome, Augustus, Emperor, and Father of his country.

It was in that memorable year—the six hundred and nineteenth of the city—in which Cicero's administration as consul ended, and in which Rome was preserved from destruction, and liberty thought to be more firmly established than ever, that Caius Octavius was born. The family of Atia, his mother (the niece of Julius Cæsar), had given many senators to Rome; but, although the Octavii were a wealthy family of Velitræ, his father seems to have been the first who obtained admission to the senate. His mother bestowed great pains on the education of the youthful Octavius, and is said to have transmitted to him much of her purity of diction and grace of manners. His own natural gifts seemed to promise fruits worthy of her care; but no one could have supposed, when at the age of eighteen he entered on public life, that he was destined to connect his name with every event of importance in the annals of the world for the next fifty-eight years, and to transform the Republic into the Empire of Rome.

Of course it would not be possible to give in an article like the present the story of a reign so eventful as that of Augustus—a reign which merits more attention than any other in the Roman history, or to trace in succession the various incidents which, during that long period, changed the destiny of nations and the aspect of the world. We do not here profess to write his life or analyse his character; nor can we attempt to depict more than some artistic and literary aspects of a court that was adorned by the illustrious band of friends who made "the Augustan era" Rome's culminating point in art, and poetry, and splendour. It was under the encouragement of Augustus that the lyric Horace wrote his matchless poems and the tasteful Virgil studied and polished his immortal compositions; in his reign Tibullus was writing his refined elegies and Ovid his flowing numbers; Dionysius of Halicarnassus, the historian, had come to Rome; Strabo was writing some of his works; and Livy was concluding his history.

The mother of Octavius seems to have dreaded his accepting Julius Cæsar's adoption of him as a son, as if she foresaw, that, in order to become the avenger and successor of Cæsar, he would grasp the consular office, and engage in a proscription of the best and noblest of his countrymen. If the imperial power of the great man whose name he now assumed was really at this period the object of the young Cæsar's ambition, he must have seen that his youth and want of military experience, not to mention the power of Antony and the strength of the friends of liberty, forbade all hope of his immediate attainment of imperial authority, and warned him, at all events, to bide his time. He had the prudence to assume—as the nephew of another great soldier and emperor in our own times has assumed—the appearance of fidelity to a republic, and for a time he seemed to be guided by the counsels of Cicero, whose patriotism was well known to be inflexible.

We who find instruction and delight in the works of that illustrious man, and justly appreciate the moral grandeur of his character, do not wonder at the influence he possessed in public affairs, and can estimate the importance of his friendship to the young Octavius. Cicero had twice saved Rome, the Senate, and the Commonwealth; the integrity of his patriotism was only equalled by the splendour of his eloquence and learning; and the sweetness of temper and charm of manners that gave him such power over all who approached him were adorned by purity of life and instinctive love of virtue.

Octavius was placed in a situation of the greatest difficulty amid the intrigues of party that followed on the events of the Ides of March; but he acted with an art and prudence that neutralised the hostility of Antony, and baffled the oldest statesmen of Rome. Cæsar's name was still a charm to the soldiery and to all whom he had promoted; his cause was espoused by all who were adventurers; and the commonalty and populace, eager for novelty, were accordingly ranged on the side of the youthful soldier, who styled himself " Son of the Deified " and " Avenger of Cæsar," while most of the patricians and men of the equestrian dignity stood by the old principles of the Commonwealth. Those writers who have taken an unfavourable view of his character, represent that at this juncture he dissembled his real aim, seeing his best chance for future empire in sharing power with others until he could grasp the whole. Be this as it may, Octavius Cæsar, notwithstanding that he had been mortally opposed to Antony, joined him and Lepidus in the ominous " Triumvirate for regulating the Commonwealth," from whose usurpation such " woes unnumbered " sprung. And now began the terrible proscription, in which each triumvir sacrificed even his own friends to the vengeance of his colleagues. A veritable Reign of Terror brooded over Rome, in which the soldiery were to become the instruments of public ruin. The best blood of her citizens was sacrificed in the long and cruel struggle that ensued; but the proscription had not a more noble victim than Cicero himself. Octavius, as his apologists affirm, strongly endeavoured to preserve him, but his death was held a necessary sacrifice to the common interest of the three, for his virtue warned them that he never could be the friend of tyrants, and his authority was such that an enemy could not be suffered to retain it. As we are not now writing the history of this short but sanguinary tyranny, it will suffice to say, that, while proscription and plunder were occupying the triumvirate at Rome, the successes of Brutus and Cassius—the Agamemnon and Achilles of the Roman legions—in Thrace, obliged Octavius Cæsar and his colleagues to encounter the champions of the republic in the field. He was doomed to witness the defeat of Julius Cæsar's veterans in their naval encounter with the forces of Sextus Pompey, the scene of which was the bay between Messina and Reggio that became memorable in English naval history for the defeat of the Spanish fleet by Admiral Byng. Octavius then proceeded to join Antony among the barren hills of Macedon. The strength of the Roman republic was there collected under Brutus and Cassius; the representatives of patricians who had been sacrificed for their patriotism had joined the camp; and the Oriental allies of the old Commonwealth were under arms in its defence, each bringing their national weapons—there were slingers from Minorca, light horsemen from Numidia, and archers from Crete.

The issue to be decided at Philippi was, whether the laws should resume their majesty, the senate its reverence, and the people their power; but, after the second battle on that memorable field, Antony and Octavius Cæsar found themselves masters of the empire. Octavius had very narrowly escaped after his defeat on the first encounter, for he had to spend three nights hid in a morass in a worse condition than Charles the Second's in the oak after the battle of Worcester. Antony, on his return from Pharsalia, carried beyond all bounds of decorum by the flow of fortune, appeared at Rome in a chariot drawn by lions—the first spectacle of the kind the Romans had ever seen; and the subjection of those fierce animals to the yoke, was looked upon (as Pliny says) as an omen of breaking the spirit of the Roman people. Antony and Octavius Cæsar, after their victory over Brutus, shared the empire, Antony taking for his portion the rich eastern provinces from the Adriatic to the Euphrates, and leaving Italy, Gaul, and Spain to his great rival.

Octavius Cæsar was now free to listen to the advice of counsellors older and wiser than himself; and, while his natural sagacity (as Tytler has remarked) enabled him to discern the character that was best fitted to gain the popular regard, his genius and versatility of temper enabled him to assume it. To his credit, he soon began to repose unlimited confidence in Mæcenas; and there is no doubt that his success, his reformation, and his future greatness, were essentially due to the counsels of that wise and faithful minister. Mæcenas, who boasted the lineage of the old Tuscan kings, was a man of noble and enlightened mind, and had sincerely at heart the welfare of the Roman people. Aiming at the salvation of Octavius Cæsar, and of Rome by his means, Mæcenas at first disguised the statesman in the man of pleasure, and he succeeded so well, that his good counsels directed public affairs, and dictated salutary legislation, as soon as the city was delivered from the confiscations and the military violence that followed the return of the victorious legions.

Those confiscations led to an incident which has an interest for every age, inasmuch as they were the occasion of Virgil being made known to Octavius Cæsar. A centurion had seized his patrimony; and Pollio and Gallus—themselves poets as well as statesmen—anxious to protect genius in the person of the young poet of Mantua, took him to Mæcenas, then governor of Rome. Mæcenas presented him to Octavius, who reinstated him in his paternal fields upon the Mincio, little conscious that his protection of Virgil was destined to procure for the world immortal works of genius, and to surround his own name with its most unfading honours. So, too, although Virgil's friend Pollio took a prominent part in the public affairs of his day, was a patriot, an orator, a poet, and a lover of learning, it is as the protector of Virgil and Horace that he has acquired his more lasting fame. To him Virgil addressed his well-known Birth-day Ode; and Horace, some years afterwards, commemorates him, as oracle of the senate and supporter of the state, and (in the first Ode of the Second Book) presents him shining with the honours of the Dalmatian triumph.

Virgil was about seven years older than Octavius Cæsar, and was at this time in his thirtieth year. At Naples, which, having been a Grecian colony, retained much of the manners and language of its Athenian founders, he seems to have acquired that taste for the polished literature of Greece of which his works afford continual examples; but after the restoration of his patrimony he resided chiefly at the capital, in favour not only with Mæcenas but with Octavius himself, and enjoying the friendship of the learned men who then surrounded the great minister. It would seem that Virgil produced his celebrated Eclogues soon after the restoration of his paternal fields. He is said to have applied himself to pastoral composition at the suggestion of Pollio, and to have taken the Sicilian poetry of Theocritus for his example. At all events, we may imagine how welcome rural images and pictures of the days of innocence must have been to statesmen and officers wearied by scenes of military usurpation and the storms of civil war.

Poetry and literature had not then become popular, and indeed are said to have stolen on the Romans against their will. Their frugal, conquering, and laborious life had been almost as incompatible with literature as with luxury. But, even before "the Augustan era," the stage, and the encouragement given by eminent men to learning, greatly influenced the public taste; and from the time of the second war with Carthage the martial Romans are said to have owned the nobler influence of the Muses. At the time, however, of Virgil's introduction to the heir of Cæsar, and for several years afterwards, the two greatest Roman poets (Cinna and Calidius, who are mentioned by Catullus and Cicero) were men whose names are now scarcely known to scholars, and even in his lifetime Virgil's fame quite outshone that of his predecessors.

Soon after he had acquired the friendship of Mæcenas, Virgil and his friend Varius showed the minister some early poems of another favourite of the muse and coheir of fame—the youthful Horace. His learning, wit, and manners so recommended him to Mæcenas, that ere many months had passed Horace, then aged about twenty-six, became his familiar friend, and his introduction to Octavius Cæsar, who was about two years younger than himself, soon followed. Most important were its results. Horace had been made a military tribune by Brutus, and was present at the battle of Philippi, but was more inclined to court the Muses' favour than that of Mars. Fortunately for posterity, he escaped shipwreck on his return from the East, and by the aid of Mæcenas obtained a pardon for having borne arms under Brutus. Although a zealous friend, he loved ease and literary leisure, and being of convivial disposition, fond of good company, and possessed of great amenity of temper and powers of pleasing, his society was much valued, and he soon acquired the esteem of the greatest men in Rome, including Octavius himself. In a letter written to Horace, in commendation of one of his writings, Cæsar expresses his wish that he had been introduced in the dialogue, so that he might appear in it to futurity. "Are you afraid," he asks the poet, "it should injure you with posterity if it should appear that you had lived with me in some familiarity?"

It would seem that at the time when Horace first came to court, Octavius, deeming his power secure, indulged in a life of vicious excess and luxury. His celebrated banquet of the deities of Olympus was certainly of itself enough to alarm his wiser friends. This was the licentious feast in which the greater gods and goddesses were audaciously represented by living revellers: Jove was there with his thunderbolt, Saturn with his scythe, and, more appropriately, Bacchus with his grapes; the "winged son of Maia" with his wand, and Mars with his shield and spear, while the young Cæsar himself played the part of the bright Apollo, his tutelary god. Six ladies personated, respectively, Juno with her sceptre, Cybele with her turret crown, and Ceres with her sheaf; there, too, was Venus, and Pallas with her helmet and spear, and Diana with her crescent diadem and her sylvan bow. But Octavius could relish less voluptuous diversions. He was a great lover of comedy and the legitimate pleasures of the stage; the public games, moreover, which he instituted in honour of Apollo, as well as the shows with which he regaled the people in the days of his imperial power, may be taken to indicate a politic, if not judicious, regard for public amusements. His celebration of the games of Venus Genetrix, in Julius Cæsar's honour, in the forty-third year before Christ, has been made memorable by the emperor himself, who, as recorded by Pliny, says it was during that celebration that the bright comet appeared "which was commonly believed to be a sign that the soul of Cæsar was admitted among the gods."*

* This famous "Julian Star" is the device on the coin of Cæsar Augustus, which is described (among coins of the Julii) at p. 96 of Admiral Smyth's *Catalogue* of the Duke of Northumberland's Cabinet of Roman Family Coins.

Mæcenas sought also to reform the political character of Octavius, and seems to have thought that his design would be best accomplished by the instrumentality of men of letters, who, without appearing to administer reproofs, might artfully lead him to prefer the power of clemency and justice to military force, and might inculcate moral lessons without the form of admonition. For these noble objects the courtly Horace was encouraged to write many of his immortal odes. His poetry was of a kind then unknown to Rome, and, while it evinces his tender, ardent, and amorous disposition, it also shows that he was a keen observer of men, a patriot, and a lover of wisdom, as well as a maker of verse. With admirable address, and a happy discernment of character, Horace conveyed instruction while achieving masterpieces of lyric composition; and, in what he wrote after Octavius Cæsar became emperor, he contrived, while invoking Clio and her sister-muses, appropriately to enforce maxims of clemency and beneficence in the language of courtly compliment and affectionate congratulation.

But while Antony, his formidable rival, divided with Cæsar the power of the state, holding as he did the eastern provinces with the most tremendous military force the world then knew, and Sextus Pompey, the champion of the old republic, was all-powerful at sea, Octavius had sterner monitors than Mæcenas and Horace to call him from sensual pleasures. The republic had been paralysed rather than destroyed at Philippi, and the large body of Roman nobles who, under proscription and banishment, had taken refuge in Sicily, flocked to Pompey's side. Sicily, the granary of Rome, was in his hands, and the supplies of corn being therefore stopped, famine amongst the people at home increased the danger of Cæsar's position. If the policy of Mæcenas had not allied Octavius and Antony by family ties, it seems probable that a conjunction between that soldier of fortune and Pompey would have been fatal to Cæsar. But his sister, the beautiful and accomplished Octavia—a woman as much distinguished by virtue and good sense as by her dignified and winning manners—had been married to Antony, and the sunniest days of his life were those he passed at Athens, happy in her love. Civil war, however, called Octavius from his feasting and diversions, and Antony from his Eastern luxury, and again covered the sea with the hostile fleets of the triumvirs and their hereditary foe. But the peace they agreed on at Miseno, while it gave to the cause of the Roman republic its final death-blow, brought a truce to the calamities that had for nine years afflicted Italy; Pompey sailed back to Sicily, and Antony to Greece, and the long proscribed and banished patricians followed Octavius Cæsar to Rome.

After the return of these noble Romans, Cæsar became surrounded by a court, but its chief ornaments were the learned men whom he encouraged to associate there. In every great family at that time, a learned native of Greece commonly resided, and brought her polished arts to soften the martial and political education of the Roman youth. Octavius had himself been bred under Athenodorus the Rhetorician, a native of Pergamos, who is said to have been one of the best and wisest men of the age, and Octavius, who could recognise virtue if he did not then practise it, treated him with particular honour. It was not only in rhetoric that he was the preceptor of his pupil, but he taught that without honour there could be no happiness; and it was he who, when aged and retiring to his native country, gave his pupil the memorable advice, whenever he should find anger rising, to repeat the letters of the alphabet (!) before speaking or writing. Here, too, might be seen Areius the Platonist, a native of Alexandria, whose refinement fitted him for courtly life; and— more illustrious than these distinguished foreigners—the noble Roman, Publius Valerius Messala Corvinus, of whom Cicero (whose disciple he was) gives a fine character, who is commended by Quintilian, and is immortalised by Horace as the most eloquent lawyer in Rome. The poet (in the twenty-first Ode of his Third Book) mentions him with peculiar distinction, and calls for his choicest wine to be poured out "in gratiam Corvini." Tibullus also was his companion and eulogist. He was a general favourite, and one of the most accomplished of the band of friends who graced the young Cæsar's court. Having been in arms with Brutus, Messala had, of course, come under proscription by the triumvirate, but he was afterwards excepted by edict. He seems to have been particularly remarkable for correctness of style as an orator, and for a dignified manner of speaking. To these accomplishments he added attainments in other liberal arts, and, while honouring the severer studies of philosophy, was himself an eminent patron of the wits and poets of the time. The favour shown by Octavius Cæsar to all learned men and votaries of the Muses, has been attributed by some writers to his having artfully sought to mask his own designs against Roman liberty under an apparent devotion to liberal arts and learning; but, whatever his motives may at first have been, the reputation of this great emperor chiefly rests on the protection he gave to learning and its votaries; and such a lustre has genius thrown over his reign that we always speak of it as the Augustan age, and regard it as the most brilliant period of the Roman state.

But, amidst all this splendour of literature and art, the home of Octavius was not without the more genial rays of female grace and beauty. Among the ladies who attended Octavia, his sister, at the ceremony of her nuptials with Antony, was Livia, the young and nobly born wife of Tiberius Nero. Tall, graceful, and lovely, with a look that inspired respect no less than love, she surpassed in the eyes of Octavius all women he had ever seen, and he determined to make her his wife. Tiberius, dreading the power which could have made Livia a widow, complied, and divorced her, but did not long survive her marriage to his unscrupulous rival. The marriage contract was immediately followed by that remarkable occurrence which was interpreted as an omen of her future greatness. As Livia was sitting in the garden, an eagle, soaring above, dropped a white hen, unhurt, into her lap, and in its mouth was found a sprig of laurel, with berries. The aruspices, being consulted, ordered the bird to be carefully cherished and the laurel spray to be planted, and this was done in Cæsar's villa on the Tiber, which was situated about nine miles from Rome, on the Flaminian Way, where the white hen's race so multiplied that the place acquired, says Blackwell, the name of the Poultry; and the sprig of bay so flourished that Octavius, at his first public triumph, took from this tree his crown and the branch he held in his hand.

But ere long the eyes of the Roman people were turned to Alexandria, then the capital of the East, where Antony—the greatest soldier of his day, the idol of his vast army, and the master of the richest provinces of the Roman empire—had become enslaved by Cleopatra, Queen of Egypt, and, far away from Octavia, his matchless consort, was leading a life of extravagant luxury and dishonour.  Octavia heard with silent sorrow of Antony's excesses in Egypt, but nobly sought to moderate the resentment which her brother, who highly honoured her, displayed.  In the hope of reclaiming Antony to his country and herself, Octavia, furnished by Cæsar with a guard of two thousand of his best soldiers, with costly presents, and warlike stores for Antony's service, sailed for Alexandria.  But, blinded by debauchery, he avoided an interview with his wife.  She returned to Rome, and devoted herself to the education not only of her own children, but of the two sons of Antony by Fulvia, in her lifetime Octavius Cæsar's enemy—conduct the magnanimity of which filled Italy with admiration.

Antony, meanwhile, as if forgetful of the Roman state itself, and of his legitimate issue, parcelled out the Eastern empire among his children by Cleopatra, and held gorgeous festivals in her honour, diverting from the people of Rome the spoils and honours that had been purchased by Roman blood.  He assumed the habit and symbols of Bacchus, and, crowned by ivy and the vine, rode through Alexandria in a chariot drawn by tigers.  His excesses only proved to Octavius—his sober and subtle rival— that the time was come for ending their partnership of power, which, inaugurated in bloodshed, now threatened fresh calamities to Rome.

The approaching rupture made Cæsar more intent on gaining the affection of the senators and the goodwill of the people; and at length, in the seven hundred and twentieth year of the city, about eight years after the battle of Philippi, he led his army to fresh military glory in a campaign against the wild and warlike people of Dalmatia; but, prudently postponing the "triumph" awarded to him for this Illyrian campaign, devoted his share of the spoils to adorn Rome with the quadruple colonnade in the Campus Martius—a stately monument of his magnificence and love of art.  This vast building contained temples, courts, libraries, and schools, adorned by Grecian masters with statues and paintings (landscape painting, according to Pliny, was first cultivated in the time of Octavius Cæsar); and in honour of his exemplary sister he called it from her name "the Octavian Portico."

But the wrongs of Octavia were to be, ere long, signally avenged, and the conflict was approaching in which Antony, and with him the very name of the Republic, was destined to fall.

By the wisdom of Mæcenas and the bravery of Agrippa, Octavius Cæsar had become master of the Western world after the naval defeat of Pompey in Sicily, which took place about two years before the Illyrian victories.* Wiser from the perils he had encountered, he had learned the instability of power founded solely on an army and not consolidated by the affection of a people. Wisdom, moderation, and humanity had now for a long time seemed to actuate all his conduct. He promoted and employed patriots who at Philippi had been in arms against him. He sent Messala to command in Gaul and humble those fierce mountaineer Savoyards the Salassi, by whose defeat he acquired and colonised the pass from Italy into France and Spain, which was afterwards, in his honour, called Augusta Prætoria—a name which, corrupted into d'Aosta, still denominates that celebrated pass of the Alps through Piedmont.† To the brave and thoughtful Strabo, whose fidelity and affection to Brutus had recommended him to the esteem of Messala, Cæsar generously gave a naval command, and he became so eminent that his figure was engraved and worn in rings, like the effigies of the greatest Romans. So, too, Publius Sextius, and other friends of liberty, were invited to honours of the state.

At length the news came to Rome that Antony, postponing his intended invasion of Parthia, was advancing with sixteen legions to the sea-coast, and might land in Italy before the end

* At page 100 of the Catalogue of the Duke of Northumberland's Roman Family Coins, Admiral Smyth mentions the suggestion that the two branches of laurel depicted on the coin of Cæsar Augustus (No. 30 of the Julii), in the possession of His Grace, refers to the honours granted on the death of Sextus Pompey. The coin next enumerated in the Catalogue seems to Admiral Smyth to have been struck on the same occasion.

† The subjection of the Salassi and the founding of the colony of Augusta Prætoria is possibly commemorated by the coin (No. 27 of the Julii) in the possession of the Duke of Northumberland, and described at p. 99 of Admiral Smyth's Catalogue.

of summer. The taxes which Cæsar was obliged to impose did not increase his popularity at home, but Antony, on the other hand, had lost the affection of every Roman by divorcing the virtuous Octavia in order to espouse the Egyptian enchantress —an act doubly unpardonable in Roman eyes, since she was a foreign princess and a declared enemy to Rome. With the manners and maxims of the Romans he laid aside the dress of his country; and, since Cleopatra assumed the attributes of Isis, Antony was represented by her side with those that characterised the Egyptian god. War being declared against Cleopatra, the armies began to move early in the spring, and the seas were covered with the gathering fleets. Antony's preparations befitted the man who held the lion's share of the Roman Empire, and commanded the wealth of Asia and the forces of tributary kings. Octavius Cæsar, on the other hand, led the might of Italy, and was accompanied by the senate and people of Rome. Guided by the fatal counsels of Cleopatra, Antony risked all upon a naval engagement, although the advantage in such an encounter was on the side of his adversary, and off

Leucadia's far-projecting rock of woe

the engagement memorable as the battle of Actium was fought. The conflict had raged for some hours, when Cleopatra, to secure her own safety, led the Egyptian part of the squadron from the bay, and the faithless and deluded Antony, following her, abandoned his fleet to the conqueror. Antony's enormous army, shut up on one side of the bay, forsaken by their chief officers and threatened by famine, soon afterwards surrendered. From this victory—achieved in the seven hundred and twenty-third year of the city—the final fall of the Republic and the rise of the Roman Empire are dated.

Octavius Cæsar did not hasten to pursue his defeated enemy, but wisely divided the force of Antony's army, gained great applause by pardoning some noble Romans who had been in arms against him, and, leaving Mæcenas to exercise supreme power as "Prefect of Italy," went to Athens to visit that ancient seat of art and learning. The fleets of Greece were gone, but historians and philosophers, the distributors of fame, still resorted to Athens, and gave it an eminence beyond that of the most powerful cities of the Roman empire. He was about to advance through Asia, when the danger of a military revolt recalled him to Rome; but having pacified the angry and murmuring army, he again advanced to complete the destruction of Antony, still leaving Mæcenas entrusted with the government of Italy and Rome.* The events that followed this campaign of Cæsar in the East are too well known to need description. He was encamped before Alexandria when Anthony rashly stabbed himself, and, being carried to the mausoleum in which Cleopatra had taken refuge, died there in her arms; and the artful queen, finding she could not move the conqueror to pity or to love, likewise destroyed herself rather than adorn his triumph at Rome. And so, within a year from the battle of Actium, Cæsar became undisputed master of the whole Roman empire. Towards Antony's family and most of his followers he signalised the clemency of which he had shortly before given a memorable example in the treatment of Herod.†

Enriched with the treasures of the Ptolemys and the ransom paid for Egypt, which thenceforth became a Roman province, Octavius Cæsar returned to Rome arbiter of the fortunes of the world, and received all the trophies that the Roman people and subject nations could bestow.‡ Temples were dedicated in his

* *Apropos* of this regency, we are reminded of the two antique gems precisely resembling each other, and on both of which was engraved a sphinx, the Egyptian emblem of strength and wisdom, which Octavius had found among his mother's jewels, and used in rings as his seals, for it was one of these that in his absence he left with Mæcenas as his representative: the seal of Mæcenas himself bore the image of a frog, and the sight of this well-known symbol of his power sufficed to make all people tremble who had anything to lose.

† Cæsar's clemency was extended, as the reader will remember, to Herod after the fall of Antony. It was when he was at Rhodes, on his way to Egypt, that Herod appeared before him, and said, " Cæsar! it was Antony who made me King of the Jews, and in his service I should have fought against you. I have not abandoned my benefactor since his misfortune, and I have discharged the duty of a faithful counsellor towards him. But God has given you the victory, and has hindered him from listening to my advice. My throne is overturned together with his fortune; but consider my fidelity, and not him to whom it has been rendered." Whereupon Cæsar bade him resume his crown, and confirmed him in his kingdom.—Josephus, de Bell. Judaic. lib. i. c. 15, cited by Blackwell.

‡ In the Duke of Northumberland's Cabinet of Roman Family Coins there is a coin inscribed CÆSAR DIVI FILIUS, the device on which possibly alludes, as Admiral Smyth (p. 27 of Catalogue) suggests, to Octavius having become sole ruler of the Roman world.

honour, and he was hailed as the guardian of the state. Magnificent triumphs were decreed to him, and Rome saw the cavalcade of her robed magistrates and senators, the tributary chiefs, the spoils of vanquished nations, the sea-green standard of Agrippa, the emblems of consular state, and the long procession of martial legions and cohorts gracing the triumphal car of her hero—then only thirty-five years of age.

Of the treasure brought from Egypt, some idea is given by the fact, that, amongst the formidable army of one hundred and twenty thousand soldiers, a sum equivalent to more than three-quarters of a million in our money was distributed, while the country places which the men were judiciously sent to colonise were largely subsidised; that a sum perhaps as large was distributed amongst the impoverished citizens; and that jewels worth even a larger sum, besides the incredible quantity of eight tons of gold, were deposited in the temple of Jupiter Capitolinus. The famous Alexandrian obelisks which Cæsar brought to Rome formed a more enduring trophy of his Egyptian spoliations.

It was to rebuke the magnificence and luxury which he feared would follow the peace enjoyed by the empire after these events that Horace wrote the ode "Persicos odi, puer," in which he deprecates the Persian luxury in entertainments, and exhorts to the old simplicity in living. The admonition, however, was not needed by Cæsar himself, for his own table was furnished with a Spartan simplicity.

Whether, as Tacitus has said, Octavius Cæsar found that the government of one person was the only remedy for the misfortunes of his country, worn out by discords and irreconcilable enmities, or whether, as his enemies alleged, the ambition of reigning was his only motive, he curbed his ambition, and artfully resolved to make the continuance of his power appear dependent on the request of the senate and people. He showed a high degree of moderation and respect for popular rights, maintained the ancient elective forms of the constitution, and professed his own functions to be merely a temporary administration for the public good. But it is probable, that, if the spirit of the old republic had not been extinct, Mæcenas would not have advised him that there could be no safety for him save upon a throne, and Octavius himself would hardly have contemplated such a change. When we look at his position shortly after his acquisition of undivided power, he seems, indeed, to have preserved (as some historian has remarked) only a spectre of liberty—a phantom that walked the Forum yearly, and frequented the senate in its shape. Meantime, he set himself to restore the dignity of that august assembly (which now numbered more than a thousand members) by clearing it of unworthy and unqualified persons, many of whom had bought their elevation during the civil wars. While the reformation of this great body was in progress, Octavius Cæsar never went to the senate house without wearing a hauberk of mail under his usual robe, or unattended by ten strong and trusty senators as a body-guard.

All his conduct now tended to the public welfare, and was distinguished by acts of prudence, wisdom, and generosity. He was a prince in all that concerned the public good, and seemed to have become a stoic in things that related to his own household and private luxury. When the senate and people voted money for statues in his honour, he devoted it to civic embellishment, and caused his silver statue (said to be the first silver statue raised) to be melted for the decoration of the temple of Apollo Palatine. With the New Year's gifts of his friends he placed statues in the squares of Rome; and in the year when the Asiatic provinces suffered by earthquakes he paid their tribute into the public treasury out of his own money. He acted as if he wished to make the Romans sensible how much a well-regulated monarchy was preferable to a turbulent liberty, and how essential his government was to the public happiness. He had become not only the avenger, but the imitator, of Julius Cæsar. When that great representative of the national spirit of Rome had become master of Italy, moderation and wisdom marked his rule, and works of legislative and social reform employed his liberal and capacious mind, and in these things also his adopted son emulated his example.

It was therefore natural that Octavius Cæsar should receive, as he did, from the grateful senate of Rome the title of IMPERATOR and appellation of AUGUSTUS, which the senate, to do him the greater honour, afterwards perpetuated by giving it to the month heretofore called Sextilis in the Roman calendar.

In the buildings of Rome before "the Augustan era" public health and convenience seem to have been disregarded; nor does any great scheme of metropolitan improvement appear to have been attempted until Octavius acquired imperial power. Had a reformed provincial municipality or a metropolitan vestry of the present day directed affairs of taste and public health in Rome, its buildings could hardly have been in a worse state than he beheld them. It is always said to have been his boast that he found the city of brick and left it of marble; but, many as were the temples he rebuilt in honour of his country's gods, he was not less sedulous to build for the poor citizens doomed to inhabit the lower parts of the city. In Augustan Rome, the heights of the Cœlian and Esquiline hills were for the most part occupied by the villas and gardens of patrician families. The villa of Augustus was called the Palatium—a name then peculiar to this mansion of the Palatine hill, but afterwards given to all royal abodes. The Palatine temple, which he afterwards built, was a famous monument of his magnificence, and he annexed to it such a library as procured for him the applause of all men of learning. In the place of a crowd of unsightly and unwholesome dwellings between the Forum and the Quirinal, he built his own new stately Forum; and, though his public buildings displaced large masses of the poorer citizens, they found more healthy abodes in the new suburban regions, the honour of enlarging Rome having been awarded to him for the victories over the Romans. The grandeur of the city under Augustus appeared not only in its increased extent and splendid buildings, but also in the stupendous aqueducts and underground works which still excite our wonder.

Amidst all this sumptuousness of art, there was epicurean luxury in living, and the wealthy Romans of the time seem to have resembled those people of Agrigentum, who, as Plato said, " built as if they were to live for ever, and feasted as if they were always about to die." The luxurious manner in which the patrician families lived in the reign of Augustus had a remarkable contrast in his own frugal simplicity. His taste was simple in this respect, as well as in dress, in which he is said to have been plain even to negligence. It might be said of Augustus, as Tacitus says of Agricola, " To soften prejudices, he resolved to shade the lustre of his name in the mild retreat of humble virtues." With this view he resigned himself to the calm enjoyments of a domestic life. Plain in his apparel, easy of access, and never attended by more than one or two friends, he was remarkable for nothing but the simplicity of his appearance; insomuch that they who knew no criterion of merit but external show and grandeur, as often as they saw Agricola were still to seek for the great and illustrious character. His modesty was an art which a few only could understand.

The poets of the court of Augustus contrast the palaces and the splendour of the city in their day with its rude beginnings. Still more striking was the extension of the Empire of Rome: a state that had been a hamlet of shepherds and refuge of the Alban colonists was become the mother of nations and mistress of the world. Her dominion stretched from the Euphrates to the Atlantic; from the land of the rising sun to the shores that "saw the burnished waters blaze" in his setting beams; from Tanais and the Danube on the north to the Lybian deserts on the south; and, ere a few more years had passed, it may be said to have been bounded only by the seas. "Who would think," well may Ovid exclaim, "that this little spot was fated to hold so wide an empire!"*

In the seven hundred and thirtieth year of the city Augustus returned from Spain, where, to secure his conquests, new colonies were settled, which became great cities (Cæsarea Augusta, for example, retains in the modern name of Saragoza a faint trace of the patronage under which it rose), and other towns that had fallen into decay were restored. For Augustus, like Romulus and the mythic heroes whom the Greeks, and afterwards the Romans, had chosen for their tutelary deities, built cities and settled colonies (Suetonius says he established twenty-eight colonies in Italy); and Horace takes care to mention the great and useful exploits in this respect of Hercules, and Bacchus, and Castor, and Romulus, as if to give a higher idea of the glory of Augustus, whose statue the Romans even in his lifetime placed with the statues of those heroes.

* In the reign of Augustus, a Roman fleet sailed round the promontory of Skagen; discovered (about 16 years after the birth of Christ) the island of Fionia, or Fünea; and is even supposed to have reached the entrance of the Gulf of Finland.

The death of the noble young Marcellus, Octavia's beloved son, to whom, three years before, the emperor had given Julia, his daughter, in marriage, and who was his hope and intended heir, happened in the year after Augustus returned from Spain, soon after Marcellus had completed his twentieth year; and the affecting lines,

> Ostendunt terris hanc tantum fata neque, ultra
> Esse sinent, &c.,

which Virgil wrote in allusion to this event, showed that he could invoke the muse to soothe the domestic grief as well as to celebrate the public glory of his patron.

To perpetuate the name of the noble young Marcellus, the emperor afterwards gave it to the vast theatre, the remains of which attest the magnificence of the Romans.

While Augustus was adorning the city at home and extending the empire abroad, Virgil—who was soon to be hailed prince of the Roman epic poets, as his illustrious friend had been hailed prince of the Roman people—was still engaged on his great poem, in which, although the adventures of Æneas are its chief subject, the glories of Rome and the fortunes of the Julian house, into which Augustus had been adopted, are skilfully interwoven. Virgil has given the Æneid an historical colouring, and connected the fortunes of Rome and of his great patron with the illustrious names of Troy.

Virgil, who seems, like Horace, to have been fond of rural pleasures and country pursuits—

> Far from the madding crowd's ignoble strife,—

had retired to Greece to finish his poem among the "Edens of the eastern wave," and was at Athens in the seven hundred and thirty-fifth year of the city, when he met Augustus on his return from the East. He appears to have been prevailed on by the emperor to return with him to Italy; but he lived only to reach Brundisium (the Adriatic terminus of the Appian Way), where he died in the autumn of that year, in the fifty-first year of his age, having appointed Augustus and Mæcenas his heirs; and it appears that for the preservation of the Æneid the world is indebted to the emperor, at whose instance Varius is said to have now revised it.

On the death of his nephew Marcellus, Augustus bestowed his chief favour on his long and faithful ally the brave and triumphant Agrippa, whom he now married to Julia, the widow of Marcellus, then in her eighteenth year—a fatal gift indeed, so far as regarded his domestic happiness, but one that more closely allied him with his imperial friend. He accomplished the reduction of Spain and of the revolted provinces of Asia; was made, on returning from his campaign, the colleague of Augustus in the office of tribune—the most powerful of all magistracies; and would probably have acquired imperial power if death had not in less than ten years put an end to his growing honours. The emperor placed in the tomb he destined for himself the remains of him who had been his Mentor through life. But not all the favour of Cæsar, or the military achievements of Agrippa, or his commanding figure in the public affairs of his time, make us regard him with so much interest, as the share he had in the architectural adornment of Rome and the building of the Pantheon—the noblest heathen temple remaining in the world—which he finished in the year that saw Cæsar hailed Augustus and Emperor of Rome.

We have mentioned the meeting of Virgil and Augustus in the East, which took place, as all will remember, on the return of the emperor from the campaign that ended in the submission of the Parthians without a sword having been drawn. It was when Augustus was in Thessaly that Horace invoked* the mild counsels of Calliope and the Muses to refresh great Cæsar's mind:

> Vos Cæsarem altum, militiâ simul
> Fessas cohortes abdidit oppidis,
>   Finire quærentem labores,
>     Pierio recreatis antro:
> Vos lene consilium et datis, et dato
> Gaudetis, almæ, &c.†

---

\* Book iii. Ode iv.

†     Ye, in some cool. Pierian cave,
      Refresh great Cæsar's mind fatigued with war,
    When home returning with his cohorts brave,
      He bids them sheathe the bloodless scimitar.
    Ye give good counsel and are glad
    When righteous deeds confound the bad.
                           LORD RAVENSWORTH's *Odes of Horace.*

And the poet made the Parthian submission the subject of the magnificent ode,* beginning

> Cœlo tonantem credidimus Jovem
> Regnare : præsens divus habebitur
> Augustus, adjectis Britannis†
> Imperio, gravibusque Persis.‡

While at Samos, Augustus received the ambassadors of the Indian kings, who brought, amongst other presents, some tigers—animals which the Romans had never seen—besides such other wild creatures as would have sufficed to set up a zoological menagerie. On his return to Rome, the emperor gave a new proof of his moderation, for the only honour he would accept was an altar which the senate and people dedicated to " Fortune Returned;" nor did he allow himself much repose among the polished and learned companions who graced his court, for he soon started on his campaign in France. The man to whom the splendour of Rome was due, and whose fame now filled the world, had become remarkable for the simplicity of his taste, the self-denying frugality of his table, and his dislike of ostentatious parade and luxury. He equally disliked all affectation and redundancy in speaking and writing; his own style was chaste and perspicuous, and marked by a correct taste—proofs how greatly he had profited by the society of the accomplished men who surrounded him. His negligence in regard to dress has been mentioned: in personal appearance, however, the emperor is described by Suetonius to have been what might be called a handsome man. He was of middle stature, but symmetrical form, and his countenance was expressive of mildness and serenity. His eyes were sparkling and piercing, and they glittered with brightness when he was animated, insomuch that the superstitious people, eager to deify

* Book iii. Ode v.
† According to Strabo, the British chiefs had now sent their gifts and submitted to Augustus.
‡     We used to think the Thunderer reigned supreme
    In heaven and earth ; but Cæsar now must be
      Our chief and present deity;
    Since subject to his rule all nations seem,
    From Britain's distant isle to broad Euphrates' stream.
                  LORD RAVENSWORTH'S *Odes of Horace.*

him, thought their lustre a mark of the divine descent that had been invented for him.

Augustus had been absent in Gaul for about three years, when Horace, in one of the most cordial, natural, and beautiful of his odes,* affectionately, and with undoubted truth, expressed the love and veneration of the Romans towards him, and their impatient desire for his return:

> Divis orte bonis, optime Romulæ
> Custos gentis, abes jam nimium diu;
> Maturum reditum pollicitus patrum
>     Sancto concilio, redi.
>
> Lucem redde tuæ, dux bone, patriæ;
> Instar veris enim vultus ubi tuus
> Affulsit populo, gratior it dies,
>     Et soles melius nitent.
>
>         *       *       *       *
>
> Nullis polluitur casta domus stupris:
> Mos et lex maculosum edomuit nefas;
> Laudantur simili prole puerperæ;
>     Culpam poena premit comes,† &c.

---

* Book iv. Ode v.

† Thus gracefully translated in Lord Ravensworth's English lyric version of the Odes of Horace:

> O Thou, from gods propitious sprung,
> Best guardian of our land, too long
>     Thine absence here we mourn;
> The sacred conclave of the state
> Thy welcome promise still await;
>     Redeem it, and return.
>
> Restore, O gracious prince, the light
> Of dawn unto thy country's night;
>     For when thy face benign,
> Like spring, hath met thy people's gaze,
> More pleasantly pass by the days,
>     The suns more gaily shine.
>
>     *       *       *       *
>
> By thee our matrons' homes are pure,
> Th' approving father owns secure
>     His likeness in his son;
> Morals and law maintain their sway,
> And justice stops the culprit's way
>     Soon as the crime is done.

So, too, in "The Praises of Augustus," which conclude the odes, the poet says no more than the historians confirm, when he tells us that law and example had abolished licentiousness and vice, and praises Cæsar, not only for defending the empire by his arms, but reforming its laws by his wisdom. Could Augustus have desired more immortal fame for the good deeds of his later reign than has been given to them by Horace? *Apropos* to the campaign in Gaul, the reader will recollect that the colony of Augustodunum (Autun), which the emperor then founded, became the seat of letters and the Athens of Gaul, and continued to flourish in the time of Constantine. The Gauls, indeed, seem to have acquired a regard for the institutions of the Romans, together with their arts and learning.

At length the universal gratitude of the people awarded to Augustus the crowning glory of his life. The illustrious Messala, addressing him in full senate, said: " Cæsar Augustus! the senate and Roman people with one voice salute you FATHER OF YOUR COUNTRY." To which the emperor, affected even to tears, replied: " Having now attained the utmost height of my wishes, what more can I ask of the immortal gods than that you may retain towards me to the last moment of my life the sentiments you now express?" It was on this occasion that Augustus for the fourth time accepted the empire. History does not present so striking a contrast as we find between the mild and beneficent splendour of his imperial reign, and the dark shadows of licentiousness, cruelty, and bloodshed that stained his triumvirate. To what extent this transformation of the character of Augustus was due to the influence and the wise counsels of Mæcenas and his illustrious friends, it would not be possible to discuss in our present limits. But, great as their influence undoubtedly was, the conduct of Augustus, when he had adopted the maxims of virtue and greatness, and resolved to become the parent of his country and people, affords another proof of the power of the human mind to become what it contemplates, and to act in unison with its object.

Independently of the imperial power, he had continued to exert the immense authority of a tribune, and the office of " prefect of the laws and manners," in which he showed zeal for the glory of the state and the happiness of the people. By adding the dignity of high-priest, on the death of Lepidus, the emperor accumulated in himself the sacred, the military, and the civil power, and it was in virtue of this office that he suppressed all books of oracles and divination. To the spiritualists of these latter days he would certainly have shown no mercy.

His victories and administrative policy had restored peace to the world, stability of government, and good administration of the laws, shortly before the era of that crowning event in human annals—the birth of the PRINCE OF PEACE, to whom, ere two centuries elapsed, regions that were inaccessible even to the Romans were subdued. Augustus was not destined to know the God of Love, who came in the time of this mortal life to redeem and visit the world in great humility: could it have been his privilege, who in his later years so nobly cast away the works of darkness to put on as a Christian the armour of light, how Christendom through all the ages would have held his name in saintly honour!

Amid the splendour of his public life, Augustus had now to mourn the loss of his beloved sister—whose life for the twelve years she survived her son Marcellus were years of mourning; of Horace, his attached and honoured friend; and shortly afterwards of Mæcenas, his faithful minister, to whose encouragement we doubtless owe no small part of the works of Horace as well as Virgil. Mæcenas and Horace, in their lives united by a mutual friendship, were not divided in their death, both being interred in the Esquiliæ, to which the celebrated gardens of Mæcenas reached. The latter years of the emperor's life were clouded by domestic ills. His daughter Julia, on the death of Agrippa, took for her third spouse Tiberius, the son of Livia by her first husband. After losing both his grandsons Caius and Lucius, the emperor adopted Tiberius, whom he promoted to the highest military commands, and bestowed on him, after his successful campaign against the Germans, the government of the provinces of the empire and the command of the armies. Augustus thenceforth sought retirement from his public cares. His conquests in Spain had been his last military exploits, and he afterwards avoided war with as much care as the Roman generals of old had been used to seek it. At length, in the seventy-sixth year of his age and the forty-fourth of his reign, when he had seen peace restored to his country, her laws reformed, her commerce extended, her colonies flourishing, her people prosperous and grateful and offering him divine honours, arts and learning carried to a height unknown before, Rome boasting a splendour worthy the capital of the world, and an empire founded that was to endure for generations, Augustus died, and his last words were from the heart: "Livia! remember our happy union. Farewell!"*

* M. Perrot, who was charged with a scientific mission in Asia Minor, recently addressed to the Minister of State a report dated at Angora (the ancient Ancyra), in which he announces the discovery, in the vicinity of the temple, of all the first part of the Greek translation of the testament of Augustus, of which Hamilton copied the end. The report is published in the *Moniteur*, and contains the following passage: " I cannot tell you all the new facts that my discovery makes known respecting the life of Augustus, the honours which he received, &c. At the end of the first column of the Latin is a blank which is made up by the columns of the Greek text. They speak of the 'absolute power αντιξουσιον αρχην' which he refused, the 'prefecture' which he exercised, the 'consulate for life' which he would not accept, the 'prefecture of morals,' and his title of 'Prince of the Senate,' all which are wanting in the Latin. The date also of his testament is given. By means of these supplements I can add much more than I had dared to hope to the knowledge and true interpretation of this important epigraphic monument. I am at this moment in negotiation for the purchase of the adjacent house, which contains the middle part of the inscription. That which Hamilton had partially pulled down only contains the end. The text which he gives begins Table 4 of the Latin. There are probably, therefore, two columns of Greek to find, in order to re-establish the text of this important inscription."

# CANTERBURY AND ITS ARCHBISHOPS.

## I. SAXON PERIOD.

[*Bentley's Miscellany*, February 1861.]

IN Dr. Stanley's engaging narrative of the landing of Augustine —a narrative which has been justly said to be written in the spirit of a poet and with the accuracy of an historian—the reverend and learned writer points out the memories that are associated with the view beheld from the hill of St. Martin's little church, near Canterbury. It is justly described as a view the most inspiriting that can be found in the world; for from Canterbury, the first Christian city of England, from Kent, the first English Christian kingdom, has flowed the Christianity of our country; and from that little hill a power went forth which in the course of a few centuries adorned England with all the glorious monuments of art which piety reared for the future and for God.

The landing of Augustine has, therefore, a continuing interest for England through every age; and, beginning with the story of that memorable event, and tracing thence the succession of the Archbishops of Canterbury, the learned Dean of Chichester has produced a work\* of national as well as great historical interest, by connecting with the biography of each primate the ecclesiastical and chief political events of his age. Dr. Hook thus presents the Church of England as a national institution, which, under its various phases, has existed from the time of Augustine, through whom is, of course, deduced that succession of the Christian ministry which connects the present Church of England, through the Gallican, with the primitive and apostolic Church of Christ. And, by giving not merely the episcopal acts but the lives of the

\* Lives of the Archbishops of Canterbury. By Walter Farquhar Hook, D.D. Dean of Chichester. Vol. I.—Anglo-Saxon Period. London: Richard Bentley 1860. Pp. 530.

archbishops, the author has embraced a large region of literature and theology, and events of political and of private life—the latter often as characteristic of the times as of the mind of the individual prelate.

Hardly any one of the lives contained in the first volume (which embraces the period—extending over about four hundred and seventy years—from the mission of Augustine to the close of the Anglo-Saxon dynasty) is without some memorable features of interest relating to the early days of the English Church and English civilisation; and it would be difficult to point out a subject of ecclesiastical controversy, usage, or legislation, from the planting of the Church in England down to the time of the Conquest, that does not receive illustration in Dr. Hook's pages. The state of the country and of the people, the progress of arts and employments, and of religion and learning, are illustrated in almost every chapter; and one cannot fail to recognise how truly in this labour of love, as in his long life of sacred duty, the learned author has himself worked in the spirit of his maxim, " that no man becomes great or really good who does not give his heart and mind to perform what his hand finds to do." His charitable judgment, his candour, and his fairness, are, moreover, not less conspicuous than his industry.

As might have been expected from such an historian, the Dean of Chichester, in tracing the Church of England back to the Italian mission and the see founded by Ethelbert at Canterbury, is not forgetful of the previous existence of the British Church, or of the earlier missionary enterprise of the Celtic Church among the pagans of the north of Britain. By whom the Church of Christ was first planted in these islands, by what missionaries the Celts, or pre-historic inhabitants, were originally converted, must probably remain for ever unknown. There is the authority of Tertullian for the simple statement that in the second century regions of Britain inaccessible to the Romans were subdued to Christ; and other authorities assert that this conquest was effected by Eastern missionaries either by direct ministrations or through the Church of Gaul. To the abundant zeal of Irish missionaries some years before the landing of Augustine, and no less than thirteen hundred years ago, the northern provinces of

Britain, which became known as Scotland, were indebted for their conversion; and very remarkable it is to see, that, at a period little antecedent to that in which Gregory the Great signalised at Rome his zeal in the cause of missions, Columba, without any communication from Rome, came from Ireland (crossing in a boat covered with the hides of oxen); and in the remote island of the Hebrides, which became famous as Icolmkill (Columba's Island of the Cells), surrounded himself with men of religious zeal and learning, who went forth to preach the gospel to the rude natives of Caledonia. The term "the Celtic Church" aptly enough distinguishes from the Italian mission established at Canterbury that branch of the Church of Christ which comprised the Irish or Scots, the Caledonians, the British, and the Welsh. The author rightly deduces from the history of the Celtic Church that it was eminently a missionary church, and his theory seems to be that the Italian mission became necessary from the unwillingness of the Saxons to be taught by the despised and persecuted Britons. Be this as it may, the British Christians seem to have regarded as hopeless the conversion of the pagan Saxons, their oppressors, the slaves of idolatrous superstitions and a terrific mythology. But the northern half of Britain owed its conversion to missionaries of the Celtic Church, and they, in the following century, passed through the Anglo-Saxon kingdoms now comprised in the counties of Northumberland, Durham, and York. As far as regards the Mercian kingdom, it appears that the British Christians had fled to Wales and to Armorica before the coming of Augustine. His success in conversion was confined to Kent and Essex; but all the branches of the Church that were planted in England by the Celtic missionaries became ultimately absorbed in the Anglo-Saxon patriarchate of Canterbury, just as the Celtic and Teutonic races have blended in the English people.

But among even the most hostile of the semi-barbarous tribes in the north and west of Europe, Rome was looked to as the representative of civilisation and excellence. Of Roman forms of government and Roman art some traces survived amongst themselves. Various works that surrounded the Saxons in England reminded them of Roman grandeur. When Christianity began its civilising work among the Anglo-Saxons, England was a thinly populated country, abounding in forests and fens, the resort of the bandit and the abode of the wolf; but towns, lighthouses, roads, and bridges of Roman workmanship remained to tell of the civilisers from Italy who had once held sway in Britain.

There was, however, a special preparation—a preparation which surely we may recognise as providential—for the reception of the Gospel in the kingdom of Kent, inasmuch as Ethelbert the king was not only a noble-hearted, liberal-minded, and intelligent man, but was married to a Christian princess—Bertha, daughter of Charibert, King of Paris, for whose enjoyment of the free exercise of her religion due stipulation had been made; and (as the learned historian of the archbishops remarks) " the ornament of a meek and quiet spirit," with which Bertha was adorned, must have predisposed the royal household to think favourably of her religion. Such was the preparation of the land when the sower came to sow his seed; and it has been truly said that we may well be thankful not only that an Augustine converted, but that an Ethelbert reigned.

In describing the circumstances which led to the mission of Augustine, well as they are known, Dr. Hook gives a new interest to them by the manner of the narration, and brings before the mind's eye every scene from the time when Gregory's missionary zeal was excited for the countrymen of the three Yorkshire lads whom he beheld in the slave-market of Rome, to the interview of Augustine at the head of his little band of monks and clergymen, with Ethelbert, the royal " son of the ash-tree," seated amidst his soldiers and wise men under an ancient oak in the Isle of Thanet. When, after Ethelbert's friendly reception of the missionaries, permission was given them to approach Canterbury, the Saxons gazed with admiration on the dark-haired and swarthy but tall and dignified Augustine, who, preceded by his silver cross and the picture of Our Saviour wearing the crown of thorns, headed the procession; and the melodious tones of a music they had never heard, as the advancing choir was led by the sweet voice of the youthful Honorius, spoke to their hearts before their minds were enlightened by the truth. The missionaries soon acquired a fixed locality in Canterbury, but the spot on which probably Augustine first celebrated Christian rites was the venerable church of St. Martin. Bertha's chaplain (Liudhard, who had been a French bishop) had received an old Roman or British church for her service, which he consecrated afresh and named after that celebrated French saint—the most famous of all the great Christian saints of whom the descendant of Clovis had heard. Ingoberga—said to be her mother—bequeathed legacies to St. Martin's church at Tours, and this is another reason for supposing that the dedication to St. Martin of the little edifice near Canterbury was a recollection by Bertha of her native land. Bede mentions this church as "formerly built while the Romans were still in the island;" and the walls of the building that now stands are full of Roman bricks*—relics, doubtless, of the church in which Bertha knelt. The chancel is built almost entirely of Roman bricks, but in the rest of the building these are mixed with later materials, and its windows belong to various periods of Gothic architecture. Tradition maintains that the edifice is as old as the second century, but its form and structure belong to a later date, though it is quite possible that parts of the fabric are coeval with the time of Bertha. At Canterbury, too, Ethelbert, after his conversion, endowed the monastery to which Augustine's name was afterwards given, and which was designed as a missionary college, a purpose to which modern piety has in our own day, happily, once more consecrated its site.

Gregory the Great intended to have two archbishoprics—one at London, which had been one of the three metropolitan sees of the British Church before the coming of the Saxons, and the other at York, once the *altera Roma* of Britain—and twenty-four bishoprics throughout England. Probably (as Professor Stanley has suggested) Gregory, to whom Britain was an unknown island, thought it might be about the size of Sicily or Sardinia, the only large islands he had ever seen. Great was the work which Augustine accomplished towards fulfilment of this purpose, although

---

\* A friend of the writer's infers from the correspondence of these bricks (or rather tiles) in length, width, thickness, and colour, with those in the old church in the Castle at Dover, which differ from those in the adjacent Roman pharos itself and in some other Roman remains, that the former were not of Roman make.

much short of the designs of the pontiff, and it seems all the greater when we reflect that it was accomplished within the short space of ten years. We shall not here follow Dr. Hook through the accurate account he gives of the difficulties that arose from the ritualistic peculiarities (attributable to the Eastern traditions, followed by the missionaries, who, coming, not from Rome, but from the Eastern Church, had originally christianised Gaul) which offended the Canterbury mission, or of the memorable conference at "Augustine's Oak," between the archbishop and his Italians on the one side, and the British bishops on the other, the object of which was to decide whether the two branches of the Holy Catholic Church then existing in the land should unite under one head, that head being the archbishop at Canterbury. Although the Celtic branches of the Church were afterwards brought under the Roman obedience, the attempts at conciliation in Augustine's lifetime were abortive, the Scots and Britons refusing to yield points which they conceived to affect their ecclesiastical independence. In narrating these and the other events of Augustine's life, the author gives us a connected narrative of actual facts, carefully sifted from the doubtful legends that have surrounded them.

The extension to Northumbria of the Kentish mission is a most interesting portion of this great chapter of English history. It was the principal event of the short episcopate of Justus, a Roman, the first Bishop of Rochester, which, notwithstanding its proximity to Canterbury, was made a separate see, it being the capital of one of the two kings of Kent (for in those days Kent was honoured with two kings), the other of whom reigned at Canterbury. It is very remarkable that in the remote kingdom of Northumbria, Edwin the king—who then ruled from the northern shore of the Humber far into the lowlands of Scotland, and westward into Cumberland—had been, by his marriage with Ethelburga, brought into contact with Christianity, as Ethelbert was by his marriage to Bertha. Like him, Edwin had conceded that his wife should enjoy free exercise of her religion, and Paulinus was sent with her from Kent by Justus on her marriage to the Northumbrian prince, and in 625 was consecrated Archbishop of York. Very interesting is the picture we have of Paulinus[*] as he appeared in

[*] His personal appearance was described by one of his converts to a friend of Ven. Bede.

Edwin's council: the lofty stature, slightly bending, the dark eye flashing, the black hair curling round his bald head, the slender aquiline nose, the thin, spare features, the dignified and venerable appearance of the civilised Italian contrasting with the long-flowing flaxen locks, blue eyes, ruddy weatherbeaten faces, and robust forms of the Saxon king's rude warrior-counsellors. The Dean of Chichester gives due prominence to Bede's account of the proceedings at Edwin's Witanagemote in A.D. 627—so interesting as the earliest report of a parliamentary debate. Edwin's baptism preluded the conversion of his kingdom; and the heart of the aged Justus, at that time archbishop, was gladdened in his then humble cathedral at Canterbury by the triumphant success of his mission. But in 633, at the fatal field of Hatfield-chase, near Doncaster, the noble Edwin lost his kingdom and his life, and with him fell in the north of England the short-lived edifice of Christianity which Paulinus, the Roman missionary, had so wondrously raised.

In narrating how Northumbria once more became a Christian country, Dr. Hook again renders due justice to the Celtic mission, and to the character of Aidan, the new bishop, an illustrious representative of the educated, self-denying, and zealous heroes of Christianity, who were sent forth by the Celtic Church, and who brought the sons of Odin into contact with the descendants of the Celtic Britons who had resisted Cæsar. In those days King Oswald reigned, and the light of the Gospel, cherished by that regal convert, shone from Bamburgh, the sea-coast fortress of Ida—"the flame-bearing"—far to the Cleveland Hills. When Oswald determined to attempt the restoration of Christianity, he resorted, not to the Archbishop of Canterbury, but to the Celtic Church; and, Aidan having fixed his cathedral on seagirt Lindisfarne, that remote island church became the pharos of Northumbria in the twilight between Heathendom and Christianity, and mother of all the churches from Tyne to Tweed. To the missionaries of the Celtic Church, even the midland (or Mercian) kingdom and all the northern territory, from the Wall of Antoninus to the Humber, became indebted for Christianity. The missionaries in Kent seem to have made no attempt to convert even the adjoining kingdom of Sussex, which was in those days a territory almost impenetrable, and it did not receive the

Gospel until Wilfrid, when deposed from his diocese of York, found employment for his active and zealous mind in its conversion, Sussex being at that time the only realm in the Heptarchy that still remained pagan. It was in the Whitby synod (at which Hilda, the celebrated abbess, and other ladies were present) that Wilfrid first displayed the powers of intellect and of eloquence which early marked him for prominence and distinction. He was a young Northumbrian Saxon, who had been educated in the Celtic Church, but had visited Rome, and now became the champion for everything Roman:

"The scenes of beauty and of grandeur, of nature in its loveliness, and of the relics of art in its perfection, overpowered," says our author, "the enthusiastic mind of the youthful traveller; and from the palaces of Rome and the vineyards of Italy he returned to the wooden hovels on the bleak hillsides of Northumbria, proclaiming his altered principles by displaying his Italian tonsure, despising everything English, and becoming a vehement assertor to the crowds who surrounded him of the superiority of all that was Roman."

Ripon, then a monastery of the Scottish monks, having been conferred upon him,

"He immediately," continues Dr. Hook, "indulged his newly acquired and expensive tastes by erecting a building, the marble and ornamental arches of which, while they faintly reminded the builder of his beloved Italy, filled the minds of native beholders with admiration."

In the Whitby synod Wilfrid secured a victory for the cause of Roman obedience in the controversy on the subject of Easter —an important step in the concession of superiority to the church of Canterbury as the English representative, in fulness of apostolic power, of the Bishop of Rome, whose recognition in England as successor of the Prince of the Apostles (about seventy years after the coming of Augustine) led to the assumption of those absolute powers which the Pope was ere long to assume.

About ten years before the Whitby synod, Honorius, almost the last survivor of the companions of Augustine, died. He was the last Italian bishop of the Anglo-Saxon Church. At that time there was no archbishop either of London or York; the bishops at London and at Lindisfarne represented the Celtic mission, and claimed no rights over other sees.

It is a remarkable fact that to the distant civilisation of Mediterranean shores, in the persons of Hadrian and of Theodorus, the one an African, and the other a native of Tarsus, in Cilicia, England—at least, in the southern province—became indebted towards the close of the seventh century for the foundation of learning. Tarsus was still a Greek city in the time of Theodorus, who acquired his learning in the same schools in which, six hundred years before (as the Dean of Chichester remarks), St. Paul was a boy learning Greek. Here, from the sailors, the youthful Theodorus may have heard of the Saxon pirates who endangered the trade that had been carried on, from the earliest periods of history, between the shores of the Mediterranean and the Cassiterides:

"Little did he think that his old age would be passed in a remote island —chiefly known by its connexion with the Scilly Islands—which these Saxons had subdued, or that his active mind would find its repose by describing to his converts there the goat-hair tents which dotted those luxuriant plains upon which, extending on one side to the sea, and terminating on the other with the Taurus, he had been accustomed to look down from the terraced roofs of his native city."

This remarkable man, who became Archbishop of Canterbury in 669, first introduced the study of the Greek language into England; and while we are indebted to Honorius, his predecessor, for our ecclesiastical music (in the chants still heard in our cathedrals), we owe to Theodorus the organ, that noble instrument, which was known in the eighth century only to the Greeks, and of which our Church appears to have been in possession before any other Church in the west of Europe. In the schools founded by Theodorus, and carried on by his successors, we find laid down the great principle—revived by William of Wykeham, and still characteristic of English schools and universities—not only to impart knowledge, but to exercise the mind; not to burden the memory, but to invigorate the intellect. St. Augustine's and the other monasteries in England were lay institutions connected with the Church; and their resemblance to our colleges in the universities became the greater when, on the whole country having been converted and the Church established, Archbishop Theodorus made them seats of learning, and laid the foundation of English scholarship. The episcopate of Theodorus was disturbed by many a controversy, and especially by that with

Wilfrid, of which, as of the other chief events of his politic and sagacious administration, a concise and interesting account is given in Dr. Hook's work.

In tracing the extension of Christianity in the northern as well as in the southern province, the learned author justly presents these early missionary bishops as the pioneers of arts and civilisation no less than of Christianity; and the music of the church of Canterbury, as well as the decorative arts of Rome, were ere long imitated by other votaries besides Wilfrid, even in the Celtic branches of the church. We learn from Alcuin, the illustrious preceptor of Charlemagne, that in his time the Northumbrian kingdom possessed written monuments of ancient genius and learning that could not be found in France; and it would appear that during the lifetime of Bede (who died A.D. 735), and the remainder of the eighth century, learning was pre-eminently cultivated in Northumbria. At York, its ancient capital, the princely Archbishop Egbert, the friend of Bede and patron of learning, founded a noble library, which he probably stored with manuscripts obtained from Rome; and at York he educated Alcuin, the most learned man of his age, who, when founding at the request of Charlemagne a school of learning in Tours, where he was then abbot and desired to raise up an Athens of France, sent to York for copies of works which could not be obtained in France, in order to transplant what he figuratively calls the flowers of Britain to perfume the palaces of Tours. The Anglo-Saxons early learned to excel all western nations in the decorative arts, and they flourished at Lindisfarne in times when the midland and western kingdoms had hardly emerged from barbarism.

It is curious that in the lifetime of Bede only eight of the present sees were existing in England. It seems to have been the wish of the kings of Northumbria and of Kent, and perhaps of all the kings of the Heptarchy, to place all the sees under the metropolitan of Canterbury; but into the disputes relating to primacy and ecclesiastical government it is not our purpose to enter here.

Years, and decades, and centuries, pass by as we turn over these historic pages: kings succeed to kings, prelates to prelates, and at length we see the petty kingdoms of the Heptarchy merge in the realm of England, and the humble mission church of Augustine and his companions expand in the stately metropolitan church of Canterbury. May its shadow never be less! Among the primates, as among the occupants of the Roman see, there have been (to use the language of our author) men, good, bad, and indifferent; some eminent for their learning, integrity, and piety; others, disgracing their station by vicious life and imbecility of mind; but, to the honour of the early archbishops be it said, that their moral conduct and exemplary lives place them in favourable contrast to the Roman dignitaries, who were too often mere politicians and worldly-minded men. Through all the turbulence and bloodshed of the time, the calm figures of Anglo-Saxon prelates shine in the troubled scenes of English history: such was Alstan, Bishop of Sherborne, that noble-minded patriot, who was a statesman as well as prelate, wise in council and brave in war, to whom we are to ascribe the ultimate successes of the reign of Ethelwulf; such, too, was St. Swithin, of Winchester, who, little as he may have had to do with July weather, had immense and beneficial influence on that monarch, and added sound discretion to religious zeal.

A long course of prosperity had followed the fusion of the British and Anglo-Saxon races, and preceded the Danish invasions. But in the first quarter of the ninth century there was episcopal indolence, and a decay of morals among public men, the traces of which are found, says Dean Hook, in the enactments of the ecclesiastical synods of the time at the courts of Ethelbald and Offa. Piety had decayed and learning had declined in the Church of England when the patriotic Alfred undertook his reforms, and the state of public affairs was menacing to civilisation as well as to Christianity. We have a terrible but not exaggerated picture of the state of the country at the death of Archbishop Ceolnoth (A.D. 870), when the Danes were devastating England. All Europe was equally disturbed, and the ninth and tenth centuries were also the gloomiest period in the history of Rome.

In the northern province, the monasteries were always the first objects of plunder by the Danes, yet the rich monastery of

St. Augustine at Canterbury was spared on both the occasions when the invaders pillaged the city in the time of Ceolnoth. Our author explains its escape by the presumption that this archbishop, who was remarkable for the quantity of money which he coined in virtue of his right of mintage, his moneyers having turned into coin all the silver on which he could lay his hands, applied this treasure to buy off or bribe the enemy.

When Alfred had defeated the Danes at " Ethandune "—one of the decisive battles of the world—the illustrious king began to acquire his right to his historical title, ALFRED THE GREAT, and added to the abilities of a military commander the prudence and sagacity of a legislator. What a pleasing picture is presented of his court, where the good king had surrounded himself with learned men attracted from all parts of Europe! From the time of Theodorus schools of learning had been engrafted on the monasteries; but Alfred founded schools that were independent of monasteries; and we may, undoubtedly, trace to his wisdom what long afterwards, under Wykeham and Henry VI. became the great blessing of his country—the system of public school education. The dean, however, has no faith in the legend which attributes to Alfred the foundation of the University of Oxford. Neither did he create the British constitution; but it was his wise and Christian policy to fuse the discordant Anglo-Saxon and Anglo-Danish races into one united people, and in this great work he was aided by the influences of the Church of England. Her revived energy was even signalised by a mission to the Christians of India, organised under the pious and patriotic Alfred, and the episcopate of Archbishop Ethelred has become perhaps chiefly remarkable for having witnessed the first intercourse between England and Hindostan.

It was in his relations to Alfred that Plegmund, a Mercian, who succeeded Ethelred as archbishop, became memorable. He is presumed to have superintended, if he did not himself transcribe, the oldest known manuscript of " the Saxon Chronicle."*

Archbishop Wulfhelm began his episcopate auspiciously, for one of his earliest duties was the coronation of Athelstan, which took

* The Plegmund manuscript is the basis of the text edited in the *Monumenta Historia Britannica.*

place in the royal camp at Moreford (an old Roman ford across the Thames), since known as Kingston. There the grandson of Alfred stood before the Witan and the people: "a thin, spare man thirty years of age, his yellow hair interwoven with threads of gold, and himself arrayed in a purple vestment, with a Saxon sword in a golden sheath hanging from a jewelled belt, the gifts of Alfred; and on a stone-seat in the market-place he was raised, the better to be seen by the people." *Apropos* of this event, the Dean remarks that the coronation service has remained substantially the same from the eighth century to the present time; and, in relation to the coronation oath, he mentions that very interesting, and perhaps only undoubted, relic of the ancient regalia of England—the Latin manuscript of the Gospels (now in the Cotton Library of the British Museum), which was sent over to Athelstan by his brother-in-law the Emperor Otho, and was given by Athelstan to the church of Canterbury. So, too, the Bible which Pope Gregory sent to Augustine—a manuscript justly regarded as the beginning of English biblical learning— was, in the year 1414, still in the library attached to St. Augustine's College, and is now in Corpus Christi College, Cambridge. Dr. Hook gives an interesting sketch of the state of England as it was left by the noble Athelstan and Wulfhelm his archbishop; and then, reverting to ecclesiastical affairs, describes the revolutionary reforms of the Benedictine party, led by Odo, Dunstan, and Thurketul. Odo was a young Dane, who had been sent by one of Alfred's nobles to study Greek and Latin, but who was of a military temperament, and was three times in the field after he became a prelate. To a bishop of the tenth century, however, military command was not inconsistent with episcopal duties: "he uplifted his right hand and girded on his armour, using— not, indeed, a sword, for that was contrary to clerical etiquette, but—a yet more formidable weapon, a club studded with spikes."

The life of Dunstan naturally occupies a lengthy chapter of Dr. Hook's work, and he has separated the real history of that remarkable man from the mass of fable with which the superstition of devotees and the malignity of enemies have surrounded it. Glastonbury—that venerable fane which was the sole inheritance of the Anglo-Saxon from the British Church, and hallowed the island, charmed of old, among the glassy streams—fed the fancy, cherished the genius, and excited the imagination of the youthful Dunstan. It was in his time occupied by scholars from Ireland, but by his exertions and endowment, after he became abbot of the royal monastery of Glastonbury, it became the great public school of England through the remainder of the Anglo-Saxon period — the Eton of those days, and, according to William of Malmesbury, no fewer than seven archbishops of Canterbury were Glastonbury scholars. The author does justice to the master intellect of Dunstan, the wonderful versatility of his talents, his natural gifts, the ardour of his character, and the variety of his accomplishments; and rightly places this celebrated man in the first rank of ecclesiastical statesmen, such as Becket, Wolsey, Laud, Richelieu, and Mazarin. As minister of Edgar, who became monarch of England at the age of sixteen, and whose reign is one of the most glorious in the Anglo-Saxon annals, he secured for his sovereign a title—THE PACIFIC—of which even Alfred might have been proud. As a statesman, Dunstan maintained peace by always keeping the country prepared for war, and under his administration (says the Dean of Chichester) " England was as a giant taking her rest, but as a giant armed and ever ready for action." The English navy was made so effectual that no enemy dared attack the coast; commerce was fostered, the authority of law enforced, the Danes subdued, and the King of England's sovereignty established even beyond the Tweed.

Elfric, a succeeding archbishop, is, perhaps, best remembered for his Homilies, which became authoritative in the Church of England: he was also remarkable as the author of a Dictionary, Grammar, and Latin Colloquies, and for a facility of composition very rare in that age.

In relating the history of Elphege (the patron saint of Greenwich, the place of his martyrdom at the hands of the Danes in 1012), Dr. Hook again enters on the department of the English historian, and concisely places before the reader the political circumstances of England at the time. By a curious revolution, London saw, ten years after Elphege had been slain, the painted and gold-ornamented barge of a Danish king receive on board the body of the archbishop, which had been interred with great pomp at London; and, preceded and surrounded by Danish courtiers and a guard of honour, it was conveyed to Canterbury, and deposited beside the reputed relics of Dunstan. It is worthy of remark, that, when the Danish army besieged Canterbury in the time of Elphege, it was sufficiently fortified to hold out for twenty days, and was then only entered by treachery.

When the author comes to the middle of the eleventh century, we seem to hear the note of preparation for the Norman invasion, and a very interesting account is given of the gradual establishment of the Norman party in England, and the bestowal on Normans of all chief preferments, by the policy of Archbishop Robert of Jumièges, in whose cloisters Dr. Hook represents the affections of Edward, surnamed the Confessor, to have been, even after he had come to the English throne. But when the exhortations of the Anglo-Saxon or patriotic party led the king to submit to the decision of a Witanagemote in which Stigand, who was the chaplain and adviser of Queen Emma, presided, Archbishop Robert was deposed. He appealed from the English tribunal to Rome; but England, although the Anglo-Saxon dynasty was drawing to a close, defied the papal decree, and Stigand was installed Archbishop of Canterbury. The most interesting events with which his name is associated were the consecration of Westminster Abbey at the close of 1065, and the coronation of "the tall, handsome, and open-handed" Harold (for crowned he seems to have been); and on this event the author eloquently remarks that Stigand, when he presented Harold to the people after the election by the Witan, and saw England once more free, and heard the people hail her champion by one long, loud, patriotic shout, must have experienced the pleasure which those enjoy who, after years of difficulty, doubt, and danger, have at length achieved, as they imagine, the great object of their sublunary ambition and desires. But Stigand was destined to be the last Saxon Archbishop of Canterbury, and the patriot and primate lived not only to become a state prisoner at royal Winchester, but to see his brave countrymen and the Church of England prostrate beneath a foreign yoke.

# CANTERBURY AND ITS ARCHBISHOPS.
## II. NORMAN PERIOD.

THE first volume of Dr. Hook's "Lives of the Archbishops of Canterbury" having brought down their history from the mission of Augustine to the close of the Anglo-Saxon dynasty—a period of about four hundred and seventy years—the Archbishops during the Anglo-Norman reigns form the subject of the second volume of this important biographical work,\* and it brings before the reader a totally new set of ideas, as well as a different race of men, and a greatly altered state of things, in Europe. It comprises historical characters and times of undying interest in the annals of this realm; for here we have the lives of Lanfranc, Anselm, Becket, Hubert Walter, and Langton, not to mention six archbishops of inferior distinction. The book occupies a period of little more than a century and a half; but the years that elapsed between the Conquest and the Great Charter, between Lanfranc and Langton, between Hildebrand and Innocent, are among the most eventful years in mediæval history. They saw the rise of feudal institutions and of the age of chivalry; they saw the rise of the universities and of our courts of law; they saw the beginning of the great struggle between the ecclesiastical and civil power, in which the Church fought the battle of the people against kings and barons; and they saw the sanguinary yet romantic warfare of the Crusades, which brought the arts and learning of the East to Europe, and aided the progress of civilisation.

In those contentious ages, when even ecclesiastics were more commonly combative than literate, the primates of England maintained the foremost place, and archbishops were ministers of state and viceroys, warriors and judges, and a bishop was seen at one time emulating the lives of saints, and at another besieging

\* Lives of the Archbishops of Canterbury. By Walter Farquhar Hook, Dean of Chichester. Vol. ii. Anglo-Norman Period. Bentley. 1862.

a castle, often acting as commander-in-chief, or seated among mail-clad barons in the royal councils. It helps one to realise the character of the stormy Anglo-Norman reigns if we remember these features of the age, and think that the cathedrals and the castles of England were then rising; that the speech of the people was still Anglo-Saxon, and the language of the court and the aristocracy Norman-French; that the only written language was Latin, and the only scholars were the clergy; that the feudal lords were generally turbulent and warlike, and wicked as well as unlettered, and knew not the refinements or the means of enlightenment that are now accessible to the peasant; that the Saxon trials by ordeal were still in use, that our judicial system was only in its dawn, and England had not yet seen the beginning of her parliament; that the lower classes of the people were for a large part in feudal slavery, and the freedom and independence of municipalities was hardly begun. No towns of portentous magnitude then spread labyrinths of streets over the fields or darkened the landscapes of England; most of the highways were those the Romans had left; a great part of the country was still forest, the abode of the bandit, the wild boar, and the wolf; and the abbeys, which received the traveller on his route, exhibited almost the only humanising influences of the time.

The Dean of Chichester prefixes to the series of biographies contained in the present volume an elaborate introductory sketch of the spirit of the age, the state of the people after the establishment of the Norman rule, and the influence of the Crusades on the progress of civilisation. He also shows the importance in those days of the monastic institutions—then the nurseries of statesmen and the homes of learning—and glances at the rise of the university system; and, for the better understanding the conduct of the archbishops, he sketches the policy of the popes and the lawlessness of the kings.

The Crusades cannot be adequately discussed in an incidental notice, but the advantages and the calamities that resulted from them (amongst the former, the abolition of slavery in England) seem to us to be very fairly stated by Dr. Hook: we must not judge them by modern standards, or measure Christian enthusiasm by maxims of political economy. It was an age when (as some one has truly said) life was earnest in its beliefs as well as stormy in its ambitions; when abbeys were reared in many a quiet vale, as well as feudal castles on many an English hill; and when the feudal chivalry, though unskilled in any art but that of war, and too often the representatives of lawless power, could glow with enthusiasm for the Holy Land, and endow churches, in which, if they lived to return from Palestine, they were laid for their final rest. But, whatever the rank of the Crusader, no considerations of worldly honour, interest, or pleasure, restrained him from the heroic enterprise, for religious zeal combined with military ardour. However depraved the state of society may have been, the Crusade appealed to the nobler instincts of human nature; from those instincts chivalry sprang; and chivalry represented all that was humanising, and softening, and self-denying, and courageous in mankind People can now talk wisely about the insanity of the Crusades, and the superstitions of what they call " the dark ages," but a lust for gold is the superstition of the present age; and we believe with Mr. Ruskin that " those who have worshipped the thorns of Christ's crown will be found at last to have been holier and wiser than those who are devoted to the service of the world." Ages may have been warlike and stormy without being dark, and men may have been rude and unlettered without being barbarous; and it certainly does not become an age that tolerates the Revivals—with their insane and revolting accompaniments, that believes in spirit-rapping and hears Spurgeon, to condemn the superstition of the middle ages or the fanaticism of the Crusades.

Dr. Hook regards the first Crusade as the termination of the " dark ages " and the commencement of a new era. Mediæval history, he remarks, extends from the commencement of the fourth century to the close of the fifteenth—a period of twelve centuries, of which, he says, " seven may be regarded as dark." But the learned author surely cannot mean to call the first seven centuries of this period " dark." That reproach cannot be applied to the age of Cyril and St. Augustine of Hippo; of Theodosius and Justinian; of St. Benedict, and Boethius, and Gregory of Tours; of Pope Gregory the Great and Augustine of Canterbury; of Aidan, and Bede, and Aldhelm; of Alcuin and Charlemagne; of Archbishop Egbert and Erigena; of Theodorus of Canterbury, Alfred the Great, Elfric, and Dunstan. Neither can the age be called "dark" in which schools of learning were incorporated into universities, and in which the monasteries began to shelter religion, literature, and art. The term is relative; and, after all, the question arises, What is meant by "a dark age?" If the want of letters, of civilising influences, and of great men makes an age dark, no doubt England passed through dark ages in the time of the first Saxon invasions, in the contests between the petty kingdoms of the Heptarchy, in the long years which preceded the missions of the Church and the Roman branches of the Church, and (in later periods of our history) after the Danish and the Norman ravages laid waste the North of England.

But the character of the age in which the archbishops lived is material to their biographies only in as much as their actions must be regarded by the light of contemporary history, and with reference to the state of society in their time. The Dean disclaims any attempt to depict the character of any one of the personages whose lives he has written, and professes to record actions and opinions only.

The noble figure of Lanfranc heads the procession of the Anglo-Norman primates. He was a native of Pavia, in Lombardy, and, having acquired proficiency in the civil and canon law, he practised as an advocate, until political troubles led him to make choice of Normandy as the place of his future labours; and, founding a school at Avranches, he attracted crowds of scholars, for he is said to have been as skilful in imparting as he was laborious in acquiring knowledge. A newly-acquired enthusiasm led him to the monastery of Bec, in which he spent some time, and which he quitted reluctantly for the court of the Duke of Normandy. Although long unwilling to exchange the studious life of the cloister for the thorny distinction of the primacy, he suffered himself to be promoted in 1070 to the archiepiscopal dignity of Canterbury. Three years before that time the Saxon cathedral had been destroyed by fire; and it is remarkable that we should owe to Italians not only the planting of the Church of

Christ in England at the end of the sixth century, but the building of the Norman cathedral of Canterbury in the eleventh. Lanfranc's edifice was destined to be, like its predecessor, not of long duration. He rebuilt also the episcopal palace, and over it placed Gundulf, a monk of Bec, afterwards Bishop of Rochester, the builder of the massive and more enduring castle upon the Medway, and the architect of the Tower of London. Lanfranc served the Conqueror in high civil office; and the ecclesiastical polity of William's reign is, no doubt, to a considerable extent, attributable to Lanfranc's counsel. He it was who separated the ecclesiastical from the civil tribunal, and in the administration of the Church he acted with prudence and justice. It was in his time that Osmund "the good," Bishop of Salisbury, drew up the service book which afterwards, throughout the province, formed what was known as "the Salisbury use," and, regulating liturgical usage, became the model ritual of the Church of England, and the basis of our Book of Common Prayer. We are glad to see that Lanfranc's literary works and services to literature are mentioned with due honour by his present biographer. If the age in which he lived was dark, Lanfranc, at all events, nobly contributed to its enlightenment.

He died in May, 1089, in the second year of the reign of William Rufus, and was succeeded by the famous Anselm, who was also one of the most remarkable men of his time. He was a native of Piedmont, for he was born at Aosta, beneath the

> Throned emblems of eternity, that rear
> Above the earth-born clouds their mitred snows.

He became a pupil of Lanfranc in the monastery of Bec, and ere long a teacher of others, and his fame attracted to that place a multitude of students, and scholars, and penitents. In 1079, when forty-six years of age, he accepted the abbot's staff from the hands of William the Conqueror, and his literary genius raised the community so high that it came to be regarded as an assembly of philosophers. Here he passed thirty-three happy years, the object of adulation, the oracle and lawgiver to all around him, though sadly indifferent to providing food for his monks, for he had a bad habit of preferring his books to his meals, and disregarded creature-comforts himself. At Lanfranc's death, the Red King had seized the temporalities of Canterbury, and filled the royal coffers by delaying the nomination of a successor. At length, however, when the profligate and avaricious oppressor believed himself to be dying, he nominated the Abbot of Bec for the vacant see, and amid great rejoicings Anselm was enthroned in 1093. We shall not follow Dr. Hook through his statement of the violent disputes which arose between the king and the archbishop, who, inflexible in his notions of duty to the Church, seems to have disregarded tact and conciliation, and he resolutely refused to yield a supremacy to the King that was incompatible with obedience to the Pope. In 1097 he took refuge in Rome, and remained in exile during the rest of William's reign. At length, on the death of the fierce and godless monarch, Anselm was summoned to England by Henry I. But his refusal to receive investiture from the king involved fresh disputes. He nevertheless assisted at the marriage of Henry with Matilda daughter of Malcolm King of Scotland and of Margaret the sister of Edgar the Atheling, by which restoration of the Anglo-Saxon line, and as a descendant of Matilda, Queen Victoria is connected with Saxon royalty. Henry, with his accustomed policy, made the talents and influence of Anselm conducive to the consolidation of his own power, and the good queen made him her spiritual adviser. In 1093 Anselm went to Rome, and a long and vexatious controversy arose between him and Henry, who at length conceded terms which the Archbishop, by advice of the Pope, accepted, and which formed the precedent for the conciliatory adjustment, some years afterwards, of the ominous controversy as to investitures. Returning to England in the autumn of 1106, Anselm was joyfully welcomed on his landing at Dover, and Matilda in person made the provisions for his comfort which his illness and age (he was now seventy-three) required. He found Prior Conrad engaged on the magnificent architectural works which superseded Lanfranc's choir, and he aided their execution nobly; but he was not destined to witness the completion of the Norman cathedral, for on the 11th April, 1109, amidst his attached friends and the monks of Canterbury, the good archbishop passed to his rest. He was acknowledged to be "mighty in Scripture," and the many literary works he produced attest his intellectual power and depth of thought.

The saintly Anselm was succeeded by Ralph de Escures, a Frenchman, who, as archbishop, was perhaps chiefly remarkable for being the patron of good and learned men. He was himself of a happy temperament, kind, affable, and joyous in spirit, and he seems to have borne with great equanimity the disputes and divisions which agitated the Church of England in his day. The last public act in which he was engaged was the marriage of Henry I. to Adela of Louvain, and the coronation of the fair young bride. His successor, William of Corbeuil, was, like him, a Frenchman, and he was elected to the archbishopric at a time when the desire of the bishops was to see in the office of primate a politician who could defend the Church from the King on the one hand and from the encroachments of the Pope on the other. The character given of him by a contemporary might really be drawn from the life at the present day: "He was a man of smooth face and strictly religious manners, but much more ready to amass money than to spend it." The works commenced by Lanfranc and carried on by Anselm were completed during his primacy, and he consecrated the cathedral on the 4th May, 1130, in the presence of such a royal and noble assemblage as had never before been seen even in Canterbury, for it included Henry I. and David of Scotland (himself the founder of many abbeys and churches in his own realm), and nobles and bishops almost without number. Four years afterwards Archbishop William crowned Stephen, and in 1136 he died, "leaving immense sums secretly hoarded in his coffers." In Theobald, his successor, Canterbury now received a third archbishop from the monastery of Bec. England was in a miserable condition of civil anarchy when this noble Norman became archbishop, and Christianity would have been extinguished if it had not been for the monasteries. But, rude and boisterous as was the time, his court soon became the centre of resort for all the learning and ability of the kingdom. John of Salisbury, one of the most classical writers of the age, was his secretary, and "in close conversation with him might be seen sitting a young man whom no one could look upon without asking who he was. In stature tall, of strength equal to any undertaking, with a keen eye, a quick ear, fluent in speech, cheerful in discourse, ready in debate, with the manners of a noble and a knight, Thomas of London, the son of Gilbert Becket, the portreeve of the city, at once commanded respect, secured attention, and won friends."

The study of the civil law had been shortly before revived in Italian universities, particularly at Bologna; and Archbishop Theobald, who was more of the lawyer than the theologian, introduced the study of the science, and attracted its professors to his court, and about the year 1144 placed a professor of the Roman law at Oxford, whose lectures were afterwards attended by persons of every rank, especially by aspirants to high office in Church or State. He discovered, encouraged, and employed the talents of the young Londoner, and enabled him to complete his legal studies by a year's residence at Bologna, and is said to have afterwards employed Becket in a negotiation with the court of Rome, in which he rendered good offices to the house of Anjou, and paved the way to the favour in which he was held by Henry II. A very remarkable concurrence of circumstances fitted Becket for the position he was destined to occupy; and his patron the Archbishop, soon after officiating at the coronation of Henry (19th Dec., 1154), commended to him the youthful scholar—then known as Thomas the archdeacon—as the fittest person to be his chancellor, and he was the first Englishman ever appointed to that office. In 1161 the enlightened, charitable, and munificent archbishop died, and was succeeded (in May 1162) by the brilliant and courtly favourite, his former pupil and archdeacon.

To the life of Becket the Dean of Chichester has evidently devoted especial care. St. Thomas of Canterbury is an ecclesiastical hero who has found so many biographers, and whose life affords such abundant materials for controversy, that the outlines of his career are tolerably familiar to most readers. His character has been viewed from different stand-points, according to the prejudices of the writer, but Dr. Hook's narrative is distinguished by its fairness and justice no less than by honest and painstaking research. The history of Becket is very conveniently arranged under the distinct periods of—first, his chancellorship; second, his primacy; third, his exile; and fourth, his return to England, so speedily followed by the martyrdom (29th Dec. 1170), which has never had a more graphic delineator than Professor Stanley. We must own a wish that Dr. Hook had himself summed up the evidence and given his own view of the character of this extraordinary man, and that he had made more apparent to the general reader the motives of conduct which often seems inexplicable. The archiepiscopal mitre seems to have transformed his whole character; and Dr. Hook's portrait of him from the time when his acceptance of the primacy placed him in a situation of antagonism to the king his former friend, as often repels our sympathy as it raises our admiration. In one scene, Becket, as the champion of ecclesiastical independence, popular, yet never basely courting popularity, loving splendour, yet indifferent to the pleasures of the world, nobly contending for his right, single-handed, against the heathen rage and might of power, engages our sympathies and homage, while in the next, his conduct is that of an aggressor towards the king, and seems marked by the most perverse and wrong-headed obstinacy and passion. But no one, impartially reviewing the circumstances of his position, can deny that his aims were most unselfish and his actions guided by high views of duty; that he was as noble, high-minded, and consistent as he was independent and uncompromising, and that he was a hero worthy of his crown in the noble army of martyrs.

Without placing ourselves amidst the controversies of his time, and realising the aims which claimed the loyalty of churchmen in the days of Hildebrand, and remembering also that to concede supremacy to the secular power in things ecclesiastical appeared to them to be to fear man rather than God, and to be a rendering to Cæsar of things that are God's, we cannot adequately appreciate the cause for which Becket fought and died. However he may have been regarded since the Reformation, we must remember that, in his day, the people, and what may be called the religious sentiment of the nation, were with him; and this was the case, not on the Continent only, where during his exile he was regarded as a Confessor for the Christian faith, but also in England, where, in the memorable conflict with the king and his council at Northampton—portrayed in the present volume with much dramatic force—and again on his return from exile, he was borne, as it were, in triumph on a wave of popular enthusiasm. In this day, a champion of ecclesiastical independence contending against the temporal power would find arrayed against him what is called the Religious World, and encounter the roar of Exeter Hall and the motley and heterogeneous Protestants who, we presume, are adverted to by the apt description of "those noisy, intolerant, ignorant, yet sincere and zealous religionists, who, by their vehemence and violence, overawe, if they do not overpower, wiser and better men."

It is to the honour of Richard, a Norman monk, the successor of St Thomas in the see of Canterbury, that he too was the *protégé* of Archbishop Theobald, and, to the last, the friend of Becket. He seems to have thought more of peace, of making parks, and preserving game, than of following the ecclesiastical policy of his celebrated predecessor; and perhaps a more amiable man, and one whose rule was more equitable, never sat in the chair of Augustine. The penance to which Henry II. submitted in Canterbury cathedral on the 12th of July, 1174, for the atrocious murder of Becket, was the first of the two memorable events of his primacy: the other was the destruction by fire, in the following September, of Conrad's choir, the glory of the cathedral. Its reconstruction was entrusted to the famous William of Sens—who was in church architecture the Scott of his day—and was completed in 1184; but shortly before the work was finished Archbishop Richard died. He was succeeded by Baldwin of Exeter, a monk of the Cistercian monastery of Ford, who seems to have been of a fervid and inconstant disposition, and who finally forsook his see and province to join the third Crusade, in company with the illustrious Ranulph de Glanville the justiciar, but not before he had crowned Richard King of England. The enthusiastic old primate, after distinguishing himself before Acre, died of grief and disappointment in Palestine, and Hubert Walter, Bishop of Salisbury, followed his friend and patron to his grave in a strange land, and, on 30th of May, 1193, to the archiepiscopal throne of Canterbury.

Hubert Walter was of noble family. He was the nephew of Ranulph de Glanville, and, like Becket, was educated as a lawyer. He must have been a perfect incarnation of British energy. After his consecration as Bishop of Salisbury, he fought valiantly as a crusader, and exhibited the military skill of a general officer, while he found in the camp a new field for his pastoral offices. When, on the advance to Jerusalem, the illness of King Richard spread a panic through the Christian host, the army owed its safety to Hubert Walter's courage and presence of mind; and Saladin himself is said to have respected in him the wisdom and prudence in which Richard was deficient—duly as he inspired respect for the " muscular Christianity" of the age. At a later period the King owed his ransom and delivery to his zealous and judicious friend, who, on his return to England, assumed the functions of the King's justiciar and vicegerent, and was elected Archbishop of Canterbury. When it became necessary to reduce the fortresses that were held by John, the King's brother, Hubert, the archbishop, took the command of the forces in person, and at length welcomed back to England the royal hero of the Crusades, who, however, again committed to Hubert the care of the kingdom.

We have not room to follow Dr. Hook into his interesting digression on the state of London at this time, and on the domestic affairs in which the Archbishop exhibited his administrative abilities. He had no sooner suppressed the formidable insurrection of the Londoners, which was raised by that strange demagogue Fitz-Osbert, known as "William with the Long Beard," than he put himself at the head of the army to check an incursion of the Welsh. Hubert, accustomed to fight by the side of prelates on the plains of Palestine, saw nothing incongruous in commanding as viceroy an army assembled for the defence of his country; but the Pope thought him too much absorbed in secular affairs, and he gladly resigned the office of justiciar to Geoffrey Fitz-Peter, but, on the coronation of John, accepted the office of lord chancellor. At his hands all people, of whatever rank, were sure of justice and protection; he was a lover of peace and of truth, and a reformer of abuses; and the magnificence of his spirit was shown in the architectural works in which he was engaged, in his gifts for the church of Canterbury, and in everything in which he was concerned. Exercising at once regal and apostolical power, this great primate held an accumulation of offices which never centred in any other individual, and he is altogether one of the most remarkable characters in the history of his time.

Archbishop Hubert died on the 13th of July, 1205, and was succeeded by Stephen Langton, one of the most distinguished statesmen this country has produced. By his varied talents and knowledge of human nature he was qualified to shine equally in the court and in the cloister. Pope Innocent had called him to Rome, that he might have at hand as his counsellor a man of piety and wisdom, skilled in law and at the same time in divinity. He reluctantly parted with him, in order that the most important see in Western Europe might be filled by the fittest man. His appointment by the Pope without the previous consent of the King roused the monarch's indignation, as well as the resistance of the Chapter. The latter, placed in a dilemma, obeyed the Pope and incurred the fierce resentment of the King, and soon England was plunged in all the troubles of the interdict, and the negotiations which ended in John's vassalage to Rome. These exciting chapters of national history are well and concisely written by Dr. Hook, who, by placing before us the active life of Langton as a politician and statesman, portrays his wisdom, his influence, and his superiority to his contemporaries; and we are to remember that it was as the adviser of Eustace de Vesci and Robert Fitz-Walter, the future general of the baronial army assembled against King John, leaders of the barons of England, that Stephen Langton became the author of Magna Charta. The splendour of his political life seems to outshine that of his primacy; but in his case the bishop was not wholly absorbed by the statesman; and the retrospect of his life might justly have been cheered by the reflection that he had ever lived for God, for liberty, and his country.

In conclusion, we congratulate Dr. Hook on these contributions to historical literature, and on the increasing interest of his work.

ON

# THE JUSTICIARS, CHANCELLORS, AND JUDGES CELEBRATED IN ENGLISH HISTORY,

FROM THE CONQUEST TO THE TIME OF LORD MANSFIELD.

A LECTURE

[Read before the members of the Durham Athenæum; the Mechanics' Institute, Chester-le-Street; and the Tynemouth Literary and Philosophical Society, North Shields.]

BIOGRAPHICAL reading is now so favourite an occupation of our leisure, and the lives of English judges have been made familiar by so many popular works, that I dare say few of the audience whom I address this evening need be told that a most interesting series of historical characters may be found in the old Justiciars, Chancellors, and Judges of England.

Among the historic shadows that border the dark stream of time, history cannot throw her pale light upon more shining and memorable forms than those which once adorned the judgment-seat of this country, or preserve the memory of any worthies more deserving of remembrance by Englishmen throughout all time, than the judges who won many of our cherished liberties, and by their influence upon the improvement of our laws contributed to make our country worthy of our pride and love.

In the lives of men who have for ages passed to the historic shadows of Westminster Hall we may view some of the noblest examples of integrity and patriotism that our history can show; and the student of jurisprudence may trace in the laws of England the influence of her bygone judges, just as he traces throughout our civil code the enduring principles of Roman law, or finds that maxims which still affect our rights prevailed in the empires of the Middle Ages.

All honour to those illustrious Englishmen who from the tribunals of justice proclaimed lofty maxims of right and principles of constitutional liberty in times when private rights and public liberties were endangered by the Crown, who could execute justice and maintain truth in times when parliaments were servile and when society was unenlightened! In the days of the Plantagenets we find judges holding that "the King's grant is of no power to prejudice the subject's interest;" that "the common law has so admeasured the King's perogatives that they shall not take away or prejudice the interests of any man;" and that "the law of God and the law of the land are all one, and both regard the common and public good of the realm." Later, we find judges declaring that "no statute is to be extended to life by doubtful words;" that "arbitrary imprisonment is unknown to the law;" that "a royal proclamation is incompetent to make new law, and cannot impose fine, forfeiture, or imprisonment;" and again, that "the air of England is so free that no slave can breathe it." And remember that these and many other assertions of the majesty of English law were heard from the lips of judges in times which compared with ours were times of barbarism—were heard in the stormy middle ages, when English had hardly become a written language; when there were neither public libraries nor printed books; when the old Saxon trials by ordeal were in use; when the feudal lords were an unlettered and warlike aristocracy, unacquainted with means of enlightenment common to the humblest artisan; when, in short, the civilization of our polished and prosperous England seems to have been in its state of infancy.

But we must not expect to find the model of a learned and patriotic judge in those early periods when the King's chancellors bore the sword as well as the pastoral staff, when the chief justices were the King's companions in arms, and feudal barons were judges of the land.

A chief justice or a chancellor was then seen at one time as an earl mounted on a war-horse and holding a sword, as we see delineated, for instance, on the early episcopal seals of Durham— at another, in his pontifical habit giving the benediction; on one day besieging a castle, on another adorning his cathedral church. In early times, military command was not thought inconsistent with episcopal duties. A bishop uplifted his right hand for other purposes than benediction, and often girded on his armour, and, although he might not use a sword, he wielded a club studded with spikes.

Although the simple institutions of Saxon judicature were not superseded at the Conquest by a system at all resembling our complicated and highly artificial jurisprudence, the feudal law of Normandy substituted intricate rules for the simplicity of Saxon tenures; the civil and the ecclesiastical jurisdictions were separated, and the bishop no longer sat with the sheriff or earl in the county court; Norman French was used instead of the English tongue in courts of justice, and the clergy were of necessity the only lawyers, as they were the only literate persons of the age. The Anglo-Norman reigns were certainly not an age of Arcadian simplicity, but lawyers at all events had not then become a separate class of practitioners, and people did not enjoy the luxury of being able to go to their solicitor. William the Conqueror seems to have designed one grand central tribunal for the whole realm, in which all causes of importance should be heard and decided, and, from assembling in the hall of the King's palace wheresoever he might be, this court acquired its name of the *Curia Regis* or *Aula Regis;* the great officers or ministers of the Crown were its judges, but the Chief Justiciar enjoyed much more than judicial pre-eminence, and was an officer of transcendent power. He was next in authority to the sovereign, represented him as viceroy, and exercised at once the functions now belonging to the Commander-in-chief, the First Minister of the Crown, and the Lord Chief Justice. Yet history shows us more than one chief justiciar of Norman England who presents the calm and dignified aspect of a judge and prelate among the mailed figures of feudal barons. Such a man was William de Carilefe, Bishop of Durham, a prelate particularly memorable in that diocese as the builder of Durham cathedral and the first great benefactor of the see. That building owes its massive grandeur to a man who eight centuries ago was a humble village chaplain in Normandy, but who was one of those favourites of heaven, those beings " gifted with celestial fire," who could not only sway "the rod of empire," but advance the kingdom of the Eternal. We see Carilefe at one time presiding in judgment, at another causing noble manuscripts to be transcribed for his church of Durham which still exist among its treasures; then sitting in the King's great council, and anon raising an edifice that has been the admiration of centuries, upon its wood-environed hill.

Like Carilefe, the early Norman chancellors too were distinguished as church builders rather than as lawyers: Maurice, Bishop of London—and he is almost the first chancellor on record—rebuilt the cathedral of St. Paul; Lanfranc, who was a justiciar, rebuilt his cathedral of Canterbury; and Osmund, Bishop of Salisbury, the Conqueror's nephew and chancellor, was a great builder of churches, and was moreover canonized as a saint, and *that* I fear is a distinction which has not been attained by any of his successors in Westminster Hall excepting St. Thomas of Canterbury, however deserving they may have been as lawyers. Carilefe was succeeded as Bishop of Durham and as chancellor by Ralph Flambard, whose character the monastic historians have certainly done their utmost to blacken, but to whose honour it must be remembered, that this man, who was a Norman of low birth and whose mother was reputed a witch and familiar of demons, rose to the highest offices, and built that grand old castle of Norham on the Tweed, where the princely bishops of Durham his successors often resided. Again, in Roger, Bishop of Salisbury and Chancellor of England in the reign of Henry I. we have another great architect, and his life was marked by romantic vicissitudes, from the time when the King heard him say mass as a village curate in Normandy to the day when he surrendered his castles to King Stephen after a career of almost sovereign power. So that you see the chancellors and justiciars of those days were magnificent churchmen. And when circuits were established for the purpose, chiefly, of trying such criminal accusations as arose in the different counties, and judges-itinerant were appointed, they were generally great barons of the province in which they were assigned to hold pleas, but probably never read a book in their lives. Thus, for Yorkshire, Durham, Northumberland, and Cumberland, in the year 1131, Eustace Fitz-John, the great Norman nobleman who built Alnwick Castle and governed Bamburgh for the crown, was appointed a justice-itinerant, and he had for his colleague Walter Espec, that great Yorkshire baron, who, when the Scottish invasion roused the northern patriots to arms, jointly commanded the English host at the Battle of the Standard, and crowned a life of valour by founding Rievaux Abbey. But the functions of these baronial judges of assize were not what we should call judicial, and no more resembled those of our judges than the aspect of the country they beheld resembled that of England at the present day. No towns of portentous magnitude then spread stony pavement and labyrinths of dwellings over the sunny fields; no populous centres of industry darkened the landscape canopied by smoke; most of the highways were those the Romans had left; castles and abbeys received the judges and their armed attendants; and a third of the country was covered by primeval wood, the haunt of the bandit, the wild boar, and the wolf.

The law itself was in a state equally rude down to the reign of Henry II.; and the administrators of justice were too commonly themselves engaged in feudal strife, or were the partisans of contending suitors. But in that reign the law became reduced to a system; the laws of Normandy had been gradually engrafted on those of England, and into this composite structure the Canonists built the enduring marble of the Roman civil law, so that it became necessary that the judges and the advocates should be skilled in law; but the chancellors and in many instances the justiciars were still ecclesiastics. I forbear to go far back in historic times, and I will notice very briefly such of these high officers as best deserve remembrance.

Two of the most memorable justiciars of Henry the Second's reign, viz. Richard de Luci and Ranulph de Granville, were feudal barons. The former was a great statesman, and governed the kingdom as well as the King's chief court of justice, before the rise and after the martyrdom of Thomas à Becket. To De Luci are due those celebrated " Constitutions of Clarendon " which formed the basis of the ecclesiastical polity of later times, for, after those enactments, criminal accusations against the clergy came to be tried in the King's courts, and suits relating to benefices came to be determined according to the common law; the clergy ceased to usurp the jurisdiction to enforce contracts, and causes were no longer carried by appeal to Rome.

It was characteristic of the times that De Luci ended his days as a monk in the monastery which he founded in a wooded solitude by the Thames, for that (as an eloquent writer has remarked) was an age when life was as earnest in its belief as stormy in its ambitions; when, if feudal castles rose on English hills, abbeys were reared in many a quiet vale; when the chivalry of England flocked to Palestine in the crusades, and if they lived to return were laid for their final rest in the churches they had endowed. De Luci's office of justiciar was shorn of its splendour as long as the genius and ambition of Thomas à Becket joined all the authority of the State to his office of chancellor. It was not until the time of Becket that the chancellorship advanced to the rank and power it has ever since maintained, but it is as a statesman and an ecclesiastic that the name of Becket is so prominent in English history. It is not in his character of chancellor that he is chiefly memorable, nor did his noble qualities, his rare and lofty spirit, shine forth until after he had resigned the great seal and become an actor in that extraordinary series of events which for ever connect his name with the civil and ecclesiastical history of England. He was the first *Englishman* who was ever appointed chancellor, and he brought to that office the knowledge of civil and canon law which was in his day only to be acquired in Italy; but the skill in hawking and the chase which, with his attractive qualities as a companion, first recommended the youthful Becket to Henry's favour, are tastes which have long ceased to be conducive to preferment in Westminster Hall.

Becket must have made a dignified and courtly chancellor, and he travelled with such unheard-of and costly state upon his embassies that the Frenchmen were at a loss to conceive what the grandeur of the King of England himself must be.

Glanville, Henry's other great justiciar, was the first judge who won both military and legal renown, and his life affords a curious example of the manners of the age; for at one time he is seen as the grave and learned civilian presiding among the bishops and other judges of the King's Court, at another, clothed in mail and leading a warlike array against Scottish invaders.

Glanville, when he was Sheriff of Yorkshire in the year 1174, performed an exploit which no sheriff before or subsequently achieved; for, when William the Lion of Scotland invaded England, Glanville raised and arrayed all the force he could collect, mustering his men on many a village green and by many a market cross, and led them against the formidable invader. I fear his volunteers did not all remain to face the Scots; but the gallant Glanville captured the king before Alnwick Castle and safely lodged him in the keep at Richmond. Afterwards, however, exchanging the spear for the pen, he became Justiciar of England, and wrote the treatise " On the Laws and Customs of the Realm," which has gained for him the title of the " Father of English Jurisprudence." This remarkable work, written little more than a century after the Conqueror's ascendancy became established, shows that England was even then "governed" (to use the language of Lord Chief Justice Coke) " by laws and customs founded upon reason and of antient time obtained," and that Henry II. at all events had the wisdom to seek for his judges " men grave in manners, familiar with the laws, and wise, eloquent, and speedy in their administration." To the advice of his distinguished Justiciar is attributed his ratification of the ancient native laws of Anglo-Saxon days, known as the laws of Edward the Confessor, and his solicitude for the due administration of justice throughout the kingdom. Glanville, however, seems to have been the first justiciar who adorned his office by legal learning and purely judicial qualities. At length, after an honourable tenure of power, he was seen in the new character of a Crusader. In 1188 the King and his council were assembled (this was about eighteen months before Henry's death), and the archbishop had exhorted them to a new Crusade, when the aged justiciar, who had never displayed any symptoms of enthusiasm, and had a wife, children, and grandchildren, the objects of his tender regard, rose up and declared his readiness to march for the Holy Land, whereupon he was solemnly invested with the Cross. At the King's entreaty he delayed his journey, and Henry never performed it; but, soon after the coronation of Richard of the Lion Heart, Glanville accompanied a chosen band of Norman knights to Palestine, where, in the following year, he ended his career at the siege of Acre,

How greatly the dying Crusader would have rejoiced if he could have seen what we see—the power of the Crescent at length drooping beneath the Cross, and England sending her peaceful sons and arts of peace to the Moslem land on which the chivalry of Christendom fought and fell!

The office of Chancellor did not rival in dignity and importance that of justiciar in Glanville's days, and it was not until some years afterwards, when the office of justiciar had been abolished under the Plantagenets and the separate equitable jurisdiction of the Chancellor acquired, that he became first in judicial rank. In the Anglo-Norman reigns the Chancellor held both the Great Seal and his place in the Aula Regis as the King's principal chaplain, confessor, and secretary, but force of personal character combined with official power in the case of other great justiciars besides Glanville to give a pre-eminent dignity to the office of Justiciar of England.

In the days of the Conqueror this diocese had sent William de Carilefe, the greatest of its early bishops, to the chief judgment-seat of England; and it is a thing worthy to be remembered here that before the close of the Anglo-Norman dynasty another of these chieftains of the law was a bishop of Durham, for the martial yet lettered Glanville was succeeded by that magnificent prelate Hugh de Pudsey, who, if he did not render himself memorable as a minister of justice, is at all events commemorated in the cathedral city of this diocese by enduring monuments of his taste and love of splendour, for he completed the cathedral church, added the unique chapel called the Galilee, and built some important edifices in the county of Durham.

Pudsey was superseded as justiciar by a still more powerful churchman—William Longchamp, Bishop of Ely, who united in himself the offices of chancellor and justiciar, and ruled England in King Richard's absence. Nothing is known of Longchamp as a judge, but the extraordinary energy of his character displayed itself in all its varied functions, and he even tried his hand as an engineer, for he constructed the ditch or moat of the Tower. His exactions oppressed both clergy and laity alike, and nearly exhausted the wealth of his countrymen, but they did not render him unpopular with people who had nothing to lose; there were no newspapers to abuse him, and the minstrels, of whom he was a liberal patron, went about singing his fame in every market-place of England. Falling at length from his almost royal state, we see him a fugitive to the sea-coast, disguised as a female pedlar, and made the sport of the fishermen and sailors while prisoner in a cave upon the English shore, which he soon afterwards quitted for ever.

He was more fortunate in making his escape than a succeeding chancellor, the brutal and daring Jeffreys, who on the flight of James II. became an object of vengeance for his own judicial atrocities, and as one of the King's evil counsellors. The unhappy ex-Chancellor was in sad consternation, and, planning an escape to Hamburgh from the river side of the Thames by a Newcastle collier, he disguised himself in a sailor's dress, and cut off the bushy eyebrows that added such terror to his frown; but, imprudently looking out of window at an alehouse in Wapping, he was recognised by a scrivener who had once undergone the terrors of his face; he was seized by the mob, taken before the Council, petitioned against by the widows of the West, whose husbands he had hung or transported on the Monmouth Rebellion, and ended his short eventful career a prisoner in the Tower of London. But, to return to mediæval judges.

After the fall of Longchamp, Walter Hubert—who from being a poor boy, educated out of charity by Glanville and his wife Bertha, had reached the dignity of Archbishop of Canterbury— became the chief justiciar of King John. As I cannot say anything about him as a justiciar, I may mention one of his exploits as a general. I do not know what we should think of an Archbishop of Canterbury in our day who should put himself at the head of an armed force, and, chasing a demagogue into one of the London churches, should drag him from sanctuary with fire and sword, hang him, and reduce the citizens of London to obedience. Yet all this was done by Archbishop Hubert when a kind of rebellion was stirred up by a formidable personage who was known in the folk-mote of the English citizens as William-with-the-Long-Beard. This strange picture of bygone times we derive from the Rolls of the King's Court—the earliest consecutive judicial records now existing; and, dry and uncouth as they appear, they afford us many a glimpse of the times; they show the thrifty habits and prosperous state of the trading and the labouring classes early in the thirteenth century, and that the people were still Anglo-Saxon in language and feeling, although the Norman tongue and manners were found in the upper classes of society, and Norman-French was the language of Westminster Hall. These records show us too—and it is more to my present purpose—that the main outlines of the common law had then become defined, and that, concurrently with the social advancement of the people of England, their judicial system was moulding the constitution, and acquiring an authority which was ever vindicated by its foundation in the law of God.

A succeeding Justiciar, the Geoffrey FitzPeter whom Shakespeare introduces in his " King John," was chiefly remarkable for his extravagant love of hawks, and for the fear with which he inspired that odious and cowardly sovereign; and his successor, Peter de Rupibus, Bishop of Winchester, and tutor of Henry III. was a man who made a great figure in the eyes of his contemporaries. It is curious to contrast the calm, nameless, and forgotten black marble effigy in Winchester cathedral which is supposed to commemorate this martial Justiciar, with the turbulent and restless life of a man whose name, when living, filled all Europe. A more remarkable justiciar was his rival and successor Hubert de Burgh, to whom Shakespeare assigns the custody of Prince Arthur, and to whom authentic history attributes the honour of having persuaded King John to grant the great Charter. His unbounded ambition and rapacity subjected him, however, to accusations like some of those which were afterwards made against Wolsey; his enemies moreover charged him not only with treason, but with poisoning some of the nobility, abstracting from the royal treasury a gem which had the virtue of rendering the wearer invulnerable, and gaining the King's favour by sorcery and enchantment—accusations curiously characteristic of the age. The seizures, escapes, and adventures of the fallen Justiciar are almost romantic; but he lived to spend the rest of his days in seclusion, and died amongst the Black Friars of Holborn, to whom he gave the house which became the palace of Whitehall.

With the reign of Henry III. we reach the time when statute law as distinguished from the old common law of England began; but Henry's ministers were generally too much occupied in measures of defence against the barons to find leisure for legal reform, and only two of their legislative measures are known, viz. " the Statute of Merton," which was passed to encourage the enclosure of waste land, and the " Statute of Marlbridge," which regulated distraint; yet in the most turbulent period of this troubled reign there was given to England the best treatise on law of which our countrymen could boast until the publication of " Blackstone's Commentaries "—I refer to Henry de Bracton's celebrated " Treatise on the Laws and Customs of England." The author is supposed to have been an ecclesiastic who had made jurisprudence and the Roman civil law his study; and it is remarkable that, notwithstanding the advancement of society in the six centuries from Bracton's time, and all the changes that England saw in that long period, the overthrow of dynasties, and the destruction of her old nobility in civil wars, it was not until the law reforms of the last five-and-thirty years that any considerable portions of Bracton's work became entirely obsolete. In these days, when a lawyer finds himself surrounded by an ever-increasing legal library, he is disposed to think with some envy of the good fortune of these old Plantagenet lawyers who needed only a few portable MSS. for reference. The spirit of jurisprudence seems to have been active in those days in France, for St. Louis the King, who used to administer justice seated amidst his council under a spreading oak on the summer mornings, graced his absolute authority by amending the judicial system of his kingdom.

I shall mention only one of Henry the Third's justiciars, Hugh le Despencer, a nobleman more celebrated for bravery than learning—which I hope no members of the Inns of Court will ever be, notwithstanding their zeal for the volunteer movement; but he is memorable as the last of those remarkable men, ancestors of some peers of England at the present day, who for more than two centuries united the sword and the gown in the political and commanding functions of Justiciar of England. Hugh le Despencer, though aged and infirm, was at the battle of Evesham, and, refusing to disgrace his ermine by flight, was slain beside the gallant Montfort, Earl of Leicester. The year in which that battle was fought, 1275, was memorable in our history, for England then saw that parliament assemble with which our representative system may be said to have begun.

The first chief justice who acted merely as a judge was Robert de Bruce, that kinsman of Scottish monarchs who is counted among the ancestors of Queen Victoria, and who presided as chief justice in the then rising tribunal afterwards called "the Court of King's Bench." The family of Bruce was Norman; but from the Conquest Skelton in Yorkshire was their chief seat, and in Scotland " their skill in the tournament and in singing romances softened the hearts and won the hands of the Caledonian heiresses." Robert was of the Scottish branch, but educated by his Yorkshire cousins, and, selecting Westminster Hall instead of the field of chivalry for the arena in which he hoped to gain distinction, he ultimately became Chief Justice of England, and, afterwards retiring to Scotland, he claimed, on the death of the Maid of Norway, to be crowned king at Scone, but Edward I. decided in favour of his formidable rival, John Baliol.

During the sway of the justiciars the King's court retained its Norman constitution, but from the time of Henry III. its functions were gradually divided, and the various courts at Westminster had their rise from that division. Still, the days had not arrived when Englishmen saw the high places of judgment adorned by the profound learning and the judicial virtues which have been so long characteristic of the English bench of justice, and it was reserved for the professionally-trained judges of later times—the Mansfields, the Hardwickes, and the Ellenboroughs —to earn our grateful remembrance for asserting some principle of law that has ever since governed rights and protected interests of their countrymen.

The lives of the Chancellors in the Plantagenet reigns belong more to the history of England than to that of the worthies of the law, for the prelate-chancellors were more prominent in affairs of the state and of the Church than in the exercise of judicial functions. What we read of one chancellor in those days is often applicable to many others—either he was a monk who won the royal favour by courtly manners and aptitude for business affairs; or who, as abbot of a monastery, gained the esteem of the brotherhood by his administrative services and his equitable rule; or was a secular priest who stepped from one preferment to another, became a bishop or a primate, negotiated treaties, and went on foreign embassies, and, when he had, like Wolsey, "sounded all the depths and shoals of honour," returned to be laid for his final rest among the fraternity to whom he owed his education, or in the calm shade of the cathedral church which he had lovingly enriched. The income of the chancellorship, however, was not at all magnificent, for this great functionary received from the Crown only five shillings a day, with certain cakes and cloth, wine and wax-lights, and lodging, besides the fees on writs and charters passing the Great Seal.

The reign of Edward I. was the era when our judicial institutions became firmly established on the basis on which they have ever since remained. The principles of English jurisprudence were then defined, and the courts for the administration of justice were established in the form they still retain. The Court of King's Bench—in which the sovereign was supposed to preside assisted by the Chief Justice—became the supreme criminal court, with a certain control over other tribunals of civil jurisdiction. The Court of Common Pleas arose from the provision of Magna Charta by which suits between party and party were fixed at Westminster in order that suitors might no longer have to follow the king as the fountain of justice in his migrations from town to town. The jurisdiction of the Court of Exchequer was at first confined to estates and revenues of the Crown, but it afterwards acquired a jurisdiction both legal and equitable, as between subject and subject; the barons its judges, however, were not necessarily lawyers, even down to the reign of Edward III. The Chancellor became first in precedence of the great officers of State, and now sat in his own court, probably even then a very sleepy domain. The old appellate jurisdiction of the Curia Regis was vested in the great Council of the Nation; and, upon the division of the legislature into two houses, remained with the Lords spiritual and temporal, who had the judges for their assessors, as they have at the present day.

Before the end of the thirteenth century a great change had

silently occurred, which has ever since proved of the greatest importance to the interests of the law. The juridical knowledge which in early times had been monopolized by the clergy had come to be emulated by laymen in the societies of professors of the law which had been established in the Inns of Court, and from them the king now selected his judges. In the reign of Edward I. also began the series of reports of cases, which, under the title of year-books, form a grand repertory of English law, less useful *now* than curious for their subject-matter and antiquity, and very unlike the professional and the newspaper reports of the present day. Then too originated that early code of law reform known as " The Statute of Westminster the first," which seems to have acquired for Edward the name of the English Justinian. On looking back at the legislative achievements of this great monarch, it is curious to see that a whole reign—a reign too which is always regarded as pre-eminent for legislation—produced fewer statutes than one Session of Parliament produces now. Yet, as Blackstone has said, there was more done in the reign of Edward I. to settle and establish the distributive justice of this kingdom, than in all the centuries since his time put together, and under Edward I. the model of the administration of justice as between party and party was settled.

Civil strife and national calamity in the feeble reign of Edward II. suspended further law reform, but the jurisdiction of the Chancery seems to have been extended, and the Chancellor's court was fixed at Westminster, where, at the upper end of the great hall, his marble chair was now exalted. Until the time of Edward III. the Chancellors continued to be churchmen, but that sovereign for the first time selected a Chancellor from among the professors of the law, who were to the common law of England what the civilians of the courts ecclesiastical were to the canon law of the Church.

The first thorough-bred common lawyer ever appointed Chancellor was Sir Robert Parnynge, but in the person of Sir Robert Bourchier, his predecessor, Edward had departed from the usage of selecting a churchman for the office, and Bourchier, who was the first layman ever made Chancellor, seems to have been better fitted for the duties of a general officer than those of a judge. He had been the king's companion in arms, and the military Chancellor resumed his proper vocation when he fought beside the Black Prince at Cressy, and gained a peerage which descended to a distinguished posterity. But Edward soon returned to the Church for his Chancellors, and one of the most remarkable men in the whole series was Richard de Bury, who had been his tutor, and was his most trusted friend, secretary, and prime minister. After a wonderful career of ecclesiastical dignities and civil employments this great and learned man became Bishop of Durham, and surrounded himself by scholars and the greatest collection of manuscripts then known in England, all which he bequeathed for the foundation of the Public Library at Oxford. De Bury had an unbounded love of literature, and made munificent provision for the preservation and advancement of learning; and the noble figure of the good bishop, both scholar and statesman, shines calmly through the eventful scenes of a warlike age and throws a lustre on the most brilliant reign in English history. One of his successors in the office of Chancellor—William of Edyngton, Bishop of Winchester—is chiefly memorable for his early patronage of William of Wykeham, who built Windsor Castle, then turned ecclesiastic, and succeeded Edyngton as Bishop of Winchester, and finally as Lord Chancellor. Whatever Wykeham's judicial merits may have been, he has achieved a sort of immortality in his architectural works; he was the great pioneer in the important educational movement which followed his time; and his collegiate foundations at Winchester and Oxford, which so nobly commemorate his munificence and love of learning, still continue to diffuse the blessings of education in his native land.

The lives of the Common Law Judges of the Plantagenet reigns present few features of general interest; yet in passing I must mention Sir William Howard, who was a Chief Justice, probably of the Common Pleas, in the reign of Edward I. and in the early part of that of Edward II., for to him the illustrious family of Howard appears to owe its rise.

With the reign of Edward III. we reach what may be regarded as the turning point of the Middle Ages in this country. His Chancellors do not appear to have originated any improvements in the law; but during the chancellorship of John de

Thoresby, Bishop of St. David's, Parliament passed the well-known statute (now in force) which defined the acts that are to be accounted treasonable. In that reign, however, trial by jury in the form in which it has come down to our own times seems to have had its beginning; juries having then for the first time assisted in the administration of justice as ultimate judges of matters of fact. From two Acts, passed early in Edward's reign, which contain the oath of the judges to disregard letters from the king touching the decision of causes, it appears that the sovereign, after he had ceased to sit in his court of justice, had been accustomed to write to the judges desiring them to decide causes be-before them in a particular manner.

It was at the same epoch, now nearly five hundred years ago, that the statute passed for the use of English in the Courts at Westminster. In 1362 we have the earliest known example of the use of English in proceedings of Parliament, but it was not until the time of Richard III. that the statute laws were given in the language of the people and were printed. The present use of Norman French in giving the royal assent to bills is, of course, a relic of the language of Parliamentary records in the Plantagenet reigns.

At the time of the chancellorships of Edyngton and Wykeham, the Chancellor's equitable jurisdiction as a judge had not become the most important part of his functions. His political office had, however, greatly increased in importance: he was in effect Secretary of State for all departments and chief adviser of the King; sanctioned all charters and grants that passed under the Great Seal; had recently acquired the right he still exercises to appoint justices of the peace; summoned and opened Parliaments; and prepared the measures which became law. When the King held his court in any provincial town the Chancellor, with the masters of the chancery, the clerks, and records, followed him; but the officers of the chancery when in the metropolis lived together in an inn or hospitium; and they seem to have been somewhat dainty in their diet, if we may judge from the fact that the King's letters of safe-conduct were obtained by a Chancellor of Edward II. for some poulterers whom he sent into different parts of England to buy poultry " for the maintenance of himself and his clerks of chancery." It is no wonder that in a subsequent reign complaint was made in Parliament that the masters were "sinecurists, over fat in body and purse." The Chancellor moreover received, as part of his allowance from the Crown, a liberal supply of wine from the royal vineyards of Gascony. Perhaps it was in consequence of an unwise abstinence from these good things, and a disregard of roast beef as the English basis of strength, that an Archbishop and Chancellor of Edward II. was weak enough to yield to the entreaties of the queen for the consecration of an unworthy favourite, and, when he heard of the papal displeasure, actually died of fear of the Pope!

So much for the Chancellors. The Chief Justices in the fourteenth century were, like them, much employed on negociations of state, and by no means confined to judicial duties. Some were eminent, a few were sadly unprincipled, and others were very ill-fated. One judge, Sir John de Cavendish, ancestor of the Duke of Devonshire, was put to death in Wat Tyler's rebellion; and another, Sir Robert Tresilian, himself underwent the last penalty of the law on an accusation of treason in 1388. Henry le Scrope, a Chief Justice of this period, demands honourable mention, for he—without the advantage of ancient lineage, and by success in the law alone—founded a family and obtained baronial honours. That he has had many successful followers in later times is sufficiently shown by the fact that no fewer than eighty-two existing peerages have sprung from the law! Other Scropes were likewise men of law and letters, and, "like good Yorkshiremen, were uniformly devoted to their own advancement." The year 1388 must have been a famous time for promotion in Westminster Hall, one Chief Justice having been hanged, and all the other judges having been attainted, deprived, or banished. Succeeding judges of those days seem to have wisely kept aloof from politics:—During tumults that convulsed the realm, they seem to have been quietly administering justice at Westminster; and the only battles witnessed by judges under the Lancastrian dynasty were those fought in the fields near Westminster Abbey by champions for the decision of trials under writs of right, when the judges attended to see that the laws of the combat were observed—a curious relic of the ordeal trials in which our Saxon ancestors believed.

The judge most distinguished perhaps of all the reverend sages of the law in Henry the Fourth's reign was Sir William Gascoigne, whose name is made familiar to us by his having committed the Prince of Wales to prison, and by his introduction in Shakespeare's play. He was of a Yorkshire family, and his ancestors were for the most part men of valour, but the future Chief Justice devoted himself to the law, and gained honourable fame for his uprightness and his disinterested performance of his duty. He showed how nobly he dared to brave the frown of power when he refused to try illegally, at the command of Henry IV., the king's illustrious captives Scrope archbishop of York and Thomas Mowbray son of the banished Duke of Norfolk, who had been taken in insurrection against him. But what has chiefly gained applause for Chief Justice Gascoigne was his dauntless ministering of justice on the royal heir of England who had presumed to insult him on the judgment-seat. Shakespeare has given dramatic effect to the scene in which the young Prince, on his accession to the throne, is represented as re-investing Gascoigne with " the balance and the sword":—

> You did commit me:
> For which, I do commit into your hand
> The unstain'd sword that you have used to bear;
> With this remembrance—that you use the same
> With the like bold, just, and impartial spirit
> As you have done 'gainst me. There is my hand;
> You shall be as a father to my youth:
> \* \* \* \*
> And I will stoop and humble my intents
> To your well-practis'd, wise directions.

But I am afraid it is now established that the young King in fact lost no time in dispensing with the services of the dauntless judge.

Henry the Fifth's reign was adorned by one of the most distinguished Chief Justices recorded in history, viz., Sir John Fortescue, author of the well-known treatise *De Laudibus Legum Angliæ*. It is refreshing to turn from the intriguing prelates and warlike barons who controlled the administration of justice in the fifteenth century to a man like Fortescue, an enlightened lover of liberty and constitutional law, who won his promotion by merit, and was not more remarkable for his professional learning than for his judicial integrity. He was advanced in years, and had long worn the robe of dignity, when he signalised his constancy in the Lancastrian cause by fighting for Henry VI. by the side of Morton, afterwards Archbishop of Canterbury and Lord Chancellor, in the field of Towton Moor—

> Where the Red and the White Rose, as all the kingdom knows,
> Were the emblems of the foes in a sad and bloody strife.

And, after the fatal and romantic events which reduced Queen Margaret and the young prince to the society of outlaws in Hexham Forest, Fortescue accompanied the royal fugitives in their exile, and wrote his admirable treatise for the purpose of instructing the heir-apparent in the duties of a patriot King. When the cause of the House of Lancaster had become hopeless, Fortescue submitted to Edward IV., but was somewhat cruelly required, as the condition of pardon, to write a treatise in support of the claim of the House of York; and when—like an old lawyer, as people will probably think—he complied, he was restored in blood, and retired to pass the rest of his days at his Gloucestershire estate of Ebrington, which gives the title of viscount to his descendants at the present day. Fortescue is regarded as having laid the foundation of Parliamentary privilege by a celebrated judgment which affirms the exclusive right of the Houses of Parliament to decide upon their own privilege—a judgment which has been followed for four hundred years.

But I must not pass from the Lancastrian dynasty without noticing three memorable Chancellors, foremost of whom was Cardinal Beaufort, half brother of Henry IV. who was a distinguished statesman during three eventful reigns, and was four times Chancellor. He boldly extended the jurisdiction of the Court of Chancery; but the control which his court then claimed over partition, dower, account, and some other matters cognizable at common law, has since continued, as well as the control which he first asserted over the marriage of infant wards. The jurisdiction of Chancery over uses and trusts had in Beaufort's days become quite established; but some of the subjects then brought before the Chancellor seem very much beneath his dignity; for instance,

Lord Chancellor Beaufort did not deem beneath his notice the revenue he derived from licensing the exportation of cheese and butter; and, as a judge, he was asked in one suit to give relief against the Sheriff of Norwich, who had imprisoned the complainant for making tallow candles with wicks of flax instead of cotton; in another, to require sureties for the peace; while in a third, an attorney prayed him to restrain the defendant from using arts of witchcraft to his prejudice. One might imagine this superstitious suitor to be identical with the attorney, in a case in the Year Books, who obtained damages for being called a fool. It is actionable to say of an attorney that he is a fool, because this is saying that he is unfit for the profession whereby he lives, but it is not actionable to call an attorney a sheep, because that imputes innocence.

But to return to the Cardinal Chancellor. Beaufort bore chief sway in England until his career closed in 1447, on that death-bed to which Shakespeare's description has given ideal terrors. The two other Chancellors conspicuous in the last of the Lancastrian reigns were, John Stafford, Bishop of Bath and Wells, who held the Great Seal for the then unprecedented period of eighteen years, and carried the Act of Parliament to confirm the foundation of Eton College, where

> Grateful Science still adores
> Her Henry's holy shade;

and William Waynflete, Bishop of Winchester, the illustrious founder of Magdalen College, who lived not only to complete that splendid monument of his magnificence and love of learning, but to see the union of the Red and the White Rose. Although classical learning was about to be restored, and the art of printing was already practised in Europe, a dark cloud seems to cover England during the struggle between the Houses of York and Lancaster—a period rife in usurpation and bloodshed, arbitrary executions, and savage manners; and during which, but for the fame of Chief Justice Fortescue and Judge Littleton, the rays of juridical science would seem to have been extinguished in this country. Thomas Littleton, a judge of the Common Pleas under Edward IV., has left a name still sacred in Westminster Hall.

He was the author of the *Treatise on Tenures,*—a work to which students of the common law were said to be no less beholden than civilians to the Institutes of Justinian; it became better known by the celebrated Commentaries of Sir Edward Coke, and has been illustrated in later times by four of the greatest of English lawyers. Judge Littleton was conspicuous for impartiality as well as learning; he was not influenced by the passions of the contending partisans of York and Lancaster, and, though he witnessed two temporary transfers of the crown, the royal disputants retained him in office. The equitable jurisdiction of Chancery made great advance in the reign of Edward IV., although it still wanted the systematic principles and independence of the courts of law which it afterwards acquired.

The most distinguished of Henry the Seventh's chancellors was Cardinal Morton—the model, as he was the precursor, of Cardinal Richelieu. As Bishop of Ely he is the prelate made familiar by Shakespeare in that scene in the Tower in which Richard III. asks Morton to send for some of the early strawberries for which the gardens of Ely House, in the then smokeless and suburban Holborn, were famous. Morton is described as of reverend aspect, weighty as well as graceful in discourse, and highly skilled in law. His successor was a prelate—Wareham archbishop of Canterbury—whose chief glory was the friendship of Erasmus, the great scholar, who has eulogized the exalted character, the penetrating judgment, and the pious life of the good and gentle primate. In 1515 Wareham was superseded by Wolsey, who, during the fourteen years for which he held the Great Seal, exercised more power than any previous or succeeding chancellor, and is quite unrivalled for the external splendour with which he surrounded his office. I need not describe the dignity of appearance, pleasing expression of countenance, and fascinating power which were so remarkable in his personal gifts; nor by what rapid steps the young Oxford student, suddenly emerging from the cloisters of Magdalen College, became Henry's favourite companion, and then his Prime Minister and Chancellor, Bishop of Winchester and Durham, Archbishop of York, and Cardinal Legate of the Holy See. His natural abilities to some extent supplied deficiencies of legal training; but as Chancellor he was not guided by those well-defined principles of equitable jurisprudence which have been the growth of a more artificial and refined state of society, yet he improved the administration of justice. We have a curious picture of the proud state he maintained in the height of his power. His household is said to have numbered eight hundred persons; an Earl of Derby was his high chamberlain, and he had quite a magnificent personage, who appeared daily in velvet or damask with a gold chain, for his master-cook; and, when the Cardinal, attired in his judge's robe of scarlet and sable tippet, went from York House to his Court at Westminster, he was received by a line of gentlemen in waiting as he passed to mount his palfrey, which stood in housings of red velvet and gold; and he was ushered by an imposing pageant, in which the Mace, Great Seal, and Silver Cross of York moved on before him to the Chancellor's marble chair. In admonitory contrast with the picture of his pride, we see Wolsey on his fall entering Leicester Abbey to find a grave among the brethren of its tranquil cloister, after surrendering all his palaces and dignities; leaving, however, in the unfinished splendour of Christ Church College—the noble foundation which he endowed at Oxford from the spoils of suppressed monasteries, and dedicated to the perpetual advancement of learning—a monument destined not to pass away.

Sir Thomas More, who was then distinguished alike for his scholastic and his legal attainments, for his genius and his virtue, was designated by the public voice as Wolsey's fittest successor. The charm of his manners and conversation was early owned by Henry VIII. who had been accustomed to familiar intercourse with him amidst his happy domestic circle before promoting him to the perilous dignity of Chancellor. He was installed in office with studied magnificence and eulogy, and his admirable discharge of his judicial duties soon reflected a new splendour on his character. It is significant of his modest piety that he was accustomed every day in term, before he sat in his own court, to enter the adjacent Court of King's Bench, and receive on bended knee the blessing of his venerable father, who was still a judge; and, instead of imitating Wolsey's proud parade, More, even when Chancellor, used to walk with his family to church, and sing among the choristers. To the home enjoyments and the literary pursuits which official duty had interrupted, he eagerly returned when the determination of the royal Bluebeard to marry Anne Boleyne, whether his divorce from Catherine should be granted or refused by Rome, obliged More to resign an office which he could no longer conscientiously hold. But his peace was soon to be invaded, and with his refusal to be present at Anne Boleyne's coronation his troubles began. A tyrannical edict, miscalled a law, made it high treason to " do anything to the prejudice or derogation of the King's lawful matrimony with Queen Anne," and required all persons to swear to maintain the contents of the statute. More, deeming the oath unlawful, refused to take it, and was committed to the Tower; but as he had said nothing that could be perverted into a semblance of the acts made treasonable the fickle tyrant could not shed his blood. Rich, the solicitor-general, thereupon undertook the infamous task of trying to betray him, in a confidential conversation, into some expression that might be called treasonable.

After a long imprisonment he was arraigned for trial, and Europe had not seen such a prisoner at any bar of justice for a thousand years. What a scene was witnessed by sympathising crowds on that May morning in 1535, when the summer sunshine fell upon his venerable form, as, aged and bent by imprisonment, he issued from the Tower gate amidst the guards, walking feebly and supported by his staff, to be tried in that great hall in Westminster where but lately he had sat in judgment! His hair it was observed had become grey since he was last seen among the people. The prosecution must have failed if Rich had not sworn that More denied the power of Parliament to make the King supreme head of the Church; and thereupon, notwithstanding that this evidence was unsupported by other testimony, and was denied by the illustrious prisoner, he was convicted, and under colour of law, to the general horror of Christendom, beheaded on Tower Hill.

In the career of Sir John Popham, one of Elizabeth's Chief Justices, there are some amusing features. While a child he was stolen and disfigured by gipsies; and the irregular habits and little respect for rules of property which marked his youth were attributed to his residence among his early captors. Traditions were then still fresh of robberies having been committed on Gad's Hill, under sanction of a too sportive Prince of Wales; and even when young Popham had become a student in the grave decorous Temple his companions out of doors were profligate, and he is even said to have assisted in taking purses on the highway; but, instead of being conducted to Tyburn for his offences, he lived to sentence others, and to become a terror to all evil-doers. His wife has the credit of having accomplished his reformation, and he became a well-conducted barrister. On attaining the degree of Serjeant-at-Law, he gave a feast of extraordinary magnificence, graced by some fine old Gascony wine, which people did say had been intercepted by him one night, many years before, on its way from Southampton to the cellars of a London alderman. Soon after his election as Speaker of the House of Commons, he was appointed Lord Chief Justice, and he presided for fifteen years, exhibiting in civil causes much learning and impartiality; but his character as a judge is sadly tarnished by his not extending that good quality to state trials, and by his conduct at the trial of Sir Walter Raleigh, when the practice of interrogating the accused in criminal trials, to which the French still adhere, prevailed in England. But few of the Tudor judges exhibited the independence and impartiality as between the Crown and the subject, which most of them showed between suitor and suitor; their subserviency, however, in state trials, is perhaps to be considered the reproach of the age rather than of the individual. Popham is also remarkable for having amassed more property than any lawyer before his time had acquired, and he became the owner of the estate of Littlecote Hall—the scene of the mysterious story of Wild Darrell.

The reign of Elizabeth does not present any chancellor of worthy memory; the Queen was often her own chancellor or keeper of the Great Seal; and perhaps the best known chancellor of that vain and capricious sovereign was her handsome favourite Sir Christopher Hatton, who may be said to have danced his way to the woolsack, and was better fitted to be a chamberlain of the household than to assume judicial duties.

I now pass to Sir Edward Coke, a Chief Justice whose life has been written by no fewer than six biographers since 1825, who has been considered the highest oracle of our civil jurisprudence and the hero of English Law. He was a scion of that ancient Norfolk family which is now represented by the noble owner of Holkham; but preferring hard study to the easy life of a country gentleman, he devoted himself with exemplary diligence to the study of the law. He rose at three, read formidable black-letter books, and went at eight to hear arguments in the courts at Westminster, which lasted until noon, then the hour of dinner; after which he attended readings or lectures and studied until supper at five, and then he heard questions debated at the moots of his Inn of Court. He finished the day in a sort of atmosphere of law, for he walked in the evening in the gardens or the cloisters of the Temple, as the season permitted, and then wrote down the information he had collected, retiring to bed at nine in order to have an equal portion of sleep before and after midnight. He never indulged in a visit to the Globe or other theatres then rising into repute, or bestowed any time in reading what he deemed so unprofitable as the poems of Spenser or Surrey, although Shakespeare and Ben Jonson were at that time in such fashion that grave lawyers wrote prologues for their plays, or assisted at the brilliant masques which then disturbed the sombre repose of the Inns of Court. Coke's progress after he was called to the bar (which was in 1578) was almost as rapid as that of Erskine two centuries afterwards, but resulted from technical skill and not from a popular eloquence. His manners were not prepossessing; his mind never opened to the liberal studies of philosophy nor owned the charms of literature; and he afforded a striking contrast to his great rival Francis Bacon, who was a polished courtier and had " taken all knowledge for his province."

Coke's reasoning was narrow-minded, his style cramped, his disposition arrogant and overbearing, his selfishness and love of riches insatiable, but his success was immense, and his practice so profitable that the Crown is said to have been alarmed by the increase of his territorial possessions. He had attained the head of his profession when he cast a longing eye on the great fortune of Lady Hatton—I fear I must say the fortune and not the lady was the attraction—though she was beautiful and young, and had besides the mysterious fascination which widows are commonly found to exercise. Her cousin, Francis Bacon, who was then a briefless barrister, though an accomplished scholar, and a man of winning address, aspired to her hand; but Coke, if not eager for the lady, was eager to prevent his professional and political rival from becoming allied with the Cecil family (she was the granddaughter of Lord Burghley), and, being preferred by her father, Coke was accepted by the lady, although there were, as the wags said, seven objections to him, viz. his six children and himself. They were privately married, for the young widow refused to be paraded in face of the church as the bride of a wrinkled attorney-general of fifty. But the sad discrepancy of their tastes soon appeared; he loved law, and hated gaiety and expense; she did not appreciate lawyers though she married one, and she delighted in hawking, in masques, and the adulation of the young courtiers who had served under Sidney, and could repeat verses of Spenser; and it is said that, while Coke banished himself to his den in Sergeants' Inn, she thronged the galleries of Hatton House with musicians, dancers, and wizards. Perhaps, if their married life had not become unhappy, Coke would not have produced the voluminous works which have given him such lasting fame, nor have plunged into the toils of public life. His first appearance as public prosecutor after the accession of James was on the trial of Sir Walter Raleigh, when Coke disgraced himself by his language and conduct, as he had done in the previous reign on the trial of the noble and unfortunate Lord Essex for his insurrection in London. In all his prosecutions, indeed, Coke's conduct was marked by servility to the Crown, an unscrupulous stretching of the royal prerogative, and a want of humanity and justice. At length, after twelve years of Crown practice, he stepped from this stormy ocean to what has been called the somnolent haven of the Common Pleas, but not until he had signalized his gigantic energy by producing five volumes of cases decided while he was at the bar. As a judge, Coke made noble amends for his conduct as attorney-general; he acted with a lofty independence, and presented the spectacle—rare in those days—of a magistrate whom neither the dread of power nor the love of applause could turn aside from duty. The diversity was hardly greater between Bacon the philosopher seeking for truth and Bacon the aspirant chancellor seeking for power, than between Coke the unscrupulous attorney-general and Coke the patriotic judge.

King James seems to have been fond of appearing in his Court of King's Bench, but when he tried his hand as a judge he became so much perplexed after hearing both sides in a cause that he abandoned the thing in despair, saying, " I could get on well enough by hearing one side only, but, when both sides have been heard, by my soul I know not which is right." The King was not content with attempting to exercise judicial functions, but endeavoured to interfere with the course of justice, to supersede the laws by royal proclamations, and to make the judges accountable to him for their decisions in civil suits. These enormities robbed the judicial bench of popular veneration, and led to that corruption of law and subservience of its administrators which was a chief cause of the horrors of the Great Rebellion, for, when judicial offices were notoriously sold, and judges became more solicitous for the prerogative of the Crown than the liberties of the people, and when those men who did venture to uphold constitutional rights suffered for their independence, the people naturally lost their confidence in the courts of justice, and the monarchy itself, deprived of those bulwarks, fell. On the memorable occasion on which James in a fury summoned the judges to scold them for having heard a cause in which he asserted his prerogative or interests to be concerned, Coke alone refused to promise that in similar cases in future justice should be delayed until the King's wishes were known: " When the case happens," he nobly said, " I shall do that which shall be fit for a judge to do." Although in the Stuart reigns a judge who gave an opinion against the Crown was pretty sure to be dismissed, Coke nevertheless continued in his high office; but he held it for only a short time longer, and it is to his early retirement that we owe the greatest monument of his delight in juridical pursuits—his " Commentaries on Littleton "— a work which has been pronounced the body of the common law of England, and the chief foundation of his fame. It is worthy of remark that his great rival, Lord Chancellor Bacon, when impeached and deprived of office, solaced himself in his fall by pursuing literature and philosophy; and that Coke, who had no taste for either, employed himself when in his turn a prisoner in the

Tower by writing his Commentaries—his library being a low chamber that had once been a kitchen. Coke, however, though not reinstated in the office of Chief Justice, was again returned to Parliament, and, to his great honour, carried the Act, still in force, for abolishing monopolies, and, moreover, framed the celebrated Petition of Right.

It is difficult for us at this day to believe that such evils as those against which the statute for suppressing monopolies was levelled can have existed in England: that one man can have enjoyed the sole right to buy and sell steel in this country; another the exclusive right to buy linen rags and make paper; another the monopoly of the business of dustmen and collectors of old clothes; and that the sale of tin, lead, iron, steel, leather, paper, currants, oils, sulphur, starch, and salt were all monopolised by favoured persons, who could suppress any competition.* Coke's statute, however, while it amended these iniquities, has ever since enabled the Crown to give an inventor the exclusive right to practice his invention for a limited time. As regards the other great monument of Coke's legislative wisdom, it is sufficient to say that when Charles I. assumed the power of committing to prison without specifying any offence upon the warrant, and the judges held that they could not examine into the legal validity of such commitment, the aged ex-Chief Justice carried resolutions, which fifty years afterwards became the foundation of the Habeas Corpus Act, and obtained the royal assent to a measure which declared general warrants to be illegal. Coke's continued vigour of intellect was such that at the age of eighty he had not closed

---

* Having mentioned the monopoly of the sale of iron and steel, it may be worth noticing that the restrictive law of the reign of Elizabeth and her successor with regard to the erection of forges and furnaces was adopted not for the advantage of a favoured individual, but on grounds of public policy. It was due to the serious apprehensions which were felt by the government that the increasing demands of the iron manufacture would exhaust the ancient forests, already much curtailed by the advance of civilization, for in those days charcoal was the combustible material employed in smelting iron; and (as a writer in the Quarterly Review has lately remarked) so unimportant did the supply of iron appear in comparison with the preservation of wood, for the comfort, the commerce, and the naval defence of the country, that more than one Act of Parliament was passed to regulate the felling of timber, and to restrict within very narrow limits the erection of iron furnaces.

his law books, and in his last retirement completed his celebrated "Institutes;" and the veteran jurist attained such length of days that, having seen in his infancy the eve of the Reformation, he saw in his old age the beginning of the Great Rebellion, and died in September 1634, in the eighty-third year of his age. In his undying reputation for learning we endeavour to forget that his vast legal knowledge was accompanied by narrow bigotry, and that, though he became memorable for patriotism, he had been capable of servility.

To the life of Francis Bacon alone a lecture might be devoted; but I need not so much regret that in a discourse embracing a long succession of judicial worthies, I can devote only a few sentences to the life of this celebrated man, for his character as a lawyer is eclipsed by his eminence as a philosophic writer, and it is from his immortal works, and certainly not from his career as chancellor, that his name derives its lustre.

He was the son of Sir Nicholas Bacon (who was Lord Keeper of the Great Seal for the first twenty years of Elizabeth's reign), and nephew of Burghley—

> The destined heir
> In his soft cradle to his father's chair.

and, being distinguished from other boys by his gravity of manners and love of sedentary pursuits, the youthful Francis was called by the Queen her "young Lord Keeper."

It was in 1598, when Bacon was thirty-seven, that he made his first appearance as an author by publishing the "Essays," which are still the most popular of his works, and seven years afterwards appeared his "Advancement of Learning." Although younger than Coke, and possessing less technical acquirement, he had won a splendid reputation when the rivalry for the office of attorney-general arose between himself and Coke; but it was not until 1617 that he was at length made Chancellor, striding over the head of his rival to the Mace and Seals, then vacated by Lord Chancellor Egerton.

Six and thirty years of toil, thought, study, disappointment, and success, though they had written (as Mr. Dixon remarks) some lines upon the broad and solid brow, had not dimmed the quick eye or quenched its kindling light, or weakened the expression of power, subtlety, and humour that overspread his countenance. The years during which Bacon was chancellor were dark and shameful years: his tenure of power was short; and the tale of his fall has been pronounced the most strange and sad in the whole history of man. Lord Campbell and Mr. Foss, the biographers of the judges of England, take, as Mr. Montagu and Lord Macaulay had taken, conflicting views of Bacon's character and conduct, and, more recently, a new champion (Mr. Dixon) has attempted his vindication, and contended that this great man was sacrificed to his enemies and rivals. I do not believe that Bacon ever accepted gifts or fees as bribes to pervert justice, but he received or allowed presents to be received for him, under circumstances wholly indefensible. Unhappily, too, there can be no doubt of the selfishness, ingratitude, and meanness which disgraced his career during the race of ambition, or of the political servility of which *he* was guilty, who could be the bold champion of intellectual freedom. But in the pursuit of philosophy Bacon showed the genius of a Solomon, and produced works which have for generations instructed mankind; even after he had been deposed from his high office, and during the nine years for which he survived his crushing sentence, the ex-chancellor in his seclusion composed works of immortal fame; and it is natural that we should now view his character through the lustre of his writings.

It was only a few of his contemporaries who suffered by his vices; it is all posterity that was profited by his wisdom; and Bacon, whom we see at one time assisting at the illegal torture of a Somersetshire clergyman, we see at another time inscribing perpetual monuments of his genius in the literature of his country: works in which he seems to be standing by us for all time, a companion in solitude and a comforter in sorrow. No man ever had more reason than Bacon had to bequeath his memory, as in effect he did, to GOD's mercy, to man's charity, and to time's verdict.

Now that the judges have long been paid by the State, it is difficult to believe that there was a time, in and long after the days of Bacon, when the chancellor and judges depended on fees of office. Yet Lord Chief Justice Coke, for example, received from the Crown hardly 225*l.* a year, though he and all the great lawyers when promoted to the bench relinquished a practice worth in the money of our days some thousands, and, as judges, kept great houses and costly state, and had a retinue of officers dependent like themselves on the suitors of the court.

I must not pass from the reign of James I. without making honourable mention of Lord Chancellor Ellesmere—the great ancestor of the noble family of Egerton—for he is justly regarded as the first founder of our system of equity, and, as a judge, was remarkable for talent, probity, and learning. The courts of common law were at that period adorned by several very able judges, many of whose decisions are still cited as authority; but equity had hardly become a system of jurisprudence, and decisions in chancery were not regarded as precedents, or even reported, as were the contemporary decisions at common law.

Speaking of the reported decisions, we may congratulate ourselves that the reports, voluminous as they have become, are no longer the old "Year Books" of our ancestors. Yet the pages of that repulsive series are not wholly filled with dead and obsolete law, and are still cited in Westminster Hall.

In the lives of judges of the reign of Charles I. there is not much to interest us. They were generally too much occupied by political broils to improve jurisprudence; but I must mention the spirited assertion by Sir William Jones, one of that learned body, of the essential independence of the judges in parliament, and of their constitutional right to deny to either house any explanation of their decisions. His words breathe a noble sense of judicial dignity:—" For my conduct as a judge I am alone responsible to God. I am myself a free man: my ancestors gave their voice for Magna Charta. I still enjoy the estate which they enjoyed. I do not intend to draw down God's wrath on my posterity, and I will neither advance the King's prerogative nor lessen the liberty of the subject."

Lord Keeper Littleton, who held the Great Seal when Charles set up his Court at Oxford, raised and took the command of a corps of volunteers consisting of all gentlemen of the Inns of Court and officers of courts of justice who were willing to take up arms for church and king; and he not only acted the part of commandant with great zeal and efficiency, but, being a tall, handsome, athletic man in a green old age, he was a very soldier-like commanding-officer. Lord Campbell has ventured to doubt whether the learned volunteers could ever have been made capable of fighting the psalm-singing troops of Cromwell; at all events, the Lord Keeper Commandant caught so violent a cold from being overtaken by a thunder storm while drilling one day, that the exhibition of his military prowess was suddenly ended by death, and Lord Keeper Littleton was the last head of the law who ever carried arms while chancellor.

Some of the republican judges were men of character and learning, and, turbulent and disjointed as the times were, showed high judicial qualities, and rendered goodly service in preserving the ancient laws of England from destruction. Some fanatical spirits of the time were for abrogating the whole fabric of our laws; they desired to substitute the law of Moses for the common law of England, to destroy all the records in the Tower, and to dispense with legal learning and professional skill. Much in the same spirit, it had been suggested, on Jack Cade's rebellion, that the first thing to be done was, to kill all the lawyers. But even during the Civil Wars, the great body of the nation, true to the traditions of Englishmen, wisely adhered to the ancient laws of the realm as their birthright and best safeguard. Reforms in legal procedure, indeed, were made during the interregnum, and certain improvements were then proposed which, after the lapse of two centuries, were adopted in the reign of Victoria, or are at this time under discussion. Criminal procedure also was improved, and in trials for felony legal rules of evidence came to prevail.

One of the most prominent of the Commonwealth Chief Justices was Oliver St.John, who as a leader on the side of the Parliament was second only to Cromwell in his influence on the events of the Great Rebellion. He had not long become Chief Justice when England saw her sovereign arraigned at the bar of a self-constituted tribunal; and, after the execution of the royal martyr, St.John failing himself to seize the office of Protector, adhered to the usurper and continued Chief Justice until the Restoration. He did nothing for English jurisprudence, and is remembered as a crafty and remorseless statesman, rather than as an enlightened judge; yet his proficiency in law, and his ability in his judicial office, contrast strangely with his " dark, ardent, and dangerous " character as a politician. But for the services of Chief Justice Rolle and some less famous judges, Cromwell's military Ironsides would have trodden out our liberties and laws. Rolle, to his honour, resigned office when the Protector admonished the judges to remember that they had no authority but what he gave them; and this Chief Justice will always be memorable—if not for the great work of his early industry known as Rolle's *Abridgment of the Common Law*—at all events for his uprightness and ability as a judge. Some of the great lawyers of those days seem to have been hardly made like other men; they studied law with entire devotion, wrote appalling compilations and bulky abridgments, conversed on law for relaxation, and passed lives of industry and self-denial.

English jurisprudence is also much indebted to Sir Matthew Hale—one of the most pure, independent, and learned of the seventeenth century judges—for, when the ancient laws of England were threatened with destruction by the military fanatics of the State, he devoted himself to their preservation, and joined some enlightened jurists in effecting legal reforms. His early training under a puritanical teacher strongly tinctured his opinions for life ; but when he was a student at Oxford the grave and studious element in his character was not in the ascendant; the visit of a company of strolling players developed his long-suppressed taste for finery and amusements, and he was on his way to serve as a volunteer abroad when a great lawyer in London on whom he called to take leave, gave a new direction to his youthful ardour, and arms yielded to the gown.

He vowed never to see a stage-play again; abjured all gay and convivial company, and devoted sixteen hours a day to study. From a love of finery, he passed to an apparel so slovenly, that, wandering on Tower-hill one day, he was captured by a press-gang for the King's service, and would have been shipped off to the West Indies if not rescued by some fellow-students. His manuscripts—which are still preserved at Lincoln's Inn—show his industry and his ardour for the acquisition of knowledge. His rise was rapid, though he had not the natural flow of eloquence and confident manner which are adapted to jury trials. When the saints of the Commons governed England without King or lords, Hale found no other object for loyalty than the laws of England; he accepted commission as a judge, and in that office his conscientious and independent conduct soon taught the Protector that he would find in him no servile instrument. The Restoration accomplished, Hale was presented to Charles on his long vacant throne; and becoming ultimately Chief Justice of England, his judicial qualities shone forth with lustre, for he showed himself familiar with every branch of law, even with the Roman civil law, and with equity; indeed, Lord Chancellor Nottingham, who is called the father of our present system in equity, is said to have reverenced Hale as his great master. It is strange that the perverse credulity of that age with regard to witchcraft should have influenced a man of his high judicial qualities, yet he charged the jury for a conviction on the trial of two miserable old women at Bury St. Edmund's, who were indicted for laying spells on children—the last capital conviction in England for the crime of bewitching.

But, be it observed, we are not entitled to look down on former ages with a self-gratulatory boast of superiority and enlightenment in this respect. Only two years ago there was a trial at the Staffordshire assizes where a host of witnesses showed that in the Midland counties, at this day, spectre dogs and witchcraft are still believed in. There is an amusing anecdote (Defoe records it) of Mr. Justice Powell, who was a judge in the reigns of James II., William III., and Queen Anne, from which it appears that the grey-haired merry old judge dealt more sensibly with some persons who were tried before him on accusation of witchcraft. To show that a woman tried before him was a witch, she was charged with being able to fly. "Ay!" said the judge, "and is this true? Do you say you can fly?" "Yes, I can," she said. "So you may, if you will, then," replied the judge; " I have no law against it." In 1752, when he tried Jane Wenham, the witch of Walkerne in Hertfordshire, the court being full of fine ladies, he very gallantly told the jury that they must not look out for witches amongst the old women but amongst the young. The jury, nevertheless, seem to have convicted the witch of Walkerne; but Judge Powell, to his great honour, got her pardoned by the Crown. Swift mentions this judge "as one of the merriest old gentlemen he ever saw, who spoke pleasant things, and chuckled till he cried." Lord Camden gives him the honourable character of being the only honest man of the four judges who sat on the trial of the seven bishops, and his honesty cost him his seat on the bench, but he was restored on the Revolution. And this leads me to mention that a very important change was made after the Restoration in the relation of the judges to the Crown, for thenceforth their commissions constituted them— not during pleasure, but—during good behaviour in office; and they thus became independent of the sovereign. Before that era the practice was capricious, some few judges holding for life, but more during pleasure only; yet we owe many maxims of constitutional liberty to judges who held their offices only during the will of the Crown, and in days, too, when public opinion and newspapers had no existence.

I must forbear to dwell on the lives of any judges of the last Stuart reigns, excepting Lord Chief Justice Holt. Although Scroggs and Saunders, Jeffreys and Wright, and a few other unprincipled and incompetent men of evil memory, disgraced the high places of justice after the Restoration, some upright and enlightened judges adorned the bench during that era, in which we behold (to use the language of Canning) the old constitutional system recovering from the revolutionary deluge, and the landmarks of ancient institutions beginning to reappear above the subsiding waves.

Holt was perhaps the most eminent of the judges appointed after the Revolution which set aside the Stuarts' hereditary right to the throne. To Holt's judicial services we may in a great degree attribute the stability of the constitutional system which was remoulded at that epoch. Unlike Sir Matthew Hale, he was early destined to the law, but, when at Oxford, was guilty of sad irregularities; and there is a well-known story that young Holt being without money to pay the reckoning of himself and his companions at a village hostelry, more than satisfied the hostess by binding on the wrist of her daughter, who was suffering from ague, a strip of parchment on which he had written some cabalistic characters; that the ague left the girl; and that, years afterwards, when Holt was Lord Chief Justice, a woman was indicted before him as a witch on the strength of a cabalistic spell she wore, upon the unrolling of which the judge told the astonished court the history of the piece of parchment, and secured the poor prisoner's acquittal.

During the twenty-two years for which Holt sat as Chief Justice he constantly rose in the estimation of his countrymen, and his great achievement in deciding on private rights was, that he adapted the common law of feudal times to the altered wants of society. When he became a judge, commerce and manufactures were rising into importance, though Manchester and Liverpool were still little more than villages, and England saw the small beginnings of that trade which English enterprise has now spread throughout the world; but important questions as to the liabilities and remedies on negociable securities, and as to the law of marine insurance, were unsettled, and it remained for him to illustrate the general law of contracts by sagaciously applying the principles of the imperishable civil law of the Romans. He laid down the principle that the *status* of slavery cannot exist in England; he put an end to the revolting practice of trying a prisoner in fetters, and of endeavouring to show the probability of his being guilty of the offence for which he was tried by proving that he had been suspected of former offences.

On state trials, too, Holt won deserved applause by his moderation and impartiality. He is memorable also for his firmness on those questions of constitutional law which brought him into collision with the two Houses of Parliament; and, when called on by the Lords to give his reasons for a judicial decision which had not been regularly brought before the House on appeal by writ of error, Holt at the peril of commitment refused to debate the judgment, and gained a triumph. In the memorable contest for election privileges after the accession of Queen Anne, when the Commons rushed into a controversy with the courts of law and the Upper House of Parliament, Holt, alone of the twelve judges, held that a court of law could inquire into the legal validity of a commitment by either House; and here I may mention that the Court of King's Bench (though not until nearly a century afterwards, in the great case of *Burdett v. Abbott*,) laid it down that, if the warrant of the House did not profess to commit for contempt, but for some other specified matter which could not be deemed contempt and was contrary to law, the judges would do justice from whatever court the warrant might have proceeded. Holt's appointment as Chief Justice had been hailed with joy by the nation, and his death was mourned by all parties in the state. I must pass over his exemplary private life, and only say with regard to it that his marriage, like Coke's second marriage, had not been felicitous, and that some people maliciously accounted for his unwearied devotion to business by his dislike to the society of Lady Holt. He was emphatically a judge of the common law, and his experience was in that branch of jurisprudence only: William III. offered to make him chancellor, but he modestly declined, saying, " Please your Majesty, I never was in but one equity suit in my life, and that I lost!"

Although after the Restoration the judges were appointed for life and during good behaviour in office, and were no longer removeable at the pleasure of the Crown, William the Third, notwithstanding the regard he professed for liberty, insisted that his judges should hold office during pleasure only; and their independence of the Crown was not finally secured until the end of his reign, when it was provided (by a sort of tack to the Act of Settlement), that the judges' commissions should constitute them for life, or so long as they should do their duty; and that they should not be removed save on the address of both Houses of Parliament—a greater improvement in a national institution was certainly never made in fewer words.

But for the length this lecture has already attained I might speak of Sir Thomas Parker, afterwards Lord Macclesfield, who succeeded Holt, and subsequently became Lord Chancellor, and of that more distinguished Chancellor, Lord Somers, a consummate lawyer and honest though Georgian statesman, who passed with unblemished honour through a base and venal age; but I must conclude these sketches, and pass to the most eminent and accomplished common law judge of the eighteenth century.

William Murray, afterwards Earl of Mansfield, first saw the light in the palace built on the site of the ancient royal abbey of Scone. As younger son of Viscount Stormont, described by

Lord Campbell as "a poverty-stricken Scotch nobleman of Jacobite sympathies," the chances were rather that he would waste his days angling for salmon in the Tay and coursing the deer among the Highland hills, or wandering an exiled adherent of King James, than that he would attain the highest dignities of Westminster Hall, and combine a taste for elegant literature with a profound knowledge of law. Dr. Johnson said that much may be made of a Scotchman if caught young, but the future Chief Justice had attained his fourteenth year before he was sent to Westminster School. Under an old ash-tree the youthful Murray received the blessing of his parents, from whom he then parted for ever, for he returned no more to his native land. He showed in after years that faculty of mind by which Lord Stowell facetiously defined "taste," the faculty, namely, which leads a Scotchman to prefer England to his own country.

His journey to London was performed on a pony, and occupied seven weeks, and the solitary youth has been compared to Gil Blas when proceeding on his uncle's mule to study at Salamanca, except that, instead of being cheated of his horse, and becoming a companion of robbers, the young Scot arrived without adventure in London, where, by the sale of his pony, a sword, two wigs, and proper equipment for Westminster School were purchased for him. First on the list of King's scholars he went to Christ Church, Oxford, where oratory was his especial delight, and he was early a votary of the muse of poetry. While studying law many of his hours of leisure were passed in the society of Pope, who might be seen sitting in the character of preceptor beside the future Chief Justice of England. He early attained eminence in his profession; and in Parliament his powers as a debater, his remarkably noble appearance, the graces of his speech and action, and the silvery tones of his voice gave him great success. His long and brilliant tenure of the office of Solicitor-General was closed by that vindication of our maritime rights in time of war which Lord Stowell always spoke of with reverence. To Murray belongs the honour of having discovered the genius of Blackstone as a jurist; it was he who advised the great commentator, then quite unknown, to read law lectures at Oxford; and the plan not only suggested to Mr. Viner the establishment of the professorship of the common law, but occasioned those immortal Commentaries which do so much honour to the judicious encouragement that led to their publication.

In 1756, on the death of Ryder Lord Chief Justice, Murray was promoted to that high office, received a peerage with the title of Lord Mansfield, and acquired an unparalleled ascendancy in Westminster Hall. One can imagine him exclaiming in the words of Blackstone's " Farewell to the Muse,"—

> Welcome business, welcome strife,
> Welcome the cares of ermined life;
> The visage wan, the purblind sight;
> The toil by day, the lamp by night;
> The tedious forms, the solemn prate,
> The pert dispute, the dull debate ;
> The drowsy Bench, the babbling Hall—
> For thee, fair Justice ! welcome all.

The system of the Courts was little different in Lord Mansfield's day from what it had been under the Lancastrian princes. Rights connected with land were still the chief care of the common law, and no rules yet existed by which the questions arising in times of extending commerce, and from the growing wants of an inventive age, could be determined. His knowledge of the mercantile jurisprudence of other nations enabled the Chief Justice to introduce, by judicial decisions, many improvements in the commercial law of England; and we owe to him the law of marine insurance, many rules since firmly established with regard to negociable securities, and such improvements in the law of evidence as caused it to be said that he found this part of our judicial system of brick and left it of marble. Without preferring his own views of justice to authority and precedent, he " never suffered justice to be strangled in the nets of form," and his efforts tended to adapt the law to the growing wants of mankind. As a statesman, Lord Mansfield's career subsequent to the death of Lord Chatham is chiefly marked by a just and liberal advocacy of measures designed to mitigate the atrocious penal laws which were then in force against that large body of our fellow-Christians who adhered to the Roman communion—measures which led to the memorable " No Popery " riots, in which the house " and lettered store " of the aged

Chief Justice were destroyed by the mob. His political career closed with the accession of Pitt to office; and, while the surges of the French Revolution were inundating France with her noblest blood, the venerable Earl was serenely meditating amongst his cedars at Kenwood near London, and his life glided tranquilly to its close in 1793, in the eighty-ninth year of his age. Five years before, he had resigned the Chief Justiceship, which he had for two-and-thirty years adorned by high judicial qualities, noble independence, and disregard of any other popularity than that which follows the pursuit of noble ends by noble means.

Lord Mansfield had for his contemporary, in the early part of his career, Lord Chancellor Hardwicke, whose chancellorship has been enthusiastically regarded as the golden age of equity, and who may be said to have fulfilled as a judge our highest idea of judicial excellence. He is memorable for the profound and enlightened principles he laid down, and for perfecting equity into a symmetrical system; but his life is perhaps more interesting to a Chancery lawyer than a sketch of it would be to a general audience. In his character of minister of the Crown, it would be well if Lord Hardwicke's memory were not unfortunately stained by the judicial severities that followed the events of 1745, which so nearly restored the Stuarts to the throne of their ancestors; but it is to be remembered, to the honour of Lord Hardwicke, that he was the author of the Marriage Act, which, with considerable modifications, remains in force, and which put an end to the irregular marriages that had led to so much social misery in the days when degraded and profligate clergymen were to be found, especially in the Fleet prison and in the Savoy, ready to marry all persons at any hours; but a great defect of the Act was, that it did not make any provisions against the marriage out of England of persons domiciled in England, so that it was easily evaded by a romantic trip to Gretna Green—as we all know, though not perhaps from personal experience.

I have of necessity confined these sketches to judges of historical celebrity who lived before the commencement of the present century, and I stop, therefore, with Lord Mansfield's time.

From the lives of these "intellectual prizemen of history," during the more modern times in which the establishment of constitutional freedom has assured the subjects of this realm against encroachment by the Crown, and in which political influences have ceased to turn aside the pure stream of justice, it has, I trust, appeared that judges have been the great improvers of our laws; and that the learning, the independence, and the judicial virtues which have long made our Courts of Justice bulwarks of constitutional liberty, have exercised a mighty and most beneficial influence upon the social advancement as well as the jurisprudence of our country.

Our judicial system, as Lord Kingsdown has justly remarked, is like our legislative system; they are both of native growth—the growth of England; they have grown with the growth of the people and, though they may have contained many irregularities, and may display some want of symmetry, yet with all these apparent defects they have conferred upon this country a greater share of order, freedom, and prosperity, and greater success in the administration of justice, than was ever enjoyed by any other country under the sun. In these days, when there are so many different Associations that kindly undertake to look after our social improvement, and go about the country to enlighten us on jurisprudence and every other subject, we hear much from the philosophers as to our want of a code of law, and we have lately spent I know not how many thousands in attempting to consolidate the statutes. But, although we are not blessed with the form of a symmetrical code of law, we enjoy the substance of justice, and without either code or consolidation the great ends of jurisprudence are effectually attained. But this is because England has produced during the last two centuries a line of judges unequalled in any country, or in any age, for integrity and learning, and they have developed a system which practically secures our rights and liberties, and gives continued vitality to the spirit and intent of the Great Charter; so that Englishmen carry with the British language and the British flag to the remotest colonies of the Empire those enlightened maxims of civil and criminal jurisprudence which are the common charter of our countrymen in every quarter of the globe.

He who takes the office of a judge as it now exists in this country, takes in his hands (to use the language of Sydney

Smith) a splendid gem, good and glorious, perfect and pure. \* \* \*
He cannot tell in what dangerous and awful times he may be
placed; but as a mariner looks to his compass in the calm, and
looks to his compass in the storm, and never keeps his eyes off
his compass, so in every vicissitude of a judicial life, deciding for
the people, deciding against the people, protecting the just right
of kings or restraining their unlawful ambition, he will ever
cling to the pure, exalted, and Christian independence which no
hope of favour can influence, and no effort of power can turn
aside. In common circumstances, the bearing of the judicial office
on the safety and security of a country is not always seen and
appreciated; but it is in periods of danger that judicial institutions are felt to be part of the inheritance we contend for; the
protection from violence, the restoration to right, the rebuke of
the oppressor, the condemnation of wrong, equal justice to the
rich and to the poor—these are privileges that men may well
come out to fight for and to defend.

The whole tone and tenour of public morals is affected (as the
same eminent divine has remarked) by the state of supreme justice; it extinguishes revenge, it communicates a spirit of purity
and uprightness to inferior magistrates; it makes the great good,
by taking away impunity; it banishes fraud, obliquity, and solicita-
tion, and teaches men that law is their right. Truth is its hand-
maid, freedom is its child, peace is its companion; safety walks in
its steps, victory follows in its train: it is the centre round which
human motives and passions turn; and justice sitting on high
sees genius, and power, and wealth, and rank, revolving round
her throne, and teaches their paths and marks out their orbits,
and carries order into a world which but for her would be a
wild waste of passions.

And so long as the pure and equal administration of our laws
is maintained by the constitutional safeguards which have descended to us from the past, so long as the independence of our
judges continues to be assured by the adjustment of royal prerogative to parliamentary privileges, so long as Englishmen shall
reverence the traditions they inherit, they may boast, that in the
majesty of English Law their liberties are secure, and that the
hand of power is paralyzed in their Courts of Justice when it is
put forth to do a wrong to the humblest subject of the realm.

# DÉSORMAIS.

## A STORY OF SKIPTON CASTLE.

[*Bentley's Miscellany*, April 1860.]

ONE of the most celebrated and remarkable women of any period was Anne Clifford, daughter of George Earl of Cumberland, and Countess of Dorset, Pembroke, and Montgomery. Her paternal name is surrounded by many poetical and romantic associations, for the Cliffords were one of the great historic families not only of Yorkshire but of England, and a Clifford is the hero of many a deed of chivalry and knightly adventure. Religious, magnificent, and literary, the extraordinary character of the Lady Anne has added its own celebrity to the illustrious name she inherited, and has surrounded with most interesting memories that famous old Castle of Skipton which was long the chief stronghold of her race.

She had certainly some very remarkable persons among her progenitors, and she inherited some of their qualities. From the days of the Plantagenets down to the wars of York and Lancaster her knightly ancestors were warriors; but "the good Clifford" who fought at Flodden Field was almost an old man before he wore his armour, and had led the life of a shepherd until his thirty-second year. The career of his son, before the latter was advanced to the earldom of Cumberland, seems to have been as violent and lawless as that of any of Falstaff's allies; and his successor fought against the Armada, and was all his life a restless sailor. Such of the Cliffords of the Tudor days as had any tranquil hours to give to the literature of the age seem to have dabbled in alchemy, astrology, and magic.

It is interesting to glance at the characteristics or the fate for which the Cliffords of the fifteenth and sixteenth centuries were chiefly remarkable. In the Lancastrian cause the family was destined to do and suffer much. Thomas eighth Lord Clifford fell at St. Alban's in 1454, in what Shakspeare calls

> The silver livery of advised age,

leaving a son, John—known as "the Black-faced Clifford"—who succeeded him, but who had short enjoyment of his patrimony and honours, for he was slain on the eve of the battle of Towton Moor. On his death the Cliffords were driven from their possessions by the victorious House of York. It was one of the children of this unfortunate nobleman who became known as "the good Clifford—the Shepherd Lord." In his childhood he was placed by his noble mother for safety, first at Londesborough, and then amongst the simple dalesmen of Cumberland, and much of his boyhood is said to have been passed at the little mountain village of Threlkeld, near Keswick, whilst the Crown usurped his lands and castles:

> Meantime, far off, 'midst Cumbrian hills,
> The *Clifford* lives unknown,
> On strangers' bounty he depends,
> And may not claim his own.

Like the Chaldæan shepherds, he seems to have early made acquaintance with the stars; and he was fond of all such knowledge and legendary lore as might be acquired among the wildest scenes of nature. As Wordsworth sings of him:

> Love had he found in huts where poor men lie;
> His daily teachers had been woods and rills—
> The silence that is in the starry sky,
> The sleep that is among the lonely hills.

Thus peacefully he passed his life until, on the accession of Henry VII., he was restored to his honours and estates, and with the rest to his ancient tower of Skipton, "too long to vacancy and silence left:"

> Glad were the vales and every cottage hearth;
> The Shepherd Lord was honoured more and more.

He indulged in after-life the taste he had acquired for studious pursuits. When he resided on his Yorkshire estates his favourite retreat was Barden Tower—a small stronghold of the Cliffords situated in the deep solitude of ancient woods in Wharfedale; his chosen companions were his neighbours the canons of Bolton Priory; and, though he could only write his name, his favourite pursuit was astronomy, to which he seems to have added judicial astrology *ad libitum*. But in 1513 the invasion of the Scots roused him to maintain the martial reputation of his race—

> Armour rusting in his halls
> On the blood of Clifford calls,

and in his sixtieth year he fought in the battle of Flodden Field. In 1523 his course was run, and he was succeeded by Henry his son, who was within two years afterwards advanced to the dignity of Earl of Cumberland. In his youth he had been prodigal, raised money by anticipation, assembled a band of dissolute followers, and turned outlaw. But he was not doomed to remain always a stranger to "all that life has soft and dear," for he had the good fortune to marry the lady Margaret Percy—an event by which the whole of the vast lordships and manors constituting "the Percy fee" in Yorkshire became vested in the Cliffords. From thenceforth all the country from Skipton in Craven to Brougham in Westmoreland, a distance of seventy miles, belonged to them, with the exception of a district about ten miles in length: and, for their chase or hunting-ground, they had around their old demesne of Skipton the vast deer-forest which then overspread the rocky central part of Craven, extending from the Wharfe to the river Aire.

It has been conjectured that this adventurous young nobleman was the hero of the ballad of "The Nut-brown Mayde"—that touching though antiquated celebration of woman's love and constancy. The ballad, however, has been regarded by some critics as older than the youthful days of Henry VIII., and the hero discovers himself as "an erlys son," which Henry Clifford certainly was not. Be this as it may, the Earl had been in youth the comrade of Henry VIII.,[*] and, unlike most other friends of

---

[*] When this young nobleman went to London, upon his creation as Earl of Cumberland, he had a retinue of thirty-four horsemen, but the cost of each man and horse was only tenpence a day in the money of those times. He was lodged at Derby House, where now the Heralds' College stands. He does not seem to have purchased

that inconstant and blood-stained tyrant, retained the King's favour so long as to receive, in 1542, a grant of the Priory of Bolton, with all the manors and lands of that famous house. But as if the gift by the royal plunderer of the Church had been fatal to the grantee, and the abbey lands had " wrought his swift decay," he lived only nineteen days after he became possessor of these rich spoils, and died at the age of forty-nine. Of his successor, Henry Clifford, little is to be said, except that he became allied to royalty by his marriage with the Lady Eleanor Brandon, and that he was not only a studious man in a generally unlettered age, but was much given to alchemy. Having had a narrow escape of being buried alive during an illness, he lived to marry for his second wife Anne daughter of Lord Dacre, and to enjoy his honours without suffering disturbance, though without acquiring renown.* George Clifford, his son, was the father of Lady Anne, and succeeded, as third Earl of Cumberland, in 1569. He was a man of noble mind, great natural gifts, and adventurous disposition. He early showed his predilection for " a life on the ocean wave," and even when at Cambridge did not care for any other learning than what might aid

> To steer the bold barque o'er the new-found main
> To the new land of glory, blood, and gain.

In his nineteenth year he married the Lady Margaret Russell, daughter of Francis second Earl of Bedford, to whom he had been betrothed in infancy; but he did not love her, and often deserted his home to engage in naval expeditions. The sea, which (as Hartley Coleridge says) he wooed for his bride, was to him a cruel mistress, and his naval trophies were bought at the expense of his fortune. He made nine voyages, chiefly to the West Indies, and, on the memorable advance of the Spanish Armada, distinguished himself in the action off Calais. This

and brought with him from London to the North any articles of luxury and amusement, except a hound and a falcon, a bugle-horn and a sheaf of arrows. He was very economical in the presents he brought to his wife, for they appear to have been confined to " a white embroidered frontlet " which cost fifty shillings, and some velvet.

* The inventory of his apparel (printed in Whitaker's " History of Craven ") affords an example of the showy and costly character of a nobleman's wardrobe at that time, and quite a picture of the interior of a great baronial castle in the middle of the sixteenth century.

high-born wanderer of the sea is portrayed by the pen of his dutiful daughter, and the pencil of an unknown limner, as a model of masculine comeliness, with an expressive as well as handsome countenance, set off by costly attire. He was possessed of great bodily strength and agility, and was skilled in knightly accomplishments. His valour and love of daring were quite romantic, and he could charm the female ear by eloquent discourse

> Of all the wonders of the mighty deep—
> Of perils manifold and strange.

James I. had been only two years upon the English throne when the Earl's adventurous career closed, at the age of forty-seven, and, on this event, the right to his lands, baronies, and honours (save the earldom, which went to his only brother Sir Francis Clifford,) descended to the Lady Anne, his only daughter and heir, then in her sixteenth year, she having been born on the 30th of January, 1590.

Our noble heroine shall now introduce herself. Writing in the sixty-third year of her age, when Time had long robbed her of her charms and thinned her flowing hair, she says:—

"I was very happy in my first constitution, both in mind and body, both for internal and external endowments; for never was there a child more resembling both father and mother than myself. The colour of mine eyes was black like my father's, and the form and aspect of them was quick and lively like my mother's. The hair of my head was brown and very thick, and so long that it reached to the calf of my legs when I stood upright, with a peak of hair upon my forehead, and a dimple on my chin, and an exquisite shape of body like my father. * * * And, though I say it, the perfections of my mind were much above those of my body: I had a strong and copious memory, a sound judgment, a discerning spirit, and a strong imagination, insomuch that at many times even my dreams and apprehensions proved to be true."

Her portrait at Knowle Park represents a youthful person of symmetrical form, with features betokening great energy of character,

> Less formed to sue than to command—

but adorned with the grace of a high-born woman. Another portrait of her, taken in later life, represents features more expressive of firmness than benignity; but, although she did possess a masculine decision of character, she was undoubtedly a person of beneficent and amiable disposition. She inherited the literary taste of some of her ancestors. Amongst the books introduced beside her in a picture in which she is represented as a damsel of thirteen, are Eusebius, St. Augustine, Josephus, and the "Arcadia" of Sir Philip Sidney.* She must have been a learned little lady indeed, if these were the books she was capable of reading! It is a pleasant relief to find that she nevertheless learned dancing and the use of the cross-bow, and took part in private theatricals.

Our sympathies are particularly engaged by finding that she had an early love for poetry and regard for literary men—a taste for which she was, doubtless, much indebted to her worthy tutor Samuel Daniel, himself historian and poet. Her noble father, sea-rover as he was, had been a patron of Spenser, and by her was Spenser's monument erected in Westminster Abbey.

The Lady Anne enjoyed the care and affection of her mother until her twenty-sixth year, and owed to her parent the defence of her inheritance and patrimonial rights.† She set up a characteristic and enduring monument of her filial love in erecting a pillar upon the spot where she took the last leave of her mother, on the road between Penrith and Appleby, in remembrance of which event she ordained that at the pillar there should be a distribution of money to the poor upon the anniversary for ever. The poet Rogers, it will be remembered, has commemorated

---

\* Written, as the reader will remember, in the classic halls of Wilton, in which the Lady Anne passed some period of her life after her marriage to Philip Herbert, Earl of Pembroke and Montgomery.

† Honourable testimony to the care of this excellent parent in forming the character of the Lady Anne is borne by her poet-tutor in the poem addressed to her, in which he says:

"With so great care doth she that hath brought forth
   That comely body, labour to adorn
That better part, the mansion of your mind,
   With all the richest furniture of worth,
To make thee highly good as highly born,
   And set your virtues equal to your kind."

> The modest stone which pious Pembroke reared ;
> Which still records beyond the pencil's power
> The silent sorrows of a parting hour.

At an early age Anne Clifford was united to Richard Sackville, third Earl of Dorset, who, although in other respects a man of sense, seems to have been a profligate spendthrift, eager to sign away her patrimonial rights for present gain. He died in 1624, leaving only two daughters, for the noble pair had been successively bereaved of their three sons; and it was by the marriage of one of those daughters to John Tufton, Earl of Thanet, that the ancient manor and castle of Skipton has descended on Sir Richard Tufton, the present owner of that historical domain.

At the mature age of forty-one, after six years of widowhood, the countess was again overtaken by matrimony. Her second husband was that memorable simpleton (as Walpole calls him) Philip Herbert, Earl of Pembroke and Montgomery, himself a widower of forty-five, whose qualifications seem to have consisted of hawking and hunting, and whose only recommendations were that he was a favourite courtier and a handsome person, for his character has been justly regarded by posterity as odious and contemptible. Yet his mother was that "Sidney's sister" celebrated as "the subject of all verse," and his brother was Lord Herbert of Cherbury, one of the most distinguished of the worthies and benefactors of Oxford, a scholar, philosopher, and hero.*

In her own account of her wedded life, the lady says of her departed lords:

"It was my misfortune to have crosses and contradictions with them both . . . so that in both their lifetimes the marble pillars of Knowle and Wilton were to me oftentimes but the gay arbours of anguish. . . . I made good books and virtuous thoughts my companions, which can never discern affliction, nor be daunted when it unjustly happens."

But soon the Lady Anne was to merge her conjugal miseries in the troubles of the civil wars. A firm royalist and faithful daughter of the Church of England, this high-spirited lady would

---

* Philip Herbert, Earl of Pembroke and Montgomery, died 23rd January, 1650. For some time before, the countess had been obliged to live apart from him.

probably have performed heroic actions had her strong castles and broad lands been in her own command during the early years of the rebellion. When she came to be actual mistress of what had been legally hers since 1643, her property was in a dilapidated state. Her Westmoreland castles—viz. Appleby, Brougham, Brough (which guarded the pass of Stanemoor), Pendragon (which commanded the pass of Mallerstang), and her Yorkshire strongholds of Barden and Skipton—were in ruins. It might be said of these as of the exiled Percy's in the well-known ballad:

> Her towers and castles, once so fair,
> Were mouldering in decay;
> Proud strangers had usurped her lands
> And borne their wealth away.

At Skipton, amidst towering rocks and dark forest, a castle had stood from the Norman days—the chief stronghold in mountainous Craven. On a plateau, bounded towards the north by a precipitous rock, and on the south by a natural dell, the Norman lords of Skipton raised their fortress. In the reign of Edward II., when Robert de Clifford acquired the castle from the Crown, he superseded the Norman stronghold by an Edwardian castle, with the characteristic circular towers which still form the oldest portion of the main fabric. To the edifice of this martial Clifford his successor the first Earl of Cumberland, more than two centuries afterwards, added the gallery, a stately range of building sixty yards in length. In this picturesque old stronghold Anne Clifford was born, but before she obtained possession of it Skipton Castle had been reduced to little more than roofless walls, for it had undergone two sieges, and had been at length savagely dismantled by the Parliament, and its tapestry, antique furniture, and embossed plate had been ruthlessly scattered. Such was its state when the noble widow, almost immediately after the death of her second husband, returned to her native castle, and set herself, with characteristic energy, to repair the damage inflicted by years of litigation, waste, and civil discord. The work of restoration was carried on by this energetic lady in a manner which shows that it was very congenial to her, and she accomplished it in defiance of Cromwell, and completed the repairs in 1658.

In her time there were fifty-seven chambers of all kinds in

Skipton Castle. Towers with winding-stairs, ghostly galleries, and the tapestried octagon chamber that was her bedroom, and might still be her presence-chamber, remain, but the interior of the castle has been much modernised. Its external features, as repaired and left by the Countess, have not, however, undergone much change in the two centuries that have since passed over them; and it presents a picturesque, though inharmonious, combination of a Tudor manor-house and more modern architecture with an Edwardian fortress. The fortified gateway of the outer bailey remains as she left it, and in its parapet, as if still proudly looking to the future, the word DESORMAIS—the motto of the Clifford family—is seen in letters of stone against the sky. Perhaps it was not until the Restoration of Charles II. (as Mr. Hartley Coleridge has suggested) that she planted in the bailey of Skipton that acorn from the oak of Boscobel—"as a symbol of the ancient loyalty of her house"—which grew to be a noble tree, long surviving the fortunes of the House of Stuart. So strictly did she restore, that in one of the courts of Skipton she planted, in the place of an old yew that the besiegers had destroyed, a yew-tree, whose spreading branches still cast their solemn shade over the inclosure. Its situation reminds the spectator that, in the palace of Latinus,

> Just in the centre of the most retired
> And secret court, a holy laurel stood,
> For many years religiously preserved.

Anne Clifford aspired to be remembered as "the repairer of the breach, the restorer of places to dwell in;" and this was the text which she set up in her inscriptions on Skipton Castle and over the entrance to Barden.

The last-named stronghold, whose grey wood-environed tower is sought by many a summer tourist in romantic Wharfedale, seems to have been a mere forester's lodge in the days when it was surrounded by the deer-park of the adjacent canons of Bolton, now the property of the Duke of Devonshire; it had been, however, enlarged for residence by "the Shepherd Lord," but had fallen into ruin before the noble widow obtained possession of her inheritance.

She also rebuilt or repaired her four other castles, besides the church of Skipton, and six other churches; for she (we are told) "would not dwell in ceiled palaces while the Lord's house lay waste." At Skipton, too, she erected a storied monument to her father, and at Appleby a marble tomb for her mother. Her affection for that good and faithful parent seems to have been the warmest feeling of her soul; and—strong-minded and free from superstition as she was—the daughter was accustomed to attribute her escape from peril to the prayers of her mother in heaven. She seems to have believed herself the object of a providential destiny, and that she was the charge of " a happy genius," acting as a presiding and directing power.

The countess resided almost wholly on her Northern domains, diffusing their produce in affording employment, hospitality, and charity. It was her great delight to succour distressed royalists, and to do such deeds of beneficence as made her a blessing in the vales of Westmoreland and among the Craven Hills. She generally resided at Brougham or Appleby (the stately lady was hereditary sheriff of Westmoreland), but occasionally visited all her castles, and seems to have exercised within her dominions little less than regal sway. Appleby Castle was chiefly her residence; there some of her manuscripts are preserved, and from thence many of her letters are dated. She was a great writer, and in her journals she has noted minute particulars relating to her own life and to her estates, and the events that happened upon them. She resided at Appleby while Skipton Castle was undergoing repair; and writing from the former place on the 10th of January, 1649, she says she should be " in pitiful case " if she had not " excellent Chaucer's book " to comfort her. In 1651 she founded an hospital for widows at Appleby, and endowed it with the manor of Brougham. She did not attempt to revive with vain parade the martial and festal splendours of the past, but took care to maintain the ample hospitality and the time-honoured customs of feudal days, and " the ties which bound the vassal to his lord's domain." For her the court of Charles II. had no attractions, nor did her sympathies embrace the political affairs of any kingdom beyond her own vast patrimony. When much advanced in life (probably about her sixty-third year) she employed an artist, whose name has not been preserved, to paint the famous family picture, in three compartments, which is now at Skipton. Her object seems to have been to have a plain delineation at one view of the features of those most dear to her; accordingly, in the centre compartment her parents and her brother are represented; in one of the wings is her own likeness when a little maiden of thirteen; and in the other wing her portrait as a widow, in the sombre habiliments of her declining years. Books are introduced in both portraits, as if to indicate that her early love of reading lasted in her age; but, while her youthful portraiture is attended by Eusebius and Agrippa "De Vanitate Scientiarum," her maturer image has the Bible, Charron "On Wisdom," and (strange decadence!) a book "Of Distillations and Rare Medicines."

Such was Anne Clifford, Countess of Dorset, Pembroke, and Montgomery. She attained the unusual age of eighty-six, with few infirmities, and seems to have remembered through her long career what her poet-tutor told her in her youth—that

> This fleeting life hath but this port of rest—
> A heart prepared, that fears no ills to come.

Her end was as peaceful as her life had been energetic; and at Brougham Castle, on the 22nd of March, 1675, she passed to immortality. Her body was interred, not in the tomb of her father and her martial ancestors at Skipton, but at Appleby, by the side of that parent whom she survived nearly sixty years, and never ceased to regard with reverential love.

# JAMES HOWELL,

## THE FIRST HISTORIOGRAPHER ROYAL.

[*The Druid—a College Magazine, Oxford,* 1862.]

ONE of the worthiest sons of the University of Oxford in the seventeenth century was James Howell, who held offices of honour from the first Stuart King, and also from Charles I. and Charles II., and who was author of many works on historical, political, and philological subjects, the best known of which are, perhaps, his "Familiar Letters" (*Epistolæ Ho-Elianæ*), written between 1623 and 1655, of which there have been many editions.

His father was Thomas Howell, minister of Abernant, in Carmarthenshire, (who died 1632,) and his elder brother was Thomas Howell, Fellow of Jesus' college, Oxford, Bishop of Bristol, and chaplain to the king. James Howell (who was one of fifteen children) was born about 1594, and received his first education at the Free School of Hereford. He was then entered of Jesus' college—the foundation connected with his native principality, and of which his elder brother was already a Fellow; and, after taking his B.A. degree in 1613, he left the University to seek his fortune, for he was " not born to land, lease, house, or office."

Writing to his father in 1619 he says—

" When I went to bind my brother Ned apprentice in Drapers' Hall, casting my eyes upon the chimney-piece of the great room, I might spy a picture of an antient gentleman, and, underneath, THOMAS HOWELL. I asked the clerk about him, and he told me that he had been a Spanish merchant in Henry the Eighth's time, and, coming home rich and dying a bachelor, he gave that hall to the Company of Drapers with other things, so that he is accounted one of their chiefest benefactors. I told the clerk that one of the sons of Thomas Howell now came thither to be bound; and he answered that if he be a right Howell* he may have when he is free £300 to help to set up, also that any maid that can prove her father to be a true Howell, may come and demand £50 towards her portion from the said hall."

Howell's "Familiar Letters" incidentally afford many particulars illustrative of his life and character, often fanciful in thought and quaint in language—*ex. gr.*

"I have (he writes) many aspirings, and airy, odd thoughts swell often in me, corresponding to the quality of the ground whereon I was born—a huge hill looking to the south-east, so that the house I came from (besides my father's and mother's coat), must needs be illustrious, being more obvious to the sunbeams than ordinary."

From these letters and from other sources, it will be interesting to collect the memorable events in his life: a few extracts from his letters will exemplify his style. In his day, gentlemen sought employment for their sons from merchants and great traders; and Howell's first employment was that of steward of the manufactory of glass established in Broad-street, London, under the patent or monopoly obtained by Sir Robert Mansell, Lord Pembroke, "and divers others of the prime lords of the Court," for making (as Howell in a letter to his father says) "all sorts of glass with pit coal only, to save those huge proportions of wood which were consumed formerly in the glass furnaces." It being necessary to obtain workmen from Italy, and the chief materials from Spain, France, and other foreign countries, Howell was selected to be the Company's travelling agent abroad for this purpose, and so was enabled to escape from the glass house "where" he says, "I should in a short time have melted away to nothing amongst those hot Venetians, finding myself too green for such a charge." Accordingly, in March, 1618, he first went beyond the seas and proceeded to the Low Countries. His letters written from Amsterdam—at that time superior to Venice in commercial activity, and her rival in the traffic with the East—and from France, and particularly from the Queen of the Adriatic (where gentlemen were in those days glass-makers), and other chief cities

* It is not known whether the good Merchant and the writer were related.

of Italy, are very interesting. Castles that are now in ruin were then bristling with arms, and Feudal Europe was seen as a visible reality as yet unchanged by advancing commerce. In these letters he gives lively sketches of foreign countries and people, interspersed with notices of current political events and with anecdotes and witty sayings.* In his foreign travel he acquired a masterly knowledge of modern languages, insomuch that he tells us it became his custom to say his prayers each day in a different language and in seven languages on Sundays; and during his connection with the glass factory he maintained a curious devotion to literature as well as business.

During his absence he appears to have been elected a fellow of his college, and in March, 1621, he writes on his return to London, to thank Sir Eubule Thelwall, the Principal, for nominating him upon his new foundation.

In 1622 he went abroad to travel, and again visited the northern Venice, and sailing on the sluggish canals, traversed the flat green meadows hardly raised above the watery level. Passing from Zealand to Holland "we might see" (he writes) "divers steeples and turrets under water, of towns that, as we were told, were swallowed up by a deluge within the memory of man."

He was now appointed to an embassy under royal commission, the execution of which destined him to be at Madrid during the negotiations for the attempted match between the Prince of Wales and the Infanta of Spain. Writing to his father 8 September, 1623, Howell says—

"I was at a dead stand in the course of my fortunes when it pleased God to provide me lately an employment to Spain, proposed to me by some of the Cape merchants of the Turkey Company."

The business to be undertaken was the prosecution of their claim arising out of the illegal seizure of a valuable merchantman on the ground of her conveying contraband of war. If Captain Wilkes had seized *The Trent*, sold the ship and cargo,

---

* The reader is referred, by way of example, to the anecdote about Count Gondomar and the Castilian Housekeeper (i. Ep. IIo-Elianæ 158, edit. 1655); How the Blasphemer was reclaimed (p. 208); the Archbishop an Admiral and the General a Divine (p. 292).

and appropriated the money as his prize, the outrage would have been somewhat similar to that which Howell was now charged to redress. He describes the matter thus:—

" A great Turkey ship, called *The Vineyard,* sailing through the straits towards Constantinople, was driven by stress of weather to put into the little port of Milo in Sardinia. The searchers came aboard of her and finding her richly laden, for her cargazon of broad cloth was worth the first peny near upon £30,000, they cavill'd at some small portion of lead and tin which was on board only for the use of the ship, which the searchers alleged to be *ropa de contrabando,* for, by article of Peace, nothing is to be carried to Turkey that may arm or vittle. The Viceroy of Sardinia hereupon seized the whole ship and all her goods, landed the master and men in Spain, who coming to Sir Charles Cornwallis, then ambassador at the Court, Sir Charles could do them little good at present, wherefore they came to England and complained to the King and Council. His Majesty sent a particular commission in his own royal name to demand a restitution of the ship and goods and justice upon the Viceroy of Sardinia, who had so apparently broke the peace and wronged his subjects."

Howell then describes the failure of three previous royal commissions, the last of which was intrusted by Lord Digby the ambassador to Mr. Cotington the secretary, but—

" He returned without finishing the work, in regard of the remoteness of the island of Sardinia, whence the witnesses and other dispatches were to be fetched. The Lord Digby is going now Ambassador-Extraordinary to Spain, and is desirous to transmit the King's Commission touching this business to any gentleman that is capable to follow it. He hath now a good round share himself in it. I go to Spain in company of the Ambassador, and I shall kiss the King's hand, as his agent touching this particular commission."

Upon his arrival in Madrid he found the papers in the law suits already "higher than himself in bulk, though closely pres't together," and the damages awarded by all the sentences of view and review came to above 250,000 crowns, most part of which the Conde del Real, quondam Viceroy of Sardinia, then Mayordomo and Lord Steward to the Infanta Cardinal, had been adjudged to pay. The esteem in which Lord Digby was held at Madrid at that time and the aid of Count Gondomar seemed favourable for the settlement of the business; but in subsequent letters written from Madrid, Howell describes the delays and evasions of the Spanish potentates, who seem to have well understood " How not to do it," and the ultimate insolvency of the dignified and delinquent Viceroy. And so ended the affair of *The Vineyard.*

He gives some interesting particulars as to the wealth of the Church in Spain, and describes the gay scenes he witnessed while the Spanish match was under discussion and the ardent Prince's wooing, which was destined to be so fruitless, was going on; and in December, 1624, Howell arrived in England in convoy of the Prince's jewels, valued at £100,000, which had been taken for marriage presents to the King and Queen, the intended bride, the ladies of honour, and the grandees. The beauty of these jewels is said to have astonished even the Spaniards. In May, 1626, the match with the French Princess was concluded— the eighth alliance of England with France since the Conquest, and Howell writes,—

"We have now a most noble new queen of England, who in true beauty is beyond the long-woo'd Infanta, for she was of a fading flaxen hair, big lipp'd, and somewhat heavy ey'd; but this daughter of France, this youngest branch of Bourbon (being but in her cradle when the great Henry, her father, was put out of the world), is of a more lovely and lasting complexion; a dark brown, she hath eyes that sparkle like stars, and for her physiognomy, she may be said to be a mirror of perfection."

In 1627, Howell was appointed Secretary to Lord Scrope, afterwards Earl of Sunderland, in his capacity of Lord President of the Council of the North, and was chosen a representative for Richmond in the Parliament which began in that year. He was subsequently appointed to the still more honourable office of Clerk of the Council to King Charles I.

For the becoming celebration of "Act" at Oxford, in June of the following year (1628), Howell like a true son of Alma Mater contributed thus appropriately:

" I send you here enclosed " (he is writing to his brother, Dr.

Howell, at Jesus College) " warrants for four brace of bucks and a stag, the last Sir Andrew Manwaring procured of the King for you, towards the keeping of your Act; I have sent you also a warrant for a brace of bucks out of Waddon Chase; besides, you shall receive by this carrier a great wicker hamper with two geoules of Sturgeon, six barrels of pickled oysters, three barrels of Bologna olives, with some other Spanish commodities."

*Apropos* to the mention of these festive provisions it is curious to observe that he sends (25 July, 1629) to Sir Arthur Ingram, of Temple Newsam, then at York, a hamper of melons from Tothill-fields Gardens, Westminster. In a letter from St. Osyth's, at that time the stately seat of his friend Lord Rivers, he mentions the Bon Chretien pear and Bergamot pear, and that Muscatel grapes grew in such plenty that some bottles of wine were sent every year to the King.

In 1532, as Secretary to Robert, Earl of Leicester (to whom Howell went at Castle Baynard, London, to receive his appointment), he accompanied the Embassy Extraordinary from Charles I. to the Court of Denmark; and here we have an example of his habit of correct observation of the men and things he saw, for he set himself to observe " the physiognomies, complexions, and carriage" of the Holstein gentlemen, as they were going in and out of the house in which the Parliament was then sitting at Rheinsburg, "and I thought verily," he says, " I was in England, for they resemble the English more than either Welsh or Scot, though cohabiting upon the same island, or any other people that ever I saw yet, which makes me believe that the English nation came first from this lower circuit of Saxony."

At home, the progress of public affairs constantly employed his pen, and he often mentions things of historical interest. For example, noticing in a letter on 30th January, 1633, the appointment of Noy to be Attorney-General, Howell says of him—

" He hath lately found out amongst the old records of the Tower some precedents for raising a tax called Ship Money in all the port towns when the Kingdom is in danger."

The private occurrences at Court in the latter part of the reign of James and in the reign of Charles I., and such foreign affairs as had reference to England are often so minutely described that some of Howell's epistles are good specimens of the "News Letter" of the period.* His letters may, indeed, be said to reflect the contemporary affairs of all Europe, and they as often contain profound and philosophical remarks as matter of obsolete interest and anecdotes of questionable delicacy. They afford perhaps the earliest collection of English epistolary literature. Familiar or formal, lively or severe, they are always manly in tone, calm, concise, and pointed; they display great reading and great knowledge of life, and in them history and philosophy are pleasantly mingled with colloquial humour. Many of the persons to whom his letters were addressed were familiar friends, and some of these were persons prominent in the history of their age. "I like," says Howell, "that friendship which by soft gentle paces steals upon the affection and grows mellow with time," and it seems to have been his lot to enjoy some ripened friendships. Several of his correspondents are noblemen of high rank, and many are men of learning, as, for example, Archbishop Usher, the Bishops of London and Rochester, Lord Herbert of Cherbury, Sir E. Thelwall, Dr. Francis Mansell, who succeeded Thelwall as Principal of Jesus College, Attorney-General Noy, "rare Ben Jonson," and Sir Kenelm Digby. By the last named friend and correspondent of Howell, mention of him is made in his "Discourse on the cure of wounds by sympathy," pronounced at Montpelier before an assembly of noble and learned men. Sir Kenelm states that Howell was wounded when interposing in a duel between two of his friends, and that he cured him by a sympathetic powder which he had derived from the East.†

In 1639 Howell went to Ireland, and in the following year to France. He appears to have been thenceforth occupied for some time in his official duties as clerk to the Council, and in his literary works. But, with the progress of the Civil War, his letters became saddened by the thickening troubles of his King and country, the sacrilegious outrages suffered by the Church of England, and the cruel and intrusive tyranny of the Puritans.

* The letters containing a relation of the death of King James, and of the assassination of Buckingham may be mentioned as examples.

† A translation of the Discourse was published in 1658, and the anecdote is related in a more familiar work, namely, in *The Lay of the Last Minstrel*. See Note W. p. 252 of the Sixth Volume of Scott's Poetical Works, ed. 1833.

At length, in November, 1643, "one morning betimes," as he writes, "there rushed into my chamber five men armed with swords, pistols, and bills, and told me they had a warrant from the Parliament for me." He was arrested, his MSS. were seized, and he was committed to the Fleet, where he remained a prisoner until some time after the murder of King Charles. Anthony Wood attributes Howell's imprisonment to debt, but there is no sufficient reason to doubt that he was a political prisoner.

A firm royalist and a churchman, Howell was disgusted by the unbridled insolence and the lawless outrages of the leaders in the Great Rebellion; and if, as is stated, he continued to be imprisoned by the Parliamentarian usurpers, his confinement was, of course, an illegal and vindictive outrage worthy of the Republican faction. He bore it cheerfully, and, like Raleigh during his imprisonment in the Tower, consoled himself with literary employment. He applied his energies to writing and translating books, as well as to continuing his letters:—

"Here," says Howell, with his accustomed pleasantry, writing from the Fleet Prison, "I purchased a small spot of ground upon Parnassus, which I have in fee of the Muses."

And, truly, his productions at this period, although written from necessity rather than choice, show readiness of wit and play of fancy. Writing in 1645, he says "nine long lustres of years have now passed over my head, and some winters more (for all my life, considering the little sunshine I have had, may be called nothing but winters), yet—I thank God for it, I find no symptom of decay."

Anthony Wood has alleged that Howell's *Epistolæ Ho-Elianæ* do not consist entirely of genuine letters, but that many of them were first written in the Fleet, after the times at which they purport to bear date, and, in fact, to gain money for relief of his necessities during his long imprisonment. There are some of the letters as to which this appears very probable, for they seem to be dissertations in the form of letters, although stated to be written at the request of the persons to whom they are addressed; and to this category, perhaps, belong such communications as the historical letter on the Dispersion and Condition of the Jews;[*] his

---

[*] *Ep. Ho. El.* p. 256, edit. 1655.

interesting philological essay on the mother tongues of the different countries of Europe;* his letter on the Beverages of different Countries, and his remarkable letter dated from the Fleet, Mayday, 1647, on the Religions of the World,† in which, speaking of Pagan superstitions, he remarks:—

" Those are the excusablest kind who adore the sun and moon, with the host of Heaven; and in Ireland the Kerns of the mountains, like some in the Scotch Isles, use a fashion of adoring the new moon to this very day, praying that she would leave them in as good health as she finds them."

Of his own devout piety and conscientious observance of Church ordinances his letter on devotional practices‡ gives a very high idea; and he was evidently as sincere and unaffected in his devotion as he was incapable of the religious cant adopted by the saints of the Commonwealth.

Charles II., on the Restoration, distinguished Howell by his favour, and cheaply rewarded his loyalty by creating the office of Historiographer Royal of England for him.

The catalogue of his works, original and translated, is too lengthy to be given in this article, and, besides, it is printed at the end of his *Londinopolis*, published in his life-time, and more fully in Wood's *Athenæ*, where some dictionaries, grammars, and various translations are mentioned. It seems doubtful whether that printed list is complete: for example, it does not include a little book on " Precedence of Foreign Ambassadors," entitled *Sir John Finett's Observations*, published in octavo in 1656, of which Howell is stated to have been the author. The reasonable rule had not then been adopted which assigns diplomatic precedence to him who has been the longest resident. His works must extend to a very considerable number of volumes, but are little known save to the lovers of old literature. His *Familiar Letters* first appeared in 1645, another collection in 1647, and both with a third in 1650; a fourth in 1655, and there have been subsequent editions, the eleventh of which was in 1754. The last of his works seems to have been his *Londinopolis: an Historical Discourse or Perlustration of the City of London*,

* *Ep. Ho. El*, vol. ii. p. 72.    † *Ibid*, p. 19.
‡ *Ibid*, vol. i. p. 273.

*whereunto is added another of the City of Westminster, with the Courts of Justice, Antiquities, and New Buildings*, published at London in folio, 1657, a work in which we may find much curious information and evidence of no small research. Prefixed to a folio, published in 1653, on the *German Diet*, is the author's portrait, a spirited and somewhat rare etching.

To the particulars now brought together as to his life (which, of course, might be greatly extended by a professed biographer,) it only remains to add that he died in November, 1666, and his body was interred in the Temple Church, where a monument to his memory was placed, which bore the following inscription:— "*Jacobus Howell, Cambro-Britannus, Regius Historiographus (in Anglia primus), qui post varias peregrinationes, tandem naturæ cursum peregit, satur annorum et famæ, domi forisque hic usque erraticus, hic fixus,* 1666." The monument is stated to have been pulled down on the repairs in 1683. Of him it may be truly said—

>    The hoary man had spent his live long age
>    In converse with the dead, who leave the stamp
>    Of ever-burning thoughts on many a page
>    When they have gone into the senseless damp
>    Of graves: his spirit thus became a lamp
>    Of brightness like to those on which it fed.
>    Through crowded courts, the city, and the camp,
>    Deep thirst of knowledge had his footsteps led,
>    And all the ways of men amongst mankind he read.

An interleaved copy of his Letters was in the possession of the Principal of Jesus College in 1823. It does not appear that this book contained any MS. particulars as to the life of this learned writer and loyal cavalier, or that any of his MSS. or other memorials of him are known to exist in the University to which he was ever so devotedly attached.

A bust of Howell, which might be modelled from the portrait, should be placed in the library of his college; and upon a tablet or some similar memorial, say in the Bodleian Library, the remembrance of this distinguished worthy should be perpetuated at Oxford.*

* This article was in the hands of the printer some time before the appearance in the *Saturday Review* (Oct. 11, 1862,) of an article which has opportunely revived attention to Howell's Letters.

# THE STORY OF RICHARD SAVAGE,
## DRAMATIST AND POET.

[*Bentley's Miscellany*, Nov. 1862.]

---

THIS unfortunate author may be said to live through Dr. Johnson's Memoir of his life rather than in his own compositions, inasmuch as his works, eagerly as they were once sought for, and great as are their merits in many respects, are now seldom read. His story enlisted the sympathy of contemporaries, and his claim to noble birth was not denied in his lifetime; but it was doubted by Boswell (who, after stating the case *pro* and *con.*, concludes that the "world must vibrate in a state of uncertainty as to what was the truth,"), and it has since been called in question by more than one writer. No one, however, seems to have taken much pains to test and challenge it until within the last four years, when Mr. Moy Thomas revived the discussion of these historic doubts.

Anne, daughter of Sir Richard Mason, of Sutton, in the county of Surrey, married Charles Lord Brandon, afterwards Earl of Macclesfield, in 1683. They separated after a union of only a few months, and in the course of time she formed an intimacy with Richard Savage, Earl Rivers, which led to the birth of a daughter, who died when a few months old, and afterwards of a son, and subsequently to her divorce from her husband. In the mean time, what had been going on came to the ears of Lord Macclesfield. She undoubtedly wished to be separated from him, and she may have acknowledged the adulterous intercourse, as Dr. Johnson states her to have done; but, lest her title and fortune should be lost, great efforts were made to prevent his obtaining evidence. In December, 1696, under the name of Madam Smith, she took up her temporary abode in lodgings in Fox Court, a passage between Brook Street and Gray's Inn Lane, and there, on the 16th of January, 1697, gave birth to the second child, a son, who was christened on the 18th by the officiating minister of St. Andrew's, Holborn, and entered on the register as Richard, son of John and Mary Smith. Lord Rivers and a Mr. Ousley stood as godfathers in person, and Dorothy Ousley, his sister, as godmother. On the following day the child was taken to Hampstead, and entrusted to a Mrs. Peglear to be nursed, and she was told that the child's name was Richard Lee. In the following summer she was visited by the wife of Richard Portlock, a baker, in Maiden Lane, Covent Garden, who claimed the nursling as their child, and, after some altercation, carried it off. It has been conjectured that the Portlocks, who did not appear as witnesses in the earl's suit for divorce, were bribed to bring up the child as their own, and were only the agents of the Ousleys in removing him. At all events, he was never again seen by Nurse Peglear, and from this time all trace of his fate is lost. The earl, without further prosecuting his suit, obtained on the 15th of March, 1698, a special act of divorce (memorable as the first ever granted without previous sentence of the Ecclesiastical Court), and the countess, reduced to her maiden name of Anne Mason, married Colonel Brett, and lived with him until his death in 1714.

Richard Savage, the poet, first appears in 1717, when he published a poem; and, as far as can now be discovered, he made his first public claim to noble parentage in 1719, when he published another work—a play—entitled " Love in a Veil: a Comedy written by Richard Savage, Gentleman, Son of the late Earl Rivers," in the dedication of which work to Lord Lansdowne he avowed himself to be " the son of Earl Rivers by the Countess of ———." His own story is that to which Dr. Johnson gave worldwide currency in his Memoir (which was published in 1744, while Mrs. Brett was still living). The outline of it is that Savage, by the agency of Lady Mason, the Countess of Macclesfield's mother, was placed in the care of a poor woman, who brought him up as her own child, and received payment from Lady Mason for her care; that his godmother, whom he calls Mrs. Loyd, died when he was only seven years of age, having by her will bequeathed to him a legacy of 300*l.*; that he was placed at a grammar-school near St. Alban's, where he received the only instruction ever given to him; that when he was about fifteen he was apprenticed to a shoemaker in Holborn, and that while in this servile condition the person whom he had always known as his mother died, and that on searching her boxes he found letters written to her by Lady Mason which revealed to him that he was the son of Lady Macclesfield, born during the wedlock of the earl and countess, but that his father was Lord Rivers, and that he was doomed to be disowned. Savage further stated this discovery of his birth to have been made after the death of Lord Rivers; that the earl, when on his death-bed, had insisted on knowing what had become of his son, and had been informed by his mother that he was dead, whereupon he revoked a legacy of six thousand pounds, which he had bequeathed in the boy's favour; and that the intention of his mother, then Mrs. Brett, had been to send him secretly to the American plantations, but that she had been hindered by her relations from executing that unnatural project, and had thereupon destined him to a life of obscurity and labour.

Those who contend that Savage personated the lost son of Lady Macclesfield, point to the many improbabilities which these statements involve, and to the fact that Savage was himself the authority for many of them. They ask, where was he during the intervening ten years? whether the person whom he calls "his godmother, Mrs. Loyd," was identical with Dorothy Ousley? how he acquired the letters of Lady Mason, which he said revealed to him the injustice he had suffered; and why, if he possessed them, they were never produced? where the grammar-school "near St. Alban's" was? who was the shoemaker to whom he had been apprenticed? and what grounds he had for stating that persons were employed to kidnap and transport him? And it has been observed that, if the secret of his birth was discovered by him at the period of his boyhood when he lost his godmother, the fact of his existence could hardly have been concealed from Lord Rivers, who died some years later, viz. in 1712. Savage stated that, on discovering who his mother really was, he sought to arouse her maternal feelings in his favour, but that she steadily refused to admit him to her presence, and that he used to walk in the dark evenings for hours before her house, in the hope of seeing her figure through the window; but she left him to grow to manhood the victim of her cruel aversion.

Those who say that Savage was a pretender, and was not the child that had disappeared, remark that the conduct of the countess towards the daughter, who died in infancy (as deposed to by witnesses in the divorce suit), was so marked by natural solicitude as to make it improbable that she would act unfeelingly towards her son, and would abandon him, and neglect all parental duties towards him. Savage himself (in " The Plain Dealer") speaks of her fine qualities; and again in the lines—

> Yet has this sweet neglecter of my woes
> The softest tenderest breast that pity knows!
> Her eyes shed mercy wheresoe'er they shine,
> And her soul melts at every woe—but mine.

But although the questions asked by objectors may not have received satisfactory answers, and the inconsistencies pointed out may not have been reconciled, there are considerations of very great weight in favour of Savage's pretensions. There is the belief of Dr. Johnson, his companion and biographer, in their validity (and we may be quite sure he concealed nothing about Savage that was known to himself); there is the belief and acquiescence of contemporaries in his story, a memoir of which, drawn up soon after the appearance of his first play, had an immense circulation, and procured for him the intercession of the Countess of Hertford on the memorable occasion which will be mentioned presently; there is the fact that the charges of cruelty and unnatural conduct were made in the lifetime of his mother, but were never refuted; and there is the conduct towards him of her own nephew, Lord Tyrconnel, who, if he had believed Savage to be an impostor, is not likely to have taken him to his house and companionship after her inhuman conduct had been publicly exposed.* There seems, indeed, to have been a very general

* It is undoubtedly to be borne in mind, as Croker has remarked, before we draw any conclusions from Mrs. Brett's forbearance to prosecute a libeller, that, however innocent she might be as to Savage, she was undeniably guilty in other respects, and would have been naturally reluctant to drag her frailties again before the public. The

acquiescence in the remark of Sir Richard Steele, that the conduct of Savage's mother had given him a right to find every good man his father; and the public interest in his behalf must have been grounded on the romantic circumstances of his early life and on the cruelty of his fate, for his works could hardly have won for him such favour on literary grounds.

Savage's first comedy (produced, as we have seen, when he was little more than twenty years of age) brought him the friendship of Steele (who, however, was little calculated to teach him either prudence or frugality), and also the friendship of Wilks the actor, which soon made him an assiduous frequenter of the theatres, and procured for him an occasional benefit. He had not attained his twenty-sixth year when he adapted the story of Sir Thomas Overbury to the stage—a work which Dr. Johnson deemed a remarkable proof not only of genius and power of imagination, but of equality of mind, for during its composition he was often without lodging and without food, and was accustomed to compose in the fields or the streets, and to beg from any shopkeeper, as he passed, the use of pen and ink to write down the scenes he had composed. The publication of his tragedy not only made him, for the first time, master of a hundred pounds, but brought him the notice and attentions of some persons of eminence and rank.

Three or four years of precarious fortune thus passed, and the aid of his generous friend Mr. Hill—a critic well known among the men of letters of his day—was advancing his reputation, when both his fame and his life were endangered by his falling, with two companions, under an accusation of murder, arising out of an affray in a tavern of discreditable resort. The evidence given on his trial seems open to much doubt and suspicion; but he was found guilty and sentenced to death, and now had no hope but from the mercy of the Crown. Earnest solicitations were made by powerful friends, but, incredible as it seems, those efforts were stated to Dr. Johnson to have been obstructed by his mother, who pretended that he had on one occasion entered her house and

story of his birth seems to have first appeared in Curll's "Poetical Register," in 1719; but that publication is not any authority, as Savage may himself have contributed the story.

placed her in bodily fear; and he would, doubtless, have been left for execution, if the Countess of Hertford had not laid before the queen the whole story of his mother's cruelty and obtained his pardon. This was in 1728.

Thus narrowly escaping an ignominious death, he resumed a life strangely divided between beggary and extravagance. Mrs. Brett's relations appear to have purchased his silence towards her, and Lord Tyrconnel received him into his family, and granted him an allowance of 200*l*. a year. Although for these benefits Savage may be said to have bartered his independence, they brought him an interval of prosperity which rendered this the golden age of his life. His merit was now invested with the glitter of affluence, and he was courted by those who desired to be thought men of taste and genius. His esteem, however, is confessed to have been no very certain possession, and he would lampoon at one time those whom he had praised at another, so that he seemed a flatterer and a calumniator by turns. Yet it must be remembered that he was a censor of great acuteness of perception, indifferent to the power or station of the persons whom he criticised, and that really exalted abilities and virtue could not find an abler judge or a warmer advocate. It is honourable to both, that Pope was his steady friend almost to the close of his life.

But the affluence which he enjoyed by the good will and hospitality of Lord Tyrconnel was not destined to long continuance—a quarrel estranged them for ever. It seemed to be the curse of his life that his misconduct or his necessities sooner or later alienated the friends whom his attractive qualities had gained; and it was but too truly said of him, that, while he scarcely ever met a stranger whom he did not make a friend, he had not a friend long before he obliged him to become a stranger. He seems to have acted in Lord Tyrconnel's house as if it had been a tavern, and to have forfeited that nobleman's good will by gross misconduct. At all events, his quarrel with Lord Tyrconnel turned him adrift upon the world, and precipitated him from plenty to indigence: those whom he had offended now returned the contempt they had suffered; those who had received favours from him did not remember them, so much more certain (as Dr. Johnson remarks) are the effects of resentment than of gratitude. When the friends of his late patron, in his justification, published the faults of Savage, his superiority of wit enlisted many sympathisers, but afforded little relief to his wants.

In 1729 he had produced his moral poem "The Wanderer," which he improvidently sold for ten guineas—as much, however, as was paid for the copyright of "Paradise Lost." Savage, now that he had lost *his* Garden of Eden, published his poem, "The Bastard," thinking himself again at liberty to expose the cruelty of his mother. There were five editions of it in a year, and it had the most general reception of all his works, for in this poem he describes sorrows and misfortunes which are not imaginary, and, writing from the heart, has written with a truth which gives the work its chief force and value. It left the unhappy writer, however, still in want of the necessaries of life: he might well have been the original of the author drawn by Pope, who

> Rhymes ere he wakes, and prints before Term ends,
> Obliged by hunger and request of friends.

A short ode on the queen's birthday procured for him 50*l*. from her majesty, with permission to write every year on the same subject, and a promise of a like yearly reward "until something better could be done for him." Nothing better *was* done, but the ode continued to be written, and the pension to be received for some years. On obtaining the money, however, Savage was accustomed to disappear from the sight of all his acquaintances until every penny had been spent, and then he experienced distress from which his pen could not relieve him: he lived by chance, most commonly at the expense of new friends formed at taverns, and lodged as much by accident as he lived, insomuch that in a cellar, or the meanest haunt of the casual wanderer, was to be found (as Johnson has said) the man whose knowledge of life might have aided the statesman, whose eloquence might have influenced senates, and whose conversation might have polished courts. Yet his distress never dejected him, or made him lose confidence in his powers of mind.

It seems to have been at this time that his visits to Cave (the publisher of the *Gentleman's Magazine*) at St. John's Gate brought him and Dr. Johnson together, and Malone treats it as not improbable that they were sometimes reduced to stroll about together all night for want of a lodging. Cave appears to have befriended Savage in his distress, but the death of the queen put an end to his hopes of advancement and to his pension, and he now accepted an offer of friends that he should retire to a cheap abode in Wales on an allowance of 50*l.* a year, which they proposed to subscribe for his support. In submitting to this exile from all the convivial society and the metropolitan life to which he had been accustomed, he intended to complete a play on which he was engaged, and to prepare his works for the press, having received several subscriptions for that purpose, and then to return to London and live on the profits of his labours. And so, with many resolutions of rigid economy, he, in July, 1739, tenderly took leave of Dr. Johnson and the rest of his friends, and went to Swansea. But he soon found the misery of his dependence, and, after living there for little more than a year, he came to look on his contributors as persecutors and oppressors, who had induced him to go into this banishment on the faith of promises which were not fulfilled. In the hope of releasing himself he went to Bristol, intending to return to London, and was caressed and entertained by the literary citizens of Bristol for some time, until his irregularities wearied the friends whom his attractive qualities had gained. He again experienced the extremes of want, and, being arrested for a debt he owed at a coffee-house, languished for some months in Bristol gaol a prisoner, supported by charity, until death released him, and threw its awful veil for ever on his frailties.

Looking back on a life of which we have now sketched the chief incidents, the reader will probably agree with Dr. Johnson that, if the miseries which Savage underwent were sometimes the consequences of his faults, his faults were very often the effect of his misfortunes. Assuming Savage to have been really the person he represented himself to be, he, born of noble parents before the divorce of his mother, and therefore entitled to be educated and provided for as a gentleman, was deprived of his birthright by an arbitrary measure, was doomed to a life of labour and poverty, and was destined by his unnatural mother to grow to manhood unfriended and disowned. The doubts and questionings which Mr. Thomas lately elaborated into a long essay, are only such as must suggest themselves to any one accustomed to the sifting of evidence, but the essay is well calculated to produce an impression that Savage's story of his birth was an imposture. Most persons will, however, be disposed, we think, to agree after all with Boswell, that it is a question to which only the Scotch verdict of "Not proven" can be applied.

As a writer, Savage had very great merit, for his works are moral in tone, have much originality, and evince poetical genius and a rare knowledge of life. He seems, indeed, to have had an intuitive perception of character, and a quickness in acquiring knowledge, which in some degree compensated for his deficient education, and enabled him to give his works the air of learning they often possess. He certainly afforded a striking example of genius and instability, and was almost equally remarkable for his weaknesses and his virtues. He had a warm and vigorous mind, rare gifts, and winning manners, but was sensual and inconstant; better qualified to acquire knowledge than riches, and more retentive of information than of his money. His ill-regulated life, his improvidence, and his literary hypocrisy justly provoke our censure, if not disgust; yet he could forcibly inculcate maxims of virtue which he was not inclined to practise, and could be the foe of all inflated pretensions, whatever the pretender's rank. Although not dejected by distress, he could be intoxicated by good fortune, and he could bear privation with heroism, though he could not enjoy prosperity with moderation. Though fickle in his friendship, he could forgive his enemies, and even do good to those who had injured him, and in his own distresses and privations he could cheer and relieve those who were still more unfortunate than himself. Finally, when we think of the extraordinary disadvantages of his birth and early years, the adverse fatality that seemed to attend his fortunes, and the fact that his sufferings were more frequently caused by the crimes of others than by his own vices, we wish to remember only what was good in the character of Richard Savage.

# EDWARD FORBES THE NATURALIST.

[*Bentley's Miscellany*, March, 1862.]

THE remarkable and gifted subject of this memoir * was born in the Isle of Man in 1815, and within the shores of that tiny kingdom he spent a third of his life, but the fame he won in after-years had nothing remote or insular in its character and limits. His great-grandfather was one of the many adherents of the Stuarts upon whose head a price was set for his loyalty, and he migrated from his native Highlands to the Isle of Man soon after the events of 1745. The father of Edward Forbes was connected with the trade of the island, and became a banker: his mother was of an old Manx family, and is described as a person of intellectual and superior mind, who took great delight in cultivating beautiful flowers and rare plants—a source, probably, of her son's early fondness for botanical pursuits.

The green romantic beauty of the valleys of Man, and the picturesque wildness of its shores and bays, told powerfully on his youthful fancy, and with the zest of a descendant of Norse sea-kings he loved the waters that encircled his island home. *He* was, indeed, a votary to whom the Muse might say:

> I saw thee seek the sounding shore,
> Delighted with the dashing roar;
> Or when the North its fleecy store
>   Drove through the sky,
> I saw grim Nature's visage hoar
>   Struck thy young eye.
> Or when the deep-green mantled earth
> Warm cherish'd every flow'ret's birth,
> And joy and music sounded forth
>   In every grove,
> I saw thee eye the general mirth
>   With boundless love.

* Memoir of Edward Forbes, F.R.S. late Regius Professor of Natural History in the University of Edinburgh. By George Wilson, M.D., and A. Geikie. Macmillan and Co. 1861.

The natural charms—the mountains, glens, sea-cliffs, and bay-indented shores of his little fatherland, were of more interest to him than its architectural remains, yet in their influence on the mind these were, in truth, unconsciously identified with the natural features, as if the fortress and the rocks together formed one natural whole. From Dr. Wilson's review of his childhood, it would seem that before he was yet twelve years of age he had without aid discovered the true scope of his intellect, and begun to employ it on the subjects which became the pursuit of his life. When a still younger child, his playmates brought him their contributions of minerals, fossils, shells, dried seaweed, hedge-flowers, and butterflies, to cheer his hours of sickness: he filled his pockets with weeds and creeping things, and appropriated another pocket to a tame lizard, and he was still a boy when he formed a museum of his own at home. Even in these early years his countenance was considered very interesting; it expressed amiability and intelligence, and a stranger, it is said, could hardly pass without turning round to look at him again. And thus in busy idleness his childhood passed:

> What liberty so glad and gay
> As, where the mountain boy,
> Reckless of regions far away,
> A prisoner lives in joy?

But it was necessary that a worldly occupation should be selected for him. His mother's highest ambition was to see him a good clergyman: he, however, felt no vocation for such a life, and would not take holy orders merely as a means of livelihood and leisure. He was fond of the arts and of poetry as well as of natural history, and it was no easy matter to say what profession he should follow. His choice being limited to the dissimilar professions of physician or painter, and his aversion to the special studies of medicine being unconquerable, he consented to make Art his profession. And so the scene now changes to the metropolis. But here his aspirations were very soon discouraged, and in the autumn of 1831, after wasting a few months in the fruitless study of Art, he quitted it to become a medical student in the University of Edinburgh. It was his destiny to return, eleven years afterwards, to London, to occupy one of its places of honour, and enter upon a career of distinction.

The lamented Professor Wilson, his friend and biographer (whose labour of love has been ably continued and completed by Mr. Geikie), casts a retrospective glance at the number and magnitude of the changes they had witnessed since the time when Edward Forbes commenced his student-life at Edinburgh. It took him three days to reach the Isle of Man from London, and three more to reach Edinburgh from the island. There was but one public railway in England. No steam-ship had crossed the Atlantic, and iron ships were novelties rarely seen. The penny-postage was not yet planned: the electric telegraph was no more than a possibility. The amazing future of photography was hidden: the physical sciences were taking immense strides, and revolutions were on the eve of occurrence. Logic and metaphysics, as taught by Sir William Hamilton, were about to throw over Edinburgh the lustre of a school of philosophy; but anatomy, the chief science on which medicine rests, was studied under disadvantages unknown to students of the present day. Chemistry was on the threshold of a great change, and at that time hardly afforded a foundation to botany as a science, or to agriculture as an art. The Botanical Garden was, however, one of the finest gardens of its kind in the country; and at Edinburgh the students possessed the advantage of being amidst a picturesque natural garden, affording a flora of great variety. One week, says Dr. Wilson, a party clambered up the Bass Rock to gather its scanty but curious plants among the perplexed Solan geese, its feathered inhabitants; another, they scoured the kingdom of Fife. Professor Jameson at that time represented Natural History in the University, and, under Dr. Hope and Dr. Reid, Forbes was a zealous student. During his noviciate, the microscope underwent such great improvements as soon led to the instruction of pupils in its use, so that while new regions of country were made accessible to botanical excursionists, new wonders of the Divine Hand were revealed in every organic structure, and the philosopher saw spread around him "the evidence that there is no one portion of the universe of God too minute for His notice, nor too humble for the visitations of His care."

After Edward Forbes had gone through a practical course of chemistry, he hesitated whether that science or natural history should be his permanent pursuit; he actually "tossed-up" with a fellow-student for the apparatus which they had bought with their common funds, and, losing the chemicals, was confirmed in his intention to devote himself to natural history.* Accordingly, we find that Forbes, when only eighteen years of age, had acquired "a clear systematic knowledge" of that branch of science: and "his power of perceiving the relation between apparently isolated facts in remote departments of nature was" (to quote the testimony of Dr. Campbell, Principal of the University of Aberdeen,) "astounding in one so young." He studied literature and science side by side, and the passages he extracted into his Common-place Book, with such great though desultory diligence, are from works which few naturalists, and still fewer students of medicine, would be found to read. It is probably quite true that, as regards natural history studies, he brought to the university more knowledge than the majority of its graduates, after four years' study, carry away with them. Of the influence of the scenery amidst which the Edinburgh student pursued his studies, Forbes thus spoke many years afterwards, when he had himself attained its chair of Natural History:

"The tastes of most men," he said, "can be traced back to the habits of their youth, and these habits are in a great measure moulded by the circumstances, physical as well as intellectual, amidst which that youth has been passed. Grand scenery suggests grand thoughts, and every ennobling thought elevates not merely for the moment, but permanently, the mind in which it dwells. It is a great gain to a university to be placed as this is amid scenes of unrivalled beauty; and the youth whose hours of relaxation are spent in their presence, carries with him into after-life the memory of their beauty and grandeur."

His early career at the university was one of the happiest portions of his life. He might truly say

        For me
Life's morning radiance hath not left the hills;
 Her dew is on the flowers.

* Dr. Charlton, of Newcastle, is the person who, when fellow-student, won the chemical apparatus.

The world's cold touch had not chilled him: his eager eyes looked forth on a bright and boundless future. Young men of genius with tastes like his own, whether students in medicine or in other faculties, had become his attached friends, and his sunny spirit and social qualities made him welcome to seniors as well as to associates. Libraries and museums were open to him; his city walks were through streets which pleased his artist-eye; his excursions carried him into a country which was to him "an Eden filled with creatures yet to be named," and his lodging (at the top of the stairs in No. 21, Lothian Street,) he called his "happy den."

When he returned in vacation to his native island, a comparison of its fauna and flora with those of Great Britain and France on the one hand, and of Ireland on the other, illustrated and confirmed (says his biographer), if it did not suggest, the doctrine of specific centres of distribution of plants and animals; and in like manner, during his early dredgings on his native shores, the doctrine of zones of submarine life, differing in character according to the depth of the sea, dawned upon him. On returning to Edinburgh for his second session, the rival claims of natural history and of medicine again struggled for supremacy; but he did not aspire to a medical degree, and, in a subsequent session, medicine was finally abandoned. Obliged to adopt a profession as a livelihood, but disowned by Art and by Medicine, his career at this point was not encouraging to his friends; but it was as a naturalist that his laurels were to be won, and the spring of 1836 saw him devote himself formally to the study of Nature. He was (as Dr. Brown of Edinburgh has remarked) in the best sense a natural historian—an observer and a recorder of what is seen and of what goes on over the great field of the world, and not less of what has been seen and has gone on in this wonderful historic earth. He was keen, exact, capacious, and tranquil, and steady in his gaze as Nature herself, and was, thus far, akin to Humboldt, Cuvier, Linnæus, Pliny, and Aristotle.

> Learned he was; nor bird nor insect flew,
> But he its leafy home and history knew;
> Nor wild-flower deck'd the rock nor moss the well,
> But he its name and qualities could tell.

Meantime, his autumnal vacation rambles were sources of great delight, for he roamed with keen eye, ready pencil, and light heart, " to gather the wonders and win the secrets of Nature." The first foreign tour he made was a pilgrimage through part of Norway. A very interesting and graphic account is given in the volume before us of his voyage from the Isle of Man. In Norway everything wore a novel aspect: the thousand isles and interlacing fiords, the endless undulations of the pine woods and the bare rocky shores, the picturesque wooden houses nestling in their green hollows or backed by far-stretching forests, were objects that he viewed with new delight. Forbes and his fellow-traveller arrived at Bergen on the festival of St. John, when the peasantry were parading the streets in every variety of costume, yet Forbes's tartan trousers soon attracted a mob. Then they plunged into the unfrequented solitudes of rock and snowfield and mountain; they visited the glacier of Folgefond, and from Bondhuus sailed up the Hardanger fiord between huge cliffs rising perpendicularly from the quiet waters to the regions of perpetual snow, and, while in Norway, boated and botanised to their hearts' content. Copenhagen, with its wide squares and numerous public buildings, palaces and churches, picture-galleries, museums, parks, rampart-promenades, and other objects of interest, delighted his artistic eye.

On his return he encountered a dreadful storm, and when he again saw the shores of England " shipwrecks strewed them like seaweeds." In the summer of 1834 he visited North Wales, and here he did little else than botanise, and, with wonderful keenness of vision and power of climbing, collect the rarer plants. The summer of the following year he spent in France, Switzerland, and Germany; and to the museum of the Jardin des Plantes, at Paris, devoted continuous study. Having here completed the winter course, he visited the south of France. He was charmed by the wildness of Vaucluse, by its bare bold rocks, its fountain—a miniature lake clear as crystal and tinted like the sapphire, mysteriously gushing from the rock, and by the inspiration which seemed to him to linger on the spot. Afterwards visiting Port Mahon in Minorca, on his way to the shores of Africa, he was charmed by the novel and almost Eastern aspect of the architecture, the picturesque dress of the natives, and the variety of nations whose vessels were in the port; and here, for the first time, he saw the cactus and the palm growing as natives of the country. But in these wanderings, as well as during his stay on the African shores, the youthful naturalist seems to have been ever intent on achieving the scientific results of travel.

Returning to Edinburgh, he gave, in the winter of 1838, a course of lectures " On the Natural History of the Animals in the British Seas." In the September of the following year he began, and in 1841 completed, his well-known " History of British Star-Fishes." He had now become a naturalist by profession, and he sought to make philosophy (to use his own expression) contribute to its expenses, by giving lectures on zoology. In 1840 the British Association met at Glasgow, and his scientific standing was greatly heightened by his papers, by the wide range of acquirements he evinced, and by the manner in which he discharged the duties of secretary. Yet, with the earnest desire to labour vigorously, every avenue towards remunerative employment seemed to fail him. For five years he had drifted from the anchorage of a professional calling, and a settled home and permanent vocation still seemed as distant as ever.

A circumstance now occurred which gave him the means of greatly extending his researches and his reputation. Captain Graves, the officer in command of the Mediterranean Survey, proposed that he should join H.M.S. *Beacon*, as naturalist to the Survey, and he left London for the Levant early in April, 1841. It had been intended to devote the summer to the coast of Candia; but beneath the white distant peaks, that seemed as the ship approached to be resting so peacefully on the deep blue sea, a native revolt against the Turks was raging, and the survey of Candia was of necessity postponed. While the *Beacon* remained off Paros he explored the neighbouring isles, pitched his tent upon the hill-sides, and partook of the rude fare, the native dances, and the picturesque life of the people. In visiting the seas and shores that had yielded their denizens to the Father of Natural History, he stood, as it were, in the shadow of the great name of Aristotle, and he viewed those isles and seas with reverence and delight. He afterwards joined that distinguished officer, Captain (then Lieutenant) Spratt, in a cruise for the prosecution of the coast survey. He found a striking similarity in the flora of all the islands, and up to three thousand five hundred feet (the highest peak he ascended) the plants of the Cyclades yielded no specimen of a sub-alpine character. The scenery presented a mingled wildness and beauty such as he had never before seen: huge precipices rising from the sea to towering peaks; and deep ravines, whose steep bare walls rose from tangled thickets of vines, and figs, and olives, and brought masses of grey and purple-tinted rock in contrast with the rich colours of the trees. He visited the great region of recent submarine volcanoes in the bay of Santorin—itself the site of an ancient crater—and found a former sea-bed at a height of two hundred feet above its present level. Among the portly, hospitable monks he visited in their rocky cells perched on the edge of cliffs, he found one recluse who had solaced himself by filling a portfolio with his own drawings, and he saw that remarkable monk, Cairi, who had visited England for the purpose of seeing Oxford. The fauna of these seas he found to be of a defined character, and different from that of any other of the marine zones, and over the two hundred miles examined an exact correspondence in productions was observed.

Forbes then visited the shores of Asia Minor, and the botanical, zoological, and geological results were combined with those of a later journey, and published in 1847 in the " Travels in Lycia," the joint production of himself and his distinguished colleague. Blending natural history pursuits with the exploration of cities that had been lost for centuries; sketching tombs, temples, and theatres; mingling amongst the peasantry; sometimes benighted amid briars, ruins, and jackals in the wild uplands of Lycia, and well-nigh wrecked among the rocks and skerries that fringe the shores, while he was exhausting the zoological treasures of that classic sea, the three months he spent in Asia Minor formed no uneventful period in his life. His Report to the British Association on the Mollusca and Radiata of the Ægean raised him to a high rank among living naturalists. He recognised in it eight provinces of depth, the lowest (about seven hundred and fifty feet) being a new marine country added by himself to the domain of the naturalist. He discovered that the species which have the greatest vertical range, are likewise those which extend over the widest areas of sea. That parallels in latitude are equivalent to regions in depth is another interesting and suggestive law of marine distribution deduced from these Mediterranean researches.

With his sojourn in Greek waters his life of light-hearted freedom may be said to have ended. In his absence, his family affairs had sadly changed: his father, hitherto prosperous as a trader and banker, had lost everything, and the young naturalist became charged with new responsibilities and duties—with solicitude for the kindred who had claims on his love and labour, as well as for his own advancement. And so, reluctantly abandoning his long-cherished wish to dredge the Red Sea, he returned to England in October, 1842, to enter on his career in London as Professor of Botany in King's College, and Curator of the Geological Society. Amid the patient gathering of facts relative to the distribution of plants and animals, he found in geology the bond that was to link those facts together in a symmetrical whole, and in carrying out this line of research he probably (as his biographer remarks) did greater service to geology than to any other branch of the natural sciences. It is his great praise that he not only did more than perhaps any man of his day to encourage a love for natural history, but more than any of his contemporaries to show how geology and natural history must be linked together.

The tone of his introductory lecture as Botany professor was such, that he seemed to have come fresh from Nature to demand for the study of her phenomena a high and honourable place among the recognised courses of mental training. His class augmented; and such was the charm he could throw round the study of vegetable structure, that his lecture-room became a source of attraction to amateurs. The rapid facility with which he sketched his illustrations while lecturing, was always a pleasing as well as striking and characteristic feature of his lectures; and whether his pencil was employed on the grotesque and humorous figures to which he loved to devote margins of letters and moments of relaxation, or on the more exact representation of scientific objects in diagrams, his graphic powers were equally ready and felicitous. The labours of his botanical session at the college, added as they were to the duties of his curatorship, which absorbed his daytime, and to the scientific work to which his evenings were devoted, would have broken down the energies of a less ardent and indefatigable labourer. Yet in 1843, when the British Association met at Cork, he acted as amateur whipper-in of geologists, naturalists, chemists, and philosophers, and amidst all this labour found time for reports and occasional papers. One of these—a paper read in the spring of 1844 before the Geological Society, "On the Light thrown on Geology by Submarine Researches"—contributed to his obtaining the hold which he never afterwards lost on the respect and sympathy of the higher class of scientific society in London, and to a government grant of 500l. towards the publication of the Ægean researches. His want of leisure to arrange for publication the mass of materials which resulted from his visit to the East seems for years afterwards to have fretted him greatly, and, unfortunately for science, the needed leisure never came. Other duties continually pressed upon him; and when at last he gained the Natural History Chair of Edinburgh, and began to put the vast mass of scientific material in order, he was cut off in the noontide of his course.

Some changes of scene and occupation in the summer of 1844 gave him new energy, which he signalised on the meeting of the British Association at York in the autumn, and by entering on the duties of his new post of Palæontologist to the Geological Survey, then conducted by its founder, Sir Henry de la Beche. This appointment brought relief to body and mind; and at the Beef-steak Dinner Club which he established under the cognomen of the Metropolitan Red Lions, he rallied round him the younger scientific men of London, and showed how thoroughly social a man of science could be, and how well mirth and earnestness could be combined. His lectures at the Royal Institution in the spring of 1845 were on "The Natural History and Geological Distribution of Fossil Marine Animals;" and at the Cambridge meeting of the British Association he contributed a paper on "The Geographical Distribution of Local Plants," in which he elucidated the doctrine that the present flora of Great Britain originated in at least four distinct geological epochs. That memoir has been pronounced one of the most masterly, as well as beautiful, generalisations to be found in British literature. Forbes believed that the plants and animals of Britain could for the most part have come only by migration, before the isolation of the British islands from the continent, during a period anterior to that of man, and when palm-trees flourished in the latitude of the south-eastern parts of England.

In the autumn he revisited the northern extremity of this realm, examined the Shetland Islands, and then, cruising among the Hebrides, dredged the deep kyles and lochs of the wild western shores.

The beginning of the year 1847 found him anxiously weighing his chances of promotion to the Natural History Chair of Edinburgh, so long the object of his desire, and which Professor Jameson was then expected to resign. The state of scientific appointments in London was such that the utmost gain he could look for was a salary of 500*l.*; and for this, his liberty, his time, and comfort must be surrendered to official trammels, and all prospect of prosecuting his own scientific work resigned. But the veteran naturalist at Edinburgh rallied from his illness to retain his professorship for another seven years.

In March, Forbes, as Palæontologist of the Survey, began his tour of inspection in Ireland. In the summer, at the close of his college lecture session, he began to prepare for the early publication of his great work, " The History of British Mollusca," which for four years occupied a large portion of his time; and the autumn was devoted to geologising, chiefly among the Silurian and Welsh rocks. It was on these excursions that his companions of the survey found his " inner life " best revealed, for genial mirth succeeded to grave debate and earnest labour. During his leisure hours in London on his return, he prepared the new Palæontological map of the British islands, which was published in Johnston's Physical Atlas in the following year. Long and elaborate contributions to the palæontology of the older geological formations occupied him during the winter; and in the spring of 1848 he made a geological tour with the surveyors in Hampshire and Dorsetshire, and returned to open his botanical lectures at King's College and to fall in love.

That a man so susceptible of the gentler emotions, and of so much sensibility to feminine charms, and who was so great a favourite in society, should be still in his bachelorhood when he reached his thirty-third year, is certainly a testimony to his prudence and judgment. There seem to have been two very serious obstacles to his following his envied comrades into the married ranks, for, first, he declared he had never met a woman he could esteem so thoroughly as to marry her; and, second, he had never enjoyed income enough to marry. It needs not to be told how impressionable by the gentler sex he ever was. Nymphs glance out in the pages of his early note-books among grim skeletons of animals and scraps of hardly drier lectures; female faces, pensive, with braided locks or laughing among curls, float through the memoranda of his London life and country rambles. His wishes were at length destined to an early fulfilment. When visiting at a friend's house in Surrey, he met Miss Ashworth, daughter of the late General Sir C. Ashworth, and the charms of " good sense, unselfishness, amiability, and accomplishments " (to use his own words), made him a lover. Circumstances favoured their speedy marriage, and on the 31st of August, 1848, he was united to the object of his choice, the philosophic bridegroom, amorous as he was, having nevertheless contrived to write two papers for the meeting of the British Association held at Swansea earlier in that month.

But the fetters of the geological survey were not thrown off on his submitting to those of matrimony, and within a week after the wedding he proceeded with his young wife to Llangollen, where he took lodgings in a homely farm-house, afterwards known among the geologists as " Honeymoon Cottage." His married life was not less nomadic than his state of bachelorhood. He had joined the survey to gain the means of living, and of giving himself eventually to the natural history work to which his life had been devoted, but it was his fate to exemplify what has been called the vanity of human wishes, for his acceptance of office only subjected him to years of labour, for very inadequate remuneration, in a capacity which brought no honour, while the field in which he hoped to win his laurels remained inaccessible.

The erection of the new museum in Jermyn-street, and the proposal to establish in it a training-school for geological science, seemed, however, to promise better things. Meantime, the arrangement of the fossils in the galleries of the new building continued to form a chief part of his survey duties down to the May of 1849. August found him, with his wife, in "the smallest possible thatched cottage" among the oolites of the Dorsetshire coast, where he devoted the rainy days and his evenings to his work on the mollusca, happy in his wife's society, and "undisturbed by ceremony or callers." His labours on the Dorset coast resulted in showing that the Purbeck strata really belong to the oolitic series; that they are divisible into three groups, each characterised by a distinct fauna, but exhibiting no traces of physical disturbance in the lines of demarcation; that air-breathing mollusca lived at the period of the deposit of the Purbeck beds, and that these strata might be expected to yield (as they have since yielded) remains of mammals. Still, with all his work, he was in no danger of shrinking to the size of a slender Purbeck column, for the sea-air fattened him, and gave him what seemed a new lease of good health, with which he returned to London—"the ugly, unphilosophical, lion-hunting centre of the universe," as he calls the great metropolis.

In 1850, the summer and autumnal rambles being over, and Forbes having returned to his post in London, he began the little volume (which he did not live to complete) on "The Natural History of the European Seas." In this little work, finished and published in 1859 by Mr. Godwin-Austen, he treated of the range of seas which extend from the icy cliffs of Spitzbergen to the sunny shores of Africa and the eastern recesses of the Mediterranean, and pointed out the characteristics of the six provinces, marked by as many distinct centres of creation, which, according to his view, they comprehend.

In the memorable year of the Great Exhibition the museum in Jermyn-street was opened by the gifted Prince whose death we have now to mourn, and Forbes entered readily into the government arrangements for organising a School of Mines. He spent part of the autumn on a geologising survey in Kilkenny and Cork, and the rest of the year in his lectures and in scientific contributions to various periodicals. And so, in work and hope, another winter passed pleasantly away, and at Easter he took a short holiday in Belgium, for the purpose, as he said, of "getting London fog out of his head." The geology of the Isle of Wight, and what he called the hatching of young geologists in Jermyn-street engaged his time during the winter of 1852. In his lecture at the Royal Institution in the following May he pointed out the general nature of his researches among the tertiary strata of the Isle of Wight, which he regarded as really the most perfect series in Europe—perhaps in the world. In the same year he undertook a course of evening lectures to working men "On the Elements of Natural History." The summer found him at warfare with the government and the Treasury commissioners touching arrangements which appeared to him to impair the educational value of the museum, and to inflict injustice on the scientific officers of the survey; in fact, he seems to have been "undergoing the horrors of slow strangulation by red tape." Later in the year, exhausted by toil, he sought rest and change of scene in France, and in the volcanic district of Auvergne spent his holidays very joyously.

At length the offered resignation of Professor Jameson afforded the opening which Forbes, during his years of labour, had never ceased to desire. Yet he hesitated to become candidate for an office which would remove him from London: the associations by which a residence of ten years had linked him to the metropolis were not to be lightly cast aside; he had, moreover, risen to high rank in the scientific world, his circle of acquaintance had widened every year, and in London fellow-labourers and many of his closest friends resided. Professor Jameson's resignation was, however, coupled with conditions which postponed the question for some months, and Forbes, meantime, employed himself in geological work, and wound up a geologist's year by joining Professor Owen and a scientific party at dinner inside the model of the Iguanodon at Sydenham on the last day of 1853.

In the spring of 1854 the Edinburgh professorship was gained, and he quitted London and all its pleasant associations to take his place as Professor of Natural History in the University which, more than twenty-two years before, he had entered as a student.

His chief inducement appears to have been the hope of leisure to reduce to order, and fit for publication, the scientific accumulations of busy years, but that leisure never came. It was destined that the energetic life which had in a few years achieved so much, and was then proposing so much for the future, should come to a sudden close. After a geologising ramble in the Highlands with a large party of his students, he came to London to complete some unfinished work at the museum; but an attack of illness warned him to return to the North. At the Liverpool meeting of the British Association in September he was elected to the president's chair in the Geological Section, and in this honourable office made his last appearance in a public capacity. His review of Sir Roderick Murchison's "Siluria," in the October number of the *Quarterly*, has a mournful interest as the last of his writings. Decreasing strength, accompanied by chills and feverish symptoms, interrupted his lectures of the winter session, and, sinking rapidly, he passed to his rest on the 17th of November, 1854. In the Dean Cemetery at Edinburgh, on a slope that overlooks the water of Leith, "among the well-explored scenes of his youth, within sight of the sea to whose wonders so much of his life had been devoted, within the murmur of the city that had witnessed the efforts of his early years," and had been from first to last the goal of his ambition and the cherished haven of his rest, the earth closed over all that was mortal of EDWARD FORBES.

THE END.

WORKS BY THE SAME AUTHOR ALREADY PUBLISHED.

*In one Volume, 8vo., Cloth, price 9s.,*

# LECTURES AND ESSAYS,

ON VARIOUS SUBJECTS,

Historical, Topographical, and Artistic.

The Author has revised and collected in this volume a variety of Essays and Reviews contributed by him to different periodicals, and has here published for the first time two Lectures—one, on " Poetry and the Fine Arts, their Affinities and Powers," and the other, on " Literature in the Middle Ages, and the Writers of English History," which were read to Literary Institutions in Northumberland and Durham. The topographical Essays comprise—a popular sketch of the History and Present State of the Inns of Court; an Essay on London, Past and Present, in which a general view is taken of the progress of the metropolis and the vicissitudes of some of its historical Edifices; a Visit to York; a Visit to Naworth Castle, in Cumberland (once the stronghold of that great Border Chieftain, Lord William Howard); a paper on Alnwick Castle and the important and costly works now in progress there; and a description of Bothal Church and Castle. The Volume also comprises an Essay on the History of the Bell, with notices of remarkable Church Bells, and various anecdotes; an Essay entitled " Leaves from Old Trees," in which mention is made of trees remarkable for age, magnitude, or historical associations; a paper on " The Stone of Destiny," in which the tradition of the famous Coronation Stone in Westminster Abbey is traced; and an article on " The Curiosities of the Number Seven." The historical papers comprise also, a review of the Rev. W. Froude's History of England, in which the pretended evidence of manuscripts discovered amongst the Public Records relating to the Suppression of Monasteries is much considered; and there are letters on some legal and ecclesiastical affairs, and papers on miscellaneous antiquities.

" A very agreeable Volume."—*The Builder.*

" The author shows extensive reading, a fine taste, and a keen perception of the beautiful. There is an extremely good article on the Inns of Court, their history, constitution, privileges, and stages of progression; the Londiniana will please all readers, pointing out the antiquities of London, spots of celebrity, changes, expansion and successive improvements. The book shows considerable literary ability, research, enthusiasm, and a highly cultivated mind."—*Morning Post.*

" Mr. Gibson discourses sensibly of art."—*News.*

" This volume indicates a comprehensive versatility in the genius of its author. He has a pleasant manner. * * The lecture on Historians and Literature in the Middle Ages is one of Mr. Gibson's good and useful papers. * * * ' Londiniana ' is replete with curious matter."—*Art Journal.*

" A valuable and interesting collection * * emanating from the pen of a very cultivated gentleman. The lectures are of especial value, as models of style in that species of composition. If all the gentlemen in England who have qualifications and opportunities in any way equal to Mr. Gibson, would devote a little of their leisure time to the improvement of the people in this manner, more might be done than by the exertions of any central organization for diffusing knowledge by rule."—*The Critic.*

" These interesting Essays have passed the editorial chairs of the *Quarterly Review, The New Monthly Magazine,* the *Illustrated London News, Notes and Queries,* the *Dublin Review, The Morning Chronicle, &c.* Essays which have stood such an ordeal, must have standard worth in them. We heartily recommend the book."—*Durham County Advertiser.*

" When you have read through the " Lectures and Essays " gathered together in this compact octavo volume, you will say that there are poetry and wit as well as learning and wisdom in the wig."—*Gateshead Observer.*

In 8vo. cloth, lettered, and embellished with Views of Naworth Castle, as restored, and of Corby Castle, near Carlisle, price 6s. 6d.

### DESCRIPTIVE AND HISTORICAL NOTICES OF
# NORTHUMBRIAN CASTLES, CHURCHES, AND ANTIQUITIES.

THIRD SERIES:—Comprising Visits to Naworth Castle, Lanercost Priory, and Corby Castle, in Cumberland ; the Ruined Monasteries of Brinkburn, Jarrow, and Tynemouth ; Bishop Middleham and the Town of Hartlepool ; Newcastle-on-Tyne and Durham Cathedral.

Previously published, in 8vo., embellished with Views of Finchale, and of the Abbey Church of Hexham, price 4s., the FIRST SERIES of the same work :—Comprising Visits to the Ruined Priory of Finchale ; the Abbey Church of Hexham ; the Parish Churches of Houghton-le-Spring, Morpeth, Bothal, Ovingham, and Ryton ; the Ancient Castles of Prudhoe and of Bothal, &c.

"Mr. Gibson has viewed the various scenes which he has visited and described with the eye of a poet, historian, and philosopher ; and his sketches, enriched by antiquarian knowledge, personal anecdotes, historical incidents, and descriptive pencillings, cannot fail to enlighten and entertain the reader."—*Newcastle Journal.*
"Many will be glad to possess these very interesting papers in a collected form, with the subsequent additions of the erudite author."—*Durham Advertiser.*
"We hail this delightful volume as another product of that goodly band of antiquaries who are doing so much to illustrate and preserve the remains in the north of England."
—*Arch. Camb.*

And also, in 8vo., 10s. cloth, embellished with a highly-finished portrait of the Earl of Derwentwater, Views of Dilston, Bamburgh Castle, Preston, &c., and several Woodcuts, the SECOND SERIES of the same work, comprising

# DILSTON HALL;
### OR,
## MEMOIRS OF JAMES RADCLIFFE,
*Earl of Derwentwater, a Martyr in the Rebellion of* 1715.

### TO WHICH IS ADDED,
### A VISIT TO BAMBURGH CASTLE; WITH AN ACCOUNT OF LORD CREWE'S CHARITIES, AND A MEMOIR OF THE NOBLE FOUNDER.

"We are delighted to meet with Mr. Gibson in a second volume of his Northumbrian Sketches. He has here given us a careful and most interesting memoir."—*Ecclesiologist.*
"A tender and chivalric interest will always attach to the name and fate of the Earl of Derwentwater, whatever be the politics of the historian or his reader. The incidents have the pathos of one of the ancient ballad stories."—*Athenæum.*
"Mr. Gibson's antiquarianism is of a very popular kind ; he has carefully collected whatever materials could be acquired for the discharge of his labour of love. The accounts of Bamburgh Castle and Bishop Crewe afford many topics of interest."—*Guardian.*
"This work fully sustains the reputation procured for the author by its predecessors. The same vivid description of scenery, correct accounts of historical monuments, and biographical information, which procured such general favour for the first series, are to be found in the present volume."—*Tablet.*

"Mr. Gibson appears to have undertaken his task from genuine enthusiasm. He determined to vindicate the memory of the generous and devoted young nobleman who formed so goodly but useless a sacrifice to the Stuart cause, and he became, for the time, a Jacobite. This volume is calculated in every way to enhance his rising reputation as an antiquary and archæologist, and deserves to be extremely popular."—*Weekly News.*

"The gifted author has applied his knowledge, judgment, and extensive acquirements to the illustration of an event, and the fortunes of a noble house, which will continue to be regarded with extraordinary interest. The work is entitled to the highest degree of estimation, and will be perused with avidity."—*Newcastle Journal.*

"The enthusiasm of the author has gilded many of its scenes and circumstances, and thrown around them an irresistible charm; his diction is chaste and elegant, and the narrative abundantly evinces his industry and research."—*Newcastle Guardian.*

"We commend this work to all lovers of ancient times and family history, a kind of reading as useful and profitable as the mind can be engaged in; and, where such a writer as Mr. Gibson is the guide, a source of instruction calculated to improve the heart, as well as to inform the understanding."—*Durham Advertiser.*

---

In 8vo. stitched, price 2s.

TWO LECTURES ON THE

## STRUCTURE & PHYSICAL ASPECTS OF THE EARTH,

*Lately read to the Tynemouth Literary Institution.*

---

In 8vo. cloth, lettered, price 3s. 6d.

AN ESSAY

## ON THE FILIAL DUTIES,

With ANECDOTES and IILLUSTRATIONS from Ancient and Modern History.

---

In 4to. reprinted from *the Archæologia,*

## A MEMOIR ON SOME ANCIENT MODES OF TRIAL,

Especially the "Judicia Dei" in the ordeals of Water and Fire.

---

Also lately published,

REMARKS ON THE

## MEDIÆVAL WRITERS OF ENGLISH HISTORY.

"In this very brief publication upon a most extensive subject, the reader will find a chronological list of all, or nearly all, the British Monastic Historians, as far as they are yet known, with a brief but lucid statement of what their writings refer to."—*Archæologia Camb.*

"The author displays great research, and an extensive acquaintance with his subject."—*Exeter Gazette.*

4

PREPARING FOR PUBLICATION, a re-issue, in one Volume, 4to., without coloured illuminations, of

## A HISTORY
OF THE
### MONASTERY FOUNDED AT TYNEMOUTH.

The first edition was produced in a very ornate and costly manner, decorated with Illuminated Pages, and Illuminated Initial Letters selected from celebrated MSS. of the Middle Ages, all which are finished by hand, in Gold and Colours, so as to be equal to the Original Drawings, and form a series of examples of ancient art; none of the copies so produced now remain for sale. The characteristic Etchings, by Mr. T. M. Richardson, representing the Ruins of Tynemouth Priory; together with Engravings, fac-simile Representations of Ancient Deeds, Seals, &c. will be included in the forthcoming impression.

"During the last three years several important and costly works have appeared on the History of Ancient Monastic Foundations in England. The volume before us is the most attractive of these contributions to English Ecclesiastical History."—*Arch. Jour.*

"A work which is destined to occupy an honourable place in the historical literature of the country."—*Newcastle Journal.*

"This is one of those laborious works which ever and anon appear, and which will live and be cherished when hundreds of others are forgotten. A gentleman, with sufficient zeal and talent, who will devote himself to the faithful elucidation of the history of an important and venerable institution cannot fail of obtaining the approbation of the discerning archæologist."—*Literary Gazette.*

---

Also preparing for publication, in one Volume, price not to exceed One Guinea,

## A MEMOIR OF RICHARD DE BURY,
### BISHOP OF DURHAM, AND LORD CHANCELLOR.

Richard de Bury was the most learned Englishman of his day, and was justly distinguished among the virtuous and worthy Ecclesiastics whose memory sheds lustre on the brilliant reign of Edward III. His services in the cause of letters conferred lasting benefits upon succeeding ages in the preservation of classical learning. His literary taste has been perpetuated by himself in his treatise "On the Love of Books," which he wrote for the students at Oxford, for whose benefit he bequeathed his vast collection of Manuscripts. This treatise—the Philobiblon—has been six times reprinted (in Latin); its style is spirited and characteristic, and it is a remarkable and unique literary monument of the fourteenth century. The Biographer has, therefore, been induced to subjoin to the present Memoir an accurate English Version of this celebrated work. But the good and learned prelate was not merely an author. The events of his life are extremely interesting and varied, as he was Treasurer of Guienne, Cofferer and Treasurer of the Wardrobe to Edward II., and Preceptor of Edward of Windsor, who evinced his love, confidence, and favour towards De Bury by bestowing upon him innumerable preferments in the Church and State, and amongst these the dignities of Dean of Wells, Prebendary of Lincoln, Sarum, and Lichfield, Keeper of the Privy Seal, Lord Chancellor of England, Lord Treasurer, and, to crown all, Bishop of Durham. He was Chaplain and Secretary of the King, and frequently his Ambassador to the Pope and to Continental Courts, on matters memorable in English History.

---

*⁎* *The Names of Subscribers for this Work are received by* MR. ROBINSON, *Bookseller,*
*Newcastle-on-Tyne.*

www.ingramcontent.com/pod-product-compliance
Lightning Source LLC
Chambersburg PA
CBHW022115300426
44117CB00007B/715